'Lasslett puts the biggest crime of all – the diverse state–corporate criminality which threatens lived communities, the rich biospheres they depend upon and the very existence of our planet – under the most critical social scientific scrutiny. This is a magisterial work, gleaned from experience across the globe and which speaks to each individual upon it. It is data-rich, fecund with conceptual and theoretical sophistication, methodologically inspiring and one which frightens and angers – but, ultimately, which bequeaths real grounds for hope and tools of resistance'.

– **Steve Tombs,** *Professor of Criminology, Open University, UK*

'You are holding a very rare book in your hands. This is empirically rich, methodologically innovative and theoretically ground-breaking. Although most researchers struggle to achieve one of those, this book is hugely impressive for its contribution on all three counts. This is a major contribution to Marxist understandings of "crime" that is meticulously researched. It shows that ignoring formal rules and norms of conduct is not merely an anti-social practice, but is part of the creative destruction inherent in urban development. In uncovering how corruption and extortion ruin the lives of ordinary people in Papua New Guinea, Kristian Lasslett makes an utterly convincing case. Here, crime is not merely a "bad" thing that "bad" people do. Rather, the crimes of urbanisation constitute a cold and calculated means of achieving class domination'.

– **David Whyte,** *Professor of Socio-legal Studies, University of Liverpool, UK*

'Kristian Lasslett's brilliant interdisciplinary study demonstrates convincingly how the urbanisation necessary to globalised capitalism is inescapably prone to the predations of state–corporate crime. The consequent human and environmental harm is here laid bare, most effectively with telling instances from Papua New Guinea that clearly show the global processes under examination. This is big-picture stuff: analytically insightful, rigorous and nuanced, methodologically innovative and empirically meticulous'.

– **Scott Poynting,** *Adjunct Professor, School of Social Sciences and Psychology, Western Sydney University, Australia*

Uncovering the Crimes of Urbanisation

From the social cleansing of cities through to indigenous land struggles at the frontline of extraction megaprojects, planetary urbanisation is a contested process that is radically shaping social life and the sustainability of human civilisation. In this pioneering intervention, it is maintained that this turbulent planetary process is also a potent space for state–corporate criminality. Market manipulation, fraud, corruption, violence and human rights abuses have become critical spokes in the way space is being transformed to benefit speculative interests. This book not only offers investigative data that documents in detail the intricate ways state and corporate actors collude to profit from the built environment; it also establishes the tools for building a research agenda that can interrogate the crimes of urbanisation on a comparative, longitudinal basis.

The author sets out an investigative methodology which can be appropriated to conduct probing research into the hidden schemas and forms of collusion that buttress state–corporate criminality in the urban sphere. Coupled to this, a theoretical framework is developed for thinking about the networks, processes and mechanisms at the heart of property market manipulation, and the broader social relationships that sustain and reward illicit speculative activity. This book concludes that researchers and civil society have a critical role to play in challenging a historical form of planetary urbanisation, marked by endemic state–corporate criminality, that poses significant threats to the sustainability of lived communities and the rich biospheres that they depend upon.

This book will be of interest to criminologists, sociologists, human geographers, political scientists and those engaged with development studies, as well as civil society organisations and urban researchers.

Kristian Lasslett is Professor of Criminology at the University of Ulster, and sits on the Executive Board of the International State Crime Initiative. He is joint Editor-in-Chief of *State Crime*, a leading international peer reviewed journal, and Editor of The State Testimony Project, the first online casebook for state crime studies.

Crimes of the Powerful
Edited by Gregg Barak, *Eastern Michigan University, USA*
Penny Green, *Queen Mary University of London, UK*
Tony Ward, *Northumbria University, UK*

Crimes of the Powerful encompasses the harmful, injurious, and victimizing behaviors perpetrated by privately or publicly operated businesses, corporations, and organizations as well as the state mediated administrative, legalistic, and political responses to these crimes.

The series draws attention to the commonalities of the theories, practices, and controls of the crimes of the powerful. It focuses on the overlapping spheres and inter-related worlds of a wide array of existing and recently developing areas of social, historical, and behavioral inquiry into the wrongdoings of multinational organizations, nation-states, stateless regimes, illegal networks, financialization, globalization, and securitization.

These examinations of the crimes of the powerful straddle a variety of related disciplines and areas of academic interest, including studies in criminology and criminal justice; law and human rights; conflict, peace, and security; economic change, environmental decay, and global sustainability.

Uncovering the Crimes of Urbanisation

Researching Corruption, Violence and Urban Conflict

Kristian Lasslett

Routledge
Taylor & Francis Group

LONDON AND NEW YORK

First published 2018
by Routledge
2 Park Square, Milton Park, Abingdon, Oxon OX14 4RN

and by Routledge
711 Third Avenue, New York, NY 10017

Routledge is an imprint of the Taylor & Francis Group, an informa business

British Library Cataloguing in Publication Data
A catalogue record for this book is available from the British Library

Library of Congress Cataloging in Publication Data
A catalog record for this book has been requested

ISBN: 978-1-138-12032-7 (hbk)
ISBN: 978-1-315-65179-8 (ebk)

Typeset in Bembo
by Out of House Publishing

MIX
Paper from
responsible sources
FSC® C013604

Printed and bound by CPI Group (UK) Ltd, Croydon, CR0 4YY

To Sandy, Eduard, Beatrix and our friends in Papua
New Guinea

Contents

Figures

Tables

Cases

Acknowledgements

This book is indebted to a large number of people who supported the research, in different ways, particularly on the ground in Papua New Guinea, where many of the key methodological innovations were developed. To protect the safety of key interlocutors, I will not thank them by name. However, suffice to say Papua New Guinea is blessed with courageous individuals of integrity, inside government, the private sector and civil society. Their diligent, honest work, often conducted at great personal risk, is rarely acknowledged or celebrated. I have been particularly amazed by the resilience and integrity of communities resisting mass forced evictions – they display a respect for fair play and rule of law, that is often not reciprocated by their state–corporate opponents. I also benefited from the hospitality of these communities – they shared their struggle and story with me, often under difficult conditions, along with a considerable volume of documentation.

However, the grass-roots do not carry the struggle on alone. During my research I had the great fortune to meet, and collaborate with, a range of international actors working in solidarity with residents and communities impacted by mass forced evictions, illegal land transactions and illegitimate property ventures.

I would like to thank Hollie Fifer and Media Stockade. They demonstrated extreme valour under fire, when documenting the stories of those impacted by forced displacement in Paga Hill (see chapter five). Thanks also go to Philippe Schneider and Olivier Pollet, artists who helped use the camera lens to tell the story of communities affected by the land deals and property developments documented in this study.

A number of NGOs and charities deserve special mention. The Bismarck Ramu Group, Act Now! PNG, Jubilee Australia, Aid/Watch, Global Witness and the Christensen Fund, have each shone a light on the land question in Papua New Guinea. They are brave, rigorous and outspoken organisations, that take on challenging topics often overlooked by mainstream civil society. I have benefited greatly from their guidance and support.

Research of this nature is always professionally and personally demanding, owing to the sensitivities involved and the considerable risks, which must be managed. I have received outstanding collegial support from the International State Crime Initiative, and the University of Ulster, both of whom steadfastly support academic freedom and applied research that benefits marginalised and persecuted communities. Ulster University's Secretary, Eamon Mullan, deserves special mention for the tireless energy he puts into safeguarding researchers, of which I am a beneficiary.

The digitally assisted analytical methods employed in this volume, were not built in isolation. Over the past five years, I have worked closely with Outlandish Coop. Their flare for data-analytics and digital innovation, helped refine and deepen the methodological tools and data-sets presented in this volume.

Of course, a book of this scope demands a patient and supportive publisher. Hannah Catterall and Thomas Sutton from Routledge have been brilliant in both respects.

During the course of this study, sadly, a number of collaborators passed away, unexpectedly. Robin Mua from Paga Hill was a towering figure in his community, an educator whose passion for children will be remembered. Poin Casper, from the Bismarck Ramu Group, was a true warrior, fighting against some of the worst international predatory forces. And finally Peter Ward, a brilliant young Australian, who was my digital magician and an unwavering friend to Papua New Guinea – he lit the fuse for a remarkable set of discoveries.

Last, but certainly not least, throughout this protracted project, with all its twists and turns, highs and lows, I have always received unwavering support from my family, which I am extremely thankful for and never take for granted.

Of course, it goes without saying, any errors in this volume remain my own.

The darkness of neon lights
Introducing the crimes of urbanisation

A new research agenda

The sprawl of our built environment extends from town to country, from sky to sea floor. It is a complex mesh of epochs, technologies and structured agglomerations. For a large part of humanity's accumulated life-history the built environment has been a modest complement to the organic and inorganic world of rivers, seas, fields, forests, wildlife and vegetation. However, the immense accumulation of productive forces over the past three centuries has inspired new scales of built life, that are so vast and resource intensive human civilisation has entered what appears a particularly tense period in its relationship with the natural world.

There is no sign that this precarious trajectory will abate any time soon. Today heaving metropolises are intensively and extensively expanding, punctuated by creative moments of destruction where 'moribund' parts of the city are levelled so new structures can emerge in their place (Harvey 1985; Lefebvre 2003). These condensed sites of production, distribution, consumption, commerce, finance, politics, culture and life, are being woven together on a planetary scale through increasingly sophisticated means of transport and communications, that are unevenly distributed across the earth's face creating a hierarchy of connectedness (Lefebvre 2003; Smith 1982). High-speed rail networks and air travel condense the space-time continuum, while fibre-optic cables facilitate high volume, virtually instantaneous information flows.

The built environment generated through the urbanisation process also winds its way out into the countryside in myriad forms. Unevenly punctuating rural spaces are intensive hubs of productive activity where energy resources, raw materials and foodstuffs are generated or extracted, then transported into industrial, commercial and residential centres, to feed the growing consumptive appetites of industry and households. As Lefebvre puts it, 'this expression, "urban fabric" does not narrowly define the built world of cities but all manifestations of the dominance of the city over the country' (2003: 3–4). Nowhere is exempt. Fleets of vessels trawl the ocean for its increasingly endangered living forms, new technologies are piloted to facilitate deep-sea mining, while state–corporate eyes are set upon the possibility of inter-planetary urbanisation. Brenner contends the 'increasingly large-scale morphologies' of urbanisation 'explode the erstwhile urban/rural divide' (2013: 87).

While each piece in the complex urban puzzle is laid out with design, as a totality this global process is prosecuted by humanity without any coherent plan or sense of destination. Buttressing this anarchic process, are legitimising ideologies which extoll the inherent virtues of expanding man's physical footprint in its many different built forms (Gellert and Lynch 2003). When vast swathes of countryside are intensively incorporated into urban centres through highways, ports, pipelines and electrical grids, so that new resource hubs can feed growing consumptive appetites, it is framed as a benevolent service to remote communities, one which brings with it 'development' and 'progress', pitched with deliberate ambiguity. As inner city tenements are demolished to make way for a high-tech industrial park surrounded by sleek postmodern apartment blocks, the language of cosmopolitanism, economic triumphalism and consumer hedonism is appropriated by developer coalitions to gloss over the intricate forms of exclusion, crime and injustice simmering beneath the surface. Those who protest against these changes on the grounds of social cleansing, environmental sustainability or cultural rights, are charged with impeding 'progress'.

Of course, it is certainly not a new thing to critically frame urbanisation as a process marked by inequality, dispossession, exclusion, violence, insecurity, environmental harm and exploitation – there is a growing literature in fields such as geography, sociology, urban studies, political economy, anthropology, planning studies and development studies, which engage with different contested dimensions of this complex process (Davis 2006; Hammar 2008; Logan and Molotch 1987; Mossberger and Stoker 2001; Porteous and Smith 2001). It is less common to find, however, sustained scholarship that investigates the multitude of actors, transactions, and commercial, political and administrative processes that organise on a molecular scale the economic and political activity that steers, speculates on, invests in and manages, this process of concentrated and extended urban expansion.

Yet when cranes lay the foundations for a luxury hotel complex, when trucks bus aggregate for a port facility, when a new downtown apartment block goes on the market, a vast edifice of organisational actors and transactions have been involved. In a capitalist political economy, the economic activity prosecuted by these actors, largely depends on its amenability to profitable forms of investment. This dynamic, though, cannot be divorced from the regimes of governance that shape the built environment. Public policy, legislation, planning codes, tax incentives, public investment (or public–private investment), urban, corporate, financial and environmental regulation, land management procedures, decision making protocols, public administration priorities, can accelerate, steer, direct and/or hinder the process of urban change. So we observe a dialectic relationship between the existing built environment (which reifies and accumulates past episodes of urbanisation), the uneven trajectories and pace of capitalist investment in spatial transformation, and the governmental regimes that draw upon a range of tools to steer how the latter and the former syncopate in new episodes of intensive and extensive urbanisation (see chapter two).

It also needs to be added that the legitimacy of these intersecting processes which organise the pace, trajectory and form of urban change, are hooked in part to their conformance with socially recognised conduct norms. Legislation, regulations, international frameworks and customary principles, establish rules that prohibit conduct which deviates from critical norms governing markets, spatial transformation, public administration and the rights of labour, minorities, consumers and indigenous peoples. When, for instance, construction companies collude to fix a public tender for a major highway, this departs from critical norms governing market competition. If a prime piece of crown land is allocated to a developer at a deflated price, shortly after a Minister's relative is given shares in the benefiting concern, this contravenes fundamental norms regulating public administration. Similarly, an attempt to circumvent planning and zoning requirements by bribing public officials breaks norms centring on public integrity. When indigenous people are forcefully evicted from custodial territories to 'free' space for a major dam, this violates an increasingly influential set of international norms protecting the rights of indigenous communities. While the employment of real-estate assets as a lockbox for the proceeds of organised crime, falls foul of norms governing money laundering.

In short, the intricate ways in which policy, public administration, markets, property and capital enmesh within the sphere of urbanisation, is a rule laden process, rooted in norms that are essential to the broader legitimacy of the economic and political activities out of which built spaces emerge, evolve and are applied. As a result, it is possible that actors involved in organising and profiting from the urban sphere, can violate critical conduct norms governing the built environment, which may become the subject of censure, whether it be in the form of prosecution by criminal justice agencies, or popular forms of condemnation enacted by civil society.

Perhaps not surprisingly it is within the terrain of civil society that we often see the most frenetic efforts to expose and condemn this activity, prosecuted by activists, journalists, NGOs, trade-unions, churches and community groups. To use the example of the UK, Global Witness and the Tax Justice Network have vocally drawn attention to the ease with which corrupt state officials and organised criminals launder money through national property markets. Along parallel lines, *Private Eye* (2015) has shone a light on the criminogenic relationship between incorporated entities established in British Overseas Territories and UK real-property assets, which facilitates money laundering, tax avoidance and tax evasion. Community groups have also proven important players. For instance, we have witnessed resident groups such as Focus E15 Mothers (2017) employ direct action to condemn forced evictions and questionable property deals buttressing the 'regeneration' of London's working class areas. Similarly, community organisations such as Thames Central Open Spaces, have worked alongside Project Compass and the Royal Institute of Architects, to campaign for an investigation into alleged impropriety in the public procurement process for London's controversial £175 million 'Garden Bridge' (see Hodge 2016). These concerns follow on from numerous other megaproject scandals, such as the *Channel 4 News* exposé, which alleged a range of improprieties relating to a £1 billion venture awarded to Chinese firm, Advanced Business Park, to redevelop London's Royal Albert Dock (Crick 2014).

Civil society mobilisation in the UK is a microcosm of much broader global activity. For example, a vibrant international movement has emerged targeting 'useless imposed mega-projects', employing a range of innovative measures that focus public attention on the undemocratic and often improper means used to facilitate large-scale infrastructure projects. The global indigenous peoples struggle – which fuses together a range of groups – has been at the very forefront of efforts that challenge forms of extended urbanisation which cause significant harm to regions of biocultural diversity, often in violation of customary rights, national laws and international norms. Green movements globally have documented and opposed forms of urbanisation that impact on spaces of important natural and cultural significance, in addition to other associated conduct, such as land-grabbing. Human displacement has also been a critical concern for a growing number of national and international NGOs, which campaign to raise awareness of the significant harms produced by development-induced evictions and breaches of housing rights. If we turn to the media, again we can find reporting on questionable property developments, infrastructure projects and land transactions. For example, *The Financial Times* has published in-depth investigations into forced-displacement precipitated by Burma's resource rush (Peel 2016), potential illicit transactions underpinning major real-estate developments constructed on reclaimed land in Bahrain (O'Murchu and Kerr 2014), and grand corruption within Malaysia's 1MDB state investment fund, which involved among other things land-grabs and money allegedly laundered through foreign real-estate (Peel and Vasagar 2016).

These efforts marshalled by civil society, however, have yet to precipitate a criminological agenda specifically focused on how the process of urbanisation lends itself to the crimes of the powerful. This book represents the first systematic and explicit attempt to build such a criminological agenda, one that is centred upon investigating, analysing and theorising illegitimate practices, prosecuted by companies, states and organised crime entities, in order to shape how our built environment is constructed, maintained, used, valued and transformed, both intensively within city hubs, and extensively in rural regions. It is the contention of this book that like other processes which have proven integral to global capitalism, including industrialisation and financialisation, urbanisation is coveted with dynamics that make it a highly criminogenic sphere of organisational conduct, which remains dangerously unscrutinised.

To build a criminological research agenda focused on the edifice of transactions and actors that coordinate and trade upon concentrated and extended urbanisation, the necessary methodological, empirical and theoretical foundations must be laid. This book will initiate this intellectual trajectory by offering a series of scholarly structures upon which future inquiry can be premised.

With that in mind, the first chapter will concentrate on defining key concepts at the heart of this research agenda. To that end, dialectical traditions of criminology, geography and urban studies, will be employed to define the antagonistic processes embodied in the concepts urbanisation and criminality, before looking at how these categories can be usefully combined to inform social inquiry. Then consideration will be given to the types of social phenomena that might fall within this area of inquiry, drawing on research conducted in a broad range of countries spanning Africa, Asia, Europe and the Americas. Finally, chapter one will conclude by introducing the four-year study which this book is based on, looking in particular at the methodology and geopolitical context.

Following this introduction to key framing concepts, chapter two broadens the conceptual focus in order to consider the socio-historical conditions that make possible and desirable the criminogenic dynamics which will be empirically examined in chapters five, six and seven. Drawing on Marx's *Capital*, it is argued that social levers exist within the capitalist political economy which enable value produced through productive sectors – a process which Marx conceptualised using the circuit of industrial capital – to be diverted into auxiliary economic circuits. This process permits certain forms of non-productive investment activity to be rewarded. With this dynamic in mind, David Harvey's work on monopoly rent will be applied to think about the levers which allow value produced through the circuit of industrial capital, to be switched into auxiliary circuits that function through land and property markets. Upon this foundation, it will be argued that organisational actors use illicit repertoires to accentuate their capacity to share in revenue flows circulating through the auxiliary circuits that function through land and property markets. In chapter two, consideration will also be given to how the organisation of governmental power shapes the intensity with which value flows between the industrial circuit and auxiliary circuits. The relationship between the opportunity structures underpinning illicit repertoires in land and property markets, and urban governance regimes, will also be examined.

Having laid out the core conceptual terrain, in chapter three an investigative framework for inquiring into the crimes of urbanisation is developed. The framework draws upon and refashions social network analysis, synthesising it with a new set of techniques called transaction mapping. Together these tools break down into concrete units of analysis the complex processes underpinning the crimes of urbanisation, which can guide clinical forms of inquiry into their social and temporal dimensions. To enhance this process a range of digital tools are introduced. Using visual intelligence and certain concepts associated with social network analysis and transaction mapping, these tools permit the researcher to model the data in ways that more effectively penetrate the opaque social worlds that administer the crimes of the powerful.

Chapter four advances the methodology established in chapter three, by introducing a range of data gathering techniques, that can populate the overarching investigative framework with rich information streams. These techniques are in part a result of methodological experimentation trialled during this study; they are also an outcome of knowledge transfer from civil society organisations and journalists specialising in investigating complex, opaque transactions. A premium has been placed on ensuring this methodology and the tools it involves are accessible to a broad range of users including academic researchers, students, journalists and civil society organisations.

Chapters five and six present two exemplary case studies that emerged out of fieldwork which applied these methodological tools. Their exemplary status is a result of the fact they displayed patterns observable in the other case studies which formed a part of the study; however, certain potent data streams were tapped which allowed the processes at the heart of these patterns to be documented in particularly rich detail, from which core theoretical constructs could be produced. With that in mind, the first exemplary case study presented in chapter five focuses on a large-scale real-estate venture, that aims to radically transform the value of harbour side land, which had previously been reserved for a national park. The venture became mired in a protracted struggle with local residents, which precipitated violent confrontation, and litigation. Chapter six investigates a former plantation that was fraudulently acquired from traditional landowners, in an area earmarked for a special economic zone which is being financed through Chinese state funding.

Chapter seven presents a theoretical framework which initially emerged out of the exemplary case studies. The conceptual construct presented through this framework is geared towards theorising the mechanisms, processes and structures underpinning the illicit repertoires employed by state–corporate actors engaged in land and property market speculation. Here we are primarily talking about forms of land speculation and property development, where returns have been secured in part through a combination of anti-competitive practices, price manipulation, fraud, corruption, regulatory non-compliance, forced evictions, home demolitions and acts of violence directed at residents, activists and civil society. The replicability of the concepts outlined in this chapter are demonstrated through a further two empirical case studies which are presented in summary form.

The conclusion reconnects these findings to the theoretical backdrop outlined in chapter two, before considering how the crimes of urbanisation may be considered a normative site of class struggle, over the way in which built spaces are organised and applied. It will be argued that investigative and ethnographic research can play important roles in both understanding and advancing such struggles for urban justice. Attention will also be given to how a research agenda centring on the crimes of urbanisation might be methodologically, conceptually and empirically advanced in coming years.

Bibliography

Brenner, N. (2013). 'Theses on urbanization', *Public Culture*, 25(1), 85–114.

Crick, M. (2014). 'Big questions for Boris over billion dollar property deal', *4 News*, 13 November. [Online]. Available at: www.channel4.com/news/boris-johnson-london-propery-deal-china-albert-dock (accessed: 16 February 2017).

Davis, M. (2006). *Planet of the Slums*, London: Verso.

Focus E15 Mothers. (2017). 'Focus E15: social housing not social cleansing'. [Online]. Available at: https://focuse15.org/ (accessed: 11 May 2017).

Gellert, P. K. and Lynch, B. D. (2003). 'Mega-projects as displacements', *International Social Science Journal*, 55(175), 15–25.

Hammar, A. (2008). 'In the name of sovereignty: Displacement and state making in post-independence Zimbabwe', *Journal of Contemporary African Studies*, 26(4), 417–434.

Harvey, D. (1985). *The Urbanization of Capital: Studies in the History and Theory of Capitalist Urbanization*, Baltimore: John Hopkins University Press.

Hodge, M. (2017). *Independent Review of the Garden Bridge Project*, London: Mayor of London.

Lefebvre, H. (2003). *The Urban Revolution*. Minneapolis: The University of Minnesota Press.

Logan, J. R. and Molotch, H. L. (1987). *Urban Fortunes: The Political Economy of Place*, London: University of California Press.

Mossberger, K. and Stoker, G. (2001). 'The evolution of urban regime theory: The challenge of conceptualization', *Urban Affairs Review*, 36(6), 810–835.

O'Murchu, C. and Kerr, S. (2014). 'Disputed land development boosts wealth of Bahrain royals', Financial Times, 10 December. [Online]. Available at: www.ft.com/content/51943274-73fb-11e4-b444-00144feabdc0 (accessed: 16 February 2017).

Peel, M. (2016). 'The great land rush', Financial Times, 1 March. [Online]. Available at: https://ig.ft.com/sites/land-rush-investment/myanmar/ (accessed: 16 February 2017).

Peel, M. and Vasagar, J. (2016) 'Malaysia: The 1MDB money trail', *Financial Times*, 15 February. [Online]. Available at: www.ft.com/content/0981b2c8-cfe3-11e5-92a1-c5e23 ef99c77 (accessed: 16 February 2017).

Porteous, J. D. and Smith, S. E. (2001). *Domicide: The Global Destruction of Home*, London: McGill-Queen's University Press.

Private Eye. (2015). 'Selling England (and Wales) by the pound', Private Eye. [Online]. Available at: www.private-eye.co.uk/registry (accessed: 11 May 2017).

Smith, N. (1982). 'Gentrification and uneven development', *Economic Geography*, 58(2), 139–155.

Chapter 1

Key concepts, empirical backdrop and research design

Introduction

The clarity, and conceptual rigour, with which we define our empirical focus, is not only essential from the standpoint of scholarly integrity, it orientates research, in subtle ways, to particular points in the empirical terrain; and thus serves to influence the type of inquiries likely to emerge out of the thematic focus. As Ward puts it: 'Definitions … are important, not because they precisely demarcate the boundaries of a discipline, but because of the questions that they prompt us to ask' (2013: 77).

With that in mind, this chapter will set out in greater conceptual detail, the processes being signposted through the concept 'urbanisation'. Consideration will also be given to how these processes may be thought of as spaces where different forms of organisational deviance can occur, triggering censure from residents, social movements, governing authorities and other stakeholders. To that end, the chapter will begin by unpacking urbanisation as an organising concept, drawing on dialectical scholarly traditions. Urbanisation, from this vantage point, will be framed as a set of dynamic and contradictory processes that create, and recreate, in an uneven and convulsive fashion, built environments on a planetary scale. This uneven and convulsive planetary process, it will be argued, is tightly bound to the rhythms of global capitalism, and a system of governance which the latter's rhythms are meditated through.

Once the process of urbanisation has been conceptually framed, we will go on to consider how the organisations and transactions that materially enact and manage this uneven, convulsive and at times destructive process, also operate within a normative terrain – itself a historical creation, with elastic fault-lines – which can generate, when contravened, resistance, censure and sanction. It will therefore be contended, that from a dialectical perspective, there is embedded in the urbanisation process, the active historical conditions for different social coalitions to direct heightened forms of stigma against targeted organisations and transactions, that inscribe upon them the quality of being criminal. Urbanisation, accordingly, is a contentious process in which a possibility exists that criminality may be inscribed on related illegitimate state and corporate activity; but if the possible is to be actualised, social mobilisation and censure must be successfully enacted, which of course occurs in a contested and uneven power terrain.

Having established the overarching conceptual framework for defining this book's focus, the potential types of illicit state and corporate activity that fit within this focus will be pointed to, drawing from a diverse range of literatures. Once mapped, the specific research backdrop for the book's methodological, theoretical and empirical contributions will then be outlined. In particular, attention will be turned to the geopolitical arena – Papua New Guinea – where the process of planetary urbanisation was studied; an arena where the impact of illegitimate state–corporate transactions on both 'town' and 'country', have become the target of social mobilisation, resistance and censure. The political-economic context of these illegitimate transactions will be outlined. Attention will then be turned to the particular way in which the case study methodology was employed, to inquire into opaque and covert state–corporate activity, with a view to generating theory that can more richly articulate the social relationships, regimes of power and institutional repertoires, underpinning forms of illegitimate urbanisation. In the subsequent chapters, the substantive discoveries that emerged from this research design will be presented.

Urbanisation, the built environment and global capitalism

'Urbanisation' is one of the essential points of reference around which this book is organised. Like other foundational concepts at the heart of interdisciplinary inquiry, it is a contested category. This intervention rests on a particular conception of urbanisation initially formulated by Lefebvre, before being further refined and deepened by a number of urban theorists, with Neil Brenner and David Harvey being among the most important interlocutors.

Engagement with this tradition of urban thought was not an arbitrary decision. It was apparent from early fieldwork and a review of the cognate literature, that many of the criminogenic drivers underpinning urban change occurring within city hubs, could also be observed in the countryside. Therefore, a conceptual arrangement was needed which could underpin analysis into geographical spheres that have traditionally been viewed through the lens of dichotomy rather than unity. Complicating matters, core criminogenic drivers contained within the process of urbanisation were closely linked to land and property market activities. It was critical, therefore, that any conception of urbanisation as a planetary process, was also acutely sensitive to how its pace, trajectory and forms are conditioned by commercial activities structured around capitalist social relations. The dialectical tradition of urban theory developed by scholars such as Lefebvre, Harvey and Brenner, offered the most fertile landscape in which to grapple with these complex issues.

To begin, it is worth noting an important distinction advanced by Lefebvre, which differentiates between urbanisation and the built environment. Lefebvre (2003) contends that the built environment may be conceived of as an object, constituted through things such as factories, office blocks, apartment complexes, highways, railways, sewerage systems, gas pipelines, port facilities, dams, and so on. Urbanisation, on the other hand, captures the social processes through which this material environment is generated, organised, connected, maintained, transformed and destroyed (2003: 16). Therefore, just as a particular commodity – say, shoes or a television set – may be conceived as a temporal material articulation of a broader set of relations and processes, so to the vast material system of built life, despite its apparent permanence, is a temporal articulation of dense social processes captured under the umbrella term, urbanisation.

Urbanisation, conceived as a set of dense social processes that cultivate, organise, connect and transform the built environment, is clearly a phenomenon that transcends any one historical epoch. Nevertheless, Harvey, Brenner and Lefebvre each maintain it is important that attempts to understand the pace, trajectory and content of urbanisation are sensitive to the fact that these variables are deeply informed by historically developed social relations, which are peculiar to particular epochs. Accordingly, if urbanisation is to be framed as a dense set of processes which drive change within the built environment – cultivating it, giving it specific meanings, transforming its depth and breadth – then its pulse is the spatial rhythms of the capitalist political economy.

It is critical, therefore, to understand the different ways in which capitalism as a system tugs at, and drives urbanisation. To that end, as this system of political-economic life progressively emerged over four centuries, then expanded across the globe, it has been at times the erratic midwife for a vast transformation in the productive forces. This has shepherded concentrated forms of production that combine highly complex industrial instruments with collective labour processes, in ways that greatly expand our aggregate output relative to labour time (Marx 1976). This immense coming together on a global scale of raw materials, machinery, buildings, labour, work processes and technology – strengthened through increasingly rapid forms of communication and transport – has heavily rested on sophisticated systems of credit. The credit system enables the centralisation of capital needed to drive vast industrial enterprises, secure major infrastructural developments and facilitate international trade and investment (Harvey 2012). Because periods of dormancy for capital represent a cost, capitalism has also triggered revolutions in the means of transport and communication, which have collapsed time through the construction of built space, that facilitates the rapid movement of people, goods and information (Bukharin 2003).

This schismatic dynamism at the heart of capitalism is inherently married to expansionary tendencies. As the social stock of capital grows, it must find ways to valorise itself. There is thus an impulse to find new areas for profitable investment. This, on the one hand, can drive industrial innovation, leaps in new technologies and foreign investment, on the other it can also fuel market speculation, out of which bubbles grow.

Attached to capitalism's schismatic dynamism are evidenced tendencies towards crisis, which have important implications for the built environment (Brenner 2013). These periods of crisis often prove particularly traumatic for working class communities, who witness their built environment being robbed of its purpose and vitality, during the downturn period. Future iterations of urban expansion that can breathe life into abandoned manufacturing districts and immiserated working class suburbs, frequently hinge on a process of 'creative destruction' where existing built environments are demolished, rezoned and refashioned, so it is congruent with a new iteration of capitalist development (Harvey 1985).

This period of urban 'renewal' often provides a crucial fix for capital during the post-crisis recovery period. For example, Smith argues suburbanisation in the United States helped enliven capitalism during the aftermath of the depressions in the 1890s and 1930s. He notes, 'with FHA [Federal Housing Administration] mortgage subsidies, the construction of highways, and so on, the state subsidized suburbanization quite deliberately as part of a larger solution to crisis' (Smith 1982: 150). Also, whether it be the gentrification of inner-city tenements, or the branching out of suburbs, these moments of urban change are a vital stimulant for consumer demand, in addition to household indebtedness, which has a range of economic and disciplinary benefits for capitalism (Harvey 2012). That is not to neglect, however, the role which increased indebtedness and urban speculation can play stewarding in new periods of crisis, as the recent Global Financial Crisis visibly demonstrated.

Of course, the dynamic and often antagonistic way the different beats of capitalism, urbanisation and population syncopate, cannot be divorced from government (Brenner 2004; Harvey 1989, 2012; Tretter 2009). Indeed, as capitalist urbanisation inspires new built landscapes, socio-demographic configurations and forms of social contention, acute governance challenges emerge relating to public health, inequality, deprivation, unemployment, crime, environmental management, organised labour, decaying infrastructure, people movement, an aging population, and so on. It might also be noted, urbanisation is not a discrete process – it is an uneven mesh that intensively and extensively expands on a global scale producing multiscalar connections between emerging agglomerations of built life. The connections, flows and circulations – which include people, money, goods, information, energy, disease – that take place through this global built edifice must be managed through policy, law, investment and intervention. How regimes of government, at multiple levels, use political instruments to strategically manage the process of urbanisation, and the metabolism that takes place through built environments, is critical both to the pulse of capitalism and the particular historical ways in which capitalist forms of urbanisation unfold (Foucault 2007; Harvey 1985; Smith 2002).

With that in mind, the challenge then becomes one of conceptualising urbanisation in a way that is sensitive to the dynamic processes pointed to in the preceding discussion. Lefebvre, for instance, coins the metaphor 'implosion-explosion', which he borrows from nuclear physics, to help capture urbanisation as a dynamic, contradictory totality. Capitalist urbanisation, Lefebvre contends, involves the 'tremendous concentration (of people, activities, wealth, goods, objects, instruments, means, and thought) of urban reality and the immense explosion, the projection of numerous, disjunct fragments (peripheries, suburb, vacation homes, satellite towns) into space' (2003: 13).

Building on this foundation, Brenner (2013) argues that capitalist urbanisation can be usefully thought about in terms of concentration and extension. On the one hand, urbanisation coagulates into heaving interconnected cityscapes that intensively integrate vast industrial, commercial, residential, finance and leisure zones, through a complex nerve system of roads, railways, trams, telegraphs, fibre optic cables, and so on. It also bursts outwards, into rural spaces that have become hubs for resource extraction, food production, biofuels, recreation, tourism and other commodifiable activities. Both processes in Brenner's conception are entwined and interdependent. He observes:

> As conceived here, therefore, urbanization involves both concentration and extension: these moments are dialectically intertwined insofar as they simultaneously presuppose and counteract one another. This proposition suggests that the conditions and trajectories of agglomerations (cities, city-regions, etc.) must be connected analytically to larger-scale processes of territorial reorganization, circulation (of labour, commodities, raw materials, nutrients, and energy), and resource extraction that ultimately encompass the space of the entire world. At the same time, this perspective suggests that important socioenvironmental transformations in zones that are not generally linked to urban conditions, from circuits of agribusiness and extractive landscapes for oil, natural gas, and coal to transoceanic infrastructural networks, underground pipelines, and satellite orbits, have in fact been ever more tightly intertwined with the developmental rhythms of urban agglomerations. Consequently, whatever their administrative demarcation, sociospatial morphology, population density, or positionality within the global capitalist system, such spaces must be considered integral components of an extended, worldwide urban fabric.
> (Brenner 2013: 102–103; see also Brenner 2000)

Framed this way, urbanisation is a differentiated totality which functions through interdependent moments of concentration and extension that take place on a planetary scale. The challenge then becomes to overlay this planetary heat map of urban change, onto geographically sensitive conceptions of global capitalism, in order to interrogate their complex relations and tensions.

Because concentrated and extended urbanisation is bonded to the geographically uneven rhythms of capitalist reproduction, it is an inherently unstable process. Urban theory, therefore, needs categories which are sensitive to the important role played by rupture and urban 'regeneration'. Indeed, as new iterations of concentrated and extended urbanisation emerge, driven by the turbines of uneven capitalist growth, they often must plough through the built legacies left by past episodes in urbanisation. This makes what Harvey labels 'creative destruction', an intrinsic feature of urban change (2003: 101). Harvey explains:

> Under capitalism there is … a perpetual struggle in which capital builds a physical landscape appropriate to its own conditions at a particular moment in time, only to have to destroy it, usually in the course of a crisis, at a subsequent point in time.
>
> (1985: 28; see also Harvey 1985: 44)

'Violence is required', he contends, 'to achieve the new urban world on the wreckage of the old' (Harvey 2012: 16).

Therefore, when we talk about the crimes of *urbanisation*, we are in effect talking about an often violent process of concentrated and extended urbanisation, that is fed by the uneven and clumpy spatial configurations of global capitalism (Ashman 2006). These processes are planetary in scope, multi-scalar in effect, and pregnant with dynamics that provoke contention, class conflict and social rupture.

Yet planetary urbanisation in its complexity could not occur unless there was a vast coming together of actors, resources and transactions, responsible for organising, at a molecular social-level, all the activities essential to its intensive and extensive drives. This organised edifice of actors, transactions and resource flows, operates through rule-laden markets and political institutions. An intellectual agenda centring on the crimes of urbanisation can, therefore, distinguish itself by studying the opportunity structures for state, corporate and organised crime that emerge from the dynamic ways in which extended and concentrated urbanisation interlock with the uneven and clumpy spatio-temporal spread of global capitalism. In particular, criminology is in a position to usefully interrogate how illicit repertoires seep into the molecular processes powering urbanisation, looking at the interests these repertoires buttress, the material changes facilitated, and the movements of resistance that emerge in opposition to illegitimate forms of urban activity.

However, such an agenda also needs to be rooted in a definition of crime that invokes sufficiently probative research questions. With that challenge in mind, we will now unpack the social processes which the category of crime denotes, looking at how they can be merged with the particular conception of urbanisation presented above.

The *crimes* of urbanisation

During a famous debate with the corporate crime researcher, Edwin Sutherland (1983), criminologist Paul Tappan warned of the dangers associated with stretching the word 'crime' beyond strict, criminal law definitions. He observed: 'The rebel may enjoy a veritable orgy of delight in damning as criminal almost anyone he pleases' (Tappan 1946: 99). Tappan continued, 'vague, omnibus concepts defining crime are a blight upon either a legal system or a system of sociology that strives to be objective' (Tappan 1946: 99). Sutherland was not, of course, arguing for a 'vague' or 'omnibus' definition of crime. His contention was of a more nuanced order. Owing to the disproportionate power corporations have to exercise influence over political decision making, Sutherland (1983) argued, their illicit conduct is frequently censured through more sedate administrative and civil law procedures. Accordingly, he suggested, if criminology is to be objective, its focal lens must take into account and compensate for power differentials, to ensure no one is excluded from criminological research on the basis of organisational influence.

This struggle to build a definitional framework that is sensitive to power dynamics, yet is capable of winning wider scholarly respect, has also been played out in the field of state crime studies (see Cohen 1993; Kauzlarich et al. 1992; Mullins and Rothe 2008; Schwendinger and Schwendinger 1975). Mindful of the fact individual states have the capacity to exceptionalise their own conduct, scholars have worked to build robust definitions of state crime using international law and human rights principles. These conceptual efforts have delineated boundaries for state crime research with enough precision to facilitate a growing body of empirical inquiry and theorisation.

However, one thread of state crime scholarship has left aside doctrinal debates over potential international criteria, to instead focus attention on the processes that have historically imprinted upon particular state conduct the quality of being a crime. Initiated by Green and Ward through a series of interventions published in 2000 and further developed by Lasslett, this tract contends that crime in this context captures a special, heightened form of social stigma that attaches to organisational activities and actors, when their conduct exceeds fundamental norms governing particular fields of practice (see Green and Ward 2000, 2004; Lasslett 2014a). So with respect to the state there are fundamental conduct-norms that make claims to state power justified and 'expressive of consent' (Green and Ward add 'exactly what this "consent" amounts to may be a very difficult question'), contravention of which will place the offending conduct outside the legitimate repertoire of political practice the state proclaims to employ and the normative values it relies on for a public mandate (Green and Ward 2000: 108–109). However, in an important qualification, Green and Ward (2000) contend, illegitimate actions only become deviant when a social audience is disposed to censure the particular transactions and apply sanctions.

This standpoint registers the fact that illegitimate activity may occur, which departs from fundamental conduct-norms, but the processes that attach stigma to such behaviour must be historically actioned through the mobilisation of censure and condemnation. This censorious activity, Green and Ward (2000) observe, is not simply the domain of state agencies, it can be enacted from below by civil society (see also Grewcock 2012). Indeed, the state crime scholarship aptly demonstrates that the terrain of civil society is among the most potent spaces where movements and actions are organised, that condemn illegitimate state practices as deviant (see Stanley and McCulloch 2012).

This approach to defining crime is sensitive to the fact that it is not an ahistorical quality inherent to an act, but rather a historically developed feature which practices acquire owing to particular social processes in which struggle is a vital determinant. Indeed, the hegemonic norms which govern fields of practice are only reified in particular phenomenal forms which hold wide-scale influence, owing to a complex process of advocacy that invariably takes place across multiple scales and terrains – this is as true for workplace health and safety as it is for human rights. Because legitimacy is a historical variable, the scope for illegitimate conduct can increase or decrease depending on the outcomes of these struggles and processes that embed fundamental conduct-norms within fields of practice. Similarly, the enactment of illegitimate practices by organisational actors does not of itself render these practices deviant, it is again a historical variable which is conditioned by the capacity of agents to mobilise credible force that can censure and sanction the conduct. In all these instances, counter-measures will of course be employed by powerful organisational actors to limit the scope of fundamental conduct-norms, conceal illegitimate activities and disrupt censuring efforts – hence emphasis must be placed on the term 'struggle' (Lasslett 2012).

It might be concluded, therefore, that when practices marshalled by state actors begin to attain the quality of being criminal, this articulates an immense coming together of historical forces, through the matrix of conduct norms – which are a legacy of previous advocacy efforts – and contemporary struggles which censure illegitimate actions as wrong. There is also no reason why we need limit this dialectical view to the state. It can be usefully extended to think about a range of powerful organisations, such as corporations and religious institutions, whose actions acquire the stigma of being criminal, only through the marshalling of quite significant social forces in the manner previously described.

Using such an approach, it might be asked, what type of research questions does this framing invite? First, it is clearly within the scope of this approach to look at the evolving normative landscape that governs institutional practices within a range of social fields, looking at the determinations which shape their form. Second, it is relevant to ask why are illegitimate repertoires employed by organisational actors to prosecute their interests, and under what conditions do they become systematic? The absence of censure in these situations does not preclude criminological inquiry; it does however demand we theorise the forces behind this absence. Third, criminological inquiry can usefully ask why certain harmful organisational activities strongly condemned by national and international civil society, are not necessarily illegitimate (Hillyard and Tombs 2004; Pemberton 2007). Relatedly, where particularly harmful practices are neither illegitimate nor indeed deviant, again there would appear to be place in the criminological landscape to ask why certain deleterious conduct becomes normalised. Fourth, illegitimacy and deviancy are not static qualities, they come about in degrees, and in different relative proportions – exploring the historical conditions behind these different configurations is a matter of importance. Of course, these are not the only research questions a dialectical framing of crime invokes. However, the above examples do demonstrate that this framing is suitably flexible to trigger diverse lines of inquiry that interrogate the sociohistorical dimensions of criminality.

With that in mind, when reference is made to the 'crimes' of urbanisation this captures dynamics that are more expansive than acts/actors found guilty of a criminal breach by a court of law. We are concerned with the complex ways in which illegitimate activities within the urban sphere come into being, are organised and concealed, and the struggles these activities precipitate across the landscape of civil society and government.

Accordingly, drawing on such framing, it may be said that this volume will empirically focus on state–corporate activity within land and property markets, concentrating in particular on land speculation and large-scale real-estate developments (some of which may be dubbed megaprojects). Such a concern requires attention be cast upon the fundamental norms governing urban planning, land and property markets, public administration, and corporate activity, in addition to the intricate networks and mechanisms used to prosecute illegitimate activities in this sector. Consideration will also be given to the complex social movements that emerge across the landscape of civil society and government in order to condemn these practices, looking at the barriers and countermeasures which can disrupt censorious actions that imprint stigma.

It might be said then, once we frame the crimes of urbanisation dialectically, a range of new questions emerge, expanding the scope of criminological inquiry, without necessarily succumbing to the 'orgy of delight' Tappan warned against. Indeed, rather than bounding inquiry by legal rules, once a dialectical approach is adopted, research takes quite a different tack, focusing on the historically elastic boundaries that give organisational practices within the urban sphere their legitimacy, looking at what motivates and allows organisations to contravene these boundaries, and the subsequent struggles this conduct provokes, as those responsible attempt to conceal their actions and disrupt organised efforts at censure.

Now that 'crime' and 'urbanisation' have been framed as a thick set of social processes, that intersect in historically specific ways – a dynamic upon which the crimes of urbanisation as a thematic rests – we will move on to consider the geographical scope and problems raised in existing research captured by this intellectual agenda.

The crimes of urbanisation: a typology

While 'crimes of urbanisation' is not yet an explicit criminological agenda, research touching upon the processes this agenda necessarily involves has been conducted within criminology and cognate disciplines. It is instructive, therefore, to survey this literature so we may specify with greater clarity the particular forms of social contention a 'crimes of urbanisation' research agenda might necessarily address. With that in mind we will begin by examining important currents within the urban planning literature, before going on to consider emerging scholarly tracts organised around the concepts of land-grabbing, forced evictions, megaprojects and environmental harm.

Turning first to the urban planning literature, we can observe a relatively small but important body of interdisciplinary contributions which consider how the decisions and rules governing space, and the economic and political reverberations they spark, give rise to certain criminogenic potentialities. To that end, Chiodelli and Moroni contend, 'corruption in land-use planning is found in many countries around the globe, and the damage that it causes is considerable' (2015: 241; see also Jiménez 2009). They argue, this in part reflects the way in which political decision making within the spheres of physical planning and construction, impacts on land and property markets. A decision to rezone land, for instance, can facilitate new forms of construction activity which precipitate a spike in land prices; the speed and rigour with which governments approve development proposals can impact significantly on construction costs. As a result, Chiodelli and Moroni (2015) suggest there is a range of financial incentives to employ bribery as a tool for reducing costs and manipulating market prices, a dynamic that is exacerbated by the low prospects of getting caught.

This dynamic has been documented in a broad range of regions. For example, Mahmud (2007) argues that while implementing agencies ostensibly charged with overseeing planned urban growth in Bangladesh are armed with credible legislation, these legislative measures have been subverted to impede construction activity and solicit bribes. This creates the environment in which urban entrepreneurs are incentivised to engage in corrupt activities to expedite approval (Mahmud 2007). In return for illicit payments, authorities are prepared to turn a blind eye towards activities that contravene zoning requirements and building regulation.

Turning to European theatres, Jiménez maintains that certain features of Spanish planning law have facilitated illicit forms of land speculation. He notes:

> Spanish planning laws have stipulated that – in the case of expropriation – rural land that becomes urban land under the municipal plan would be given a value as if it were already fully developed (urbanized and built on) simply by the plan being approved.
>
> (Jiménez 2009: 258)

A strong incentive is thus created for land speculators to work in tandem with public officials in an effort to manufacture urban plans and expropriate rural property for considerable profit. This feature of Spanish planning law, Jiménez observes, has been 'an extraordinary source of speculation and corruption' (2009: 258).

The social consequences of corrupt urban planning processes can be particularly high. For example, Green notes that a process of market liberalisation and patronage politics facilitated a construction boom in Turkey during the 1980s and 1990s, where 'it was possible to build wherever and whatever one liked, with no adequate regulatory control' (2005: 530). Subsequently, between 1999 and 2003, a series of earthquakes took 40,000 lives across Turkey and destroyed 300,000 homes. Green (2005) contends, the loss of life and property was directly linked to unregulated construction activity, which dramatically increased the earthquakes' human impacts. As a result, she concludes, the natural disasters' toll can 'be attributed in large part to government and industry corruption, gross negligence and state links to organized crime, or in other words, to state-orchestrated organizational deviance' (2005: 528).

The illegitimate manipulation of urban planning processes, however, is not only a field for enacting economic crimes. For instance, Smith and Green (2014) have catalogued the role which urban planning plays in Israeli state efforts to persecute and displace Palestinian communities (see also Green and Smith 2016). Following fieldwork in East Jerusalem, Ramallah, Jordan Valley, Yafa, Tel Aviv, Hebron, Bethlehem and the Negev Desert, Smith and Green uncovered a significant volume of cases where the Israeli state abused zoning regulations to render residential Palestinian communities illegal. As a result, affected communities have been denied access to basic amenities, and must live under the constant spectre of forced eviction, which is frequently enacted, with brutality. This same spectre is widened even further through the systemic practice of denying Palestinian households permission to expand homes. Smith and Green observe of the West Bank, '94% of the 3,750 requests for planning permission made by Palestinians between 2010 and 2012 were rejected by the Israeli authorities' (2014: 12). As a result, 'Palestinians wishing to extend their homes or expand their communities in order to accommodate family and population growth face impossible bureaucratic barriers and have no other option but to build without a permit' (Smith and Green 2014: 12).

Complementing and intersecting with this literature on physical planning, urban governance and corruption, is a growing tract of research organised around the concept of 'land-grabs'. This research centres, in particular, on certain international dynamics, which have facilitated large-scale redistribution of landholdings from local owners in the Global South, to transnational organisational actors. This asset redistribution, it is argued, has been primed by a global process of land-market liberalization, which has expedited the pace with which landholdings have been commodified and alienated (White 2012; Zoomers 2010). This process of market liberalisation has fused with transnational systems of production that have shepherded significant capital flows into ventures that profit through stakes in minerals, biofuels, foodstuffs and other raw materials. The literature on land-grabs concentrates on theorising these dynamics and the 'large-scale, cross-border land deals' they depend upon (Zoomers 2010: 430).

Given that these deals are often punctuated by forced evictions and allegations of resource theft, the literature on land-grabs invariably intersects with more established scholarly tracts on development-induced displacement, forced evictions and the enclosure of the commons.

It is apparent from these multiple tracks, that land-grabs, resource theft and development-induced displacement are global problems, which take different, historically distinct forms. We find evidence for this from all continents. Klopp, for instance, observes that Kenya has been gripped by a 'land grabbing mania' (2008: 298), where prime plots of state land in city centres have been leased or sold well below market price, through irregular transactions that suggest acts of fraud and corruption, facilitated through political patronage networks. Shifting the context to Asia, similar dynamics have been evidenced in Cambodia. Mgbako et al. report that Cambodian officials:

> have benefited from the high price of land by unlawfully granting land title to private developers in exchange for compensation. Once these officials have granted land title to developers, they forcibly evict from the property existing residents, who mostly come from poor and marginalized communities.
>
> (2010: 40)

The forced evictions associated with land-grabs flag a range of important human rights concerns (Farha 2011). The evictions themselves can be brutal, conducted with little or no notice, with homes being demolished *en masse*. Compensation payments offered to affected residents are often non-existent or derisory and can contain significant discriminatory dimensions. Where alternative living arrangements are offered, they usually involve locations on the urban periphery with minimal access to services, infrastructure and employment. Developer coalitions sanitise these deleterious acts through discourses that stigmatise displaced residents through pejorative labels, which is set against the proposed development, cast in terms of development, modernisation and improved living standards. As a result, Farha (2011) concludes, forced evictions target:

> the most marginalized and vulnerable populations, most often with far-reaching implications with respect to their housing, employment, education, physical and mental health, family life, culture, and overall well-being. Moreover, forced eviction deepens poverty, destroys communities, and irrevocably adversely impacts the future of millions of people.
>
> (Farha 2011: vii; see also Porteous and Smith 2001).

The scale of the problem presented by development induced displacement is pointed to by Neef and Singer (2015). Looking at Asia, they observe, 'in the second half of the twentieth century over 45 million people were displaced by development projects in China [alone]'. Neef and Singer continue, 'in India, it is estimated that almost 60 million people were displaced between 1948 and 2008' (Neef and Singer 2015: 602–603). Although post-war Europe and North America have not been traditionally identified with mass displacement on this scale (Farha 2011), the Global Financial Crisis and the subsequent austerity policies, have precipitated a wave of forced evictions across both continents, which have disproportionately affected low-income households, ethnic minorities with a foot in the private housing market and those reliant on social housing (European Action Coalition for the Right to Housing and to the City n.d.; Wyly et al. 2009).

Of course, not all resources grabs or forced evictions are economically motivated. For example, Hammar (2008) finds that the forced displacement of residential communities in Zimbabwe has on occasions been employed by the Mugabe regime to reconstitute the geopolitical landscape. She observes:

> At different moments, people accused of being 'enemies of the state' (mostly for being, or assumed to be, opposition party supporters) have been forcibly and often brutally removed from farms, rural villages, informal urban housing, factories, non-formal business enterprises, local council offices, schools, churches and NGOs.
>
> (Hammar 2008: 421)

The evicted are often then replaced, Hammar (2008) contends, by party loyalists. The impact can be colossal. In one notable instance during 2006, Operation Murambatsvina rendered 700,000 people in Harare homeless – which is over double the size of the famous Maroko eviction in Nigeria (Agbola and Jinadu 1997).

In contexts marked by rising property prices and clientelistic political regimes, a number of interventions suggest organised crime groups are especially well placed to prosper through bribery and violence. In her research on Mumbai, Weinstein found a record rise in property prices led the local state to begin 'making certain highly valued lands available for development through a series of industrial land conversions, slum clearance schemes, and the de-reservation of certain public lands' (2008: 22). Mumbai's organised crime groups took advantage of this opportunity to diversify their illicit portfolios and enter the property-development business. Drawing on their connection with political parties and transnational business networks, Weinstein observes that bribes, violence and 'black money' were employed by these organised crime groups 'to finance land acquisition and property developments' (2008: 32).

Switching focus to South America, Grajales (2011) notes that paramilitary groups in Colombia have synthesised their capacity to marshal violence, with their extensive reach into the Colombian state, in order to prosecute forced evictions and land-grabs. The forms of violent and social capital wielded by paramilitaries, Grajales (2011) argues, allows them to forcefully expel peasant communities from rural landholdings using terror; the stolen assets are then laundered with assistance from government agencies. This provides paramilitary lieutenants, or their proxies, with formal land titles. Once these titles are washed of their illicit origins, the land can be sold off to agribusiness for considerable profit. As a result, Grajales concludes, in Colombia we witness the conversion of 'spurious capitals into legal ones' (2011: 789).

Given their immense scale, lucrative features and heavy debt to political decision makers, megaprojects have proven vulnerable to the themes discussed above. The term itself is coined to capture those large-scale built ventures that require an extensive marshalling of resources and which, in turn, exact a significant imprint on the host terrain (Flyvbjerg 2014). Megaprojects might include transport infrastructure such as high-speed rail, tourist ventures such as a theme-park, and energy projects, such as mines, gas pipelines and hydroelectricity dams, to name just a few examples. Common to all is their scope, the fine political-economic mesh they must pass through, and their tendency to displace biophysical landscapes and human communities (Gellert and Lynch 2003). These dynamics are pregnant with a number of criminogenic potentialities.

For instance, in a paper on megaprojects in Brazil, Brandão Timo argues that such 'projects are being executed in the country at an unbridled pace and in disregard for the basic principles of the democratic rule of law' (2013: 138). An expansive list of deleterious impacts is compiled by Brandão Timo. She contends, megaprojects have targeted poor and marginalised communities, violated rights to housing, polluted the biophysical environment, undermined community health, damaged sustainable development practices, restricted the right to information and consultation, and led to the intimidation of community leaders and activists by police. Shifting attention to North America, Olds' (1998) study of megaprojects in Canada – including Expo 86, the Calgary Winter Olympics and the Toronto Summer Olympics – found that lax laws and speculative activity precipitated wide-scale evictions, that had a distinctly disproportionate impact on poor and low-income households living in residential hotels. The human rights violations associated with megaprojects occur, Olds (1998) concludes, because these ventures achieve strong government backing rooted in a belief they will stimulate private capital flows, urban regeneration and international prestige; coupled to which is their significant (complex) scope, compressed implementing period and the substantial mass of capital hooked to the project's success.

It would be remiss at this stage to overlook the important contributions made by green criminology. This criminological field has drawn attention to the multiple ways in which the industrial and urban footprint of human civilisation has harmed delicate biospheres, in addition to the complex normative questions such harm precipitates, or fails to trigger (White 2013). Critically, green criminologists have examined how harmful forms of social conduct – such as toxic dumping, deforestation and habitat destruction – overlap with other forms of state–corporate criminality, such as corruption and land-grabbing. As a result, there is an opportunity to study further the connection between the crimes of urbanisation and green crimes, which frequently flow out of the former.

To conclude, it can be observed through the above literature that while an intellectual agenda centring on the crimes of urbanisation is a new enterprise, clearly it rests upon important research produced within both criminology and cognate fields. This research reveals that the crimes of urbanisation are global in scope, with heavy empirical footprints across Asia, the Middle East, Africa, Europe and the Americas. Furthermore, the research also demonstrates that these crimes produce a human, financial and biophysical toll, far greater in magnitude than street crimes, which elicit the majority of policy attention.

By leading an interdisciplinary research programme into the crimes of urbanisation criminology can challenge this trend, by visibly exposing the intricate nexus of actors, mechanisms, institutions and transactions such crimes involve, and the important movements of resistance they trigger. Furthermore, if this can be done in a comparative fashion, the field can begin to fashion analysis that determines whether the diverse forms of illicit activity pointed to above are potentially connected by shared transaction sequences, in addition to common market, social and political structures.

On that note, we will now turn to the empirical study on which this book rests. It offers the first large data-set specifically designed to build a criminological research agenda focusing on the crimes of urbanisation.

The empirical context and research design

It has already been noted that this book aims to establish a solid conceptual, methodological and theoretical foundation for advancing research into the crimes of urbanisation. One essential prerequisite for achieving this objective is the production of robust empirical data-sets. This was achieved through a four-year study, completed in early 2016. The study focused on practices employed by organisational actors engaged in large-scale land speculation and real-estate developments. These practices were documented in order to determine the frequency of illicit transactions and to study the role such transactions play in prosecuting state–corporate interests. The type of illegitimate conduct evidenced through fieldwork included anti-competitive practices, price-fixing, fraud, bribery, land law violations, physical planning breaches, company law violations, unlawful eviction exercises, property destruction, and attacks on activists. The movements of resistance that emerged in response to this illegitimate conduct was also documented, including the practices and counter-practices employed during struggles to censure the illegitimate conduct as deviant.

The scope of the empirical research was informed by a broader theoretical agenda directed towards unpacking the social network structures, institutional mechanisms and transactional sequences that aid illegitimate activity in land and property markets; in addition to the historical processes that make these criminogenic forces a systematic feature of the capitalist political economy. Of course, to successfully execute these different theoretical aims, the collected data-sets needed to provide a clear window into the transactions and actors organising land speculation and real-estate development, one that is wide enough in scope to forensically and systematically capture over extended time periods the full range of social determinations informing relevant state–corporate activities.

Given these aims, a choice was made to design the research employing the theory building, case study methodology (Dul and Hak 2008; Eisenhardt 1989; Eisenhardt and Graebner 2007; Iacono et al. 2011; Løkke and Sørensen 2014). This particular branch of case study research is suited to emerging areas of inquiry, where there is a lack of conceptual scholarship from which to build a diversified intellectual agenda. While the crimes of urbanisation have certainly been considered in a number of scholarly tracts, it has never been done in a unified fashion with a view to developing theory that can explain the role illicit practices play in the contentious process of concentrated and extended urbanisation. Accordingly, the theory building, case study approach was congruent not only with the study aims but the existing scholarly terrain.

To enact this methodology multiple case studies must be produced. Case studies are selected using theoretical sampling, which prioritise cases on the basis of their potential to generate concepts relevant to the research propositions being explored. Case studies selected on the basis of this sampling approach, are then put together by tapping a diverse body of data-streams, which can facilitate triangulation. Once collected the triangulated data is then analysed using within-case and cross-case methods, from which theoretical concepts can be generated, and refined through an iterative process. Replicability is an important dimension of this approach to case study research. The more convincingly concepts can be intimately linked to the data emerging from multiple case studies, the stronger is the claim to generalisability.

However, a particular challenge confronts researchers enacting this approach to theorise the crimes of the powerful. The rich empirical data required to conceptualise essential agents, relations, processes, mechanisms and structures, are often closely guarded by organisational actors who have the legal and institutional power to conceal their activities from public view (Lasslett 2012). Where a study threatens to expose illicit activities in a way that may significantly impinge on the interests of political and economic elites, the degree of difficulty is heightened even further. Accordingly, when constructing a range of criminological case studies that probe land speculation and real-estate development prosecuted by high profile actors, it quickly became apparent that conventional data-collection methods alone were not going to be sufficient. As a result, this study required considerable experimentation with different investigative research techniques, some of which were pioneered during fieldwork, while others were transferred from cutting-edge work being conducted in civil society organisations and the investigative media.

Given the overarching methodology, the degree of difficulty involved, and the experimental data collection methods required, a decision was made to focus on a particular region in which the author had built up considerable field experience, Papua New Guinea. This may, in the first instance, strike someone unfamiliar with Papua New Guinea as an odd choice for a study on urbanisation, given that orientalist media accounts frequently focus on 'exotic' or 'brutal' themes set against a remote tropical island backdrop. However, for reasons that will soon become apparent, it is actually a strong candidate for such a study and the sampling method it rests on.

Indeed, Papua New Guinea is a vibrant, micro-ethnic polity made up of over seven million people. During the past two decades it has experienced significant bursts of concentrated and extended urbanisation. With high levels of concentrated urban growth extending back to the 1960s (Koczberski et al. 2001), 'the PNG urban population in 2010, estimated as approximately 1 million persons, is more than the entire populations of the Pacific sub-regions of Polynesia (663 795 persons) and Micronesia (547 345 persons)' (Jones 2012: 148). And even though 85% of the nation's population still remains situated outside cities, they are certainly not exempt from the impacts of urbanisation. Stimulated by global demand for Papua New Guinea's rich body of natural resources which includes minerals, oil, gas, timber, biofuels and fisheries, select rural areas have been sites of intensive, extended urbanisation. This has been a highly contentious process for rural communities dependent on sustainable agriculture. The most extreme example took place on Bougainville, where extended urbanisation rooted in global mineral demand, helped to spark a war that left approximately 20,000 people dead (Lasslett 2014b).

In Papua New Guinea concentrated and extended urbanisation is overseen at a governance level by a democratically elected parliament, which works alongside an executive and judiciary, modelled upon the Westminster system (see May 2004). However, patronage politics and clientelistic forms of public administration, have become an enduring feature of government in Papua New Guinea for a range of complex reasons (Kombako 2007; Kurer 2007; Standish 2007). In part it reflects an ethnically fractured, self-reliant population who vote on the basis of relationships with particular parliamentary candidates, which are cemented through promises of infrastructure and services that can aid household reproduction strategies (Kurer 2007). On the other hand, it is symptomatic of the mechanisms through which the business and political elite organise their affairs, which is heavily reliant on speculative commercial repertoires, enacted through client networks based on quasi-ethnic forms of solidarity. As a whole, these processes have prompted a system of parliament that webs together through personal alliances that allow individual MPs to obtain Ministerial positions, offering access to resources and decision making vehicles, that can satisfy supporter and client obligations (May 2004; Standish 2007). These governing alliances though are often fickle affairs; even within a coalition there can be multiple cliques that operate semi-autonomously from each other, which can lead to schisms and parliamentary votes of no-confidence.

A number of organs are charged with responsibility for overseeing the execution of public office, including the Auditor General's Office, the Ombudsman Commission, the Public Accounts Committee, the police anti-fraud squad, and up until recently a special multi-agency body known as Investigation Taskforce Sweep. While there are serious concerns over the vigour with which corruption is prosecuted in Papua New Guinea, there is nonetheless a rich body of reporting. This reporting has unveiled a complex mesh of networks that span business and government through which a range of corrupt practices are enacted (see, for example, Barnett 2002; Davani et al. 2009; Numapo 2013; Public Accounts Committee 2006, 2007; Sawong 2007). In short, business figures from within the private sector forge alliances with public officials in cognate departments or ministries, using these links to expedite approvals, win contracts, obtain valuable assets and misappropriate public funds, through practices that contravene the *Criminal Code Act* 1974, *Public Finances (Management) Act* 1995 and the *Leadership Code*. The proceeds from crime will then be shared out between organisers, patrons and fixers, in various proportions. Because Papua New Guinea's high levels of transparency are married to low levels of prosecution, often a visible public spotlight is placed on these criminal activities without any subsequent political effect, much to the chagrin of the national population.

Land administration and urban governance is managed by a range of public agencies. The Department of Lands and Physical Planning and the Office of Urbanisation, in particular, are charged with responsibility for ensuring urban change conforms to physical planning regulations, land laws and urbanisation policies. Practically speaking, the Office of Urbanisation has historically had limited capacity to fulfil its mandate to oversee the orderly expansion of towns and cities in Papua New Guinea, owing to budget constraints, human resource challenges, and its low status within government (Kep 2013). With respect to land administration and physical planning, the Department of Land and Physical Planning has also struggled to perform its duties, albeit for different reasons. Audits and anti-corruption inquiries have consistently revealed the department suffers from endemic corruption, serial record mismanagement and impunity sanctioned at the highest levels (Barnett 2002; Davani et al. 2009; Numapo 2013; Public Accounts Committee 2007). As we will observe in chapters five, six and seven, these dynamics are not accidental – to the contrary, this institutional culture constitutes an important, cultivated asset for influential networks using anti-competitive practices, price manipulation and fraud to increase their returns on land and property market transactions.

The opportunity structure for this type of speculative activity in Papua New Guinea's land and property market has been buttressed by a period of consolidation in the national economy. Following several decades of stagnation and crisis, the last decade in particular has seen Papua New Guinea enjoy solid levels of GDP growth (exceeding 5%), underpinned by inward investment in major resource projects such as PNG LNG, in addition to large-scale infrastructure projects funded through debt financing (Barker 2014; Batten 2014). This has been accompanied by a significant rise in land and property market prices. Some of the highest spikes have been witnessed in Papua New Guinea's capital, Port Moresby, which acts as a central hub for the nation's commercial and political activity. Gouy et al. observe, 'one of the unexpected surprises that new residents and investors to Port Moresby find is the extraordinary price of unimproved and improved property in all categories' (2010: 15). A survey of sales data solicited from real-estate companies in Port Moresby, revealed that two and three bedroom residential properties in the capital's most salubrious areas were selling for K1.9 million (US$703,000), while four-bedroom apartments were leased on average for K425,000 (US$157,250) annually, putting them in the league of 'New York, London or Tokyo' (Gouy et al. 2010: 19). Even more modest areas lying outside the capital's salubrious hubs have experienced significant growth. Chand et al. observe, 'in Gerehu, a suburb of the NCD [National Capital District] with majority owner-occupied residences, [prices] more than doubled between 2008 and 2013' (2014: 2). Evidence presented in the empirical chapters, suggest similar buoyancy in those rural land markets impacted by extended urbanisation.

Another reason for bullish land and property market prices, lies with particular features of the property regime governing Papua New Guinea's landed estate. Owing to the colonial 'settlement' reached between Britain, Germany, Australia and indigenous communities, a tenure system emerged which prevented customary land in Papua New Guinea from being alienated. As a result, it is estimated that customary tenure today covers approximately 97% of the national landmass. State land in contrast only constitutes approximately 2% of the national estate (Armitage 2001). However, rather importantly it includes many significant tracts of land situated in cities, towns and prospective rural areas (Kimas 2010). Under the *Land Act* 1996, state land can be leased to private actors for up to 99 years, in accordance with provisions contained in the act, *Land Regulation* 1999 and the *Physical Planning Act* 1989. As a result, it has become a prime commodity for land and property market speculation.

In a national context defined by upward swings in land and property markets, where plots are in limited supply, adept business figures who can leverage clientelistic relations, have been in a prime position to profit from speculation in state land. This activity has primarily taken two forms. First, we have witnessed investors purchase state leases. The land is then left dormant, frequently in violation of improvement covenants stipulated in the lease. A profit is then realised by selling the leasehold title – or the company holding the lease – when its market value has increased. The second approach involves more active investors, who are prepared to improve the property through soliciting interest from developers. As fixers for these landed improvements, the investor then shares in the enhanced value of the leasehold title with commercial partners and political patrons.

In either case, the investment can prove socially contentious. Owing to the prohibitive price of rents in the formal housing market, many living in Papua

New Guinea's urban centres have had to lease or purchase properties in the informal housing sector. Remarking on the situation in Port Moresby, Jones reports, the capital's 'informal [housing] settlements are located on both State and customary land, with approximately 40 per cent being customary and 60 per cent being freehold or State land' (2012: 152). The significant rate of growth in these informal housing agglomerations since independence (1975), is pointed to by Chand and Yala who observe:

> on average a new informal settlement was established each year over the 20 years to 2000 [in Port Moresby] and the settlement population grew at an annual rate of 7.8 per cent—twice the population growth rate of Port Moresby overall—in this period.
>
> (2008: 91)

Similar growth rates have been observed in other urban centres including Lae, Mount Hagen and Rabaul (ICCC 2010).

Complicating matters, informal settlements built on state land have often been established with the explicit or implicit permission of the state, with politicians seeking to solidify their electoral support base through offers of infrastructural improvements. This does not, however, prevent the government from subsequently leasing the land, without any provision for existing residents. This places settlements in conflict with business figures speculating on the property titles. Commonly conflict is resolved through forced evictions, executed by the Royal Papua New Guinea Constabulary or private security. Eviction exercises often involve mass-destruction of property, violence against residents and a range of human rights abuses, whose burden falls hardest on women and children (Goddard 2005; OHCHR 2010).

Given the range of dynamics pointed to above, Papua New Guinea contains social features which make it an appropriate candidate for a methodology whose sampling method places a premium on cases that congeal theoretically significant dynamics. Indeed, thriving land and property markets, clientelistic political cultures, inward injections of capital into property development, and urban contention in the housing sector, have combined to produce a lamentably large number of cases in Papua New Guinea that can help advance theory into the crimes of urbanisation.

To that end, in total six in-depth case studies were produced during the fieldwork period (2012–2016). Four of these case studies relate to real-property situated in the capital Port Moresby, while two of the case studies are located in rural Madang on Papua New Guinea's north coast, a region that has been earmarked for a special economic zone facilitated through Chinese state loans. It was important that the cases featured enough empirical variation to build concepts that are sensitive to common threads and core distinctions. To that end, three of the case studies in Port Moresby involved state land hosting informal residential settlements. In these three cases leasehold titles over the state land were issued to companies incorporated in Papua New Guinea, two of which were foreign owned, while the third's shareholders were nationals. In all three cases, the companies attempted to accentuate the value of their leasehold title by attracting investments from real-estate developers. The fourth Port Moresby case involved a recently built public housing complex, populated by leasehold tenants. The apartment block was abruptly sold off by the state to a private developer, with residents being driven out by police and street gangs.

The research in Madang involved two large plots of state land in a region earmarked for a special economic zone, known as the Pacific Marine Industrial Zone. One of the plots, Mililat plantation, hosts villages made up of the land's customary owners, who are entitled to leasehold title over the plantation under a land redistribution scheme set up during the 1970s. This right led a local business leader to draw on his own customary influence to grab the land with financial support from an Australian investor, albeit one who was unaware of the fraud taking place. The second plot of researched land is known as Vidar Plantation. Abutting Mililat, it has been selected to host industrial facilities associated with the Pacific Marine Industrial Zone. Vidar is also home to an informal residential settlement made up of former plantation workers, who have lived on the land since the 1960s.

These cases were initially identified using a combination of mechanisms, including civil society contacts, professional informants, media reports, blogs and social media commentary. A decision was made to focus on these six cases because they met the core criteria guiding the research. That is, all the cases were significant plots of land, in centres of concentrated and extended urbanisation, which were the subject of speculative repertoires, contested by local actors. There were, thus, potent signs these cases would generate empirical data that could help answer core research questions, and generate theory.

Case studies were populated using a number of investigative data-collection methods which are explained in chapter four. In particular, data was extracted through documentary research that cross-referenced a range of company, land and anti-corruption records, which were triangulated with interviews, observation and experiments. The full range of documentary and oral sources employed, and the analytical techniques used, are highlighted in chapter four. In total, 54 semi-structured interviews were conducted, which included 37 interviews with community representatives (affected by mass forced evictions), six lawyers defending impacted communities, two NGO officials, three executives from developer coalitions, three officials from the Lands Department and the Office of Urbanisation, one Ombudsman Commission official, one official representing the police, and one Member of Parliament. Given that the study's focus was on collecting, modelling and analysing data relating to social networks, distributions of power, the execution of complex transaction chains and state–corporate criminality, interviews tended to provide important context and leads, while forensic documentary research was where the concrete particulars were established.

To enhance the study, within-case analyses were performed using a number of pioneering techniques set out in chapter three. In particular, the author repurposed social network analysis to an investigative context, and augmented it using a new technique, transaction mapping. Together these digitally enhanced analytical methods permitted each case study to be broken down into common units of analysis, and subjected to different forms of data modelling, from which a series of explanatory concepts could be generated.

Once the case studies had been analysed using these techniques, a process of cross-case analysis took place. This allowed patterns to be observed with respect to relationships, processes, mechanisms and transactions. Then through an iterative process, these patterns shaped the generation of theoretical concepts, which aimed to enrich understandings of the generalised structures and historical conditions informing the observed illicit repertoires.

To support the process of theory generation, certain modifications had to be made to the overarching methodology, as a result of the particular challenges crimes of the powerful research presents. In particular, it became apparent that the technically complex, opaque nature of land and property market speculation, when combined with the acute power of organisational actors to conceal their activity, made for an uneven empirical terrain. Although each case study was populated by a significant volume of triangulated data, which allowed within-case and cross-case analysis to occur, it became apparent that two cases contained a specifically rich breadth and depth of data that allowed them to exhibit with particular clarity the patterns observed across all cases. Because of their exemplary character, these two case studies played an important role in the theory construction process.

In particular, the exemplary case studies were employed in the first instance to inductively generate theoretical concepts which help define the fundamental social forces underpinning observed forms of illegitimate activity taking place within land and property markets. Additionally, the exemplary case studies were used to build a theoretical framework that could help explain the historically developed structures that reward certain activity in land and property markets, through levers that divert value from the productive economy, thus providing the basis for speculative profits. The remaining four cases were then used to test and refine the hypotheses generated using the exemplary studies.

This alteration to the orthodox case study research design is reflected to an extent in the chapter structure. During chapters five and six the two exemplary case studies are presented in rich narrative form. A theoretical framework is then advanced in chapter seven, which conceptualises the core relations, enacting mechanisms and social processes, that had proven critical to the illegitimate activities employed to facilitate land and property market speculation. The replicability of these dynamics is then demonstrated through a shorter empirical presentation, focusing on two further case studies.

It also should be noted, that when cataloguing the illegitimate practices employed to prosecute certain land and property market deals, a caveat must be added that applies to all the case studies. When approximating opaque processes, with potentially illicit characteristics, it is rare to extract confessions from the organisational actors involved. Given that researchers are rarely able to view the events concerned first hand, in lieu of a confession it is impossible to say with absolutely certainty that a particular illicit transaction occurred. However, the researcher can triangulate primary sources, applying forensic rules to test their credibility. And where relevant, these findings can be corroborated employing robust secondary sources and the grey literature.

Accordingly, when the case studies are presented in the following chapters, they will be supported by a large body of primary evidence, secondary sources and grey literature. This will allow a range of potentially illegitimate practices and relations to be identified, but clearly it is impossible to definitively say X or Y occurred. Instead, the empirical analysis and theory generation components of this study rely on the clinical set of methodological techniques used to evaluate and corroborate sources. With that in mind, while it is impossible to make a direct allegation that a particular illegitimate practice occurred, appropriate levels of methodological rigour allow compelling evidence based approximations to be made of the events, from which theory can be developed.

One other caveat needs to be added. How civil society interprets, organises and challenges the illegitimate repertoires explored through crimes of the powerful research, has rightly become an increasingly important area of inquiry. Organised through the rubric of resistance, a growing number of criminological studies are focusing on how state and corporate crime are publicly challenged through campaigns of censure and reform. Certainly the empirical evidence presented here, bears testament to the important role which civil society actors plays in censuring and challenging illegitimate processes prosecuted through land and property markets. This evidence reflects the considerable time spent with displaced communities in the field, collecting their oral accounts and documentary materials. However, owing to certain spatial constraints full justice cannot be done to these conversations here. A fuller account of the resistance campaigns noted in this volume will be presented in future outputs linked to the study.

Of course, it might be observed by way of one final note, research that is confined to a single geopolitical region will always face limits with respect to the generalisability of its findings. That said, it has already been noted that Papua New Guinea is certainly far from being anomalous with respect to the process of extended and concentrated urbanisation, or the criminogenic dynamics contained in the national political economy. Nonetheless, it is certainly true that the findings of this research prompt a range of new research questions, that can only be answered through further international, comparative research. This matter will be addressed in more detail during the book's conclusion.

Conclusion

In this chapter foundational concepts essential to understanding the crimes of urbanisation have been introduced. We then scoped the broad range of inter-disciplinary interventions that exist in the literature, which are potentially captured by the former thematic, while also acknowledging the lacunas and limits that make this new intellectual agenda important and necessary. Finally, attention was turned to the geopolitical context and research design of the study underpinning the methodological, empirical and theoretical innovations set out in this volume, which as a whole offer a framework for investigating and understanding the crimes of urbanisation.

Now we will turn towards unpacking the substantive discoveries made. To that end, the theoretical lens which emerged from the research will be set out, rooted in the work of Marx, Foucault and Harvey. In particular, chapter two will examine how the labour theory of value can be married to other critical theoretical concepts, such as class monopoly rents and governmentality, in order to conceptualise the historical conditions under which illicit repertoires deployed in land and property markets are incentivised and validated – this will help to frame subsequent criminological inquiry within a broader political economy. Following on from this theoretical tract, a systematic methodological framework for inquiring into the crimes of urbanisation will be presented, before the empirical results such a framework can generate are set out through in-depth case studies. This will lay the foundation for a second theoretical chapter, which concentrates on the organisational mechanisms and processes employed to prosecute, at a micro level, concentrated and extended urbanisation, with a focus on explaining the role illicit repertoires play.

Bibliography

Agbola, T. and Jinadu, A. M. (1997). 'Forced eviction and forced relocation in Nigeria: The experience of those evicted from Maroko in 1990', *Environment and Urbanization*, 9(2), 271–288.

Armitage, L. (2001). 'Customary land tenure in Papua New Guinea: Status and prospects'. [Online]. Available at: http://dlc.dlib.indiana.edu/dlc/bitstream/handle/10535/589/armitage.pdf (accessed: 26 February 2017).

Ashman, S. (2006). 'From world market to world economy', in Dunn, B. and Radice, H. (eds) *One Hundred Years of Permanent Revolution*: Results and Prospects, London: Pluto Press.

Barker, P. (2014). 'PNG's economy 2014 – Past, present and future prospects'. [Online]. Available at: www.inapng.com/pdf_files/PNG_Mining_Petroleum_Conference_2014. pdf (accessed: 17 February 2017).

Barnett, T. E. (2002). Report of the Commission of Inquiry into the National Provident Fund. [Online]. Extracts available at: web.archive.org/web/20060923050634/http://www.postcourier.com.pg/NPF%20inquiry/npf116 (accessed: 16 February 2017).

Batten, A. (2014). 'Papua New Guinea', *Asian Development Outlook*. [Online]. Available at: www.adb.org/sites/default/files/publication/31241/ado2014-png.pdf (accessed: 17 February 2017).

Brenner, N. (2000). 'The urban question as a scale question: Reflections on Henri Lefebvre, urban theory and the politics of scale', *International Journal of Urban and Regional Research*, 24(2), 361–378.

Brenner, N. (2004). *New State Spaces: Urban Governance and the Rescaling of Statehood*, Oxford: Oxford University Press.

Brenner, N. (2013). 'Theses on urbanization', *Public Culture*, 25(1), 85–114.

Bukharin, N. (2003). *Imperialism and World Economy*, London: Bookmarks.

Chand, S., Ondopa, J. and Nao, L. (2014). 'Use of land leases as collateral for accessing formal sector finance in Papua New Guinea', *The National Research Institute Issue Paper*, Issue Paper No.7, Port Moresby: The National Research Institute.

Chand, S. and Yala, C. (2008). 'Informal land systems within urban settlements in Honiara and Port Moresby', in Wawrzonek, S., Fitzpatrick, D., Levantis, T. and O'Connor, P. (eds) *Making Land Work*, Vol.1, Canberra: AusAID.

Chiodelli, F. and Moroni, S. (2015). 'Corruption in land-use issues: A crucial challenge for planning theory and practice', *Town Planning Review*, 86(4), 437–455.

Cohen, S. (1993). 'Human rights and crimes of the state: The culture of denial', *Australian and New Zealand Journal of Criminology*, 26(2), 97–115.

Davani, C., Sheehan, M. and Manoa, D. (2009). *The Commission of Inquiry Generally into the Department of Finance: Final Report*, Port Moresby: The Commission.

Davis, M. (2006). *Planet of the Slums*, London: Verso.

Dul, J. and Hak, T. (2008). *Case Study Methodology in Business Research*, London: Butterworth-Heinemann.

Eisenhardt, K. M. (1989). 'Building theories from case study research', *The Academy of Management Review*, 14(4), 532–550.

Eisenhardt, K. M. and Graebner, M. E. (2007). 'Theory building from cases: Opportunities and challenges', *Academy of Management Journal*, 50(1), 25–32.

European Action Coalition for the Right to Housing and to the City. (n.d.). Eviction Across Europe. [Online]. Available at: https://housingnotprofit.org/files/EvictionsAcrossEurope. pdf (accessed: 16 February 2017).

Farha, L. (2011). *Forced Evictions: Global Crisis, Global Solutions*, Nairobi: UN-Habitat.

Flyvbjerg, B. (2014). 'What you should know about megaprojects and why: An overview', *Project Management Journal*, 45(2), 6–19.

Foucault, M. (2007). *Security, Territory, Population: Lectures at the Collège de France 1977–1978*, Basingstoke: Palgrave Macmillan.

Gellert, P. K. and Lynch, B. D. (2003). 'Mega-projects as displacements', *International Social Science Journal*, 55(175), 15–25.

Goddard, M. (2005). *The Unseen City: Anthropological Perspectives on Port Moresby, Papua New Guinea*, Canberra: Pandanus Books.

Gouy, J., Kapa, J., Mokae, A. and Levantis, T. (2010). 'Parting with the past: Is Papua New Guinea poised to begin a new chapter towards development?', *Pacific Economic Bulletin*, 25(1): 1–23.

Grajales, J. (2011). 'The rifle and the title: Paramilitary violence, land grab and land control in Colombia', *The Journal of Peasant Studies*, 38(4), 771–792.

Green, P. (2005). 'Disaster by design: Corruption, construction and catastrophe', *British Journal of Criminology*, 45(4), 528–546.

Green, P. and Smith, A. (2016). 'Evicting Palestine', *State Crime Journal*, 5(1), 81–108.

Green, P. and Ward, T. (2000). 'State crime, human rights, and the limits of criminology', *Social Justice*, 27(1), 101–115.

Green, P. and Ward, T. (2004). *State Crime: Governments, Violence and Corruption*, London: Pluto Press.

Grewcock, M. (2012). 'Public criminology, victim agency and researching state crime', *State Crime*, 1(1), 109–125.

Hammar, A. (2008). 'In the name of sovereignty: Displacement and state making in post-independence Zimbabwe', *Journal of Contemporary African Studies*, 26(4), 417–434.

Harvey, D. (1976). 'Labor, capital, and class struggle around the built environment in advanced capitalist societies', *Politics and Society*, 6(3), 265–295.

Harvey, D. (1985). *The Urbanization of Capital: Studies in the History and Theory of Capitalist Urbanization*, Baltimore: John Hopkins University Press.

Harvey, D. (1989). 'From managerialism to entrepreneurialism: The transformation in urban governance in late capitalism', *Geografiska Annaler, Series B, Human Geography*, 71(1), 3–17.

Harvey, D. (2003). *The New Imperialism*, Oxford: Oxford University Press.

Harvey, D. (2012). *Rebel Cities: From the Right to the City to the Urban Revolution*, London: Verso.

Hillyard, P. and Tombs, S. (2004). Beyond criminology? In Hillyard, P. Pantazis, C., Tombs, S. and Gordon, D. (eds) *Beyond Criminology: Taking Harm Seriously*. London: Pluto Press.

Iacono, J. C., Brown, A. and Holtham, C. (2011). 'The use of the case study method in theory testing: The example of steel emarketplaces', *The Electronic Journal of Business Research Methods*, 9(1), 57–65.

Independent Consumer and Competition Commission. (2010). *PNG Housing and Real Estate Industry Review*, Port Moresby: Author.

Jiménez, F. (2009). 'Building boom and political corruption in Spain', *South European Society and Politics*, 14(3), 255–272.

Jones, P. (2012). 'Pacific urbanisation and the rise of informal settlements: Trends and implications from Port Moresby', *Urban Policy and Research*, 30(2), 145–160.

Kauzlarich, D., Kramer R. C. and Smith, B. (1992) 'Toward the study of governmental crime: Nuclear weapons, foreign intervention, and international law', *Humanity and Society*, 16(4) 543–563.

Kep, M. (2013). Office of Urbanisation, Personal Communication, 26 July 2013.

Kimas P. S. (2010). 'Administration of land held under formal tenure', in Yala, C. (ed.) *The Genesis of the Papua New Guinea Land Reform Program: Selected Papers from the 2005 National Land Summit*. Boroko: The National Research Institute.

Klopp, J. M. (2008). 'Remembering the destruction of Muoroto: Slum demolitions, land and democratisation in Kenya', *African Studies*, 295–314.

Koczberski, G., Curry, G. and Connell, J. (2001). 'Full circle or spiralling out of control? State violence and the control of urbanisation in Papua New Guinea', *Urban Studies*, 38(11), 2017–2036.

Kombako, D. (2007). Corruption as a consequence of cultural and social idiosyncrasies in a developing society. In Ayius, A. A. and May, R. J. (eds) *Corruption in Papua New Guinea: Towards an Understanding of Issues*. Boroko: The National Research Institute.

Kurer, O. (2007). 'Why do Papua New Guinean voters opt for clientelism? Democracy and governance in a fragile state', *Pacific Economic Bulletin* 22(1), 39–53.

Lasslett, K. (2012). 'Power, struggle and state crime: Researching through resistance', *State Crime*, 1(1), 126–148.

Lasslett, K. (2014a). 'Understanding and responding to state crime: A criminological perspective', in Bantekas, I. (ed.) *International Criminal Law and Criminology*, Cambridge: Cambridge University Press.

Lasslett, K. (2014b). *State Crime on the Margins of Empire*, London: Pluto Press.

Lefebvre, H. (2003). *The Urban Revolution*. Minneapolis: The University of Minnesota Press.

Logan, J. R. and Molotch, H. (1987). *Urban Fortunes: The Political Economy of Place*, London: University of California Press.

Løkke, A. and Dissing, Sørensen P. (2014) 'Theory testing using case studies', *The Electronic Journal of Business Research Methods*, 12(1), 66–74.

Mahmud, A. (2007). *Corruption in Plan Permission Process in RAJUK: A Study of Violations and Proposals*, Dhaka: Transparency International Bangladesh.

Mahmud, T. (2010). '"Surplus humanity" and the margins of legality: Slums, slumdogs, and accumulation by dispossession', *Chapman Law Review*, 14(1), 1–73.

Marx, K. (1976). *Capital*, Vol. 1, Harmondsworth: Penguin Books.

May, R. (2004). *State and Society in Papua New Guinea: The First Twenty-Five Years*, Canberra: ANU E Press.

Mgbako, C., Gao, R. E., Joynes, E., Cave, A. and Mikhailevich, J. (2010). 'Forced eviction and resettlement in Cambodia: Case studies from Phnom Penh', *Washington University Global Studies Law Review*, 9(1), 39–76.

Mullins, C. W. and Rothe, D. L. (2008). *Blood, Power and Bedlam: Violations of International Criminal Law in Post-Colonial Africa*, New York: Peter Lang.

Neef, A. and Singer, J. (2015). 'Development-induced displacement in Asia: Conflicts, risks, and resilience', *Development in Practice*, 25(5), 601–611.

Numapo, J. (2013). *Commission of Inquiry into the Special Agriculture and Business Leases: Final Report*, Port Moresby: Commission of Inquiry into the Special Agricultural and Business Leases.

Office of the High Commissioner for Human Rights. (2010). *Housing Rights Assessment Mission to Papua New Guinea 29 June–9 July 2010*, Suva: Office of the High Commissioner for Human Rights.

Olds, K. (1998). 'Urban mega-events, evictions and housing rights: The Canadian case', *Current Issues in Tourism*, 1(1), 2–46.

Pemberton, S. (2007). 'Social harm future(s): Exploring the potential of the social harm approach', *Crime, Law and Social Change*, 48(1–2), 27–41.

Porteous, J. D. and Smith, S. E. (2001). *Domicide: The Global Destruction of Home*, London: McGill-Queen's University Press.

Public Accounts Committee. (2006). *Public Accounts Committee Report to Parliament on the Inquiry into the Office of the Public Curator*, Waigani: National Parliament of Papua New Guinea.

Public Accounts Committee. (2007). *Public Accounts Committee Report to Parliament on the Inquiry into the Department of Lands and Physical Planning*, Waigani: National Parliament of Papua New Guinea.

Sawong, D. (2007). *Report of the Commission of Inquiry into the Management of the Investment Corporation of Papua New Guinea and the Investment Corporation Fund of Papua New Guinea and all Matters Relation to the Conversion of the Investment Corporation Fund of Papua New Guinea to Pacific Balanced Fund*, Port Moresby: Commission of Inquiry.

Schwendinger, H. and Schwendinger, J. (1975). 'Defenders of order or guardians of human rights?', in Taylor, I., Walton, P. and Young, J. (eds) *Critical Criminology*, London: Routledge and Kegan Paul.

Smith, A. and Green, P. (2014). Forced Evictions in Israel-Palestine, June. [Online]. Available at: statecrime.org/data/2014/07/20140709_ForcedEvictionsInIsraelPalestine. pdf (accessed: 17 February 2017).

Smith, N. (1982). 'Gentrification and uneven development', *Economic Geography*, 58(2), 139–155.

Smith, N. (2002). 'New globalism, new urbanism: Gentrification as global urban strategy', *Antipode* 34(3), 427–450.

Standish, B. (2007). 'The dynamics of Papua New Guinea's democracy: An essay', *Pacific Economic Bulletin*, 22 (1), 135–157.

Stanley, E. and McCulloch, J. (eds) (2012). *State Crime and Resistance*, London: Routledge.

Sutherland, E. H. (1983). *White Collar Crime: The Uncut Version*, London: Yale University Press.

Tappan, P. (1946). 'Who is the criminal?', *American Sociological Review*, 12(6), 96–102.

Timo, P. B. (2013). 'Development at the cost of violations: The impact of mega-projects on human rights in Brazil', *International Journal of Human Rights*, 10(18), 137–158.

Tretter, E. M. (2009). 'Cultures of capitalism: Glasgow and the monopoly of culture', *Antipode*, 41(1), 111–132.

Ward, T. (2013). 'State crime and the sociology of human rights', *Revista Crítica Penal y Poder*, 5, 77–89.

Weinstein, L. (2008). 'Mumbai's development mafias: Globalization, organized crime and land development', *International Journal of Urban and Regional Research*, 32(1), 22–39.

White, R. (2012). 'Land theft as rural eco-crime', *International Journal of Rural Criminology*, 1(2), 203–217.

White, R. (2013). *Environmental Harm: An Eco-Justice Perspective*, Bristol: Policy Press.

Wyly, E., Moos, M., Hammel, D. and Kabahizi, E. (2009). 'Cartographies of race and class: Mapping the class-monopoly rents of American subprime mortgage capital', *International Journal of Urban and Regional Research*, 33(2), 332–354.

Zoomers, A. (2010). 'Globalisation and the foreignisation of space: seven processes driving the current global land grab', *The Journal of Peasant Studies*, 37(2), 429–447.

Chapter 2

Fictitious capital, class monopoly rents and urban governance

Theorising criminogenic opportunity structures and incentive schemas

Introduction

The forthcoming empirical chapters (5–7) present a range of case studies which document complex land and property market transactions, which have been seriously affected in part by different combinations of corruption, market abuse, anti-competitive practices, fraud and mass forced eviction. At the outset it ought to be acknowledged that when empirical research is conducted through the case study method, there is a risk that the analysis produced will skew theoretical explanation towards the immediate organisational activities, mechanisms and decisions which informed the event(s) under consideration. This comes at the cost of incorporating the latter determinations within a broader social theory of the historical arrangements which they have emerged out of, and depend upon for their integrity.

Put more concretely – given our current subject matter – theoretical explanation can consume itself, for instance, with the task of explaining why a developer consortium was able to illicitly build a major dam, focusing on matters such as state–corporate decisions, political goals, regulatory lacunas, market incentives, and so on. While, no doubt, these are important factors in need of conceptualisation, nonetheless if pursued with singular focus this framing risks overshadowing other critical questions. For example, what are the defining historical characteristics of the seemingly inherent arrangements – markets, capital, government, and so on – that enabled this activity to occur, in the style and format being considered?

This particular theoretical concern has been given explicit voice by Tombs, in his work on state–corporate crime (see also Lasslett 2010). Tombs contends that research in this thematic area conducted through the case study approach, has tended to 'focus upon what are essentially forms of *discrete joint ventures* between corporations and states' (italics added) (2012: 175). Thus, he argues, such research abstracts 'events from ongoing [social] relationships and wider contexts, each of which may require theoretical comprehension in their own terms as well as to perceive adequately the original event(s) under consideration' (2012: 174).

In order to avoid empiricist vectors, Tombs maintains that case studies must be 'generated as vehicles which are operationalised through both theoretical frameworks and their related, internally consistent, conceptual tools which ground such cases in more fundamental relations and processes of contemporary capitalism and its dynamics' (2012: 175). Put another way, historically developed market and governance structures should not be framed as stable, natural processes in which 'discrete joint ventures' take place. Instead, they too must be problematised, and subjected to scrutiny, so that it may be better understood how state–corporate 'ventures' depend upon, and syncopate with, social relationships and regimes of power, that emerge from the capitalist system, framed as a historically developed social totality.

For example, if we take the subject matter that will be dealt with in the forthcoming chapters, it is tempting to concentrate primarily on the particular ways in which the illicit land and property market transactions have been organised and executed, taking into account factors such as: the commercial and political repertoires employed by actors; the organisational structures and environments these repertoires were incubated within; and the regulatory cleavages that ensured impunity.

Of course, these are vitally important social determinations, and thus are dealt with in detail during chapters 5–7. Nevertheless, to focus on these issues alone leaves aside certain critical questions. For instance, why is it that the act of delimiting space and rendering it into a private monopoly, can in turn produce a financial asset, and market, which generates significant profits for a class of property investors/speculators? Furthermore, how is it that the trade in property titles – through sale and lease – can deliver significant gains for investors, without actually being conducive of value, that is, if we accept materialist theories which root value in the productive dimensions of human labour? Given this contradiction, are there social mechanisms which can be pointed to that permit value generated elsewhere in the economy, to be redirected into land and property markets, providing the necessary substance for profits – and if so, in what ways do urban governance regimes accelerate or dull this *switching* process? Finally, it might also be questioned how these factors, as a whole, generate the historical conditions in which illicit repertoires can come into being within land and property markets.

Against this backdrop, the following chapter intends to theorise some of the essential historical conditions which support the criminogenic dimensions of land and property markets. To that end, a conceptual framework will be developed drawing on Marx, Foucault and David Harvey. In particular, it will be argued that the switching process alluded to above can be usefully theorised drawing on Marx's approach to the circuit of industrial capital, where he distinguishes *capital* from other forms of investment by delineating its active property of being productive of value and surplus value. We will then turn to Marx's work on fictitious capital, a category which captures a range of auxiliary economic circuits where latent capital can be invested and valorised, without necessarily being productive of value or surplus value. It will be argued that real-estate markets may be usefully conceived of as a circuit for fictitious capital, a process that is indebted to the particular way space is delimited and commodified under capitalism. David Harvey's work on class monopoly rents – which is grounded in capitalist property relations – will then be forwarded to help conceptualise the switching mechanisms that see value transfer from productive to unproductive circuits. As a whole, it will be contended that these theoretical concepts help explain how value may be drained more rapidly from the circuit of industrial capital, by employing certain manipulative land and property market practices.

Of course, investor freedom to engage in these types of activity is dependent to an extent on how governmental power is exercised. Accordingly, in the second part of this chapter Foucault's late work on governmentality will be blended with the theory of capitalist relations set out by Marx in *Capital*, to help build an explanatory framework that casts the art of government as an integral component mediating the switch of value between economic circuits (see also Lasslett 2015). This synthesis of Marx and Foucault – complemented by innovations developed in radical geography – as a whole lays the foundations for historically situating the state–corporate activities that will be documented in greater detail during the forthcoming empirical chapters.

Industrial capital and fictitious capital: a dialectical view

To begin it is worthwhile restating the problem under consideration. The apparent contradiction we are trying to make sense of in this chapter centres on the historical conditions which allow a strata of investors to speculate on expected price shifts in land and property markets, which they accentuate through a range of illicit and licit practices. Evidence will be presented in the forthcoming chapters, illustrating that quite substantial rates of profit can be realised through this activity, without the prosecuting actors being directly involved in the economic circuits which are productive of value. It would seem, therefore, that in a capitalist class context there is a strata of actors who enjoy an ability to realise surplus value without being involved in its generation.

This apparent contradiction dovetails with an important question Marx broached in the opening part of *Capital* (Marx 1976). Here he conceptually unpacks the elementary source of value within the capitalist mode of production, which forms the inner content of more complex economic phenomena such as profit, rent, interest and wages. In this conceptual tract Marx draws a critical distinction between the production of value, and the realisation of value. Setting aside vulgar explanations, Marx argues that the growing revenue flows generated by the capitalist mode of production would be impossible to sustain were they merely a result of different capitalists cheating each other by buying commodities below their exchange value and selling them above their exchange value. Instead, Marx contends, it is feasible that all capitals in a commodity chain can valorise their investment, from the industrialist through to the merchant, without any link swindling the other. He argues this is the case because surplus value is extracted from a labouring class through a range of opaque mechanisms. This surplus is then circulated away from the site of exploitation – again through complex, opaque mechanisms – and realised by actors standing outside the immediate production process. Therefore, embedded in the nucleus of capitalism is a systemic possibility that actors who have no direct role in the production of surplus value, can nonetheless share in it through certain revenue forms.

While it is impossible to fully unpack Marx's theoretical thesis in this chapter, nevertheless, certain key points can be extrapolated from his work salient to our primary focus. We can begin, in this respect, by surveying volume one of *Capital*, where Marx presents his labour theory of value. Put simply, Marx contends that it is human labour which forms the underlying basis of value. By labour Marx means the exertion of energy and intellect over a finite period. Within the capitalist mode of production, Marx argues, labourers are forced to exert this energy under conditions of market mediated competition. As a result, a commodity's exchange value is materially determined by the socially average labour time required for its production.

Upon this foundation, Marx then plots a theory of surplus value that explains how many different capitals can see a return on their investment, without necessarily cheating each other. This can occur, Marx contends, because under capitalism there is a labouring class which has been divorced from the means of production[1] through a historical process of dispossession – a systemic inequality that has been historically sealed through private property regimes. In order to purchase the means of subsistence essential to the household's reproduction, dispossessed workers must sell their labour-power – that is, their capacity to labour – an act which can take place through diverse labour regimes. In this fundamental transaction lies capitalism's essential foundation – the remuneration which the capitalist pays to use labour-power over a particular duration, contains less value than what the purchased labour-power can produce over this set period. This difference, Marx argues, congeals surplus value, which is eventually appropriated by those who command capital in its different forms, in addition to the state through taxation.

It is important to note, that when presenting his theoretical assessment Marx does not adopt the vantage point of the individual worker and individual capitalist. Instead, the process of exploitation is conceptualised from the vantage point of classes as interdependent masses. These class unities are made up of vast agglomerations of workers and capitals – in a multitude of concrete forms – which are busily engaged in metabolism that congeals, through millions of streams, surplus value to the capitalist class as a whole, before being redistributed via particular revenue streams, which are collected by the different stratas of capital.

In volume one, Marx also conceptualises the mechanisms that help accentuate the critical difference between the amount paid for labour-power, and the value it produces when put to work. For example, the rate of surplus value can be augmented by increasing the work day, or through lowering the price of labour-power by cheapening the consumption fund working families depend on. Again, to appreciate Marx's argument here one has to conceive this process on a global scale, where many millions of capitalist enterprises are operating, and increasing the rate of surplus value extraction through these mechanisms, delivering up a growing mass of surplus value to be shared out via the different social mechanisms that determine revenue forms.

By the conclusion of *Capital* volume one Marx has set out a theory which explains how the moment of production, generates the essential surplus needed to oxygenate capitalism without capitalist cheating capitalist. In volume two, Marx (1978) broadens his theoretical lens in order to frame the moment of production, as part of a broader totality, which he labels the circuit of industrial capital. With that in mind, Marx observes that if capital as a sum of value – extracted through previous rounds of exploitation – is to successfully impregnate itself again with surplus value and accumulate, it needs to transit through a series of different phenomenal forms. First, capital must assume the money-form, so it can make the transition to productive capital which takes place through the purchase of labour-power and the means of production. Once it has assumed a productive form, capital can then be fertilised with surplus value through the mechanisms Marx theorised in volume one. This fertilised mass of capital now takes a new form, commodities pregnant with surplus value. These commodities must be circulated and then sold, so capital can return to the point of departure, money, but with an addition supplied *gratis* by labour. This cyclical motion through which capitalist relations of production are operationalised and reproduced, is what Marx calls the circuit of industrial capital.

The circuit's unimpeded revolution is, in Marx's view, essential to social reproduction in its capitalist form.[2] Over the remainder of volume two Marx focuses on conceptualising how transitions within the circuit of industrial capital are expedited by capital's frenetic search for surplus value. In addition, he looks at the tensions that emerge in the circuit as a result of the way complex, interdependent productive units are historically organised under capitalism through privately owned, competing capitals.

Turning to volume three of *Capital*, here Marx theorises the social mechanisms which regulate how surplus value is finally distributed in different revenue forms, such as profit of enterprise (productive capital), interest (financial capital) and ground-rent (landed capital) (Marx 1981). It is important in this respect that we do not assume the immediate saliency of the category ground-rent to the problem being explored in this chapter. The theory of ground-rent Marx presents in *Capital* centres on the determinations which shape how a certain portion of the surplus value cultivated through rural production is deducted as ground-rent. The companies that feature in the forthcoming empirical chapters – which are broadly reflective of many land and property market actors – do not directly participate in the production of surplus-value, nor are they absorbed directly, in any substantive sense, within the circuit of industrial capital. Yet in each case the titleholders can still levy a charge for accessing/acquiring the property, that will be paid for out of the revenues which have accrued to the lessor/purchaser. A theory of this particular dynamic is better rooted in Marx's chapters on fictitious capital (Marx 1981).

In Marx's usage, fictitious capital is a term of art that is married to a particular historical conception of capital. It will be recalled, in this respect, that Marx distinguishes industrial capital through the particular way it circulates. To be considered industrial capital, a sum of value must transit through a series of forms which allow it to generate surplus value during the moment of production, which is then transformed via a series of mediating steps back into money-capital, fertilising the investments of different stakeholders involved in this process. Accordingly, for Marx, capital is not a thing – a certain amount of money in a bank account – it is a social process, whereby value seeking its own expansion, passes through a set of forms which facilitate this feat through an injection provided *gratis* by labour.

Where an investment eschews this circuit, in Marx's conception it is not capital in the historically distinct form that is indigenous to the capitalist mode of production. Instead, he reserves the name fictitious capital for certain investment circuits where the original sum is valorised, without being a direct part of the process that fertilises the capitalist system with surplus value. Valorisation can occur, in this instance, because of certain switching mechanisms. That is, once the surplus value generated by the circuit of industrial capital is congealed in certain revenue forms, economic mechanisms exist which allow auxiliary circuits of fictitious capital to be valorised through making a secondary claim on these revenue sources. Marx considers some of the particular mechanisms that allow this switching process to take place.

There are, he contends, titles of ownership that investors can purchase, which give the holder a right to share in future revenues, ultimately generated by the circuit of industrial capital. This occurs without the holder necessarily making any contribution to the circuit of industrial capital. For example, an investor in possession of dormant capital may decide to loan the state money at a certain rate of interest, which the government concerned then expends on a foreign war. This sum of money does not productively enter the circuit of industrial capital. Nevertheless, through a mediated path the investor is able to acquire a share of the surplus value generated by industrial capital. This is because a proportion of the surplus value generated by industrial capital is distributed to the state in the form of taxation. The government bond formalising the loan then acts as a lever, which gives the investor a right to share in a certain percentage of this revenue, as determined by the agreed rate of interest. This allows the initial investment to be valorised, without being directly immersed in the circuit that percolates surplus value into the capitalist system.

Marx (1981: 595) explains:

> The state has to pay its creditors a certain sum of interest each year for the capital it borrows. In this case the creditor cannot recall his capital from the debtor but can only sell the claim, his title of ownership. The capital

itself has been consumed, spent by the state. It no longer exists. What the state's creditor possesses is (1) the state's promissory note for, say, £100; while (2) this note gives him a claim on the state's annual revenue, i.e. the proceeds of the year's taxation, to a certain amount, say £5 or 5 per cent; (3) he is free to sell this promissory note to anyone he likes.

As a result, Marx (1981: 595–596) argues:

> [I]n all these cases, the capital from which the state's payment is taken as deriving, as interest, is illusory and fictitious. It is not only that the sum that was lent to the state no longer has any kind of existence. It was never designed to be spent as capital, to be invested, and yet only by being invested as capital could it have been made into a self-maintaining value. As far as the original creditor A is concerned, the share of the annual taxation he receives represents interest on his capital, just as does the share of the wealth of the spendthrift that accrues to the money-lender, but in neither case has the sum of money lent been laid out as capital.

Marx uses other examples to exhibit the diverse forms fictitious capital can assume. For instance, he argues, when stocks are purchased the investor obtains a right to share in the future revenues of a company through the mechanism of dividends. What gives these stocks a market value is not their connection to the capital handed over by the purchaser, which is relinquished, rather it stems from the shareholder's right to make a claim on the company's future earnings. It is quite possible this claim will allow their stock portfolio to expand in market value, beyond the actual subsequent amplification of their relinquished capital. This disjuncture, Fine observes, 'gives rise to the potential for speculative booms in which the prices of assets, such as shares, rise disproportionately but can then come crashing down' (2014: 51).

Nevertheless, it is important to acknowledge that fictitious capital is not merely a parasitic or toxic phenomenon – it can play a valuable role in switching dormant capital into auxiliary circuits in ways that aid social reproduction. For instance, the issue of state bonds has been critical to the financing of large-scale infrastructural improvements, which in turn buttress global circuits of industrial capital. To use another example, establishing a liquid market in housing finance provided a vital stimulant for the post-WWII boom in the United States, whilst having a crucial disciplinary effect on labour (Harvey 2012; Smith 1982). Clearly there is a dialectical interplay of forces here. On the one hand fictitious flows of capital can aid stability, growth and reproduction, on the other, they can fuel speculation, bubbles and crisis.

To summarise then, industrial capital in Marx's conception is distinguished by the historically distinct properties associated with its effervescent transition between the money, productive and commodity forms. If successfully navigated, this process stimulates flows of surplus value – provided by labour – which are then distributed throughout the capitalist system in distinct revenue forms. Alongside this process, and feeding off it, are auxiliary circuits of fictitious capital. Here dormant capital is invested in assets which give the holder a claim over future revenues. Numerous levers exist in this respect for switching flows of revenue into auxiliary circuits, ranging from interest through to dividends. These legal claims can also be sold, yielding the vendor a potential capital gain. To the extent that this allows the original capital invested to be augmented, it can be said to have been valorised. However, owing to the type of switching mechanisms already highlighted, this can occur even though fictitious capital has not directly participated in the process that extracts surplus value from labour.

With these points in mind, the following section will contend that land and property markets constitute a potent site of investment for fictitious capital. This claim will be rooted in David Harvey's theory of class monopoly rents. It will be suggested that class monopoly rents act as the switching mechanism which enables these fictitious flows of capital, pooling in land and property markets, to feed off the revenues generated by the circuit of industrial capital. Once this relationship between class monopoly rents and fictitious capital has been conceptually unpacked, we will examine the role illicit activity plays in accentuating the returns yielded to fictitious capital invested in land and property markets.

Class monopoly rents, fictitious capital and illicit real-estate market activity

In the preface to his chapters on ground-rent, Marx examines certain changes to rural property regimes precipitated by the transition to capitalism, which are worth noting. The capitalist mode of production, he contends:

> detaches landed property completely from relations of lordship and servitude, while on the other hand it completely separates the land as a condition of labour from landed property and the landlord, for whom moreover this land represents nothing but a certain monetary tax that his monopoly permits him to extract from the industrial capitalist, the farmer.
>
> (Marx 1981: 754–755)

As a result, 'the landed proprietor can spend his entire life in Constantinople, while his landed property remains in Scotland. Landed property thus receives its purely economic form by the stripping away of all its former political and social embellishments and admixtures' (Marx 1981: 755).

This captures something of a general tendency within capitalism. Its drives strip away forms of real-property ownership rooted in personalised ties, replacing them with freely exchangeable property titles that render to their owner a monetary yield grounded in a particular form of (landed) monopoly. However, in *Capital* Marx's primary focus is the economic relation underpinning the 'monetary tax' placed on farmers. He did not consider the charges levied by real-property owners on users outside the process of rural production. To stimulate thought on the latter front, David Harvey has forwarded the concept of class monopoly rents.

At its most elementary, Harvey observes, 'rent is, in effect, a transfer payment realized through the monopoly power over land and resources conferred by the institutions of private property' (Harvey 1974: 240; see also Harvey 2012: 90–91). In practice, this can be quite a difficult transaction to pinpoint. For example, when a property developer constructs a luxury apartment complex, the charge levied on consumers will incorporate payment for the housing commodity which is mixed with a monetary tax rooted in monopoly rents. Nevertheless, these payments are distinct. Moreover, Harvey (1974) contends, it is the monopoly rents which property owners can levy that constitute the key driver for real-estate market activity, rather than the profit accrued from commodity production.

Accordingly, it is important to ask, how is it that real-property owners can systemically levy a monetary tax, without necessarily being involved in the process of value production? It is clear, for the reasons already outlined, that monopoly rent is not a deduction from the surplus value extracted using the land concerned – this applies to the capitalist farmer, but not to the landlord leasing an apartment complex, or a speculator providing vacant land to a hotel chain. As a result, Harvey (2012) contends that monopoly rents are in fact a deduction from revenues, which creates the sustained economic basis for this charge. In other words, property titles confer upon their owners an important monopoly power over space and the built environment, which can be employed as a lever to extract revenues from those wishing to access this monopoly. Harvey is careful to note that this power is rooted in capitalist class relations, which places socially cultivated assets under private control through exclusive property regimes (Harvey 1974, 2012). Broadly speaking this regime is essential if labour is to be confronted by the value it creates in the alienated, disguised form of capital, which stands over it in relations marked by domination and exploitation. It is this same exclusive regime which confers upon the real-property asset owner a power that allows them to share in future revenue flows. Because this power is ultimately rooted in class relations, Harvey (1974) labels the tax levied by real-property owners, class monopoly rents.

When considering the rate at which class monopoly rents may be levied, a number of determinations are pointed to by Harvey (2012). First, the charge levied to access or acquire a particular piece of real-property may be derived, in part, from its proximity to infrastructure, commercial centres, financial districts, a large suburban residential population, a newly rezoned district, and so on. The uneven way in which the process of concentrated and extended urbanisation distributes these opportunities for rent extraction, creates the possibility of differential rates in class monopoly rents being levied over a space-time continuum.

Monopoly rents may also be affected by certain unique features the property possesses, which give it distinction – such as a water views, or a bespoke design created by an internationally acclaimed architect. In reality, the uniqueness of a property, and its urban proximity, synthesise in complex, evolving ways to form a critical determinate of the monopoly charge that can be levied on the consumer.

A third factor that ought to be taken into account is the distribution of revenue flows. For instance, the substantive flow of revenue to a particular geo-graphically rooted class stratum will generally have a positive impact on the monopoly rents charged for those properties marketed to this constituency. That said, there need not necessarily be a direct correspondence here, between the monopoly rents charged and the geographic location of those in receipt of substantive revenue flows. For instance, London property developers have enjoyed a substantial windfall by courting international investors, with dormant revenues, seeking stowage in secure, upmarket properties in Western Europe. This, in part, has rested on their ability to market these properties globally to revenue hot-spots, whether it be China's ballooning 'middle class', members of Russia's elite or indeed home-grown speculators, who frequently minimise their taxation obligations using the UK's thriving offshore sector (Martini 2017).

Because class monopoly rents are a flexible lever, which investors can exploit to valorise their dormant capital, Harvey (2012) contends that this investment cycle can be usefully interpreted through the lens of fictitious capital, adopting the definition outlined in the previous section. In other words, through the mechanism of monopoly rents, property titles in effect confer on their owners a claim on future revenues, just as a loan to the state gives creditors a share in future tax revenues through the mechanism of interest. This claim on future revenues, facilitated through the medium of monopoly rents, thus creates a lever for switching surplus value congealed in revenue form, from the circuit of industrial capital, to an auxiliary circuit of fictitious capital functioning through land and property markets.

Furthermore, real-estate market investors can, of course, augment their return by influencing the rate of monopoly rent, through improving the prop-erty itself, and by becoming part of coalitions lobbying for favourable changes to the urban environment, and urban governance regimes. The latter coali-tions tend to involve a diverse cast of actors with a material stake in monopoly rents and property values, including for instance city councils, developers, real-estate firms and finance capital (Logan and Molotch 1987; Mossberger and Stoker 2001). Anderson (2014: 18) contends that these organisational actors 'are now centrally involved in setting the terms for realizing class monopoly rents through gentrification'.

If we return now to the problem framing this chapter, it can be argued that the theory of class monopoly rents advanced by Harvey, illuminates how surplus-value produced through the circuit of industrial capital, distributed in particular revenue forms, can be switched into auxiliary circuits of fictitious capital, creating a stable economic basis for land and property market activity. And it is within this social dynamic that the illicit repertoires, presented in the forthcoming chapters, must be situated.

To that end, it may first be observed that such illicit repertoires are targeting revenue flows through the mediation of land and property markets using the lever of monopoly rents. Second, they are often looking to expand the net used to capture these revenues, so that a greater share is diverted into the circuit of fictitious capital and appropriated by the speculative network concerned. However, the challenge here is to identify the different, often obscure ways this can occur, linking it back to the underpinning social theory. To explore this point, several examples will now be employed.

In a number of the case studies featured in this volume there is evidence to suggest that certain illegitimate tactics were used by corporate actors to acquire 99-year state leasehold titles – a common legal mechanism for alienating property in Papua New Guinea (see chapter one) – at a reduced cost. Subsequent steps were then taken to increase the title's market value, by courting large-scale, multi-use property ventures. For example, Papua New Guinea's Public Accounts Committee (2007) argues that the Paga Hill Development Company (PHDC), and its predecessor (Paga Hill Land Holding Company), secured title over portion 1597 – a Port Moresby based national park, zoned open space – without first obtaining the necessary approvals from the Physical Planning Board, thus reducing acquisition costs (see chapter five). It was also alleged that the company retained possession of its title despite failing to pay annual rent – even after it had been illegally reduced. Nor did it complete the K300 million improvement covenant required to obtain a 99-year business lease, that was issued anyway to a new Australian owned corporate vehicle linked to the developers, which did not appear to have the requisite foreign certification, essential under Papua New Guinea law. In addition to these factors, company records suggest that two of the developer's shareholders enjoyed a direct commercial tie with the Tourism Minister Michael Nali, who originally sponsored the project in Cabinet, and later became a shareholder (see chapter five).

It would thus appear, through a range of measures, PHDC and its predecessor was able to deregister a national park, and mitigate competitive pressures, in order to obtain a prime harbour-side plot. It achieved this, in part, by making contractual promises – K300 million in improvements – which were not delivered on, and through strategically leveraging direct ties with a senior political champion, who later became a shareholder. This mix of questionable measures helped PHDC obtain title over arguably Port Moresby's most exclusive portion of vacant land – in a highly competitive environment – thus giving the company an opportunity to capture sizable revenue flows commanded by a small international elite headquartered in Port Moresby, through the lever of monopoly rents. Then, PHDC held the leasehold title at a discounted rate – rents owed to the state were alleged to be in significant arrears (Publics Accounts Committee 2007) – over a considerable period while it courted investor interest.

Similar dynamics were found in the case of portion 1564, a 12.1 ha plot which abuts Papua New Guinea's national parliament (see chapter seven). In this instance, evidence suggests that Macata Enterprises acquired the land in 1989, initially through a Town Subdivision Lease, at a time when the company's principal was a Member of Parliament. Subsequently it was converted into a 99-year business lease during 1995. Lands Department records suggest Macata Enterprises has only been charged a nominal annual rent of K100 for this 99-year state lease. Under the *Land Regulation* 1999 annual rent for business leases should be set at 5% of the unimproved land value.

The land leased by Macata has lain largely dormant for over two decades, with no visible signs of development activity. Then, in or around 2012, after Port Moresby had experienced a considerable rise in real-estate prices, Macata Enterprises secured a Chinese investor. The exact size of the payment made to Macata Enterprises for accessing the land is unknown, but it was enough to prompt a schism between the company's husband and wife owner. Indeed, the latter party has been excised from the company, seemingly without lawful approval from the court.

It would thus appear a corporate entity has managed to again monopolise an exclusive space in Papua New Guinea's capital, under state leasehold title, for a discounted price. Furthermore, the company was able to hold this prime urban land for two decades, without adding any significant improvements. Macata has been well positioned to protect its interests in this respect owing to the close links its principal has enjoyed with a range of political power brokers.

To this it might be added that Macata Enterprises and PHDC, both organised eviction exercises in an attempt to remove long-standing informal communities resident on their land portions. These evictions involved house demolitions, police violence and the presence of private security. They also both occurred as legal challenges proceeded in the National Court. In the case of portion 1564, no provision was made by Macata Enterprises or the Papua New Guinea government for displaced residents. In the instance of Paga Hill, an agreement was made with a customary landowner from the 6-mile region in Port Moresby, to open up a customary land portion for rehousing Paga Hill residents. However, significant concerns have been raised over conditions at the site, and the limited security of tenure relocated residents enjoy.

Now if we connect the above facts to the theory developed in this chapter, it may be noted that the monopoly over vacant land plots in Port Moresby gave the corporate title holders a potentially significant claim over the future revenues flowing to high-end consumers wishing to purchase, or access, these prime plots. There is evidence to support the contention that this claim was secured through anti-competitive practices, and questionable forms of political influence.

For those investing in Papua New Guinea's land and property market through the mechanism of state leases, a portion of this claim on future revenues is shared with the state through annual rents hooked to the land's unimproved value. In both the Paga Hill and Mililat case, the share owing to the state was significantly reduced, through practices that potentially breach the *Land Act* 1996 and *Land Regulation* 1999. This decreased the overall asset acquisition costs for the companies concerned. As a result, the titleholders were relatively free to pursue investor interest over a prolonged period, so the land could be improved in ways that would capture high-end consumers, who at the time were paying monopoly rents on par with New York and London.

In the North Waigani and Mililat cases that feature in chapters six and seven, the evidence points to a different set of concrete specificities. In the instance of Mililat, a limited liability company, Selon Limited, obtained a 99-year state lease over a former plantation, by fraudulently holding itself out to be a customary landowner vehicle. This fraudulent acquisition signalled a complex chain of underpinning transactions, organised by the company's principal – an influential, local power broker – in fractured, contentious circumstances. As a result of these manoeuvres, Selon obtained the title to Mililat at a significantly discounted rate, illegitimately benefiting from past payments made under the Plantation Redistribution Scheme by a deregistered customary landowner vehicle. Having acquired fictitious capital belonging to local landowner groupings, Selon Limited proceeded to subdivide the land and valorise its investment through sales to a missionary organisation, New Tribes Mission, and a private company, Aces Ventures Limited. The latter was heavily involved in a neighbouring special economic zone.

In chapter seven we will examine the North Waigani case, which involves a National Housing Corporation apartment block. The latter entity is a statutory organisation responsible for the management of public housing. Evidence obtained by displaced residents suggests public housing valued at approximately K37 million was sold by the government for K11.1 million. To free the property for sale, a range of misleading tactics were employed by National Housing Corporation officials to dislodge tenants. Although no evidence was uncovered to show that the purchaser, DAC Real Estate, was involved in price fixing, Public Accounts Committee reporting suggests that National Housing Corporation stock is frequently sold off with the proceeds being misappropriated by public officials. In the North Waigani case, a severe constriction of land supply in Port Moresby had produced a housing bubble, particularly in the region's more salubrious areas, which allowed titleholders to levy high monopoly rents. It would appear reasonable to conclude from the available evidence that government officials were prepared to offload the North Waigani block at a discounted price, in order to privately appropriate the still sizable revenues that could be obtained in a buoyant market. In other words, fictitious capital belonging to the state was very likely expropriated by public officials, through discounted sale to private investors.

Accordingly, while the Paga Hill/Waigani, and Mililat/North Waigani cases contain different commercial repertoires that will be teased out in finer detail during chapters 5–7, they nonetheless are rooted in a set of common historical presuppositions. In the former examples there is evidence of price manipulation, anti-competitive practices and human rights abuses, which allowed the companies concerned to obtain exclusive, sizable land plots in a highly competitive market. These companies then held the plots over a prolonged period, at a discounted rate, while management courted investors in a bid to increase the monopoly rents that could be levied. On the other hand, in the Mililat and North Waigani cases there was no immediate ambition to increase monopoly rents. Rather, the main aim of the actors concerned was to acquire, at a heavily discounted price, what was in substance fictitious capital belonging to another, and then sell it on, even below market rates, so the misappropriated asset could be converted into monetary form. The lure of the assets in these cases was their vulnerability to expropriation.

Yet in *all* four examples we can observe that those in possession of spatial monopolies were able to make a claim on revenues shifted from the circuit of industrial capital, through the lever of monopoly rents. This creates the possibility of valorisation without surplus-value creation. And it was upon this historical foundation that certain institutional frameworks, organisational vehicles and commercial repertoires – which are the focus of chapters 5–7 – were developed, in order to help engorge and capture, via illicit means, the share of revenues being switched into Papua New Guinea's land and property market, where fictitious capital circulates.

At this juncture in the argument, it needs to be added that when considering the enabling structure for illicit land and property market activity, the field of state power cannot be ignored. Indeed, the policy, institutional, legal and material infrastructure through which state power functions, mediates in critical ways how the different circuits of capital operate and interact. Therefore, government should not be framed as an activity extraneous to the functioning of capitalist social relations; to the contrary, it must be viewed as an integral, internal feature. Accordingly, any attempt to understand the historically distinct ways that state power functions through the apparatus of urban governance, including the mediated impact it has on market behaviour, requires conceptual framing that roots state power in a theory of capitalist social relations. On that note, the remainder of this chapter will set out such a conceptual framing drawing on the late work of Foucault, before applying it to help think about dynamics which can be observed in real-property markets.

The role of government

In volume two of *Capital*, Marx breaks down the circuit of industrial capital into a series of sub-circuits – focusing on money-capital, productive capital and commodity-capital – each of which is an essential moment in a larger totality.

To this he adds further auxiliary circuits of investment in volume three, which feed off this industrial core. As a whole, Marx is attempting to conceptually capture the complex cyclical passage value takes, from the moment of its entry into the circuit of industrial capital through to its distribution in often quite convoluted phenomenal forms. And it is the vigorous processes which churn value along, so that it can covet its essential other (surplus value), which are the lifeblood of capitalist society. They keep the wheels of social reproduction turning, which is essential if the system's human participants are to satisfy their historically conditioned, class relative needs.

Of course, these processes are also socially tumultuous, replete with internal antagonisms, class struggle and impending rupture. Yet to oxygenate the social system with surplus value, industrial capital must successfully transit through its essential forms of existence unimpeded. If successful, this process allows surplus value to be extracted and then distributed in different revenue forms, which also provides sustenance for auxiliary circuits of investment. Needless to say an expansive material apparatus of institutions, infrastructure, tools, inputs and actors, is required if this system of transiting value flows, so elementary to the life of capitalism, is to function. For instance, labour must be provided in the right quantity and quality; there must be a regular, reliable supply of raw materials; machinery, technology and knowledge must be produced and distributed; communication and transport infrastructure must be built and maintained; credit systems must be operated with security and predictability; labour tensions and other political strife must be mediated; nation-states must contend with the complex nexus between international geopolitical rivalries and transnational economic flows using bilateral and multilateral forums; and that is just to name a few examples of the delicate material and institutional processes that are essential to the circuits at the heart of capitalism. There is also a host of associated social challenges and risks cultivated by industrialisation, urbanisation and globalisation, such as crime, deprivation, people movement, pollution and public health, which cannot be allowed to threaten the vast material metabolism essential to social life in its capitalist form.

Put simply the complex, intersecting, oxygenating circuits that as a totality produce and distribute value, must be constantly fed by a managed supply of material elements, infrastructure and institutional supports. Where significant problems emerge which prevent the circuits of value from transitioning through these different material conduits, the system as a whole loses its source of oxygen, leading to economic hypoxia and potentially, major crisis. Problems can arise from many different angles. Marx (1981) most famously talks about the falling rate of profit, which cultivates overproduction on the one hand, and lack of demand on the other, thus paralysing the circuit of industrial capital – with consequential effects on dependent auxiliary circuits. Only a painful process of sweeping devaluation can reboot the system.

However, at a less grand scale, cleavages prove to be a perpetual, multi-scalar dimension of capitalism that require constant attention and recalibration – labour shortages must be countered, interruption in raw material supplies must be cleared, aging infrastructure must be renewed, new technologies must be produced, consumer confidence requires stimulation, ailing credit systems must be flushed with liquidity, and so on.

Perhaps not surprisingly given this sensitive social ecosystem, in Marx's view government, as a set of practices, has an integral place in the everyday operation of the capitalist mode of production. It was envisaged by Marx that a volume of *Capital* would be reserved for the state system (see Heinrich 2012). Although it was never written, we may nevertheless draw on Marx's existing theoretical legacy, to think about how governmental power forms part of capitalism's interior. To that end, a fertile source of stimulation can be found in Foucault's late work on governmentality presented in his lectures delivered at the *Collège de France*. Although expansive in scope, a significant portion of these lectures reflect on an emergent form of governmental power stewarded into being by industrialisation and the transition to capitalism.

With the latter historical shifts, Foucault contends, power circulating through the nation–state has a new historical impetus, and logic, that needs to be carefully distinguished (Foucault 2007, 2008). While he does not borrow explicitly from Marx's conceptual framework, Foucault's work does closely reflect on the relationship between this new logic, and the delicate social balance struck between the material economy and the value that flows through it, which as a whole is essential to capitalist reproduction.

For Foucault government, as a field of practice, is not so much concerned with the passage of self-realising value – rather its policies and repertoires focus instead on keeping the material economy of things, which value flows through, in motion and in balance. In this sense governmental power does not directly target value in its transformative movement, it only registers value's motion indirectly, via the vitality and pace through which labour is working, raw materials are moving, factories are producing, banks are loaning, and so on. In this context, governmental power acts by stimulating, steering and securing material metabolism.

Yet a critical relationship still exists between the circuit of capital, and governmental power. Value flows signal their health in coded form through this readily apparent material economy of things, while government, using law, policy and practice, registers these signals and applies measures that attempt to secure a pace and balance within the material economy congruent with value's transformative journey (Foucault 2007). The latter ambition never assumes an explicit form, rather it is indirect, articulated through a desire to bring about the right economic indicators that signal good fiscal health.

Foucault's concern is to conceptualise the logic and repertoires informing this historical form of statecraft, which he designates governmentality. With this in mind Foucault argues, government must confront the challenge of:

> allowing [many different] circulations to take place, of controlling [regulating] them, sifting the good and the bad, ensuring that things are always in movement, constantly moving around, continually going from one point

to another, but in such a way that the inherent dangers of this circulation are cancelled out.

(2007: 65)

Yet this modality of power, in Foucault's view, does not work through dictates or decrees that prescribe how capital, money, raw materials, machinery, manufactured goods, landed resources, labour, and so on, move and combine. The 'immutable' laws and drives underpinning market metabolism – their 'natural regulation' (which is capitalist social relations in mystified form) – must, from the vantage point of government, be respected (Foucault 2007: 353). The impetus then is to use policy, public administration and law, as strategic measures that work with these 'immutable' laws to achieve desirable outcomes by guarding against the dangers of stagnation, saturation and rupture.

Foucault explains:

> It will be necessary to arouse, to facilitate, and to *laisser faire*, in other words to manage and no longer control through rules and regulations. The essential objective of this management will not be so much to prevent things as to ensure that the necessary and natural regulations work, or even to create regulations that enable natural regulations to work.

(2007: 353)

Foucault uses the example of the grain trade to concretise his point:

> English politicians ... from the end of the seventeenth century ... developed, and got Parliament to adopt, a legislative package that imposed or accepted the free circulation and commerce of grain, with, however, a support and a corrective. The first was freedom of export, which, in prosperous periods, and so in periods of plenty and good harvests, should make it possible to support the price of wheat, of grain in general, that was in danger of collapse due to this very abundance. Not only would export be permitted to support the price, but it would be helped by a system of subsidies, establishing a stimulant to this freedom. Second, to avoid an excessive import of wheat into England in favourable periods, import taxes were established so that the surplus of abundance coming from imported products did not cause price to fall.

(2007: 34)

In this example employed by Foucault laws, subsidies and tariffs are strategically used to secure and stabilise the circulation of wheat over different cyclical periods, using price as a signal. The objective of government, however, is not to override natural regulations. Instead it works with the underlying commercial calculus of trade, adding certain stimulants and correctives that help to get its parts to pull together, creating a foundation for freedom and security. Foucault observes:

it is not a matter of imposing a law on men, but of the disposition of things, that is to say, of employing tactics rather than laws, or, of as far as possible employing laws as tactics; arranging things so that this or that end may be achieved through a certain number of means.

(2007: 99)

It needs to be said, while economic management features heavily in his lectures, Foucault's framing of government is broader than that. Foucault sees this historically developed art operating in the arenas of public policy, social policy and public administration. Indeed, from the standpoint of governmentality crime, welfare, public health, urbanisation, and so on, can all be conceived of as distinct social realities like the economy. They evidence an internal nature through sustained empirical patterns and predictable cycles. We are able to observe, for example, in morbidity and mortality rates, systematic health dynamics that emerge from the social way human biophysical rhythms become articulated through historically developed dispositions, habits, lifestyle and environments. Again, government cannot change the public's nature, instead it must work with it. Accordingly, law, policy and administrative interventions may be used to optimise levels of public health by stimulating desirable forms of activity, such as exercise and balanced diets, while introducing correctives to deleterious habits such as drug-use, smoking and high intakes of salt and sugar.

Foucault also considers the special role knowledge plays in the exercise of governmental power (Foucault 2007, 2008). Whether the field is social policy or economic management, he argues, governmental power seeks to act intelligently, by knowing the target's dispositions and calibrating its actions so that government does not intervene too little, or too much. We have here a form of power that attempts to systematically limit itself in accordance with the nature of its object. This, Foucault observes, creates the foundation for an alliance between practitioners of government and science – which he captures through the conceptual phrase governmentality. Only by listening to science and using scientific analyses, can practitioners of governmental power administer the economy and society intelligently, ensuring they do not act excessively or insufficiently. We thus witness governance according to truth, rather than justice.

The consequences of this historically specific marriage between power and knowledge are teased out by Foucault, during a survey of the French physiocrats:

What the physiocrats deduce from their discovery is that the government must know … [economic] mechanisms in their innermost and complex nature. Once it knows these mechanisms, it must, of course, undertake to respect them. But this does not mean that it provide itself with a juridical framework respecting individual freedoms and the basic right of individuals. It means, simply, that it arms its politics with a precise, continuous, clear and distinct knowledge of what is taking place in society, in the market, and in the economic circuits, so that the limitation of its power is not given by the respect for the freedom of individuals, but simply by the evidence of economic analysis which it knows has to be respected.

(2008: 61–62)

And here we see quite explicitly an important tension at the heart of governmental power. In order to intelligently generate the particular forms of freedom critical to the inner 'nature' of economy and society, governments must be prepared to deploy correctives and stimulants that undermine individual and collective rights. For example, Foucault observes:

There must be a free labour market, but again there must be a large enough number of sufficiently competent, qualified, and politically disarmed workers to prevent them exerting pressure on the labour market. We have then the conditions for the creation for a formidable body of legislation and an incredible range of governmental interventions to guarantee production of the freedom needed in order to govern.

(2008: 64–65)

Banning of unions, and the targeted killing of labour activists, in this sense represent correctives designed to effect the disposition of the worker, so they are more responsive to coercive market forces – out of which emerges a 'free' labour market. Similarly, if capital and commodities are to freely flow in the global economy, particular forms of economic and military coercion must be used to effect the disposition of target states in ways that ensure, for instance, the regulated supply of strategic natural resources. Accordingly, self-limiting government committed to certain forms of freedom, remains congruent with the systemic application of coercion and violence.

At this point in the argument it is helpful to recall the theoretical arrangement Marx employed in *Capital*, in order to consider how governmentality can be used to advance understandings of the capitalist system as a whole. To that end, it can be argued, regimes of governmental practice intervene at the complex interface between the primary and auxiliary circuits of capital that channel flows of value in their different economic forms, and the vast material infrastructure and movements which value transitions through in its turbulent cyclical journey towards valorisation. Governmental power, in concrete, historically specific ways, aims to: secure the mobile material edifice value transitions through; optimise social metabolism, by creating incentives, correctives and enabling environments that intelligently stop social sepsis from setting in; guard against paralysing forms of saturation; and inspire modes of behaviour that help produce desirable freedoms and aggregate outcomes.

In so doing, government is in a cat and mouse game with circuits of value, and the relations they rest on, which form the hidden engine behind the targeted social metabolism and its 'immutable' laws. The tendencies, cycles and trajectories these circuits and social relations inspire are systematically modelled through science, and then effected through governmental interventions, which seek to intelligently stabilise, regulate and secure the economy and society, without necessarily glimpsing the class orientated structure beneath the material semblance being targeted. So we are talking here of a mediated relationship between governmentality and the circuits of capital – the circuits of capital function in covert ways only sending out overt signals in reified forms, which science systematises, and government reacts to. Nevertheless, both capital and government are essential to the other's activity, even if this activity also has its own distinctive drives, which creates the potential for antagonism and rupture.

It also ought to be noted that governmentality, as a determinate layer of reality at the interior of capitalist relations, cannot necessarily be viewed as being synonymous with the nation-state. Nation-states – which are complex, multi-scalar entities – certainly act as primary organisational hubs for a global governance framework. However, the art of governmentality is also dispersed beyond the nation-state. It is prosecuted by a range of connected, but distinct organs, ranging from international financial institutions through to NGOs. It is this complex, uneven global weave of institutions, as a heterogeneous and often antagonistic global whole, that administers the interventions constitutive of governmentality.

This global weave, of course, is not removed from class struggle. Each hub articulates class power, and is a site for struggle between different, vying class forces.[3] In other words, how these varied organs execute governmentalised interventions is neither informed by a universal script, nor is it necessarily going to be what is best for the system as a whole – assuming such a judgement could be made. Instead, what is deemed to be necessary and desirable from a governmental perspective, is a judgement that is the subject of struggle between class rooted social groupings, seeking to shape the common sense of practitioners.

It should be emphasised, in this respect, that influence occurs in myriad ways. While formal lines of democratic communication may exist between the public, and political actors, class power may also be exerted forcefully through informal networks of influence and decision making, involving senior politicians, high level bureaucrats and central business figures (see Jessop 2007; Poulantzas 1978). These shadow networks of influence can act as the opaque organising framework for establishing what is desirable in government circles, while formal democratic processes become something of a deceptive semblance. Accordingly, any attempt to make sense of how governmentality is conceived of, and applied, at a historical juncture, must acknowledge the role class struggle has played in this moment, looking at both formal and informal mechanisms of influence.

If we now turn to the question of urban governance, it is possible to appropriate the above conceptual framework to better understand the historical foundations essential to illicit activity in land and property markets. To that end, we might first note that as surplus value circulates through primary and auxiliary circuits of capital, in mediated economic forms, the levers of urban governance become a determinate layer that shape how this takes place. In other words, real-property regimes, urban development policies, taxation measures, the administration and enforcement of regulations, infrastructure investments, to name just a few factors, will stimulate the intensity with which circuits of fictitious capital operate in land and property markets, as well as their relative capability to draw sustenance from the revenue flows generated by the circuit of industrial capital. All of which impacts in precise ways on the reward structure open to real-property investment, and the incentives for enacting illicit repertoires.

Of course, the urban governance terrain cannot be surveyed in abstraction from the broader regimes of governmentality it is part of, which again are heterogeneous affairs replete with rivalries, antagonisms and ruptures. Nevertheless, how these regimes, as a unified whole – conceived of on a multi-scalar continuum – mediate social reproduction is a critical determinant that shapes the ways in which surplus value is percolated and distributed through the circuit of industrial capital, and then switched via a range of levers to auxiliary circuits.

For example, in the case of Papua New Guinea, the evolving regime of governmentality there, organised primarily through the nation-state framework, is a complex articulation of influence exerted through formal and shadow spaces, administered at a national, provincial and local level. In particular, we have witnessed over the past four decades an increasingly adept class of speculative capitalists, engaged in practices designed to build informal governance regimes at all levels of government in an effort to secure the improper award of important legal rights over natural resources, principally logging, fisheries and land (Barnett 1989; Numapo 2013; Public Accounts Committee 2007). In addition, they have succeeded in coordinating schemes that redistribute public assets into private hands, through mechanisms such as sham consultancies, inflated service contracts and fraudulent law suits against the state (Barnett 2002; Davani et al. 2009; Public Accounts Committee 2006; Sawong 2007). These informal networks, in effect, have cultivated a bureaucratic and political culture, which strategically uses a combination of illicit and legal mechanisms to stimulate the flow of material resources and revenues into speculative circuits of capital, which have become a central pillar for the reproduction of Papua New Guinea's ruling class. No aggregate data exists on the total loss incurred through these different forms of grand corruption, but given the documented scale and breadth of these schemes, most commentators have assessed it would be very significant.

However, there would be little point misappropriating state land or enacting schemes to defraud public funds, unless there were muscular flows of revenue to make these different illicit enterprises rewarding. One particularly important industry that enables Papua New Guinea to share in the proceeds of global capitalist production, is the extractive sector, principally gas, oil and minerals.

It has been a key challenge for successive governments at a national level to keep industrial capital moving into this sector, ensuring it can transit through its productive and commodity forms, without facing significant barriers from landowners or other sources of local resistance. To that end, a range of legal and institutional structures have been put in place, including tax holidays, 'business friendly' regulations, and heavy handed paramilitary units, to help stimulate, manage and regulate the material movements essential to the flow of industrial capital within the extractive sector, assisted by international donors and corporate consultants (Connell 1997; Dinnen 2001; Fletcher and Webb 2012; May 2004; Namaliu 1995; Standish 1994). This has stewarded into being a number of large-scale extractive projects, ranging from a liquefied natural gas venture in the Southern Highlands, through to nickel mining in Madang. While these industries impact deleteriously on local ecologies and communities, they have nonetheless been a significant source of government receipts, foreign export earnings, and an important, albeit temporary, stimulus for the service and construction sectors (Asia Development Bank 2015; Barker 2014; Batten 2014).

So on the one hand we witness in Papua New Guinea a formal regime of resource governance, which has been enhanced over time in an effort to stimulate, regulate and secure the material conditions essential to a buoyant extractive sector. This has allowed revenue streams generated by international circuits of industrial capital to be distributed into Papua New Guinea's national economy. Married to this is a more opaque, shadow regime of governmental power. It strives to enact measures which progressively allow a significant portion of national revenues to be diverted into auxiliary circuits of fictitious capital, in which a powerful clique of political figures and their business associates have a significant stake. Land and property markets are an example of this dynamic.

Formally speaking, Papua New Guinea boasts an impressive range of laws, regulatory mechanisms, institutional structures and policies, which have been designed to manage urbanisation in ways that balance economic growth, social need and environmental management. However, behind this formal edifice is an informal regime of urban governance typified by clientelism, corruption and fraud – which has permeated key institutions, including the Department of Lands and Physical Planning, the National Land Board and the National Housing Corporation (Barnett 2002; Davani et al. 2009; Numapo 2013; Public Accounts Committee 2007, 2009). Successive investigations conducted by commissions of inquiry, the Public Accounts Committee and Auditor General, have consistently confirmed the existence of this shadow regime.

This regime, on the one hand, tends to restrict the supply of state land to a privileged strata of politically connected speculators who hold land with minimal real obligations. On the other, it also facilitates the misuse of certain exceptional legal measures to stimulate the circulation of customary land, so it can feed forestry and agroindustry.

However, it would be a mistake to characterise this dynamic as a breakdown in urban governance. It is simply an alternative model for doing urban governance, one that for instance permits politically privileged investors to commandeer lucrative sources of monopoly rents – state leases – and the significant claim they give title holders over national revenues. Furthermore, when it comes to more peripheral real-estate, the subject of extended urbanisation, this shadow regime, for instance, allows forestry companies to access large customary landholdings at a considerable discount, with modest payments being made to local fixers and their associates. We see here something of a sensitive and intelligent form of urban governance design, if looked at from a class perspective. On the one hand, it slows down and inhibits the circulation of state land, so a stratum of politically connected speculators can lay a growing claim on national revenues through the mechanism of monopoly rents; on the other, it helps to stimulate the circulation of customary land – which would otherwise be off the market – allowing forestry companies to access lucrative plots at often heavily discounted prices, denying to landowners owed monopoly rents. Speculative capital and forestry capital in these instances are the chief beneficiaries, while working class families and the peasantry face reproduction challenges owing to inflated costs of living and reduced claims on revenues.

With that in mind, the core contention advanced here is that governmental power, acting through the state edifice, helps to conduct the complex material flows and social processes that are the most visible articulation of capitalist social relations. In so doing, this modality of power regulates how circuits of capital sequence through different essential forms of existence in the quest to be valorised. It may be hypothesised then that the class-laden way governmental power is exercised can act as a crucial stimulant for the investments, assets and market metabolism, which switch surplus value in revenue form into circuits of fictitious capital. Out of this emerges the opportunity structures and incentive schemas found to precipitate illicit land and property market activity, which again governance regimes can stimulate or deter, through a range of strategic measures. Therefore, any attempt to theorise the historical conditions which make illicit land and property market activity a rewarding, systemic process, must register how governmental power mediates the relationship between circuits of capital and the frenetic economy of material flows these circuits must necessarily act through.

Conclusion

At first glance, the conditions of existence for different forms of illicit activity in land and property markets – which will be teased out in subsequent chapters – are the sizable profits which these ventures can generate. However, theoretical inquiry cannot cease at this point in the explanatory process. It needs to be asked how economic activity which generates no value, can nonetheless realise sizable returns. It has been the contention of this chapter, that a holistic reading of Marx's *Capital* offers novel theoretical devices that help explain why investment repertoires in the real-estate sector can congeal sizable returns on a sustained basis, without necessarily generating value.

This explanation is rooted in the labour theory of value, and a distinctive framing of capital as value-in-motion, which is fertilised through a process of surplus-value extraction. In particular, it has been suggested, drawing on Marx, that the extraction of surplus value occurs through, and oxygenates, the circuit of industrial capital. This circulatory process as a whole percolates the revenues which can then be potentially redistributed through auxiliary circuits of fictitious capital investment.

With that overarching conception in mind, it has been argued that real-property titles may be viewed as a form of fictitious capital, employing Harvey's theory of class monopoly rents. In effect, the latter mechanism – a charge rooted in the monopoly power generated by property regimes – allows surplus value extracted from the labouring classes, to be absorbed through a set of mediated steps, into auxiliary circuits of fictitious capital, where actors can speculatively valorise their 'capital'.

However, if this process is to be concretely approximated an adequate theory of governmental power is needed, that builds on and deepens the treatise set forth by Marx in *Capital*. To that end, a starting point was found in Foucault's late work on governmentality. Although open to multiple interpretations, it has been argued here that governmental power as conceptualised by Foucault has a certain distinctive logic of action – albeit one that can have many different concrete expressions – that is articulated through sites of practice that span a range of social and political institutions. These regimes – in conversation with the sciences – appropriate policy, laws and public administration, to stimulate, regulate and steer those visible aggregate tendencies constitutive of the economy and society. And in so doing they condition, in a mediated fashion, how value flows through the circuits of capital. Out of this process emerges certain opportunity and incentive structures critical to illicit land and property market activity.

On that note, attention will now be turned to a systematic, comparative methodology which can be employed to document such illicit activity. This framework's application, it will be argued, can robustly generate data-sets and data-analysis that help to disclose how the governmentalised, economic circuits which emerge out of the historical dynamics theorised in this chapter, become sites of sustained illicit practices that impact in significant ways upon concentrated and extended urbanisation. The focus of this methodology, and subsequent empirical chapters, will thus be on better documenting the granular networks, institutional mechanisms and commercial/political repertoires used to effect this illicit activity, from which a systematic framework will emerge for theorising the latter determinations.

Notes

1 That is, the tools, fixed assets and raw materials essential to production processes.

2 Although he is careful to note there are many internal contradictions that obstruct this process.
3 Class here articulates the way in which human subjectivity enters the world as potential, and then actualises through historical engagement with social practices, which renders this subjective potential into concrete human form (see Bensaid 2009; de Ste Croix 1981; Mikhailov 1980). These concrete forms articulate a particular social positioning, within an overarching order rooted in the production and redistribution of wealth structured around class relations, out of which emerges various, distinctive senses of interest and purpose. This creates the foundation for forms of class solidarity and class antagonism. It is not necessary, of course, for this solidarity or antagonism to materialise in the consciousness of participants as 'class'; a whole complex set of discourses and narratives mediate these experiences in the minds of actors. Nor should we imagine that life experience prompts interests and purposes that coagulate into neat groupings; the reality of class and social practice is more muddy.

Bibliography

Anderson, M. B. (2014) 'Class monopoly rent and the contemporary neoliberal city', *Geography Compass*, 8(1), 13–24.

Asia Development Bank. (2015). 'Papua New Guinea 2016–2020'. [Online]. Available at: www.adb.org/sites/default/files/institutional-document/157927/cps-png-2016-2020.pdf (accessed: 17 February 2017).

Barker, P. (2014). 'PNG's economy 2014 – past, present and future prospects'. [Online]. Available at: www.inapng.com/pdf_files/PNG_Mining_Petroleum_Conference_2014.pdf (accessed: 17 February 2017).

Barnett, T. E. (1989). *The Commission of Inquiry into Aspects of the Forestry Industry*, Port Moresby: Commission of Inquiry into Aspects of the Forest Industry.

Barnett, T. E. (2002). Report of the Commission of Inquiry into the National Provident Fund. [Online]. Extracts available at: web.archive.org/web/20060923050634/http://www.postcourier.com.pg/NPF%20inquiry/npf116 (accessed: 16 February 2017).

Batten, A. (2014). 'Papua New Guinea', *Asian Development Outlook*. [Online]. Available at: www.adb.org/sites/default/files/publication/31241/ado2014-png.pdf (accessed: 17 February 2017).

Bensaïd, D. (2009). *Marx for our Times*, London: Verso.

Connell, J. (1997). *Papua New Guinea: The Struggle for Development*, London: Routledge.

Davani, C., Sheehan, M. and Manoa, D. (2009). *The Commission of Inquiry Generally into the Department of Finance: Final Report*, Port Moresby: The Commission.

de Ste Croix, G. E. M. (1981). *The Class Struggle in the Ancient Greek World*, London: Duckworth.

Dinnen, S. (2001). *Law and Order in a Weak State: Crime and Politics in Papua New Guinea*, Honolulu: University of Hawai'i Press.

Fine, B. (2013). 'Financialization from a Marxist perspective', *International Journal of Political Economy*, 42(4), 47–66.

Fletcher, L. and Webb, A. (2012). *Pipe Dreams: The PNG LNG Project and the Future Hopes of a Nation*, Sydney: Jubilee Australia.

Foucault, M. (2007). *Security, Territory, Population: Lectures at the Collège de France 1977–1978*, Basingstoke: Palgrave Macmillan.

Foucault, M. (2008). *The Birth of Biopolitics: Lectures at the Collège de France 1978–1979*, Basingstoke: Palgrave Macmillan.

Harvey, D. (1974). 'Class-monopoly rent, finance capital and the urban revolution', *Regional Studies*, 8(3–4), 239–255.

Harvey, D. (1985). *The Urbanization of Capital: Studies in the History and Theory of Capitalist Urbanization*, Baltimore: John Hopkins University Press.

Harvey, D. (2012). *Rebel Cities: From the Right to the City to the Urban Revolution*, London: Verso.

Heinrich, M. (2012). *An Introduction to the Three Volumes of Karl Marx's Capital*, New York: Monthly Review Press.

Jessop, B. (2007). *State Power*, Cambridge: Polity Press.

Lasslett, K. (2010) 'Scientific method and the crimes of the powerful', *Critical Criminology*, 18(3), 211–228.

Lasslett, K. (2015). 'The state at the heart of capitalism: Marxist theory and Foucault's lectures on governmentality', *Critical Sociology*, 41(4–5), 641–658.

Logan, J. R. and Molotch, H. (1987). *Urban Fortunes: The Political Economy of Place*, London: University of California Press.

Martini, M. (2017). *Doors Wide Open: Corruption and Real-Estate in Four Key Markets*, Berlin: Transparency International.

Marx, K. (1976). *Capital*, Vol. 1, Harmondsworth: Penguin Books.

Marx, K. (1978). *Capital*, Vol. 2, Harmondsworth: Penguin Books.

Marx, K. (1981). *Capital*, Vol. 3, Harmondsworth: Penguin Books.

May, R. J. (2004). *State and Society in Papua New Guinea: The First Twenty-Five Years*, Canberra: ANU E Press.

Mikhailov, F. T. (1980). *The Riddle of the Self*, Moscow: Progress Publishers.

Mossberger, K. and Stoker, G. (2001). 'The evolution of urban regime theory: The challenge of conceptualization', *Urban Affairs Review*, 36(6), 810–835.

Namaliu, R. (1995). 'Politics, business and the state in Papua New Guinea', *Pacific Economic Bulletin*, 10(2), 61–65.

Numapo, J. (2013). *Commission of Inquiry into the Special Agriculture and Business Leases: Final Report*, Port Moresby: Commission of Inquiry into the Special Agricultural and Business Leases.

Poulantzas, N. (1978). *State Power Socialism*. London: Verso.

Public Accounts Committee. (2006). *Public Accounts Committee Report to Parliament on the Inquiry into the Office of the Public Curator*, Waigani: National Parliament of Papua New Guinea.

Public Accounts Committee. (2007). *Public Accounts Committee Report to Parliament on the Inquiry into the Department of Lands and Physical Planning*, Waigani: National Parliament of Papua New Guinea.

Public Accounts Committee. (2009). *Inquiry into the National Housing Corporation and State Home Ownership Schemes*, Waigani: National Parliament of Papua New Guinea.

Sawong, D. (2007). *Report of the Commission of Inquiry into the Management of the Investment Corporation of Papua New Guinea and the Investment Corporation Fund of Papua New Guinea and all Matters Relating to the Conversion of the Investment Corporation Fund of Papua New Guinea to Pacific Balanced Fund*, Port Moresby: Commission of Inquiry.

Smith, N. (1982). 'Gentrification and uneven development', *Economic Geography*, 58(2), 139–155.

Standish, B. (1994). 'Papua New Guinea: The search for security in a weak state', in Thompson, A. (ed.) *Papua New Guinea: Issues for Australian Security Planners*, Canberra: Australian Defence Studies Centre.

Tombs, S. (2012). 'State–corporate symbiosis in the production of crime and harm', State Crime, 1(2), 170–195.

Chapter 3

The crimes of the powerful and urbanisation

An investigative framework

Introduction

In order to understand the role that illicit transactions play in building the cities and rural environments we inhabit, a substantive body of empirical data is needed. To complicate matters, built environments are managed through a diverse range of property, planning and environmental regimes, which are distinct to particular socio-historical contexts. So at a very minimum, any thematic focus on the crimes of urbanisation, demands a rigorous body of evidence that documents these contexts, regimes and the state–corporate transactions they facilitate. To do this in a way that produces concrete, comparative data-sets, from which generalisable theoretical approximations can be developed, requires distinctive units of analysis that help forge a shared empirical focus, with congruent methodologies.

However, a further layer of complexity exists peculiar to crimes of the powerful research, of which crimes of urbanisation are a subset. First, the organisations and individuals implicated in these crimes tend to wield considerable economic, political and cultural resources, which they can deploy to cloak their behaviour and shape public perception. Second, the transactions which facilitate these crimes are often rendered objectively opaque by the sheer technical complexity they involve.

Therefore, at the minimum we need to build an investigative framework that can be enacted through units of analysis that illuminate these hidden worlds, and bring to the fore crucial factual determinations that shape how they function. To do this, such a framework requires data-collection methods that can challenge the different forms of opaqueness we encounter when researching the crimes of urbanisation. It is not the case that the often covert nature of such transactions close off research; however, it does mean that we need to develop innovative tools and frameworks that can crack these illicit event chains and the actors that stand behind them, while conforming to requisite standards of scholarly rigour and professional ethics.

With that challenge in mind, this chapter will present social and temporal units of analysis that can be used to think clinically about the crimes of urbanisation, and more effectively interrogate the closed social worlds that organise these illicit processes. Attached to these units are a number of new methodological tools pioneered during this research; they are married with more established social science instruments, which have been repurposed using new digital and forensic advances to give them an investigative edge.

To start, a position is adopted in this chapter – based on the empirical research – that the crimes of urbanisation presuppose sophisticated social networks that empower actor coalitions to command space in a particular way, regardless of formal rules or conduct norms (Coles 2001; Kriegler 2014; McIllwain 1999; Van der Hulst 2009);[1] it is also presumed that these social networks contain forms of competition and contention, the outcome of which is closely linked to the influence, resources and solidarity of the groups concerned. A social network, in this sense, is a unified, contradictory whole populated through a constellation of organisations, individuals, assets and events, materially connected through diverse ties, such as business partnership, political patronage, strategic alliance, ownership, agency, friendship, family, solidarity, locality, competition, opposition, and so on (Kriegler 2014; Wasserman and Faust 1994). These relationships facilitate the circulation of wealth, assets, information, expert knowledge, moral support, prestige, opposition and stigma between actors. Of course, none of this could take place without thousands of social transactions being organised that trigger ties, manage relationships and facilitate flows, over different temporal periods.

The complex, changing architecture of actors, ties and flows empower coalitions to champion and realise their objectives with a certain probability of success, in social environments marked by multiple forms of competition and resistance. In other words, a complex economy of power exists, which is conditioned by the way socially grounded actors use their respective positions to solidify relations, command resources, accumulate knowledge, mobilise forces, perfect tactics, and so on (Tilly and Tarrow 2007). Furthermore, this is not a mere conjunctural matter; we can observe patterned processes which suggest there are logics in the economy of power as it operates in the field of urbanisation, which can be documented and understood.[2]

Against this backdrop, the following chapter is premised on the contention that we can build data-sets that progressively trace these social constellations, and the economies of power that circulate through them, beginning with the more elementary adhesives that bind networks together, moving progressively towards more complex network dynamics that involve increasingly complicated social intersections of forces. To do this a particular methodology will be introduced, called investigative social network analysis. As the name implies, this framework is indebted to the social network analysis (SNA) literature, which has developed techniques for visualising, analysing and measuring networks that populate different social fields. However, the SNA framework has been modified and repurposed here to meet the specific demands of investigative fieldwork into the crimes of urbanisation.

With that in mind, this chapter will argue SNA graphing methods can be appropriated as an investigative tool to build network models in the field, that help scrutinise critical actors, groups, assets and events, the ties which bind them together, and the processes these ties facilitate. An important role is reserved here for visual intelligence; that is, using data visualisation to think about a large number of variables with a degree of accuracy and control that would be difficult in the absence of visual aids. Drawing dialectically on SNA methods, including associated forms of data-visualisation, it will be suggested that progressively richer approximations of the social networks at the heart of contentious urban processes may be produced. These emerging data-sets and associated visual models can then be further refined through more complex analytical techniques developed in the SNA literature. These techniques allow the researcher to identify, analyse and weigh network characteristics, which have been found to possess a range of significances.

However, the emphasis here is on strengthening investigative inquiry; in other words, using SNA techniques and concepts to uncover actors, processes and ties that often opaquely underpin the crimes of urbanisation. For practical and subject specific reasons less emphasis is placed on the quantitative tools found in the SNA literature. While these quantitative measures are valuable, it will be apparent that investigative SNA builds thick qualitative data-sets, which owing to the opaque subject matter, are not uniform – this means they are often incompatible with the metrics employed in quantitative analyses, or even where there is compatibility the uneven character of the data-set renders the measure inaccurate. Therefore, while some quantitative techniques will be referenced in this chapter, with caveats, the focus will be on extracting analytical principles from SNA that can aid qualitative, investigative inquiry.

The second part of this chapter builds upon this framework for investigating the social networks organising the crimes of urbanisation, by shifting the focus to techniques that have been developed through this study for plotting, visualising and analysing temporally dispersed transactions. Extended and concentrated urbanisation is executed over time, through complex transaction sequences out of which networks emerge, and objectives are prosecuted. Even a modest change to the built environment often involves thousands of transactions, prosecuted over ten or more years by a range of organisationally situated actors, from the public sector, business and civil society. There is a need, therefore, to develop a method that enables the researcher to systematically code and graph the data, so that a large body of temporal determinations can be visualised in ways that aid investigative interpretation and the discernment of patterned forms of organisational behaviour (Aminzade 1992; Griffin 2007). To do this, a new qualitative graphing technique will be introduced, transaction mapping. Attached to this data-visualisation method are a number of analytical concepts outlined in a bid to help researchers distinguish, analyse and interpret particular types of transaction patterns appearing within the timeline. To increase the rigour of this approach, the process tracing method will be used to strengthen the hypotheses employed to explain transaction sequences.

In the next chapter fieldwork techniques for collecting data that can populate this overarching methodological framework will be explored, drawing again on investigative traditions of social research.

Investigative social network analysis

Succinctly put, SNA is a body of analytical methods designed to interrogate the net of ties that bind actors and facilitate the circulation of material and immaterial assets, ranging from friendship through to trade (Scott 2001; Wasserman and Faust 1994). The SNA literature is vast and interdisciplinary; it is also informed by quantitative methods that are designed convert data-sets into measures that can record the shape, intensity and features of the network under study.

The typical SNA study would be rooted in a fieldwork methodology that systematically elicits a data-set on a number of core variables (Scott 2001; Wasserman and Faust 1994). For example, a researcher may ask a class of students who in the room they like and dislike; or, they may look to measure trade between states (Wasserman and Faust 1994). The information is then inputted into a data-matrix; which can, in turn, be converted into a graph and subjected to different formulas that convert network data into specific metrics. For example, SNA research might investigate who in the classroom is the most prestigious individual, a designation determined by the sum of student choices mediated by the respective popularity of those making the choices (i.e. the student with the most prestige would be the one who is liked by a large number of well-liked students).

Investigative SNA (ISNA) draws on these core tools, but embeds them in a very different set of methodological practices. There are a number of reasons for this. First, because of the opaque nature of the processes under study, it is difficult to predict in advance of fieldwork the type of actors who will be examined, the assets which will feature or the ties that will be unpacked. Furthermore, there are going to be actors who have an interest in keeping their network position, assets and ties hidden. Therefore, a raft of investigative tools will need to be deployed; and even then, there will be data-gaps. Accordingly, designing methodologies in advance of fieldwork that will produce a uniform data-set is difficult. Equally, it would be nearly impossible to evenly collect data on actors, assets, events and ties, given the considerable challenges that beset research into the crimes of the powerful.

Accordingly, in this section a new method for applying SNA is proposed – ISNA – that enables the researcher to engage in penetrating fieldwork, while circumventing some of the problems pointed to above. Rather than framing SNA largely as a tool for processing network data, it will be argued here that its principles, techniques and graphing methods can actually be integrated into the fieldwork process in ways that enhance investigative inquiry. To that end, it will be maintained that network models can be generated in the field using easily accessible software, which can process large volumes of biographic and social data on actors, assets, ties and flows, in ways that allow the data to be more clinically handled and more effectively scrutinised for new leads and loose ends. In this sense, ISNA becomes a mechanism for interrogating social networks at the heart of urban contention, so we can begin to systematically establish what we know, what we don't and what we must find out.

As investigations progress, the volume of information being handled increases exponentially. ISNA graphing techniques help researchers appropriate visual intelligence in ways that allow complex network data to be rapidly computed, in a fashion that the mind alone could not easily handle. Finally, ISNA introduces categories that can be employed to interpret the emerging network data, by first focusing on elementary determinations, progressively moving to more complex approximations of plotted data, which as a whole allows a richer appreciation of the power economy to be developed.

These different dimensions of ISNA will now be explained. The two exemplary case studies noted in chapter one – and documented in full during chapters five and six – will be drawn on to help exemplify core ISNA techniques.

Investigative social network analysis: the basics

SNA, at its most basic, begins with two elementary units, actors and ties (Kriegler 2014; Mcillwain 1999; Van der Hulst 2009). Actors might include a business person, company, government agency, politician, country, civil society organisation or a student. Ties capture the links that bind members of the network together. This can include, for instance, friendship, investment, opposition, rivalry, a common location, kinship, business partnership or political solidarity. There is also the potential to include within SNA modelling, events and assets, which actors are affiliated to in some way. For example attendance at a specific conference, membership of a club or ownership of a particular piece of land (Wasserman and Faust 1994). These different units can be plotted onto a graph, sometimes referred to as a sociogram. A dot or icon, known in graph theory as a node, designates actors, events and assets. Ties are captured by lines connecting the different nodes, which are sometimes referred to as arcs. The particular place on the graph where nodes and lines are drawn has no special significance in graph theory.

Before the discussion proceeds further, it is important to introduce a software package, Maltego Casefile (Casefile). Casefile allows the researcher to progressively generate sociograms during the course of fieldwork – even with uneven or incomplete data-sets. Furthermore, it does not require uniformity in data-sets. Nevertheless, it retains the core underlying principles of SNA, which are built into the program's analytical functions. Critically, unlike a lot of advanced SNA software, a fully functional community version (not-for-profit) of Casefile has been made freely available. As a result scholars, students and community researchers can access an investigative tool that is user-friendly, visually rich and analytically powerful.

For investigative inquiry, a strength of Casefile is that it permits actors, assets, events and ties to be coded on the graph in a way that registers rich qualitative detail. For instance, it includes a sophisticated pallet of icons – which can be expanded – that allows nodes to be coded inductively according to distinguishing characteristics the actor acquires from their position in the network under study.[3] A node may be coded business leader, for instance, owing to the actor's position of high status and influence within a particular commercial community; more straight-forwardly an institution in the network might be designated offshore company, or bank, because of its commercial function. Ties can also be coded to capture a complex range of relations using colours and patterns. Coding, in this respect, may be done inductively, based on emerging types of tie, such as shareholder, business partner, consultant or advocate. Table 3.1 comprises the code sheet used to map ties in the exemplary cases featured in chapters 5–7. As the network begins to emerge Casefile also has analytical tools rooted in SNA theory – which will be discussed shortly – that can be used to identify important features and processes within the emerging model.

Casefile can be helpfully complemented by Visual Investigative Scenarios (vis.occrp.org), an online, freely available tool. While Casefile offers arguably a more powerful engine for enacting investigative inquiry, VIS's interface is more visually polished. Therefore, when it comes to public presentations and publications, data-sets modelled through Casefile can be helpfully converted into visually dynamic sociograms using VIS.

Of course, other tools exist which replicate to varying extents the functions of Casefile and VIS. Critically engaging with the strengths and weaknesses of different packages is an important task for crimes of the powerful research. However, for our current purposes, both Casefile and VIS are accessible and appropriate digital tools, that allow the researcher to enact ISNA techniques, a method which we will now consider in more detail.

It has been noted that nodes allow actors and assets to be plotted on a graph. However, because this is a network, nodes will presumably be affiliated in a range of ways. To that end, sociograms typically feature three types of ties: non-directional, directional and valued (Scott 2001; Wasserman and Faust 1994). Non-directional ties reflect links between actors, where there is no clear orientation in the tie from Actor A to Actor B. For instance, a set of actors may be linked by their residency in the same neighbourhood. Directed ties – which are plotted on the sociogram using arcs, that is → – involve Actor A, the origin, who makes a particular type of choice, which establishes a tie with a destination, Actor B, that is, A→B. For example, a company may elect to acquire shares in another concern, or a Minister may choose to act as a political patron for a particular business. Of course, it is quite possible that actors will be connected through multiple directed ties, some of which may be reciprocal, while others may be unilateral – as a whole these ties constitute the relationships between actors. Valued ties involve those instances where the link can be weighted according to a value, for instance levels of exports and imports between nations. One limitation of Casefile is that it is programmed to construct directed and weighted ties. However, when researching the crimes of urbanisation, the primary focus tends to be actors and directed ties – so this is not a particularly significant drawback. Sociograms that are focused on directed ties between nodes are known as digraphs (directed graph).

When plotting nodes and arcs on a digraph, in dense social environments, a sampling method is required that includes certain facts as being relevant to the network under study, while excluding others. Given that our goal is to uncover the complex processes through which the crimes of urbanisation are organised, a purposive sampling method can be used. As a result, it is not the case that the researcher will necessarily be plotting every single actor involved in episodes of urban contention, or every single tie. Value judgements, backed up by clear inclusion/exclusion criteria, need to be employed in order to input those nodes and arcs that help illuminate the crimes of the powerful, while excluding those determinations which would generate unnecessary convolution. For example, if a Lands Minister and the CEO of a company vying for a tender over state leasehold land are close schoolboy friends, that is a potentially

Table 3.1 Code sheet for social ties used in Maltego Casefile

Shareowner	Green
Associated with company	Dash green
Appointed Director/Secretary	Dark grey
Appointed Executive Manager	Light grey
Employee or member	Light blue
Creditor	Red
Donor	Red dotted
Payment or bribe	Red dash dot
Subsidiary	Orange
Appointed consultant/contractor	Dark blue
Business partner/collaborator	Purple
Rival	Purple dash
Political patron	Red dash
Professional contact	Orange dash
Advocate	Black dash
Investigator or litigant	Black
Property owner	Mauve
Friend	Light green
Family	Light green dash
Shared location	Green dash
Resident	Mauve dash
Application	Dark grey dash
Award	Dark grey dot
Rejection	Dark grey dot and dash

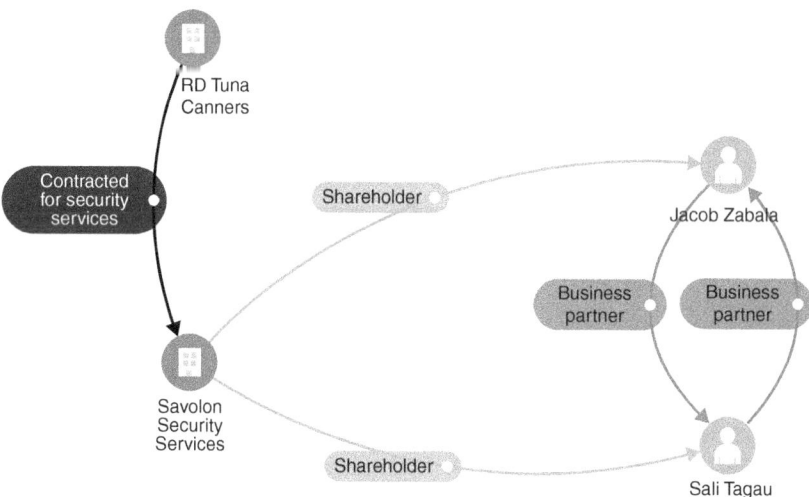

Figure 3.1 Snapshot, Savolon Security Service

significant tie. On the other hand, it would be excessive to include in a digraph the CEO's housekeeper, unless data emerges suggesting their inclusion helps to explain the potentially criminogenic ways in which the company is pursuing its landed claim (for instance, were it discovered that the housekeeper's uncle was the Lands Minister).

To demonstrate the basic features of a digraph, we will now use an empirical example. In Figure 3.1 we see a discreet snapshot from a social network underpinning the Mililat case study – see chapter six – which centres on a 416.9 ha plot of land, known as portion 237. The land is situated within Papua New Guinea's Madang Province, in an area that has been earmarked for a special economic zone known as the Pacific Marine Industrial Zone (PMIZ). Filipino multinational the RD Group, which has sizable Tuna processing interests in the Madang region – through its subsidiary RD Tuna Canners Limited – strongly lobbied for the special economic zone. In 2000 portion 237 was granted to a local company, Selon Limited, through a special government scheme which had been set up to return land alienated during the colonial period, to its traditional owners. Selon Limited's Managing Director, Sali Tagau, convinced the Department of Lands that his company represented the traditional owners of portion 237. In reality, the company was owned by Tagau and his business partner, Jacob Zabala. When the state lease was granted to Selon Limited, Tagau subdivided the land; a large section was sold off to Aces Ventures Limited, a company currently (2017) managed and part-owned by former politician Gabriel Kapris. Kapris was the Minister responsible for initiating the special economic zone through a credit agreement with the Chinese state.

In Figure 3.1 we can observe a discrete number of individuals and corporate actors bound together by a variety of ties. In Casefile, the actors can be coded through three distinct icons. For instance, RD Tuna Canners and Savolon Security Service Limited can be coded on the digraph through the company icon, Jacob Zabala may be mapped as a business person, while Sali Tagau can be designated using the business leader icon, in recognition of Tagau's local commercial status. VIS has similar codes for designating nodes, however, we lack an actor code for capturing elevated status.

In the digraph we may observe a series of unilateral ties, that capture decisions made by actors in the network. For instance Sali Tagau and Jacob Zabala elected to establish a company, Savolon Security Services Limited, with equal shareholdings. RD Tuna chose to award a security service contract to Savolon. On the other hand, the arc between Savolon's two shareholders captures a reciprocal tie between Zabala and Tagau, because the men concerned have selected each other as appropriate partners in a range of commercial pursuits, including through Selon Limited, and its real-estate interests.

In SNA terms, the corporate actor Savolon Security Services Limited is adjacent to three nodes, RD Tuna, Jacob Zabala and Sali Tagau, because there is a direct tie linking them. As it stands, Sali Tagau is not adjacent to RD Tuna, but there is a clear, mediated path between them – that is he is the part-owner of a company contracted by RD Tuna. A fieldworker might reasonably ask on the basis of this snapshot, whether Tagau had direct ties with senior officials within RD Tuna Canneries; and if so, did these relations strengthen Tagau's political influence at a provincial and national level. Similarly, it might be questioned whether there are direct connections tying RD Tuna, the former Minister Gabriel Kapris and Sali Tagau. It would also be relevant to know what assets, connections and abilities Tagau and Zabala fused to make a successful partnership that spanned a number of businesses.

Here we can already see the relationship between SNA and investigative inquiry; as we progressively plot determinations, network features can be analysed, producing questions that inform future fieldwork activity. In so doing, our objective is to progressively bring to the fore, with greater clarity, the network architecture that links actors, the power dynamics that underpin these ties, and the material/immaterial flows they facilitate. In order to do this more effectively, embedding qualitative data in the network model proves important. To that end, Casefile allows the researcher to incorporate into the digraph documents, files, notes and online content, which helps add texture.

To demonstrate how this texture can transform the interpretation of digraph components, we will turn to another example from the Mililat case, depicted in Figure 3.2. Figure 3.2 contains two companies, Panuluan Holdings and Gudi Investments. These corporate entities partnered during 1999–2000 in order to obtain the state lease over portion 237, in direct competition with Selon Limited. Like the latter concern, Panuluan Holdings informed Lands Department officials it represented the traditional owners. The company belonged to three

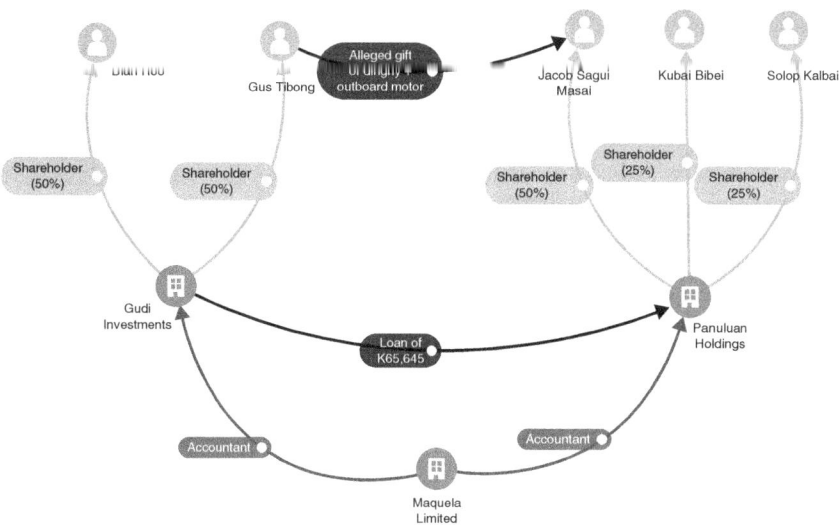

Figure 3.2 Gudi Investments and Panuluan Holdings

individuals, Jacob Sagui Masai, Salop Kalbai and Kubai Bibei, all of whom were members of clans with customary claims over portion 237. One barrier, however, impeded their claim – to secure the leasehold title they needed to refund the amount which the state incurred reacquiring the land under a plantation redistribution scheme.

Gudi Investments agreed to loan the outstanding, K65,645. Gudi Investments was owned by two businessmen, Gus Tibong and Dian Roo. In addition to loaning the money, Gus Tibong is also alleged to have 'gifted' a dingy and outboard motor to Jacob Sagui Masai, who possessed the largest shareholding in Panuluan Holdings.

So far we can see that Panuluan Holdings and Gudi Investments are connected by two material ties – a loan, and an alleged gift to its largest shareholder. Both firms are also indirectly connected by Maquela Limited, who does their respective accounts and company filings.

From this emerging model it is apparent that each corporate subgroup possesses a form of power, the other lacks. Panuluan's shareholders are traditional landowners with customary claims over portion 237. This gives them cultural legitimacy when appealing for the state lease. However, they lack the requisite capital to complete the transaction. Gudi Investments possesses the capital, but cannot apply for the land in its own right, owing to a lack of cultural legitimacy.

However, more qualitative detail is required if we are to fully appraise the power dynamics underpinning this corporate partnership. The addition of individual and organisational biographical detail gives the snapshot important new complexions. One thing to note in this respect, is the date of Gudi Investments and Panuluan Holdings incorporation. Company records show both companies were incorporated on 1 December 1999. This implies there is more to the corporate relationship than a credit arrangement. This contention is further supported by the geographical spread of the subgroup. Panuluan Holdings and its shareholders are based in a rural area outside the town of Madang, whereas Gudi Investments and Dian Roo, are located in the city of Lae, Morobe Province. Roo's business partner, Gus Tibong, resides in the township of Madang, thus creating a potential bridge between the two worlds. The company records and submissions for both companies are lodged by Maquela Limited, a firm situated in Lae. These organisational details would appear to suggest the corporate partnership is led by Gudi Investments, rather than Panuluan.

Further texture can be added by considering individual details. Both Gus Tibong and Dian Roo were fifty years old in 1999, whereas the owners of Panuluan were all over seventy-five. This would mean the latter grew up during a period when the colonial regime provided very little in the way of education; knowledge, culture and productive systems were instead in the hands of village custodians. In contrast, Tibong and Roo grew up during the post war period, when Australia invested significantly more resources in education and 'development' (Downs 1980; Hawksley 2006). As a result, they formed part of the first generation heavily involved in governmental politics and market activity. Indeed both Tibong and Roo were active in a large range of businesses – a fact uncovered through a search of scraped company registry data, triangulated with other commercial sources. Whereas no other corporate association was found for Masai, Kalbai or Bibei. This would again appear to strengthen claims that Gudi Investments were the driving force in this arrangement. So we can see from this example how additional qualitative texture can transform in crucial ways how we interpret network architecture.

If we now draw back and consider all of the above examples, it is apparent that digraph construction is a generative exercise, where layers of meaning are gradually plotted along three core dimensions – nodes, ties and qualitative context. By plotting these different social forces a data-set emerges that can facilitate analyses (see below) which determine how actors, assets, events, ties and material/immaterial flows come together to create coalitions varying in strength, capability and ambition. The progressive plotting of data also prompts hypotheses and questions for further exploration, creating the foundation for more probative fieldwork.

Of course as the digraph is populated, the complexity of the social constellation being modelled grows. It is possible for digraphs to emerge that contain hundreds of nodes and ties. Carefully breaking down cases through the use of analytical aids is critical for comprehending such complexity. To that end, SNA provides a series of conceptual tools that analysts can employ to help think about the dynamics and relations shaping the network under study, a matter to which we will now turn.

Analysing social network dynamics

One of the most elementary concepts in the SNA canon is the dyad. Although elementary, it nonetheless captures arguably the most critical adhesive of any social network – namely the ties that bind adjacent actors together (Van der Hulst 2009). These ties can facilitate flows of information, assets, money, prestige, influence, expertise, friendship, institutional support, and so on, between different actors in the network. Of course not all ties are built on collaboration, they can also be rooted in relations of rivalry, exploitation or opposition. In which case the ties may encompass actions designed to disrupt flows of information, support or wealth.

Figure 3.3 (over page) presents an overview of the dyadic ties enjoyed by the Paga Hill Development Company (PHDC). To summarise the key facts, in 2000 PHDC was awarded a 99-year state lease over a 13.7 ha plot of land at Paga Hill in Papua New Guinea's capital city, Port Moresby. The land, which had formerly been reserved as a national park, enjoys panoramic harbour views, and is in close proximity to the capital's central business district. Since incorporation, PHDC has been led by its current CEO, Gudmundur Fridriksson. To date, Fridriksson's various business dealings have been censured in four Public Accounts Committee inquiries, two Auditor General reports, a Commission of Inquiry, in addition to a range of investigative articles published in *The Australian*, Papua New Guinean and Icelandic media.

With respect to Paga Hill, the irregularities surrounding the land acquisition process prompted Papua New Guinea's Public Accounts Committee to label the developer a 'foreign speculator' (2007: 60), who they claimed acquired the land through 'corrupt dealings' (2007: 70). PHDC's public image took a further blow when it helped organise a demolition exercise designed to remove existing residents from the site in 2012. During the exercise, police opened fire on unarmed residents who had peacefully congregated – a documentary filmmaker captured the events on film and the video subsequently went viral, attracting international condemnation (see chapter five). The demolition exercise was stopped prematurely, by a court injunction. Residents then mobilised against PHDC and the Papua New Guinean state with an unprecedented level of sophistication – public protest, political lobbying, litigation, art and performance were fused to mobilise popular and institutional support behind their struggle to restore Paga Hill's former national park status. Despite the sophisticated character of this campaign, and the considerable stigma that had attached to the company, residents were forcefully displaced during 2014 by city authorities in violation of a Supreme Court order – although PHDC denies any involvement in the latter exercise.

Figure 3.3 helps explain why the company was able to persevere in this contested environment, especially given their mandate was alleged to have been tainted by corruption and illegal activities.

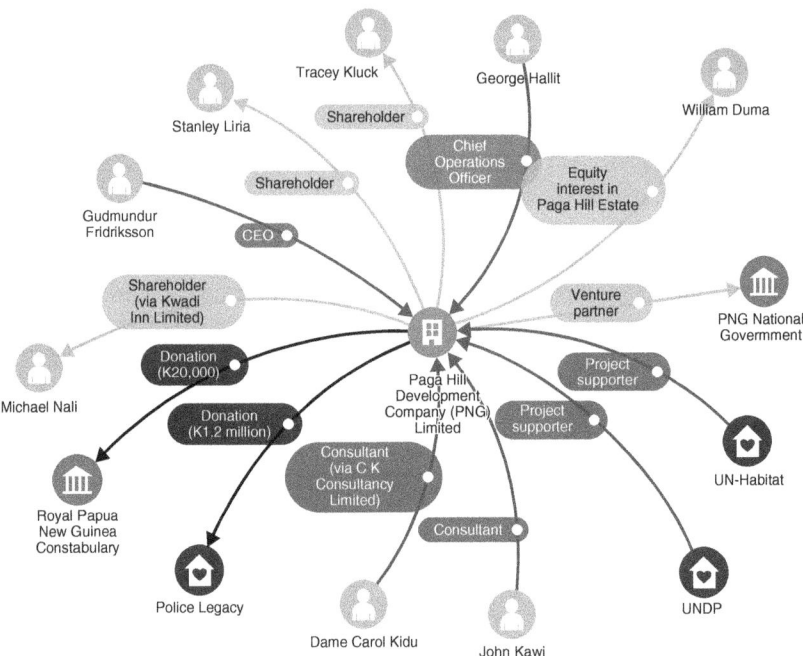

Figure 3.3 Paga Hill Development Company's dyadic structure

Looking at the digraph, it is apparent PHDC has enjoyed dyadic relations with a wide range of highly influential individuals and organisations both in Papua New Guinea and the wider region. Shareholders in the company have included the former Deputy Prime Minister of Papua New Guinea, Michael Nali, an actor closely linked to Papua New Guinea's current Prime Minister, Peter O'Neill; the wife of a prolific Australian indigenous advocate, Noel Pearson; and a well-connected local lawyer, Stanley Liria. It is also claimed that the current (2017) Minister for State Enterprises, William Duma, has an equitable stake in the venture (see chapter five). Furthermore, PHDC has made significant donations to a number of organisations, including the Royal Papua New Guinea Constabulary, which has repeatedly applauded the company for its largesse and corporate social responsibility. In addition, the developer has contracted a number of influential consultants, including the lawyer John Kawi who would go on to become a National Court Judge, and Dame Carol Kidu, one of Papua New Guinea's foremost human rights advocates, and a former Minister for Community Development (2002–2011). When attempting to forcefully relocate Paga Hill residents, the company managed to garner support from the UNDP, and UN–Habitat; while 'friends' inside Papua New Guinea's anti-corruption squad are alleged to have tipped PHDC off over an investigation into its CEO. Thus, we can see, a close examination of the dyadic ties enjoyed by PHDC, helps to reveal why the company proved resilient in the face of a highly organised social movement, and a long list of negative findings delivered against its executives by state agencies, journalists and researchers.

Of course, dyadic ties represent the minimal unit of a social network; our abstractive lens can be widened to think about more complex arrangements. For example, SNA employs the category triad, to think about ties that bind together three actors (Wasserman and Faust 1994). Once we move beyond three nodes, the category subgroup is employed. However, it is important to emphasise here that concepts such as triad and subgroup are used to think about qualitatively distinct dynamics that may pertain to the tied actors as a unity – in other words these categories do not merely register the cumulative result of multiple dyads. For example, if we return to Figure 3.2, we can see that it would be impossible to understand the power relations underpinning Panuluan Holdings' bid for Portion 237 if we merely focused on the company's dyadic tie with Gudi Investments Limited. By expanding our analytical lens to include their respective shareholders and Maquela Limited, a distinct group dynamic was revealed that enriched our understanding of the transactions being prosecuted by the corporate coalition.

One particularly important dimension of SNA, are categories designed to detect actors who are critical conduits, gatekeepers or playmakers in the network under analysis. To that end, two key concepts used to measure a node's network significance are centrality and prestige (see Knoke and Yang 2008; Van der Hulst 2009; Wasserman and Faust 1994). Before the latter categories can be unpacked, it is helpful to distinguish between a node's indegree and outdegree (see Scott 2001). Using the notional Actor A as an example, outdegree would identify and measure the number of ties they have initiated with other nodes in the network; while indegree identifies and measures the ties with Actor A, initiated by other network nodes.

With that in mind, at its simplest centrality measures the outdegree of nodes featured in a network. This can help the analyst identify particular actors who have established a wide range of ties with others nodes in the network, which increases the likelihood they are a player of importance (Van der Hulst 2009). For example, it may be that in an autocratic regime a particular government agency concentrates decision making power – such as the Office of the President – which gives it a capacity to unilaterally approve official appointments, oversee the application of budgetary resources and vet policy initiatives. This gives the office a position of centrality within government. Those seeking to commercially benefit from the autocratic application of governmental power, know then it is the Office of the President that must be reached through fixers and the offer of material incentives.

Centrality measures can be honed through a series of associated conceptual tools. For example, rather than measuring a node's centrality on the basis of their connection to adjacent entities, we may choose to include nodes where there is a greater degree of separation. Degrees of separation are calculated by the number of arcs between nodes. For example, in the following diagram there are two degrees of separation between the first and last node: •→•→•. By broadening centrality to measure all the nodes reached by Actor A on the basis of say two or three degrees of separation, we can determine which actors are more capable of influencing the greatest number of nodes in the network. In other words this is a measure of *closeness* (Prell 2012; Wasserman and Faust 1994), a determination which can have a range of significances.

For Casefile users, as data is inputted into emerging digraphs the software produces an 'entity list' that can be filtered according to centrality. Furthermore, Casefile's investigation toolbar permits researchers to interrogate a particular node's centrality by choosing 'select children'. This will identify all adjacent nodes connected by outdegree. If analysts then press shift, ctrl (cmd for Mac), ↓, they can see nodes separated from the actor by two or more degrees of separation. It may be the case that an actor enjoying strong local centrality – measured by the number adjacent nodes connected by outdegree – may not necessarily have a high score for global centrality; that is their ability to reach a large number of nodes in the network through relatively short paths (determined by degrees of separation). Varying measures, therefore, can uncover different forms of potential power.

With that in mind, betweenness is another important centrality measure used within SNA to help identify nodes who may be significant, even when they have scored low in terms of their local or global centrality. Betweenness focuses on those nodes that connect together two or more subgroups, in the absence of which, there would be no path between them (Scott 2001). It is possible that some nodes are central within a network because they fuse together a number of important subgroups. For example, the brother of a Prime Minister might be a core target for bribes, because he acts as a bridge between the Prime Minister, government officials and the business community. Therefore, this measure may not necessarily uncover the most prolific actor in the whole network, but it may nevertheless locate critical players who accrue power from gatekeeper or fixer roles, a matter which we will return to in just a moment. That said, it is of course very possible that those with significant levels of local and global centrality, also mediate different subgroups.

What these different measures of centrality share is a capacity to detect particular forms of power that congeal within a network, because of how a node links itself to a wide range of other actors. Certainly in the Paga Hill and Mililat cases (see chapters five and six), when organisations were found to be locally and globally central, this had important analytical implications. For example, at a public institutional level, the National Court and the Department of Lands and Physical Planning are primary playmakers in Papua New Guinea whose decisions have critical impacts on the allocation and application of the national landed estate; this, in turn, has a reverberated impact on the interests of a wide range of actors involved in land and property market activity. For instance, the Lands Department manages the tendering of state land, the award of state leases, land administration, physical planning, zoning and development approvals, and many transactions associated with customary land. This key agency has also become a central site for bribery, clientelism, and fraud, perpetrated by speculators looking to build an institutional environment primed for price fixing and anti-competitive practices.

Similarly, because activity within Papua New Guinea's land and property market is punctuated by illegality, commercial schisms, social contention and community resistance, which frequently end in litigation, court decisions also influence how land is allocated and applied. As a result, its organs become a critical site of struggle, for a range of actors, looking to leverage/mitigate National Court decisions. Given the centrality of the Lands Department and National Court, it became important during the research process to understand the formal and informal rules governing their decisions, the institutional cultures shaping how the rules are administered, and why certain subgroups were more adept at navigating these contexts than others.

However, not all actors in a social network are important because of their institutionally inscribed power to command, for instance, how assets or state support is apportioned. Actors can also accumulate network significance because they are the target of decisions made by other nodes in the network. This type of significance is helpfully captured within SNA using the category prestige (De Nooy et al. 2011; Wasserman and Faust 1994). Like centrality, prestige may be measured in multiple ways; each method attempts to capture different forms of esteem actors can enjoy. At its most elementary, prestige may be measured by simple indegree; that is the number of adjacent actors in the network that choose to establish ties with the entity under study (represented by directed lines). For example, a businessperson who has been appointed to the Board of Directors in a wide range of blue-chip companies enjoys commercial esteem, which makes them a potentially very valuable actor for a company seeking expert advice, or influence. However, we can widen our search by measuring prestige on the basis of paths involving more than one degree of separation. Here it is important to note that a node's *closeness* measured by *outdegree*, will most likely be different to their degree of *proximity* measured by *indegree*.

Another prestige measure is known as rank or status prestige. It looks not only at the prestige a particular entity enjoys, but also registers the prestige of other actors in the network who choose this entity. The hypothesis here is that actors have greater prestige when they are chosen by other nodes in the network who themselves enjoy significant prestige, as opposed to mere peripheral players. For instance, an actor connected to a wide range of peripheral players in a network may accrue less power than an actor connected to a small number of players, who nonetheless boasts a wide range of senior level contacts in government, business and the courts.

An interesting insight into the potential role prestige can play in determining case outcomes, may be observed in the Paga Hill study. One of the most important individual actors in this network was the Icelandic-Australian businessman, Gudmundur Fridriksson. Over the course of two decades he had accumulated significant prestige across Iceland, China and Papua New Guinea – however, this was often a result of other actors in the network making negative assessments of his commercial actions. For instance, in Hong Kong, a hotel and residential apartment complex attempted to sue Fridriksson for alleged unpaid bills. In Papua New Guinea, his businesses had been censured in a significant number of public inquiries into corruption and public mismanagement, while his actions had also been criticised by a number of decorated journalists who themselves enjoyed significant prestige. While Fridriksson had managed to steer through these controversies, without PHDC losing control of Paga Hill, nevertheless, the stigma associated with these negative assessments had impeded PHDC's ability to solicit international investment for their luxury real-estate development. The CEO's prestige, in this instance, had proven a barrier to the achievement of PHDC's core organisational goal.

Another important player in the Paga Hill network was Dame Carol Kidu. An Australian by birth, Dame Carol married a young Papua New Guinean who later became Chief Justice of Papua New Guinea's Supreme Court; Dame Carol went on to have a successful career in national politics as an MP and long-serving Minister. During this time, she built up a reputation as a strong advocate for good governance, human rights and gender equality. Following her retirement in July 2012, Dame Carol enjoyed a range of appointments at prestigious policy institutes, charities and international companies, which cemented her strong credentials in both the national and international human rights community and the corporate sector. Initially, Dame Carol had strongly championed the residents' cause in Paga Hill, accusing the developer of corruption and fraud. However, PHDC's CEO asked Dame Carol to work for the company when they met on a flight; subsequently, Dame Carol's company CK Consultancy Limited became a consultant for PHDC. This allowed PHDC to draw on Carol's national and international prestige within civil society, the private sector and government. Dame Carol's image was liberally spread across the company's website, and she featured prominently in carefully curated media events organised by PHDC. This even included a documentary film which premiered at Papua New Guinea's Human Rights Film Festival in 2014. With one of Papua New Guinea's foremost human rights advocates as its public face, the company found itself in receipt of praise from organisations such as the UNDP, whose Head declared the forced relocation of residents from Paga Hill to the area of 6-Mile a 'world first' ('UN at PHDC's Official Handover to the Tagua Community' 2014). It thus appeared through a somewhat unlikely, but astute commercial transaction, that PHDC had found an effective antidote for the stigma generated by the negative assessments of its CEO's past commercial activities. This is just one example, but it demonstrates how thinking about prestige can offer an analytical path for understanding the currents and counter-currents underpinning legitimacy, in situations of urban contention.

Of course, it should be noted that there is always the potential for overlap between centrality and prestige. An actor enjoying positive prestige from central actors who have the capacity to make important decisions on the allocation of capital, resources or other material/immaterial flows, is in a potentially particularly powerful position within the network, especially if their rival's prestige emanates from less central characters. Indeed, in cases of urban contention, developers looking to acquire property and displace residents, frequently enjoy a number of positive ties with central decision makers within the state. On the other hand, resident coalitions tend to draw their prestige from civil society. Although they may lack the ability to directly influence key decision making organs in government, residents can nonetheless wield forms of power through mass participation in a social movement.

So far we have considered dyads, triads, subgroups, centrality and prestige. The first three concepts help us to think about the elementary ties that create the framework for flows of wealth, information, influence and diverse resources; the latter two concepts draw off these determinants to pinpoint critical junctures in the network where power or stigma pools. Now we will turn to the categories of paths and semi-paths, which help researchers detect more complex linkages that can span the network.

As sociographs emerge during the fieldwork process, it becomes apparent that actors who are not necessarily adjacent are nonetheless connected by a series of arcs (directed lines). In effect we can walk between them on the graph. Where the walk can take place through a series of arcs that point in the same direction, that is •→•→•→• we call this a path (Scott 2001). On the other hand where the walk involves a series of opposing arcs, such as •→•→•←•→• we call this a semi-path (Wasserman and Faust 1994). The number of arcs that must be traversed in a walk to arrive at a destination is measured by degrees. The path plotted above consists of three degrees, while the semi-path features four degrees. The SNA literature suggests the closer and more direct the walk (i.e. a path), the greater the likelihood that lines of communication exist between actors. The case for this assessment becomes even stronger, where a path between node A and node B can be walked in both directions.

To demonstrate how these concepts can be applied to think about the potential lines of influence that shape complex property transactions, we will turn again to the example of Paga Hill. It was apparent when researching this case that PHDC was the recipient of prestige emanating from the government of Papua New Guinea. Indeed, shortly after an international report was published revealing the controversial commercial history of PHDC's executives – which triggered front page media coverage – the Papua New Guinea government's private real-estate arm announced it would partner in the Paga Hill development, while Cabinet declared the project one of national significance.

Given this surprise move came during a low ebb in PHDC's corporate history, it seemed pertinent to probe the company's potential lines of communication with key decision makers in government. One focus was Papua New

Guinea's Prime Minister, Peter O'Neill, in whom significant power is pooled owing to the historical nature of the country's political system. With the available data, four potential walks were identified – two will be focused on here. The first walk linked the Prime Minister to former Deputy Prime Minister Michael Nali, through the People's National Progress Party, which O'Neill heads. Nali stood for election in 2012 on a People's National Progress Party ticket. In addition, both men had been in Cabinet together when part of the former Somare government. Michael Nali, in turn, is the owner of Kwadi Inn Limited, which held at the time a 9% stake in PHDC; he also championed the project when in government. So here we have the following walk: Prime Minister O'Neill ← People's National Progress Party → Michael Nali → Kwadi Inn → PHDC. An alternative walk was discovered when scrutinising data scraped from the corporate registry (see chapter four). It was apparent that Nali, through Kwadi Inn, owned shares in a company part-owned and managed by the Prime Minister, Peter O'Neill via a holding vehicle LBJ Investments Limited. This produced the following walk: Peter O'Neill → LBJ Investments Limited → NIU Finance Limited ← Kwadi Inn → PHDC.

The second walk involved the company's major shareholder and Director, Stanley Liria. According to news reports in 2005 O'Neill had chosen to launch Liria's book on Papua New Guinea's legal system, and petitioned his parliamentary colleagues to purchase the volume. So here we see the following path: Prime Minister O'Neill → Stanley Liria → PHDC. It was also alleged by a senior associate of PHDC that Liria had grown up in the Prime Minister's household, which suggested the following path: Prime Minister O'Neill ← O'Neill family → Stanley Liria.

Clearly when assessing paths and semi-paths allowances must be made for the durability, intensity and length of the walk involved. For instance, in the above examples, there is compelling evidence to suggest that Nali and O'Neill enjoyed both commercial and political ties, which could potentially provide a powerful line of communication between the two actors. On the other hand, Liria and O'Neill appeared in the first instance to only have a superficial connection. However, allegations volunteered by a PHDC associate suggests the book launch noted above might be a symptom of a deeper line of communication between the Prime Minister and PHDC shareholder. Of course, for reasons already noted in chapter one, it is impossible to say that these lines of communication were improperly employed by either shareholder to curry favour within the O'Neill government. However, it is within the researcher's ambit to note that durable, intensive walks exist between key corporate and political actors in the social network under examination.

Moving on, if we now combine the measures of centrality and prestige, with the categories of paths and semi-paths, it becomes possible to identify another critical dimension of a social network – the cut point. When analysing dyads, triads and subgroups, and the different walks between them, it is often the case that there is one node which ties together two or more groupings within the graph. Cutting this node would thus remove the only line of communication between these groups.

An example of a critical cut point can be found in the Miiliat case. Here the Madang based business leader, Sali Tagau, connected a range of different subgroups in the network. It will be remembered Tagau was the Managing Director and joint-owner of Selon Limited, a company who eventually acquired a lucrative state lease over portion 237 in 2000. His position as a vital cut point was no accident. Tagau carefully positioned himself so that he was the interface between the customary landowners and a range of different groups. For example, he managed relations with the creditor, Tropic Timbers Limited, which was providing a mortgage facility essential to securing the lease; Tagau also monopolised ties with strong supporters within the provincial government's lands branch. Entrenching further his position of power, Tagau oversaw the management of company documentation for Selon Limited, and interfaced with the Investment Promotion Authority, who administers the country's corporate registry.

By acting as the circuit board mediating the connection between these different stakeholder groups, Tagau was in a powerful position to selectively communicate information. For example, he advised both the creditor and customary landowners that the latter were the proprietors of Selon Limited. Company records show this was not the case. When Selon Limited's creditor discovered this fact, his attempts to establish ties with customary landowners were forcefully rebuffed by Tagau, who guarded his position carefully. In this instance, Tagau's cut point status allowed him to mislead a number of parties, which gave him a competitive edge in acquiring the land as a personal financial asset. Cut points may have other significances. For instance, in the Paga Hill case it was discovered that the residents' coalition trying to save the former national park depended on a cut point, Dame Carol Kidu, for a considerable amount of political, professional and financial support. When this cut point was abruptly removed and acquired by PHDC, it disrupted the movement's capacity to organise, and put the developer on the front foot. Cut points, therefore, tend to capture a node in the network that pools significant forms of power, essential to a range of dynamics lying behind the crimes of urbanisation.

At this point, it needs to be emphasised that this chapter can only touch upon some of the major SNA categories relevant to the subject matter. There is a large and informative literature out there, that drills down further into the reservoir of concepts and metrics used to conduct SNA, which can be applied or repurposed for ISNA. Clearly, there is more scope for work on this front. For our current purposes the focus has been on core tools that employ visual intelligence and certain analytical categories, to facilitate investigative inquiry into the social networks standing behind criminogenic processes. In this respect we began by looking at some of the more elementary determinations, such as dyads and triads, before examining categories capable of capturing more complex determinations, such as centrality, prestige, paths and cut-points.

During the introduction it was noted, by absorbing SNA into an investigative paradigm of research, the methodology is given a different complexion. Investigative research is incremental and exploratory. Researchers are attempting to uncover the network, relations and flows at the heart of urbanisation, in a field context marked by opaqueness and power imbalances. SNA tools become part of the fieldwork process. They allow researchers to systematically document and graph what they know, and need to find out. Using visual intelligence, coded data and versatile modelling tools, researchers are able to develop testable investigative hypotheses, and think more richly about the social significance of the emerging network data-set being plotted. By the time fieldwork is concluded – through a frenetic back and forth movement between the data and the field – a point is reached where the researcher hopefully has social network data that is complex, and already part enriched by theoretically informed analysis.

Yet one drawback of this approach is that SNA models tend to be temporally flat. That is, it is difficult to build into digraphs the dimension of time, so that we can begin to map the choices that create and build links between actors, and facilitate critical forms of accumulation and loss. Of course, there are techniques for developing longitudinal snapshots of networks, but this will not alert us to the temporally bound sequences of transactions that build ties, facilitate flows and generate contention. In other words, we cannot plot the everyday transactions that form the lifeblood of living social systems, circulating flows of information, influence, capital, support, expertise, and so on. As a result, a pilot form of analysis is going to be introduced that draws on visual intelligence to temporally map transactions so that hundreds of everyday decisions and flows can be modeled into sequences; this, in turn, will be married to a range of categories that helps us interrogate transaction patterns, and spreads, critical to the historical trajectories underpinning the crimes of urbanisation.

Investigative transaction mapping

Over the past three decades a range of techniques for thinking about how social transactions accumulate over time to form part of causal chains, have been developed within historical sociology and the political sciences (Aminzade 1992; Axinn et al. 1999; Collier 2011; Griffin 2007; Mahoney 2012). Transactions here encapsulates temporally bound events where an action or exchange takes place involving one or more actors. Examples associated with the subject matter at hand might include, the transfer of money from a business account to a personal account, the purchase of shares in a company, the grant of development approval by a physical planning board, a breakfast meeting between business partners, or a violent confrontation between police and residents. However, it is less common to find in the literature techniques for plotting, visualising and analysing transaction sequences, which is an important process to undertake if we are to rigorously compute complex transaction data. Certainly in areas of criminology which are focused on mapping longitudinal patterns in offending, there has been a definite turn to data-visualisation as a method for enhancing data-analytics (Harris 2012; Maltz and Mullany 2000). With that in mind, the forthcoming section will introduce experimental techniques for building an analytical framework that can do for temporally bound constellations of transactions, what ISNA does for social networks.

The software employed to construct transaction timelines during the research, Tiki-Toki, is not specifically engineered for the analytical tasks outlined here, but it contains enough features to act as a helpful starting point (other applications exist that do similar tasks, such as Aeon Timeline). Critically, Tiki-Toki allows transaction data to be plotted on a timeline as 'stories'. Data can be coded on the graph according to date and transaction author. Coded data appears as story boxes on the timeline, which provides an abbreviated summary of the event; the full story is embedded within the box and can be accessed by clicking 'more'. Accordingly, as with Casefile, graphs can be generated, and embedded with rich qualitative data. In Tiki-Toki there is also an analytical toolbar, that allows the researcher to manipulate the plotted transactions in different ways by including a vertical axis and through focusing on specific actors.

An immediate advantage of plotting transactions on a timeline is that it allows complex historical moments, populated by a large range of transactions authored by multiple actors, to be visualised in ways that can enhance the researcher's capacity to spot important relationships and processes. It follows, the investigative potential of timelines is enhanced when the visualised data is married to concepts capable of thinking about important sequences and patterns. With that in mind, a number of elementary concepts will now be introduced to facilitate such an analysis, ascending gradually towards more complex categories capable of articulating denser transaction sequences.

To begin, a basic sequence that forms the building block for more complex currents is what we can call the transaction chain. Transaction chains designate a series of actions, unified by an intended outcome they collectively help facilitate. These transaction chains might be authored by a single entity, creating an arrow chain, or it may be constructed by multiple authors, forging a pyramid chain. Identifying an arrow chain can be fairly simple. For example, a developer seeking to remove residents from its landed property, achieves this goal by bribing local leaders, obtaining a consent order from the court, and then organising a demolition exercise with assistance from private security guards – we can see here the events are connected by a fairly apparent causal logic. However, things often become more convoluted with pyramid chains.

To use an example from the Paga Hill case (see chapter five). Having experienced formidable resistance from residents, in the space of several months during 2014 the communities living at Paga Hill were successfully cleared from the site, leaving PHDC in vacant possession of the property. This occurred despite the fact residents had acquired a Supreme Court order declaring that the properties populating reclaimed land along the harbour foreshore area lay outside the developer's lease. This meant they were excluded from the eviction order. Nevertheless, they were all successfully removed. This outcome was the result of numerous transactions authored by a range of bodies.

First, shortly before the initial eviction exercise took place, a promotional article appeared in the national newspaper, celebrating the developer's relocation plans for residents. Two days later on 29 May, residents living on middle/upper Paga Hill lost their court appeal, paving the way for the relocation exercise. However, a Supreme Court appeal organised by residents living on reclaimed land along the harbour foreshore, remained in play. On 29 May, police arrested Joe Moses, a key Paga Hill community leader, who had spearheaded the Supreme Court action. It was claimed by police that the anthropology graduate and university administrator had discharged a firearm. Over the following weekend, residents from middle/upper Paga Hill were evicted and relocated by police and private security – it was alleged threats of violence were employed to deter residents from taking pictures. Police, however, issued a press release lauding a 'peaceful' relocation exercise, commending PHDC for its 'humane and responsible actions' (Royal Papua New Guinea Constabulary Metropolitan Superintendent 2014). On 3 June, police claimed Joe Moses had made a daring escape from custody; a press statement on the man-hunt was released by police. Fearing for his life, Moses went into hiding. The following day a gazettal notice was published. It stated that the national Land Board had awarded a Special Purpose lease over the reclaimed land at Paga Hill to Andayap No.5, a company fully owned by PHDC. Several weeks later on 1 July, residents won their Supreme Court battle, and the reclaimed land was declared to be outside the developer's lease; seemingly neither the court nor residents were aware PHDC had just acquired a lease over the reclaimed land. Then on 22 July, a demolition exercise took place along the harbour foreshore, in violation of the court order. Homes and important historical sites from WWII were levelled. PHDC strongly condemned the exercise, even though the company staged a similar style demolition during May 2012. Responsibility for the 2014 exercise was attributed in the press to the city authority – the National Capital District Commission (NCDC) – and a contractor responsible for building the Paga Hill ring road. Following the successful eviction of Paga Hill residents, groundwork began at the site. Later it was announced by the developer, that the NCDC and PHDC were partnering with a Chinese consortium to develop the Paga Hill Estate.

There are multiple ways of reading this sequence of events standing behind the successful forced eviction of Paga Hill residents. On the one hand, it could be viewed as a series of arrow chains, that simply temporally overlapped in a sympathetic way. That is, while PHDC attempted to secure leasehold title over the harbour foreshore (which in effect neutralised the Supreme Court decision), the NCDC was collaborating with the road contractor to evict the community. Independent of these activities, police were pursuing allegations against the public face of the Paga Hill campaign, Joe Moses, at the same time that the national newspaper chose to publish a supportive piece on the developer's relocation strategy. When these events merged, PHDC was the beneficiary of serendipity. Then once the land was cleared, PHDC and NCDC joined forces to court Chinese investor interest.

Alternatively, it could be argued, with justification, that the transactions are suggestive of a coordinated pyramid chain, rather than a series of sympathetic arrow chains. The timing of the newspaper article and the arrest of Moses; the unusual steps taken by police to publicly laud the first eviction and indeed the developer; PHDC's efforts to contest the community's legal argument over the reclaimed land, while seemingly approving of it in practice through acquiring a lease over the property; the subsequent collaboration between PHDC and the authority allegedly responsible for evicting the community and damaging historical sites; PHDC's failure to take legal action, after the NCDC trespassed on its land with a contractor and damaged important historical artefacts; put together, these sequences are suggestive of potential collusion between the various parties involved in these events.

Rigorously plotting the transactions and assessing this hypothesis has important analytical implications. If we see evidence in this case, and in others, that government, police, media and companies are colluding to legitimise and enact violent eviction exercises designed to displace residents impeding land speculation and property development, this impacts on how we theorise the structures and repertoires underpinning the crimes of urbanisation. Consequently, meticulously mapping and analysing the transaction data has relevance beyond description.

On that note, we will move on now to consider a number of other concepts that can help hone attention on important timeline features. Where transactions – whether in arrow or pyramid form – are a response to the action of rivals or community opposition, they become part of what we can call a wave of contention. This visual metaphor captures how rivalry, or opposition, creates its own unique forms of momentum. That is, when a developer or politician is organising, for instance, certain transactions that will precipitate a particular urban project, if they face rivalry from within their own strata, or opposition from the community, it can alter in fundamental ways how they behave and pursue their objectives. It is important, therefore, to identify waves of contention within the transaction timeline, and think about how the character, intensity and impact of the transactions, are affected by the particular forms of rivalry or opposition being experienced.

To again use an example from the Paga Hill case (see chapter five). During 2012, PHDC suffered significant loss of public face, when its attempt to forcefully evict residents precipitated a vocal campaign to save the former national park. Coming in behind the Paga Hill community were a range of international civil society actors. Collectively, this generated a strong public current of interventions that drew attention to PHDC's contested title, and the record of its executives, which constrained the company's commercial movement.

In response, PHDC's CEO made a number of poorly judged remarks to the media, demeaning residents, while a company Director appeared to freeze on Australian radio when presented with evidence on the CEO's commercial record.

However, this wave of contention did not lead PHDC to abandon the project. Nevertheless, it did cause the company to devote considerably more resources to public image management. Public relations and social media specialists were appointed by the company, who created an elegant online presence for PHDC and its key personnel. An impressive number of articles also appeared in the national media, applauding PHDC and its efforts at Paga Hill. The company began donating money to charitable organisations and sponsoring public events. Furthermore, they also attracted support from a range of bodies that could strengthen their image of corporate social responsibility, including the UNDP. More ominously, PHDC and its associates began issuing legal threats to critics, and in one case launched litigation against a documentary filmmaker working with Paga Hill residents.

It was apparent that the landmark campaign organised by residents had important impacts. It caused the developer to engage in a series of transactions designed to acquire expertise in the areas of public relations management, social media presence, corporate social responsibility and strategic litigation. This, in turn, had important consequences for the civil society coalition campaigning to save Paga Hill, revealing important structural inequalities that were to the developer's advantage. Therefore, paying close attention to waves of contention that appear in timeline data can help to build understandings of how agency and structure meld in the urban sphere, in ways that create power imbalances critical to contentious outcomes.

On occasion, the transactions plotted on a timeline will form part of an established, time bound sequence of events, prescribed in law, regulation or custom. For example, when state or crown land is earmarked for private development, in many jurisdictions there is a precise sequence of events governments must initiate and oversee, if the process is to be lawful. The land, for instance, should be advertised in a certain manner, there must be a competitive tender process, formal approvals must be given in a certain way, decisions must be gazetted, and so on. When an event is plotted that forms part of a mandated process, we can call this a prescribed transaction sequence. Where detected such transactions invite us to investigate whether the regulated sequence has indeed been observed. Such investigations can again alert researchers to deeper structural issues supportive of elite malfeasance.

For example, in both the Paga Hill and Mililat cases, it was observed during fieldwork that PHDC and Tropic Timbers Limited began life as locally owned shell companies. Not long after their incorporation both companies experienced a change in shareholdings, which made the concerns foreign enterprises. The change in status triggers a set sequence under the *Investment Promotion Act* 1992, where the foreign enterprise must, within 15 days, apply for a certificate to operate. In neither case did this apparently occur. Such failures are an offence under the Act, and render any contracts entered into by the company void. Despite this, both companies have successfully conducted business in Papua New Guinea. It appears the Investment Promotion Authority was either unaware of these violations, or failed to act. This suggests that there is a lack of capacity within the Investment Promotion Authority to rigorously police corporate regulations, which in turn has fostered a weak compliance culture within the international business community. Scrutinising prescribed transaction sequences can thus offer critical insights into both the lawfulness of transactions witnessed in the immediate case, and the prevailing compliance culture.

Where a particular story plotted on the timeline is seismic in nature, precipitating a significant range of transaction sequences, which have major long term impacts, we can call this a spark event. To give an example, the previously mentioned 12 May 2012 demolition at Paga Hill proved to be such a moment. It triggered transaction chains at a local, national and international level which turned a localised land dispute into a landmark struggle, that continues to have reverberations in Papua New Guinea and abroad. Identifying this type of spark-event in the timeline data and assessing what transforms say, an everyday injustice – that may occur ordinarily with banal regularity – into a catalysing force, constitutes an important theoretical task, from both a scholarly and practical perspective.

Of course, on occasion, a potential spark event fizzles out unexpectedly; it becomes what we might call a damp squib. Detecting damp squibs can also be an important diagnostic tool. For example, during the course of the research into land and property markets it was found many of the private and public actors under scrutiny had been the subject of strong censure by the Public Accounts Committee, the Auditor General's Office and numerous Commissions of Inquiry. None of the referrals to the Fraud Squad, or the suggested reform packages submitted by these authorities, appear to have been implemented. Therefore, during the research process it became increasingly apparent, despite the often thorough and compelling character of these inquiries, their recommendations were repeatedly damp squibs. This, in turn, said something about the political culture at the highest levels of power in Papua New Guinea. Therefore, even where a transaction sequence peters out, which in other circumstances might be a spark for significant change, explaining why this occurred can be an important task.

Another helpful diagnostic tool is a sequence trace. A sequence trace is a category that captures a plotted event or events that imply a series of other transactions that may be quite difficult to uncover. For instance, on 24 April 2014, the Royal Papua New Guinea Constabulary announced that PHDC had donated K20,000 to the police; this occurred shortly before the RPNGC forcefully evicted residents at Paga Hill on 31 May, a demolition exercise, we will recall, that was prefaced by a very public attempt to arrest the most active community leader. The controversial donation was, surprisingly, made with public fanfare.

Notably, senior officers issued a press release praising the company. For this known sequence of events to have transpired it is reasonable to deduce there would have been preceding transactions. At the minimum, representatives of the company would have met with RPNGC officers, to discuss and provide the donation. Given standard organisational practice, it would also be reasonable to deduce that the media release would have been issued by mutual consent. Accordingly, this trace transaction implies a degree of collegiality between the two organisations. It also places into question police governance; after all, PHDC was a corporate entity embroiled in a series of legal controversies, while the police were supposed to be an impartial force. From this example, we can see how carefully plotting and detecting trace transactions can help identify the existence of broader ties, and contexts, that illuminate social dimensions of the case under study.

The final category we will consider in this introduction to transaction mapping, is approximate transactions. Approximate transactions involve events plotted on the timeline that are roughly adjacent, but are not explicitly connected in any direct way. Nonetheless, the temporal proximity of these two events is important either because it effects the emerging trajectory under examination, or because the approximate transactions potentially signpost hidden connections. To demonstrate this point we can again turn to the Paga Hill case. On 6 April 1998, an Urban Development Lease over Paga Hill was granted to the Paga Hill Land Holding Company Limited. To win this award, the latter proposed to construct a K300 million development at the site which would include a luxury hotel and a large marina for cruise vessels. The Chair of the Land Board awarding the leasehold title was Ralph Guise, a figure subsequently condemned by a Commission of Inquiry into the National Provident Fund (Barnett 2002). The latter inquiry found his chairmanship to be tainted by bribery and fraud.

On 25 October 1998, 6 months after the Urban Development Lease was awarded to the Paga Hill Land Holding Company, Guise acquired a company, Noko No.36. Noko No.36 held leases over land on the foreshore abutting Paga Hill's lease. It would appear reasonable to suggest this adjacent land would increase significantly in value from the proposed development. Therefore, on the basis of these approximate events, at the very least, it can be hypothesised that the Land Board Chairman used inside information to speculate on land. Of course, the proximity of these transactions could also generate a range of related hypotheses that might be tested. Nevertheless, the core lesson is, scrutinising approximate transactions, even if there is no explicit chain linking them, may help to disclose hidden connections.

Of course, in the discussion so far only a general introduction to transaction mapping has been possible. It is a new and experimental methodology, that requires further technical refinement and conceptual development. Nevertheless, its employment now in a range of fieldwork environments,[4] has demonstrated the benefits that come from graphing transactions, using visual intelligence and honed analytical categories to carefully scrutinise the emerging sequences. In so doing important new hypotheses can be generated and tested during the fieldwork process. It also has the ability to uncover social dynamics, critical to theory building.

There are a range of sympathetic methods that can be synthesised with transaction mapping to increase rigour. One example is process tracing, a methodology designed to test potential relations of causation in complex environments. The core categories employed in process tracing are straw in the wind, hoop test, smoking gun and the double decisive test. Straw in the wind tests identify circumstantial evidence in the case under examination, that make the hypothesis more or less likely. Collier (2011: 826) observes that 'straw-in-the-wind tests … provide *neither a necessary nor a sufficient* criterion for accepting or rejecting a hypothesis, and they only *slightly* weaken rival hypotheses'. For example, it may be hypothesised that the company TS Limited, owned by Jane Smith, is really a front for laundering bribes to the President. This hypothesis would be strengthened by the fact Jane Smith is close friends with the President's mother. However, it is certainly not definitive proof.

A hoop test sets a necessary condition for a hypothesis to be true; if a hypothesis passes this test it considerably strengthens it, while if it fails this test it can be excluded. For example, using the previous hypothesis, we would expect a front for laundering bribes to be in receipt of significant payments. If TS Limited was receiving large payments into its Swiss bank account, it passes the hoop test. The smoking gun test, as the name suggests, involves the presence of evidence that would be sufficient for proving a hypothesis; however, the absence of this evidence does not necessarily disprove the hypothesis. So for instance, a suspect caught holding a smoking revolver over a victim is sufficient – although not absolutely definitive – proof of the hypothesis that they are the guilty party, but the absence of a weapon on the suspect would not exclude them from the investigation. So if, for instance, we found out that money paid into TS Limited's Swiss account was used to pay for a luxury New York apartment, held in the name of the President, the original hypothesis passes the smoking gun test. However, the absence of such a smoking gun would not disprove it. Finally there is a double decisive test, which employs the three outlined tests to exclude alternative hypotheses, so that there is only one necessary and sufficient explanation left.

In effect, what process tracing allows us to do is create a transparent system for weighing competing hypotheses in complex environments where the researcher will rarely have access to complete data-sets. It also helps to inject rigour into research decisions, by creating a common reference point for explaining why a hypothesis was viewed as compelling, or at least reasonably likely, compared to other explanations.

Of course, there is room for further innovation and synthesis. ISNA and transaction mapping, however, offer a starting point for scholarly conversations devoted to building rigorous methodologies that can effectively uncover the crimes of urbanisation.

A note on information management

Clearly the techniques noted in this chapter demand an effective information management system. Each researcher will have their own preferences in this respect. However, to offer one perspective, a brief outline of the techniques used in this study will be provided – again the emphasis here is on accessible software, rather than more expensive packages only available to researchers based in higher education institutions. To that end, Excel was employed to organise the raw data. The bibliographic details of all documents and interviews relating to a case were logged in a spreadsheet, in chronological order. Each source was given an identification number, which was then used in all the subsequent analytical systems. That way, the original sources, which were all digitised, could be accessed from a numerically ordered file index if needed.

Before logged data was plotted in either Casefile or Tiki-Toki, it was coded and inserted into a central spreadsheet, labelled the data-organiser. The vertical axis of the spreadsheet was organised by theme such as 'land acquisition process', 'community history', 'eviction process', 'key actors', 'public accounts inquiry findings', and so on. Then the data corresponding to these thematic codes were embedded on the horizontal axis, where possible, in chronological order, with page references included to allow quick access to the original sources.

Once plotted in the database, the information could then also be inserted into the relevant digraph and timeline, using the cognate software. It was found that this approach to data organisation allowed nimble movement between the Excel file, Casefile and Tiki-Toki.

Conclusion

Distilled down, the methodological framework set out in this chapter serves two core purposes. First, it provides a mechanism for organising complex social sequences in ways that allow the mind to think more clinically about the dynamics being investigated. In effect a complex series of happenings are turned into uniform data-sets, which are forensically processed using congruent units of analysis and data-modelling tools. Second, the framework provides a range of concepts that train the mind to hone in on tendencies within the social and temporal currents being investigated, to identify important processes in need of further scrutiny and theorisation. As a whole, the framework developed here helps researchers to generate questions, hypotheses and insights, that can enhance investigative fieldwork; while also offering tools that can convert the results of fieldwork into uniform data-sets capable of facilitating robust comparative and longitudinal research, on which rigorous theorisation may be based.

However, to maximise the benefits of such a framework, the researcher must, of course, be able to tap rich currents of data. On that note, the next chapter will introduce a range of methods and techniques for cultivating such data streams, in a fieldwork context often marked by secrecy and power imbalances.

Notes

1 These assumptions reflect the findings presented both here and in the wider literature (see chapter one).
2 Of course, speaking more generally this position has precedent in a wide range of socio-logical traditions that attempt to understand the logics of power informing social conten-tion (see Bourdieu 1986; Lukes 2005; Poulantzas 1978; Tilly and Tarrow 2007)
3 Where new data changes our appreciation of an actor's social role, researchers may elect to recode an actor.
4 It has been deployed to research urban content in Papua New Guinea, and corruption in Central Asia.

Bibliography

Agbola, T. and Jinadu, A. M. (1997). 'Forced eviction and forced relocation in Nigeria: The experience of those evicted from Maroko in 1990', *Environment and Urbanization*, 9(2), 271–288.

Aminzade, R. (1992). 'Historical sociology and time', *Sociological Methods & Research*, 20(4), 456–480.

Ashman, S. (2006). 'From world market to world economy', in Dunn, B. and Radice, H. (eds) *One Hundred Years of Permanent Revolution*, London: Pluto Press.

Axinn, W. G., Pearce, L. D. and Ghimire, D. (1999). 'Innovations in life history calendar appli-cations', *Social Science Research*, 28, 243–264.

Barnett, T. (2002). Report of the Commission of Inquiry into the National Provident Fund. [Online]. Extracts available at: web.archive.org/web/20060923050634/http://www.post-courier.com.pg/NPF%20inquiry/npf116 (accessed: 16 February 2017).

Bourdieu, P. (1997). 'The forms of capital', in Halsey, A. H., Lauder, H., Brown, P., and Wells, A. S. (eds) *Education: Culture, Economy, and Society*, Oxford: Oxford University Press.

Brenner, N. (2000). 'The urban question as a scale question: Reflections on Henri Lefebvre, urban theory and the politics of scale', *International Journal of Urban and Regional Research*, 24(2), 361–378.

Coles, N. (2001). 'It's not what you know, it's who you know: Analysing serious crime groups as social networks', *British Journal of Criminology*, 41(4), 580–594.

Collier, D. (2011). 'Understanding process tracing', *PS: Political Science and Politics*, 44(4), 823–830.

De Nooy, W., Mrvar, A. and Batagelj, V. (2011). *Exploratory Social Network Analysis with Pajek*, Cambridge: Cambridge University Press.

Downs, I. (1980). *The Australian Trusteeship: Papua New Guinea 1945–75*, Canberra: Australian Government Publishing Service.

Griffin, L. J. (2007) 'Historical sociology, narrative and event-structure analysis: Fifteen years later', *Sociologica*, 3, 1–17.

Harris, D. A. (2012). 'Using life history plots to visualize criminal careers', *Criminal Justice Review*, 38(1), 94–109.

Hawksley, C. (2006). 'Papua New Guinea at thirty: Late decolonisation and the political economy of nation-building', *Third World Quarterly*, 27(1), 161–173.

Knoke, D. and Yang, S. (2008). *Social Network Analysis*, London: Sage Publications.

Kriegler, A. (2014). Using Social Network Analysis to Profile Organised Crime. [Online]. Available at: www.issafrica.org/uploads/PolBrief57.pdf (accessed: 4 October 2017).

Lukes, P. (2005). *Power: A Radical View*, Basingstoke: Palgrave Macmillan.

Mahoney, J. (2012). 'The logic of process tracing tests in the social sciences', *Sociological Methods & Research*, 41(4), 570–597.

Maltz, M. D. and Mullany, J. M. (2000). 'Visualising lives: New pathways for analysing life course trajectories', *Journal of Quantitative Criminology*, 16(2), 255–281.

McIllwain, J. S. (1999). 'Organized crime: A social network approach', *Crime, Law and Social Change*, 32(4), 301–323.

Poulantzas, N. (1978). *State Power Socialism*, London: Verso.

Prell, C. (2012). *Social Network Analysis: History, Theory and Methodology*, London: Sage Publications.

Public Accounts Committee. (2007). *Public Accounts Committee Report to Parliament on the Inquiry into the Department of Lands and Physical Planning*, Waigani: National Parliament of Papua New Guinea.

Royal Papua New Guinea Constabulary Metropolitan Superintendent. (2014). 'Police pleased with Paga Hill resettlement exercise', media release, 1 June 2014.

Scott, J. (2001). *Social Network Analysis: A Handbook*, London: Sage Publications.

Tilly, C. and Tarrow, S. (2007). *Contentious Politics*, London: Paradigm Publishers.

'UN at PHDC's Official Handover to the Tagua Community'. (2014). YouTube video, added by Paga Hill Development Company. [Online]. Available at www.youtube.com/watch?v=oJ60h-bATUc (accessed: 28 February 2017).

Van der Hulst, R. C. (2009). 'Introduction to social network analysis (SNA) as an investigative tool', *Trends in Organized Crime*, 12(2), 101–120.

Wasserman, S. and Faust, K. (1994). *Social Network Analysis: Methods and Applications*, Cambridge: Cambridge University Press.

Chapter 4

Uncovering the data trail

Accessing, handling and triangulating sources

Introduction

When conducting investigative fieldwork into the crimes of the powerful, researchers frequently face a range of barriers. Not only will the transactions under scrutiny often be of a complex, convoluted nature, they are prosecuted by a set of powerful organisations endowed with the legal capacity and material resources to conceal their conduct from public scrutiny (see Tombs and Whyte 2003; Whyte 2012). Therefore, for this type of research, rigour has a relative meaning. It must, in part, be measured by the inventiveness of the researcher, and their capacity to penetrate highly opaque processes and institutions through systematic probing, using established methodological knowledge, along with innovations that draw on cutting edge technologies and techniques (Green et al. 2012).

With respect to established methodological knowledge, it tends to be dispersed across a wide range of written and living sources, that are not always easy to locate or access. Some of the richest sources of knowledge are investigative professionals working within the media or civil society organisations. Access here depends on establishing personal contact and rapport. However, we are starting to observe the systematic dissemination of investigative techniques and technologies by this professional contingent, through workshops, conferences, handbooks and online guides. The International Consortium of Investigative Journalists, Centre for Investigative Journalism, the Organized Crime and Corruption Reporting Project, Corporate Watch, and Global Witness, are examples of organisations that construct investigative repertoires, and share this knowledge publicly. All of which needs to be drawn on and systematised if an overarching methodological framework is to be created, capable of penetrating the opaque processes and institutions underpinning the crimes of the powerful.

With this in mind, it was argued in the previous chapter that such a framework rests on the development of units of analysis that pinpoint more exactly the moving components and processes around which illicit activity is organised. For example, it was observed that we need to understand the social network architecture buttressing transaction chains, and resistance; the material and immaterial flows that circulate through particular networks and subgroups; the pooled resources which see power accrue to certain nodal points; the transaction patterns underpinning critical events; and the connection between these patterns and particular outcomes. By helping orientate researchers to these types of core social process constitutive of the crimes of urbanisation, a vantage point is created from which to systematically inquire.

For inquiry to pay dividends, rigorous data collection methods are needed. To that end, this chapter sets out a systematic approach for collecting data pertinent to understanding and theorising the crimes of urbanisation. It is, in part, informed by a range of experimental techniques that have been developed by the author during fieldwork for this study, and over the course of his research into the crimes of the powerful,[1] alongside knowledge exchange activities with investigative journalists and civil society organisations.

This chapter will begin by exploring methods for acclimatising to the field environment, before setting out key documentary sources that can feed the analytical tools presented in chapter three. When considering documentary sources, an emphasis will be placed on locating, reading and storing the relevant data. Attention will then turn to relevant methods for handling sensitive oral sources and conducting field experiments.

Of course, this chapter is not intended to be a definitive statement on relevant data collection techniques. Rather, it is a contribution to a growing conversation which is taking place within criminology and civil society, on investigative methodologies for uncovering the crimes of the powerful.

Arriving in the field and building a support network

It may be obvious to say, but nonetheless it is still important to emphasise, when initiating research into the crimes of urbanisation building ties with actors who are confronting the relevant activity is a key first step in charting orientating points for data collection. Important actors, in this respect, may be resident coalitions, community activists, unions, journalists, NGOs, professionals, professional bodies, public servants and politicians (Lasslett 2012). Even at a preliminary stage in the research process, it is possible to identify some of these interlocutors, through press searches and online inquiry.

All of these actors, of course, are nodes in broader social networks, that will exhibit degrees of interconnectedness, and disconnection. For example, building ties with an NGO that enjoys strong links to residents and activists protecting a heritage site, may help create a bridge for accessing those resisting a land-grab. On the other hand, there might be discrete professional actors with specialist knowledge on the illicit phenomenon under investigation, who can only be accessed by traversing elite-actor networks. It, therefore, pays dividends to apply the key principles underpinning social network analysis, in order to strategically identify potent conduits for snowball sampling.

When establishing a support network of contacts in the opening phase of fieldwork, it is advisable to be circumspect. There will be rivalries, tensions and alliances in the social fabric being navigated, which the researcher may only be faintly aware of, if at all. Furthermore, there will be hidden histories, which may influence how different stakeholders engage with academic researchers, civil society and journalists. Gently testing the water is important, during this initial phase, as is building meaningful relationships with stakeholders, drawing on their local knowledge to map those issues that may need to be handled sensitively, or with caution.

With these caveats in mind, there is nonetheless scope when establishing a foothold in the field, to build genuinely collaborative relations with different groups impacted by the activity under investigation, each of whom may be considered condensed sites of experience, knowledge and ties. For example, a residents coalition resisting displacement will almost certainly have critical insights into the corporate entities, and political actors, driving this existential threat to their community. It might merely be rumour, or educated guesswork, nevertheless, this information can generate important lines of inquiry. Similarly, quite often experienced journalists are aware of the hidden patronage networks that exist in a particular region, which can help the researcher to build a tentative social network model, that can then be verified or modified through subsequent fieldwork. Complementing this, NGOs and sector professionals may have a strong understanding of the technical processes standing behind the property transactions under examination – for instance, land acquisition and development approval procedures – and can thus advise the researcher on methods for accessing data from relevant government agencies. In some instances, these actors may even be able to share documents obtained through legal discovery, or professional inquiry, which can give fieldwork a critical initial boost.

Indeed, the researcher's power to uncover is not merely a dichotomous relation between the individual investigator and those organising the illicit conduct. Rather, it is an evolving, dialectical process, embedded in a much wider social fabric. Accordingly, the researcher can subtly change the power balance by building ties with groups commanding particular forms of social capital, such as community knowledge, particular technical expertise or investigative resources, such as professional databases. Furthermore, the power balance can also be shifted by locating pathways into the elite network prosecuting the conduct under investigation, which can potentially congeal leaked data or insider knowledge (see below).

However, it is important when building collaborative relations, especially with residents, community activists and NGOs, that the researcher establishes a shared expectation of what cooperation will produce. For example, often the sequence of events critical to the interests of residents, will occur at a greater pace than the research process, which means the investigators may be unable to supply finished results in time for them to impact on an advocacy campaign. This needs to be communicated at the outset. Nevertheless, the research may still have valuable legacy impacts, which residents might wish to support. It is also important that enduring lines of communication are maintained. The simple act of sending to communities a policy brief, or advising them of delays impeding a publishing deadline, helps to validate their investment in a research project.

Of course, building ties with civil society, professionals and elite actors, is only the first step in fieldwork. It launches a broader process of inquiry, that aims to meticulously tap a range of documentary and oral sources. On that note, the sources pertinent to crimes of urbanisation inquiry will now be mapped, looking in particular at the issues of discovery, access and analysis.

Accessing, reading and analysing data sources

Company records and the hidden stories they tell

When investigating the actors, networks and transactions central to particular forms of illicit conduct permeating the urbanisation process, it is probable that key commercial relationships have, in part, been organised through incorporated entities. These entities can generate a significant documentary trail (see Table 4.1), in the form of memos, emails, reports, contracts, commercial plans, proposal documents, to name just a few examples. Unless leaked, or tabled publicly, access to these records will ordinarily be restricted. However, a public reporting requirement may be legally enshrined in the jurisdiction's company regulations. If handled carefully, these publicly tabled records can be an important source of data. Of course, the level of public disclosure which companies must comply with will vary between jurisdictions.

An important source of guidance is the Financial Secrecy Index (FSI), which is administered by the Tax Justice Network (www.financialsecrecyindex.com). The FSI sets out the levels of transparency and accessibility offered by corporate regimes in over 100 jurisdictions. Researchers can also use the Investigative Dashboard (investigativedashboard.org), an open-source tool for accessing corporate data. The Investigative Dashboard contains links to dozens of corporate registries, and other related databases. In addition, it has its own integrated database that houses data scraped from a large range of business registries, official sources such as government gazettes, leak archives, the grey literature and certain secondary sources.

Of course, the level of transparency offered by different corporate regimes is an evolving matter. For example, Companies House in the United Kingdom (UK) recently removed paywall barriers (beta.companieshouse.gov.uk). This has made company records more accessible to civil society and university researchers. Additionally, laws have been enacted in the UK that now require companies to publicly table a register of beneficial interests.[2] However, transparency levels vary significantly between jurisdictions. Therefore, while company records may be accessible in one jurisdiction, such as New Zealand, the researcher may nonetheless face barriers when tracing back commercial networks to holding companies incorporated in the British Virgin Islands, where corporate information is not ordinarily accessible to the public. Or the data trail may lead to a jurisdiction where corporate information is ostensibly open to the public, but shielded by prohibitive paywalls. Australia is a notable example in this respect.[3]

However, even when researchers enjoy access to corporate records, it may be that company registries only permit restricted search strings. This is the case, for instance, in Papua New Guinea. Although the corporate registry – administered by the Investment Promotion Authority – is freely available online (ipa.gov. pg), searches must be conducted using either a company name or number. It is impossible, therefore, to implement record searches using, for instance, individual names or a particular address connected to an individual (a technique used for detecting proxy vehicles).

This type of restriction places a significant barrier in the way of investigative research. For example, it prevents researchers from constructing comprehensive lists of companies that are either owned or administered by key individuals in the jurisdiction under investigation. In turn, such a list is an important resource for mapping commercial networks, and conducting certain forms of forensic data analysis and data modelling.

A social network graph compiled using corporate registry data, for example, can at the very minimum indicate who a target is commercially tied to (that is, key associates). Modelling data this way can have a range of benefits. It may

Table 4.1 Company records and their potential uses

Types of document	Potential uses
Application for registration	Ownership structure of corporate vehicle.
Certificate of incorporation	Executive structure of corporate vehicle.
Company extract	Documenting commercial ties between actors.
Historical extract	Individual biographical details such as date of
Annual return	birth, nationality and address.
Share issue	Corporate biographical details including assets,
Transfer of shares	liabilities, personnel, owners, activities and
Appointment/change in Director	location.
Appointment/change in Secretary	Date and content of key organisational
Charges and encumbrances	transactions, including changes in ownership
Change in registered address	and executive structure.
	Identification of company law breaches.
	Assessing rigour of regulatory agencies responsible for compliance.
	Uncovering hidden beneficial owners.
	Evaluating the accuracy of oral testimony and documentary evidence collected during fieldwork.

be discovered, for instance, that Businessperson A, who is the recipient of a government contract, and Politician B, the key decision maker, are partners in a consultancy firm. A clear conflict of interest has, therefore, been detected. Furthermore, it may be possible to see who the target is connected to by a degree of separation. For example, a target's business partner in Company A, may be the Director of Company B, which is owned by the Lands Minister. We can thus now trace a direct line of communication between a target, and an influential decision maker in government.

Of course, lists of companies associated with a target can, in part, be constructed using other tools, such as LinkedIn, media reporting databases, Google and leak archives. However, this approach hinges on the target's name, and the associated company, being connected in a public footprint. Comprehensive lists ultimately depend on open, robust corporate registries (which display beneficial ownership), with flexible search strings.

Where a corporate registry is open, but its usability is curtailed by limited search strings, options are available for improving data flexibility. For instance, in the case of Papua New Guinea a data scrape of the corporate registry was conducted.[4] This scrape allowed the data contained on the Investment Promotion Authority website to be downloaded and projected in an Excel spreadsheet. The spreadsheet contained a full list of companies registered in Papua New Guinea, including their name, registered address, postal address, in addition to the names and addresses of directors, shareholders and secretaries. It was then possible to model this data in order to produce detailed lists of entities associated with a target, using a range of search strings, including their name, address, and the name of family members or known proxies.

However, accessing and searching corporate registries is only one part of the challenge. Once records have been located, the researcher must be able to read and collate them in ways that maximise the record's intelligence potential. Record literacy, on the one hand, involves understanding what different technical terms mean (e.g. charges, share class, assets, liabilities, etc.), and knowing the rules that govern how companies operate and report on their activity (i.e. company laws will prescribe reporting requirements, and administrative procedures, which companies incorporated in the jurisdiction must adhere to). It also points to the multiple ways a record can be read to extract data. For instance, a share transfer form in Papua New Guinea, most obviously contains information on a share transaction, including the number of shares sold, and the amount paid. It also includes biographical data on the nationality, date of birth and registered address of the purchaser. Finally, the form contains the executive's name approving the transfer, in addition to the name and address of the entity submitting the record.

At first glance, some of this information may sound trivial, yet carefully handling such detail can enhance research rigour. For example, knowing an individual's date of birth can have important uses. It may help to distinguish an individual with a common name – such as John Smith – or, it might signpost unusual transactions. A company owned and directed by a 20-year-old who is in receipt of $US300 million in consultancy payments should raise concerns that this person is a proxy, and that these consultancy contracts are potentially shams. A target's registered address – or addresses – can have important uses too. It allows company searches to be conducted using an alternative form of identification – as opposed to a name. This could reveal entities owned or administered by a close family member, a proxy, or indeed the target, but under a different name or with a different spelling of their name.

Other, arguably even more subtle, examples can be pointed to of 'minutiae' mattering. For instance, when surveying the records of a company administered by multiple directors, it may be difficult to know who has a more hands-on role in the business. Observing whether the same director signs the majority of company records can help to evidence their centrality in the corporate network. Even noting the consultancy company or accounting firm that submits a corporation's records to the relevant registry can have important analytical consequences.

For instance, during the Papua New Guinea research it was discovered that the firm lodging records for a target company had been censured, alongside key personnel from the target company, in a government anti-corruption report. While both groups were alleged to be involved in the same type of illicit scheme in this report, the reporting agency did not identify any link between them. The uncovering of a direct link, by noting this subtle cue in the company records, led to the discovery of further information showing close commercial relations between the two groups at the centre of the aforementioned government inquiry. Therefore, sometimes seemingly innocuous information can have significant analytical implications. Learning how to read records in ways that maximise their full intelligence value, therefore, is a critical skill to master.

The intelligence value of company records can be further enhanced by deploying techniques that allow the extracted data to be modelled and analysed in a systematic fashion. Crucially, it is important that the extracted information is collated centrally in integrated databases, so cross-referencing can take place. Through cross-referencing data feeds, information fragments dispersed over a range of sources can be connected – often producing a sum greater than its parts – which helps the researcher construct more coherent images of the networks, transactions and processes under examination. This is where the analytical tools outlined in the previous chapter have an important role to play. By coding and storing data using digraphs, transaction maps and a central database – employing software such as Excel, NVivo, Maltego Casefile and Tiki-Toki – dynamic opportunities are opened up for cross referencing the information retrieved from corporate registries, and triangulating these datasets with intelligence extracted from other sources (see below).

For example, during the Papua New Guinea research a list was kept of registered addresses associated with target individuals and companies. Keeping track of these addresses proved important on multiple occasions. In one instance it was discovered that a corporate vehicle developing shorefront land in Papua New Guinea's capital was owned by an Australian holding company. The latter's shares, in turn, were held by a Perth based accountancy firm. When the data was cross-referenced with a list of addresses associated with one of the developer's foreign directors, it was revealed that they shared a registered address with this Perth based firm. The Perth address was used by the director in records associated with a separate Papua New Guinea holding company they had an interest in. It was thus possible to hypothesise that the director and the accountancy firm were linked.

Of course, the intelligence value of company data is more potent when it is triangulated with other information sources, such as court judgements/documents, arbitration decisions, land records, anti-corruption reporting, interviews and news reporting. For instance, during the Papua New Guinea research searches were conducted on organisational entities closely linked to key individuals prosecuting land deals and development ventures. This was a two stage process. First an associate list was compiled using scraped corporate data – supplemented by a trawl of the internet and news reporting – focusing on companies the target was linked to through corporate office or shareholdings. Once an associate entity list had been compiled, searches were then conducted of the anti-corruption reporting, court judgements and news reporting, using the names of linked entities and business partners. This frequently returned important details on previous criminal convictions, corruption allegations, partnerships with ex-convicts, and schisms between business associates.

The reverse is also true. Data extracted from other sources can be triangulated with company records in ways that maximise their value. For example, in two of the cases researched for this volume, key executives made public statements about the ownership and management structure of the company they were representing, which was recorded in meeting minutes and media reporting. These statements were designed to legitimise certain property transactions the companies were a party to. However, once the statements were cross-referenced with the company data, they were revealed to be false. This had two important implications. First, it indicated the corporate officers concerned were issuing misleading statements, which raised concerns over their credibility and *bona fides*. Second, it also pointed towards potentially unlawful conduct.

The handling and analysis of corporate records can be further enhanced by acquiring a working knowledge of the relevant company laws and regulations. For example, in Papua New Guinea the *Investment Promotion Act* 1992 and *Companies Act* 1997 place certain governance and accounting requirements on incorporated entities and foreign investors. The former act, in particular, requires that foreign enterprises – that is, companies majority owned by foreign nationals – acquire certification from the Investment Promotion Authority prior to conducting business in Papua New Guinea. Before granting this certification, the Investment Promotion Authority must be satisfied that the company has the finances and experience to engage in the proposed line of business, and that they are in good commercial standing. Until certification is granted, any business conducted by the company is unlawful, attracting a maximum penalty of K100,000.

During fieldwork it was revealed that two foreign developers, centrally involved in the cases under study, were conducting business in Papua New Guinea without certification. In one instance, this fact was explicitly acknowledged by the Managing Director of the Investment Promotion Authority. However, it appears no effort was made to prosecute the company. This is a recurring theme in Papua New Guinea. That is, foreign companies implicated in a range of illicit enterprises are not correctly certified, nor for that matter are they observing reporting requirements set out in the *Companies Act* 1997 – yet no action is taken against them. In effect, these companies enjoy de facto impunity owing to lax enforcement.[5] Accordingly, as this example demonstrates, attentiveness to the relevant company laws allow corporate records to be read in ways that also say something more general about the oversight system, whether it be the vigour of regulatory agencies, or broader inequalities in the national legal regime.

To summarise, company records are an important source of data which can help investigators document the actors, networks and transactions critical to understanding the criminogenic dimensions of intensive and extensive urbanisation. That said, accessibility is an enduring challenge, given that public accounting requirements for companies vary considerably between jurisdictions. And even where records are accessible their intelligence value depends on the systematic way in which data is extracted from the records, and then collated/analysed. In this respect, cross-referencing records, the triangulation of data, and reading information against a particular regulatory backdrop, are all techniques that can help maximise the intelligence value of company documents. As we will now see, these general lessons also apply to the handling of other documentary sources.

Property related records

When scrutinising real-estate transactions, property developments, infrastructure projects and extractive ventures, there will potentially be a range of property related records that can be examined (see Table 4.2) – again, with variations between jurisdictions. For example, most government land registries will contain data on the property under examination, and related commercial transactions. This will generally include property size, boundaries, type (zoning) and location, the vendor, purchaser, date of sale(s), amount(s) paid and tax information. Stipulated improvement requirements and annual rental may be discoverable where leasehold property is concerned. Furthermore, land registries – or cognate departmental agencies – will maintain important technical documents, such as land surveys, and zoning maps.

When a major real-estate, infrastructure or extractive venture is being scrutinised, researchers will also find there are numerous procedural documents

Table 4.2 Property related records and their uses

Types of document	Potential uses
Land survey	Data on land size, land type, land boundaries and zoning.
Contract of sale	
Title deeds	Transaction history of land/property.
Lease	Identification of vendor, purchaser, lessor, lessee, witnesses, authorised signatories and relevant public officials.
Tenancy agreement	
Scoping study	
Tender document	Terms and conditions of sale, lease or development.
Public notices/advertisements	
Gazettal notices	Public tender criteria, tender evaluation process and justifications for bidder selection.
Development proposal documents, such as masterplan and environmental impact statement	
	Data on proposed development including size, economic impact, environmental impact, urban impact, investors and business model.
Land Board, Physical Planning Board and Departmental records	
Building approvals	
Land Registry files	Hearings/meetings convened by approving agencies, including outcomes.
Physical planning/zoning records	
Rental statements and land-tax statements	Compliance of approval/award process with relevant laws/regulations.
Notice to vacate	
Summary eviction notice	Compliance with sale/lease terms, zoning laws/regulations and land laws/regulations.
Eviction order	
	Eviction details, including date served, legal mandate, involved parties and approving authorities.

linked to project approval and project implementation. This may begin with a scoping study, before moving to a public consultation or public tender phase. In the latter instance, bidders will submit numerous proposal documents. Once an award has been made, or a private real-estate venture has been initiated, the developer will generally navigate a range of official approval processes, before starting the project. Then during the construction phase, audits, progress reports and project reviews will frequently be produced. Where access to these various documents can be obtained, the researcher can learn, for instance, about the project's scope, objectives, technical details, key personnel, conditionalities, monitoring procedures, progress and finances.

In cases where land is compulsorily acquired, or where residents are evicted, important administrative and legal records will often be generated. For example, in Papua New Guinea state leasehold title owners can apply to the district court for an *ex parte* summary eviction order, where those occupying the land are deemed to be squatters. On the other hand, if residents have a legal or equitable right to occupancy, natural justice must be afforded through a national court hearing. In the latter instance, the court can issue a notice to vacate, or a

consent order may be entered into. These various records may disclose important information about those resident on the land, and the eviction process
itself, including whether prior warning has been given and any compensation
package offered.

Of course, each jurisdiction will have its own rules which govern public
access to such records. Some of the documents already mentioned will likely
be made available to the public, as standard. Others may only be available upon
request, using freedom of information legislation, or by attending the court
registry.

Outside these procedural records, most real-estate transactions, property
developments, infrastructure projects and extractive ventures generate a significant volume of confidential documentation. For instance, there are contracts of sale, mortgage facility/finance agreements, formal correspondence and
emails, to name just a few examples. If any of these documents pass through
the hands of public organisations, they could potentially be acquired through
a freedom of information request (although legislated exemptions may hinder
such requests). Alternatively, it may be possible to source a leak from someone
within the organisation prosecuting the transactions, or a professional interme-
diary (see below). Where litigation has occurred, these internal records could
potentially be found in the case file, if they have been employed as an exhibit.

Of course, as with company records, simply locating these documents is not
enough. The record's intelligence value will vary depending on the reader's
technical literacy, and their capacity to collate extracted data for the purposes
of cross-referencing and triangulation. To enhance record literacy levels, it pays
to develop a working knowledge of the laws and regulations governing property developments, land transactions, infrastructure projects and forced evictions, as well as key policy documents and procedural manuals. This will enable
researchers to more effectively spot gaps, inconsistencies or unlawful transactions within the documentary trail.

For example, during the Papua New Guinea fieldwork, elementary legal/
procedural literacy, combined with data triangulation/cross-referencing, helped
identify a range of illicit transactions. In one case study, a copy of the developer's
Urban Development Lease was obtained. Document markings show it was
issued on 6 April 1998. A sweep of the government gazette, however, revealed
that the land was still zoned open space in 1998. To pinpoint the problematic
character of this transaction sequence, working knowledge of the *Land Act* 1996
is needed. The latter law stipulates that land must be appropriately zoned for
the type of proposed use, before a matching lease can be issued. Therefore, it
appeared in this instance that the Urban Development Lease was unlawfully
granted.

In another case study, a survey of the government gazette revealed that the
developer under examination had been awarded a 99-year business lease by
the national government over prime real-estate in Port Moresby, a city whose
premium areas fetch rents akin to London or New York. A check of the

Lands Department's electronic registry, revealed that the developer was paying an annual rent of K100. Yet according to the *Land Regulation* 1999 annual
rent should be levied at 5% of the land's unimproved value. Therefore, in this
instance it appeared that the developer was sitting on prime urban real-estate
for pepper-corn rents.

Triangulating sources, again, can pay dividends. For example, in one case
study homes were demolished by police on the basis of an eviction order
approved by the National Court. The eviction order covered land portion 1597.
Examination of the official land survey for this area, however, revealed that
many of the demolished homes actually lay on reclaimed land outside portion
1597 – thus rendering the police actions unlawful.

Property related records may also have a range of significances beyond the
immediate case study under consideration. Careful examination of these records
could, for instance, disclose details relevant to understanding the prevailing
governance and regulatory environment mediating land and property market
transactions. Patterned evidence of flawed tender processes, illegal development approvals, notably opaque decision making processes, or unsanctioned
forced evictions, for example, signpost systemic failings within a lands administration. These findings can be further deepened by triangulating property
related records with any grey literature on the lands administration, produced
by bodies such as auditors, commissions against corruption, the ombudsman,
the courts, researchers and NGOs.

Yet arguably property related records remain one of the most difficult to
access within the crimes of urbanisation cannon. There is generally a lack of
strong civil society literacy in this area. Furthermore, we rarely witness the same
level of public pressure being placed on governments to ensure such records
are digitised and freely available. Accordingly, access can be cumbersome, non-
existent or dependent on assistance from professionals in the sector.

Despite these barriers, the fact remains property records are a rich source of
technical and commercial data, integral to detecting and analysing the illicit
transaction sequences underpinning the urbanisation process. In addition to
this, they are an important primary source for gauging the broader regulatory
and governance context in which transaction sequences take place.

Court records

Ventures, projects and decisions, essential to the urbanisation process, owing to
their complex and contentious nature, will often leave behind a legal footprint
in the courts (see Table 4.3). The accessibility of court documents will vary
between regions. For example, many court judgements delivered in Australia,
New Zealand, the United Kingdom and the South Pacific can be accessed
through the AUSTLII, BAILII and PACLII websites respectively. Commercial
archives, such as Lexis Nexis and Westlaw, can also be employed to access judgements by researchers with institutional library privileges. Of course, in some

Table 4.3 Court records and their potential uses

Types of document	Potential uses
Statement of claim/complaint Indictment Motion Amicus brief Affidavit Exhibit Court judgement	'Biographical' details of individuals, companies and government agencies, including their background, characteristics, modus operandi and prior illicit behaviour. Political, administrative, legal, commercial, financial and managerial transaction data. Particular conversations, statements and actions undertaken by target individuals. Financial and commercial data on the ties between entities, and the resource flows between linked concerns. Information on the precise institutional mechanisms and processes employed to facilitate property related transaction. Details of the harm(s) suffered as a result of particular transaction sequences. Governance and compliance data on state agencies and commercial sectors. Details of the legal rules governing political, commercial and social transactions. Judicial opinion on the integrity of individuals, agencies and organisations. Judicial opinion on corruption, governance and commercial activity within particular sectors/areas.

countries judicial decisions may not be available at all – this was found to be the case when conducting research in Uzbekistan.

When available, judicial decisions will generally offer the researcher a factual background to the dispute, a reiteration of the competing claims, an outline of the relevant law, and a determination of which argument forwarded by the parties is most compelling factually and legally. Court judgements, as a result, can potentially disclose important data relating to transactions, networks, institutional processes and illegal activities relevant to the study. They may also offer critical insights into the modus operandi, and background, of research targets. Certainly during the Papua New Guinea research, judicial decisions proved instructive in nearly all the case studies. For example, National and Supreme Court decisions documented relevant criminal histories, past acts of dishonesty, sustained institutional malfeasance, in addition to the legal, commercial and administrative particulars of the cases under scrutiny.

Of course, locating relevant court decisions may require inventive searches that draw on lists of targets, and associated entities. While the target 'John Smith' may not appear in a search of the court archive, their company 'JS Limited' could have been the subject of civil litigation or liquidation proceedings, thus rendering an important result. Furthermore, if a researcher is trying to learn more about the operating environment in a particular sector, or whether the abuse of an administrative mechanism is systematic, again the search results will hinge on the search strings employed.

For example, in Papua New Guinea a particular administrative mechanism, 'certificates of inexpediency', are used to circumvent public tender requirements. Searching the National/Supreme Court archive by the phrase 'certificate of inexpediency' demonstrated that the abuse of this mechanism was widespread, and directly linked to corrupt transactions. Similarly, it was discovered during the Papua New Guinea fieldwork that state leases were being issued to companies under conditions indicative of fraud. A search of the court archives using the terms, 'actual fraud' and 'constructive fraud', revealed a large body of judicial review cases all of which suggested that the Lands Department had frequently issued state leases under conditions that were so unusual, the courts concluded that fraud was involved.

Judicial decisions are also important sites of legal interpretation, which can illuminate how different laws, regulations and common law precedents, have been applied by the courts in practice. This is not only a matter of concern for legal scholars. It has already been noted that a researcher's capacity to critically read data, depends in part on their understanding of the regulatory and legal landscapes mediating the transaction sequences being scrutinised.

For example, an important aspect of the research findings presented in chapters five, six and seven, centre on forced evictions. However, in order to more precisely analyse the displacement process, an appreciation of the legal terrain governing evictions was needed. To that end, a stream of case law has been developed in Papua New Guinea on informal tenure arrangements. A distinction is made in this case law between squatter communities and settlements, attached to which are different rights and eviction procedures. Understanding this distinction helped determine whether governments and developers had observed legal procedure when conducting mass forced evictions. The case law also illuminated a sharp disparity in the legal protection offered to property owners – even those with titles obtained through illegal processes – and lawful residents, some of whom had enjoyed half a century of tenure at the property.

To summarise, at a minimum court judgements need to be read from three different angles, if their analytical value is to be maximised. First, they are a forum for reporting on important factual and legal statements relating to the case study under examination. This may include historical data on the commercial and governance repertoires employed by target individuals, entities and institutions. Second, court judgements can disclose information on institutional bodies and mechanisms, that form part of the enduring structure underpinning systemic illicit conduct. Third, judicial decisions offer instructive legal interpretation and commentary, which can help researchers to better understand the regulatory terrain governing the urbanisation process.

However, court decisions are condensed summaries behind which often stand voluminous case files made up of submissions, affidavits, exhibits and interim judgements. Where the legal action involves substantive questions of fact and law, hundreds of exhibits may be submitted to evidence the claims, and counter claims. This can include confidential sources such as memos, meeting minutes, emails, contracts and internal reports, to name just a few examples. Additionally, there will generally be a series of affidavits submitted by those with an immediate knowledge of the case, and very often by expert witnesses. On top of this, submissions made to the courts by legal counsel are often themselves detailed documents, which draw on evidence provided in the affidavits and exhibits.

The accessibility of these different court documents, and the procedure for securing access, will vary between jurisdiction. In the United States, case files are available online through the PACER website, which includes a paywall of 10 cents per requested page. However, a range of online archives store US court files downloaded from PACER by users, making them available free of charge. In a jurisdiction such as Papua New Guinea, where there is no electronic case management system, researchers will need to visit the court registry in order to physically inspect case files.

Not all jurisdictions, however, will offer case file access to the public. When blocked, researchers will need to approach an individual party to the proceeding, in order to gain access. Approaching parties in a legal dispute likely to be sympathetic to the research is a useful tactic regardless of the jurisdiction. The case files retained by lawyers may be more detailed than those stored in the court archive. Furthermore, law firms can be an important staging point for obtaining the contact details of parties and experts, who can usefully comment on the transactions being examined.

Of course, when analysing court documents it is important that the context of their composition is kept in mind. Affidavits and submissions are produced in order to persuade the courts of a particular position. Therefore, it is possible that these documents will embellish or omit facts to strengthen their case. Accordingly, a sufficiently critical lens must be maintained when reading court records.

It is also important that the methods and techniques outlined in the previous chapter are utilised in order to meaningfully extract and model data contained within court documents. As technical records designed for a particular forum, the full intelligence value of court documents is often only fully realised when core content has been extracted and modelled using bespoke tools. Once this extracted data has been plotted in social network maps, transaction timelines and thematic databases, it can then be cross-referenced and triangulated, further enriching its research value.

Public oversight reports

Although there will be variation in size, scope and rigour, in most jurisdictions where the crimes of urbanisation take place there will be institutions set

Table 4.4 Public oversight reporting and its potential uses

Types of document	Potential uses
Audit report	Detailing relevant financial, political and legal
Parliamentary committee	transactions.
hearing transcript and/	Information on network actors, and the ties
or report	connecting nodes.
Ombudsman/Inspector	Evaluation of institutional and market environments.
General report	Data on internal institutional structures, processes
Commission of inquiry	and mechanisms.
transcript and/or report	Details on the past conduct of individuals, companies
Judicial inquiry transcript and/	and government agencies.
or report	Detailing laws, regulations and policies governing
Anti-corruption commission	particular sectors/processes.
(such as ICAC) hearing	Information relating to the deviant schemas and
transcript and/or report	mechanisms used to engage in corruption,
Serious organised crime/anti-	misappropriation and other illicit activity.
fraud squad case report	Detailing compliance weaknesses.
Civil society organisation	Evaluation of institutional response to illegal activity.
report/resource	Success/failure of reform efforts.

up to investigate, report on, and combat corruption, abuse of power, market malfeasance and other forms of related illicit behaviour. Examples include the public auditor, parliamentary committees, independent commissions against corruption, the ombudsman office, sector regulators, and law enforcement agencies. Investigations conducted by these bodies can generate a large volume of documents including hearing transcripts, submissions, exhibits and reports (see Table 4.4).

Given their civic mandate the resources produced by these bodies will often be publicly available. Ideally they will be accessible online through an institutional website. That said, researchers may have to approach libraries, or the institutional author, for a hard copy, particularly when it comes to less contemporary investigations. The intelligence value of hard copy reports can be increased, if scanned and rendered searchable using Optical Character Recognition (OCR) software. There are a range of affordable OCR software packages available, in addition to online processing centres, such as DocumentCloud, which provide this service free of charge.

Where fieldwork demands an extended engagement with a particular jurisdiction, it can help to collate all the available public oversight reporting into a central repository (browsers such as Chrome and Firefox have extensions which facilitate batch downloading, where an institution has published a large number of reports online). In effect, a database is created that can be searched via the name of individuals, companies, government agencies or institutional mechanisms, in a bid to systematically locate the relevant reports touching upon these entities or processes. At its most elementary such a database can simply consist of a folder on the researcher's hard drive, which can be batch searched using Windows search, OS X Spotlight or Adobe search. Databases can also be managed using more complex software, such as DocFetcher, that has greater analytic capabilities.

Triangulating the public oversight reporting with company data is often a useful technique. While a target individual may not feature directly in the anti-corruption reporting, searching for associated companies in a linked entities list may return hits. For example, a search of Papua New Guinea's anti-corruption reporting using the name of a key actor featured in chapter five, only returned one result from the author's database. When companies owned or managed by the actor were included in the search criteria, a total of seven reports were returned, which evidenced patterned commercial behaviour that had been censured by a diverse range of public oversight agencies. In the same case study, a database search also revealed that a key decision maker chairing the Land Board – a body responsible for awarding state leasehold title – had featured in the anti-corruption reporting for a range of illicit actions, including forgery, fraud and bribery. Collectively an image emerged of systemic market abuse and governmental complicity.

In addition to documenting the historical record of target entities and key decision making institutions, the public oversight reporting may also include details relating to the particular transaction, venture, project or decision being investigated by the researcher. This will be a rarer occurrence. However, if the venture or project has precipitated a major scandal, public oversight bodies may have been prompted to investigate. In which case the researcher may then be able to obtain insights garnered by agencies with the privileged capacity to subpoena witnesses, and obtain confidential documentation.

Beyond their value as sources of information on target individuals, organisations and processes, the public oversight reporting can also contain evaluations that help to document the broader institutional environment prevailing within government, and particular markets. It may also be possible to obtain from the reporting information on commonly exploited institutional mechanisms, or legal loopholes.

Of course, as with court records, it must again be emphasised that these documents are produced in accordance with specific terms of reference. Accordingly, the constraints these terms of reference place on the reporting needs to be kept in mind when reading oversight documents. Furthermore, the reporting format adopted by the oversight institution concerned can affect the document's immediate research value. If a commission of inquiry, for instance, publishes a 1,000 page report, along with 20,000 pages of inquiry transcripts, it then becomes imperative for the researcher to selectively extract data relevant to their investigation, and model it in ways that facilitate cross-referencing and triangulation (see chapter three).

Indeed, while the public oversight reporting is often voluminous in scope, the strategic use of search strings, database tools and data modelling techniques can render this resource a powerful means for deepening investigations into the networks, transaction sequences, institutional environments and market structures underpinning the crimes of urbanisation.

Sourcing and handling leaks

When attempting to document illicit transactions, and the organisational repertoires they depend upon, internal records often offer the most intimate insight into the strategies, decisions, motivations, pressures, network architecture, resource flows and institutional mechanisms, essential to the activity under consideration. The capacity internal records have to shine light on the nefarious dealings of powerful actors has most recently been demonstrated through the Panama Papers, and numerous archives published by WikiLeaks (see Table 4.5). That said, these mega-leaks tend to involve a degree of serendipity – which is not to discount the efforts certain organisations expend positioning themselves to harness these chance moments. Nevertheless, when conducting focused research on particular regions and markets, serendipity cannot be relied on to secure internal documents. Researchers require tools and techniques that can help them to tap sources which may provide access to records of public interest, such as emails, written correspondence, contracts, approval documents, meeting minutes, reports, and so on.

Where state agencies are enmeshed in the transactions under study, an initial avenue for accessing internal documents may be found through freedom of information (FOI) regulations, if they exist within the jurisdiction. Most FOI schemes, however, provide responsible officers with considerable discretion,

Table 4.5 Internal records and their uses

Types of document	Potential uses
Meeting minutes	Detailing key transactions integral to the broader event sequence under study.
Email, facsimile and written correspondence	Particulars of the individuals, organisational entities and mechanisms essential to deviant transaction sequences.
Contracts	
Internal memorandums	
Internal reports	Evidencing ties and lines of communication between entities, including communication content.
Approval records	
Financial records	
Audio-visual recordings	Detailing the methods entities use to conceal activity and ties.
	Documenting the motives and aims of entities.
	Evaluating the centrality, prestige and reach of actors.
	Assessing legal and regulatory compliance.
	Obtaining 'smoking gun' evidence on illicit activity and conspiratorial relations.

including numerous grounds on which the request can be rejected, ranging from national security, through to commercial in confidence. That said, a growing number of instructional resources exist to help applicants navigate this process (see, for example, Montague and Amin 2012). It is also worthwhile trying to build a relationship with the relevant FOI officer: receptive FOI officers can help applicants frame the request in ways that enhance their chance of success.

Once we step out of the public arena, few formal conduits exist for obtaining access to internal organisational records. The main exception in this respect occurs when the entity concerned has been involved in litigation. If publicly available, court submissions may include exhibits featuring relevant internal records (see above). However, in the absence of such an avenue, the researcher will generally have to source access through an organisational insider.

To that end, investigative social network analysis (ISNA) (see chapter three), is one tool that can help researchers trace lines of communication within a network, and potentially vulnerable incision points that can be used to locate a willing source. It will be recalled, in this respect, that ISNA aims to model network data iteratively over the course of the fieldwork, so emergent models can be employed to hone new rounds of investigative inquiry. These emerging models can, of course, also orientate the researcher to potential nodes with access to internal records.

A number of analytical considerations will come into play when trying to identify relevant nodes. First, researchers will initially want to identify actors who are a part of, or directly tied to, the subgroup under investigation; the assumption is, they may be privy to internal information flows. When surveying the network subgroup, it helps to differentiate nodes that would likely be the recipient of important information flows, without necessarily possessing high levels of institutional loyalty linked to positions of centrality. Office managers, consultants or subcontractors, for example, are relevant nodes who may be privy to flows of information, without being in a position of centrality that might dictate high levels of group loyalty.

However, given that many network subgroups prosecuting complex forms of criminality experience internal schisms, even central actors may be willing to assist. Therefore, it can help to register rivalries or discontent within target groups, which could provide leverage for access. Another factor to take into account is temporal distance. Once actors retire from a network, their loyalty to adjacent actors can dilute over time. This may increase the opportunity structure for accessing relevant historical records from a retired source's period of tenure.

Even when actors are located who are willing to share internal records, the institutional and legal consequences of doing so can cause hesitancy. The individual concerned, for instance, could be in breach of private contractual obligations which would leave them open to civil litigation. Furthermore, there may also be the risk of retributive violence, or criminal prosecution – in Switzerland, for instance, punitive sanctions exist for bank executives who reveal a client's identity, even when motivated by the public interest. Accordingly, most willing sources will only provide access to internal records if they are confident that the recipient is credible, ethical and has the capacity to protect their identity.

It is important, therefore, to gradually build rapport with sources. Furthermore, regardless of whether the source explicitly outlines their concerns over the risks associated with providing access, it is important that researchers establish a transparent protocol for protecting the source's identity, which is in compliance with their own institutional and disciplinary ethical/governance requirements. Protocols should include a communications strategy. For example, employing email service providers that are protected by strong privacy laws and encryption software, can help to enhance the confidentiality of communications with sources. Similar precautions should be taken with file-sharing.

When a source of access to internal records cannot be located, a tactic known as 'shaking the tree' may be usefully employed. 'Shaking the tree' involves making a visible public intervention in a deliberate attempt to elicit contact from insider sources. This intervention might take the form of an article in a newspaper or popular blog, raising concerns over the legitimacy of a venture being investigated. It is important that the article's author is clear, including contact details where possible. A broad beacon has then been created which can fish for interest from concerned/aggrieved employees, government officials or professionals with first-hand knowledge of the events. Certainly during the Papua New Guinea fieldwork, visible news articles and blog pieces, shared through the social media, repeatedly secured direct communications from insider sources wishing to share information. Of course, when shaking the tree, the researcher will now be visible to target actors, which will likely limit any future front-door access. Accordingly, it is a tactic that is often best reserved till after all other options have been exhausted.

As with the other documentary sources surveyed so far, once internal records have been accessed, their intelligence value can be maximised by carefully coding, modelling and triangulating the data. Modelling such data on thematic, network and transactional lines not only maximises the intelligence value of internal records, it also often pollinates the value of other data sources collected during fieldwork, giving them new significance.

Elite interviews

Although the scholarly literature on investigative research methods is limited in scope, a more established body of work exists on elite interviewing, which need not be rehearsed here (see, for example, Dexter 2012; Richards 2007; Williams 2012). That said, it still should be underlined that corporate and political elites will frequently be a key source, when investigating the crimes of urbanisation.[6] And, of course, where the transactions under examination are of a distinctly illicit or illegitimate nature, there will often be a hesitancy over meeting with researchers.

Obtaining access to senior officials, therefore, is itself a challenge. Reaching out directly in a personable format can help initiate contact. Unsolicited emails, for instance, are often ignored, while interview requests sent to risk averse public relations officers may lead to a blanket denial of access. Often the ideal entry point is to secure a personal referral from a mutual acquaintance. In lieu of a personal connection, other personalised methods for initiating contact can still be utilised. For example, in the digital age sending the target official a letter in an envelope with a handwritten address is a distinctive form of communication. In some cultural contexts it may be acceptable to initiate a personal introduction at the person's office, with a view to setting up a future appointment.

Even when access is granted, the interview will generally still be a challenging situation. The subject matter being discussed, for instance, can be technical and convoluted – this is certainly the case with land frauds and illicit infrastructure projects. Furthermore, if the conduct has distinctly illegal dimensions, implicated elite actors will have strong a motivation to provide information that is designed to conceal, obscure or mislead.

That said, there are exceptions to this rule. For instance, where illicit repertoires have become habitual features of a professional environment, their deviant quality may no longer be as apparent to practitioners – leading to surprising admissions in an interview. Or it may be that the participant's impunity is so assured, there is no need to be elusive. In other instances elite actors may be prepared to acknowledge illicit transactions, but deploy techniques of neutralisation in order to contest normative definitions branding their conduct as wrong. It may also be possible that an elite actor is so aggrieved with a venture partner or former political ally, that they are prepared to divulge self-incriminating information.

In light of the various scenarios that might be faced, designing interviews in a way that helps ascertain a source's credibility is important. Indeed, researchers will frequently hear multiple, contradictory accounts. Accordingly, having reliable methods for testing which account, and source, is the most credible, can help researchers out of this impasse.

To that end, conducting the first iteration of documentary research in advance of the interview – modelled using the types of technique set out in chapter three – provides an evidentiary foundation for testing source credibility. That is, having a reliable approximation in place of the core transaction sequences, and the constellation of actors organising them, allows strategic questions to be asked. For example, open ended questions can be employed to test how forthcoming the participant is in volunteering information on certain events and transactions, which they would reasonably be expected to have knowledge of (that is, based on the documentary evidence). More direct questions may also be asked focusing on the particulars of transactions and events, in order to test whether the participant is willing to deceive the interviewer. Given that many senior state and corporate officials are skilled at image management and public relations, having clear evidence of dishonesty can help the researcher neutralise attempts to blindside the investigation.

An example of an open ended question might be: 'Can you tell me about the processes you had to navigate in order to obtain development approval from the Physical Planning Board?' The response given can then be triangulated with other oral and documentary sources, to see whether it is a credible representation of the actual processes navigated by the interviewee. Direct questions, on the other hand, will tend to have a black and white answer. For instance: 'Residents claim you are in business with the Finance Minister, do you actually have commercial links with the Minister?' Assuming the researcher has strong proof that such a relation exists, this type of question will help diagnose whether the source is prepared to lie in an interview.

Of course, regardless of the question type, diplomacy is an imperative. Accusations do not cement rapport. Even probing questions can be delivered in the spirit of politeness, and gentle inquiry. Furthermore, in those scenarios where it is clear that an interviewee is lying, openly challenging their account may not always be the best course of action. Even if their interview does not provide an accurate account of events, it nonetheless may offer important data on the narrative and framing being employed to diffuse criticism; while finishing the interview on a pleasant note may lead to the provision of assistance in the form of further contacts, or accessing certain documents.

Field experiments

It is worth noting that on occasions field experiments can play a productive role when investigating the crimes of urbanisation. They may be deployed on varying scales. In some instances field experiments may be at the core of an investigative project. An example of this is Sharman's research on secrecy jurisdictions. In order to conduct the study, Sharman (2010: 129) attempted to set up 'anonymous corporate vehicles without proof of identity' and then 'establish corporate bank accounts for these vehicles', in 22 different countries. Strict procedures were used to ensure the data was comparable. This, of course, is an example of a more onerous field experiment. It is also possible to draw on smaller-scale experiments, that act as a complement to other data collection methods.

For instance, during the Papua New Guinea research, data on potentially illicit transactions was collated and submitted to different regulatory bodies, in order to observe their reaction, and the rigour of any subsequent inquiry. To that end, a complaint was lodged with a lauded anti-corruption unit, Investigation Taskforce Sweep (ITFS). This led to a series of unexpected findings. It was discovered that an ITFS agent leaked the complaint to an executive at the centre of the submission, who then provided Sweep with exculpatory evidence, including a statement produced by one of the government agencies alleged to be complicit in the illegal transactions. A case report was then issued by

ITFS, drawing heavily on this evidence. It, in effect, cleared the companies concerned of any wrongdoing. Additionally, ITFS accused the Auditor General's Office and Public Accounts Committee of having previously conducted flawed inquiries, which were highly critical of the companies. As a result, their findings were discounted. A subsequent evaluation of ITFS's case report revealed serious errors of fact, law and methodology, that notably departed from procedures applied by Sweep in other investigations. This alerted the researcher to potentially serious institutional weaknesses within a body that was being described as the 'most successful anti-corruption agency in Papua New Guinea's history' (Cochrane 2015).

Thus, while field experiments of the type designed by Sharman will often produce significant findings, even more modest studies applying this approach can help to produce case study data that enhances diagnostic work. In addition, field experiments may also have important strategic and practical implications for those communities and organisations confronting the illicit transactions, giving them practical insights into the institutions and actors they are contending with.

Counter-research activities

When investigative research successfully illuminates opaque processes central to illegitimate or illicit activity authored by powerful individuals or entities, researchers should expect that organisational efforts will be marshalled to discredit the study. Given that the research, if rigorously executed, will be premised on robust sources, which have been carefully corroborated and triangulated, counter-research activities will tend to centre on discrediting the researcher's reputation through smear campaigns, and marshalling different forms of coercive action designed to intimidate and silence. It is important, therefore, that protocols are established which help mitigate these types of threat.

For researchers working within a bureaucratic organisation, such as a university, it is tempting to simply circumvent institutional red tape when conducting sensitive investigations. However, if the study does produce results that impinge significantly on powerful interests, it is highly likely that the researcher's institution will be a target of counter-research activities. Accordingly, it is important to secure institutional support in advance of releasing the study's findings, by ensuring relevant line-managers and legal officers have been apprised of the research, and research outputs.

A range of issues will need to be considered in consultation with institutional managers. For instance, which legal entity is formally publishing the research? What types of indemnity policy do they have? What steps can be taken to mitigate the threat of legal action? Are there other anticipated lines of attack, which require defensive measures? It is also, of course, important to ensure that the research has been conducted in conformance with the institution's research governance policy.

All of which presupposes that there are a range of ways a researcher can be targeted via their institution. It may, for instance, occur through legal threats, ethical complaints or personal smears. Furthermore, the counter-research activities may not necessarily be prosecuted directly by those seeking to silence/ discredit the study. Given that powerful state and corporate actors will often enjoy ties with esteemed individuals and bodies in a range of sectors, attacks may be delivered indirectly through institutions enjoying greater civic esteem, once removed from the affairs under investigation.

During the Papua New Guinea research, for instance, some of the most vociferous interventions came from unexpected institutions and individuals. For instance, when investigating a major property development at Paga Hill, discussed in chapter five, critique was made of ITFS – for the reasons noted above. When this critique was published, ITFS's Chairman wrote to Ulster University. He claimed that the criticism had exposed his agency 'to hatred, contempt and ridicule, causing them to be shunned, avoided or lowered in the estimation of right-thinking members of the society generally' (ITFS 2016). The letter continues, 'Dr Lasslett had an improper motive', grounded ITFS argues in 'spite, ill-will, or publication for personal gain' (ITFS 2016). The government anti-corruption agency, the letter suggests, has 'suffered and continue to suffer considerable damage/injury to their reputation' (ITFS 2016). As a result, ITFS's Chairman warns Ulster University, 'we are in the process of instructing our lawyers in the UK to take up this matter further' (ITFS 2016). In this instance there was no evidence on record to suggest that ITFS sent the letter on behalf of the developers, or their political partners.

Later in 2015, however, an injunction was taken out against a documentary film which closely covers key findings emerging from the Paga Hill research. In this instance the action was launched by Dame Carol Kidu, a widely respected human rights advocate who initially appeared in the film as a critic of the property venture. During the subsequent court hearing, it was discovered that the developer had paid Kidu's company, CK Consultancy Limited, A\$178,000 for consultancy work associated with the forced relocation of Paga Hill residents (*Carol Anne Kidu v Hollie Fifer* [2016] NSWSC 982). In addition, the developer also 'agreed to indemnify the Plaintiff [Kidu] in respect of her costs of … [the] proceedings and also has paid the [A]\$250,000.00 [in security]' (*Carol Anne Kidu v Hollie Fifer* [2016] NSWSC 982, para.45).

Personal smears are another method commonly used to discredit research. For instance, an article on the Paga Hill development was published in the *Post-Courier*, Papua New Guinea's national newspaper, in which it is implied that the author of this volume had misappropriated K100,000 in artwork produced by a prominent local artist (Pakawa 2016). During 2014, when a study was published airing community concerns over a major mining venture situated on the island of Bougainville, smear pieces were issued by the Autonomous Bougainville Government, and tied political figures, which included accusations of racism, dishonesty and Trotskyite conspiracies, directed against this author and civil society collaborators (see, for example, Autonomous Bougainville Government 2014; Pentanu 2014).

Depending on the levels of media independence, the smeared researcher may be given a right of reply. Often the best defence, particularly when attacks come from politically esteemed figures, is research rigour. Keeping the narrative firmly focused on the findings and underpinning evidence is key, ensuring that critics are forced to cite specific errors in the work. Of course, if the abuse reaches an unacceptable level, the matter is often best handled at an institutional level by the relevant legal officer.

Harassment and smears can also be delivered through anonymous emails and social media messages, including threats of violence. Certainly during the Papua New Guinea fieldwork anonymous 'trolling' occurred on social media. More worryingly a hand-written death threat was left on the office desk of a local collaborator. Needless to say, these are again moments where researchers should alert their institution.

Anticipating diverse forms of counter-research activity through a robust protocol is one method for handling these challenging situations. Additionally, the researcher can make matters more difficult for those seeking to supress their work, by also adopting a cautious communications strategy. For instance, where there is a risk that communication facilities could be hacked, using encrypted email servers, situated in jurisdictions with strong privacy laws, may help to protect confidential conversations with contacts and colleagues.

Being circumspect when composing written correspondence, making telephone calls and entering into field based conversations is also advisable, given that each communication format may be recorded, whether the researcher is aware of it or not. It is difficult to predict where or when this may occur. Indeed, the researcher will not be privy to all the complex, and often hidden ties underpinning the networks they are investigating; accordingly a cautious approach to communications is needed. This warning extends to potential allies and collaborators in the field, at least until a long-term working relationship has developed. Indeed, unexpected schisms can suddenly emerge owing to unseen political alliances or new commercial ties. The researcher needs to ensure they are not compromised in such situations, owing to a hasty moment of candidness with an initial collaborator in the field.

Therefore, to help minimise leaks which might harm the research, it is important that communications are carefully managed, keeping in mind that what is said may one day feature in a formal complaint, or legal proceedings. Furthermore, it is vital that source confidentiality is strictly maintained, and efforts are made to ensure assets and techniques being used to uncover illicit transactions – the divulgence of which may aid counter-research activities – are kept private. Additionally, all written communications, including texts, should be safely stored, in case needed on a future occasion to verify a conversation or claim.

Investigative research is a rewarding process, but clearly it does not come without challenges. Counter-research activity is often the most stressful, owing to the considerable animosity it can generate. Nevertheless, with a good support network, institutional backing and sound protocols, researchers can place themselves in a stronger position to protect the integrity of their work.

Conclusion

This chapter, and chapter three, rest on a core thesis – namely, research on the crimes of urbanisation requires robust analytical techniques, that are married to rigorous methods for sourcing credible information. In this chapter attention has primarily been focused on introducing methods which help researchers to locate, handle and process data-sources that can enhance our understanding of the networks, transactions, institutional environments, political/commercial repertoires, discourses and broader social structures which lie at the heart of the crimes of urbanisation.

Of course, there remains ample scope for further innovation, experiment and knowledge-transfer from cognate fields and professions. Indeed, it has already been noted that the methodological literature underpinning research into the crimes of the powerful remains in a nascent state. This is especially the case when we turn to economic crimes that involve complex regulatory, financial and corporate machinery, and intricate transaction sequences. Yet there remains here an opening for criminology to take the lead in systematising and deepening methodological techniques in this area, so as a discipline it is uniquely placed to produce data, and concepts, grounded in the fine pores of illicit state–corporate activity, which can inform broader efforts to tackle corruption, land-grabs, market abuse, racketeering and fraud, to name just a few examples.

In the next three chapters, case studies will be presented that demonstrate the type of intricate empirical data that emerges when the techniques and approaches presented both here, and in the previous chapter, are applied. On the basis of these intimate data-sets, a number of theoretical innovations will then be presented in chapters seven and eight, which exhibit the intimate connection that exists between method, empirical data-sets and theoretical precision. Put simply, robust methods liberate data-collection, while liberated data-collection opens up new spaces for theoretical innovation, which then fertilises the empirical data with a layer of conceptual richness, that deepens our comprehension of the structures and processes underpinning criminogenic sequences in the urban sphere.

Notes

1 For instance, since 2004 the author has conducted research into state–corporate crime within Papua New Guinea's extractive industries. This has involved interviews with elite political, bureaucratic, military and corporate actors, alongside investigative research targeting documentary sources. More recently (2009–) the author has embarked on a broader programme of research into the transnational dimensions of grand corruption

in Eurasia and the South Pacific, which has involved targeting highly opaque actors and regimes, using leaks, insider sources, forensic documentary research and novel data modelling tools. In both cases survivors and civil society have played a critical role, including as collaborators and witnesses.

2   On the other hand, proposals are in place to delete the records of dissolved companies after six years, which would be a notable step backwards for corporate transparency in the UK.

3   As a result of the uneven transparency landscape, a global campaign has emerged challenging corporate secrecy, buttressed by groups such as the Financial Transparency Coalition, Global Witness and the Tax Justice Network. For practical and political reasons, crimes of the powerful scholars have a direct stake in the success of campaigns initiated to improve the transparency and accessibility of corporate data, which are growing in the aftermath of major exposés such as the Swiss Leaks and the Panama Papers.

4   Data scraping involves the use of codes to systematically download all the information on a website. Data scraping specialists can be contracted to conduct this work.

5   In contrast, it was found that the law was enforced much more rigorously against residents contesting real-estate developments.

6   Of course, elites are not the only source for oral data on how suspect transactions sequences were organised. Particularly where a real-estate venture, or major infrastructure project has elicited resistance, community activists may have emerged with intimate insights into the networks, transactions and mechanisms employed to facilitate the venture.

Bibliography

Autonomous Bougainville Government. (2014). Letter from Chief John L. Momis, President, Autonomous Region of Bougainville, to Members of the Board, Jubilee Australia, NCCA Officers, Level 7, 379 Kent St, Sydney, NSW 2000, Australia, 2 November.

Cochrane, L. (2015). 'PNG anti-corruption taskforce broke after making allegations against prime minister Peter O'Neill', ABC News, 4 February. [Online]. Available at: www.abc. net.au/news/2015-02-04/png-anti-corruption-taskforce-starved-of-funding/6070170 (accessed: 13 February 2017).

Dexter, L. A. (2012). *Elite and Specialized Interviewing*, Colchester: European Consortium for Political Research.

Green, P., Lasslett, K. and Ward, T. (2012). 'The advance of state crime scholarship', *State Crime Journal*, 1(1), 5–7.

Investigation Taskforce Sweep. (2016). Letter from Sam Koim, Chairman Investigation Task-Force Sweep, to Professor Patrick Nixon, Vice-Chancellor & President, Room H204, Ulster University, and Professor Simon Gaskell, President and Principal, E127, Queens' Building, Queen Mary University of London, 29 February.

Lasslett, K. (2012). 'Power, struggle and state crime: Researching through resistance', *State Crime*, 1(1), 126–148.

Montague, B. and Amin, L. (2012). *FOIA Without the Lawyer: Freedom, Information and the Press*, London: Centre for Investigative Journalism.

Pakawa, D. (2016). 'Settler backs Dame Carol, denounces motive of film', *Post-Courier*, 1 April.

Pentanu, S. (2014). 'A Bougainville voice: Let not outsiders pit us against ourselves', PNG-Attitude, 7 October. [Online]. Available at: asopa.typepad.com/asopa_people/2014/10/

a-bougainville-voice-lets-not-outsiders-pit-us-against-ourselves.html (accessed: 2 March 2017).

Richards, D. (1996). 'Elite interviewing: Approaches and pitfalls', *Politics*, 16(3), 199–204.

Sharman, J. C. (2010). 'Shopping for anonymous shell companies: An audit study of anonymity and crime in the international financial system', *Journal of Economic Perspectives*, 24(4), 127–140.

Tombs, S. and Whyte, D. (eds) (2003). *Unmasking the Crimes of the Powerful*, Oxford: Peter Lang.

Whyte, D. (2012). 'Between crime and doxa: Researching the worlds of state–corporate elites', *State Crime Journal*, 1(1), 88–108.

Williams, C. (2012). *Researching Power, Elites and Leadership*, London: Sage Publications.

Cases

Carol Anne Kidu v Hollie Fifer [2016] NSWSC 982

Chapter 5

The crimes of urbanisation and megaprojects

Investigating a 'tourism city'

Introduction

On 12 May 2012, Papua New Guinea's social media broadcast pictures of demolished homes along the harbour foreshore at Paga Hill in the nation's capital Port Moresby. Displaced families could be witnessed picking through the wreckage for salvageable personal effects. As darkness fell a Port Moresby artist, Jeffry Feeger, stepped through the rubble to speak with residents, who sheltered under sheet metal and blue tarpaulins. In the dim candlelight, he filmed their story. The next day these vignettes were uploaded onto YouTube. In the videos residents condemn the destruction, which they allege was perpetrated by the Papua New Guinea state on behalf of a private developer ('Paga Hill at Night, Aftermath of Eviction' 2012).

Raw video footage of the demolition soon emerged ('Dame Carol Kidu Arrest Threat' 2012). Commanding officers from the Royal Papua New Guinea Constabulary (RPNGC) could be seen rebuffing the Member of Parliament for Moresby South, Dame Carol Kidu.[1] She had demanded a stop to the exercise, until a special National Court sitting on the matter was concluded. In a dramatic turn of events, RPNGC officers pointed assault rifles at residents and opened fire. An irate Dame Carol was frog marched from the scene. It was not uncommon for Port Moresby's residents to be violently displaced from their homes in such a manner; it was unusual for a rich multi-media footprint to be left by the destruction.

The 12 May demolition exercise was enacted to clear the way for the Paga Hill Estate, a luxury property development – which is currently under construction – that will include an integrated residential, commercial and marina complex, and a much vaunted 'six-star' hotel (www.pagahillestate.com). The project is spearheaded by the Paga Hill Development Company (PHDC), a Papua New Guinea registered firm. Its ownership and executive structure has a complex and revealing history.

Shortly before the demolition exercise, PHDC advertised its vision for Paga Hill in the national papers. The real-estate development would, they promised, 'promote a way of life not yet seen in Papua New Guinea' (PHDC 2012a). PHDC claimed:

> With tourists and visitors staying at the Hilton Hotel, residents of the site, together with city visitors enjoying the waterfront retail, restaurants and marina complex, the area will be a buzzing melting pot, creating a new image for a progressive Papua New Guinea.
>
> (2012a)

In contrast to this cosmopolitan vision for the Paga Hill Estate, PHDC's Australian based CEO, Gudmundur Fridriksson, reserved pejorative labels for the hill's residents, describing them as 'squatters and settlers and criminals' (cited in Robinson 2012a: 1). Their homes, he insisted, were 'illegal dwellings' (Fridriksson cited in Robinson 2012a: 1). 'There would not be more than three houses there that qualify as a house', Fridriksson maintained, 'it is just rocks on top of corrugated iron held down by nails. It's like Rio de Janeiro or Manila' (cited in Robinson 2012a: 1).

The developer's language echoed Papua New Guinea's colonial past. Since the first annexation of Papua New Guinea by German, British and Australian colonialists, the acquisition of land, urban development, the stimulation of commodity markets, and the emergence of public administration through state-hood, have been framed as benign efforts to modernise and civilise an archi-pelago made up of 'primitive' natives, prone to 'savage' excess (*Administration of the Territory of Papua and New Guinea v Doriga and Guba* [1973] PGHCA 1). The colonial process extolled and rehearsed at all levels an ideology that flattened the accumulated achievements and rich advances in civilisation built by Papua New Guinea's ethnically diverse rural communities. In its place was a narra-tive that implanted into the national consciousness a sense of deficit, one that frames the village as a site bereft of economic development, law and order, or the markings of modern civilisation (Barnes 1969; Donaldson and Good 1988; Hawksley 2007; McCasker 1966).

Dimensions of this framing are adeptly maintained by national politicians today, who champion a 'progressive' vision for a 'developed' and 'modern' Papua New Guinea, one that is a hub for cosmopolitan ventures and international investment, which will gradually see the country shake off a derogatory third-world title (Connell 1997; Gewertz and Errington 1999). Those who resist this forward march into development, centralised government and modernity, through drawing strength from culturally distinct values of development, bal-ance and custom, are frequently marginalised as ignorant, backward and a bar-rier to progress (Donaldson and Good 1988; Gewertz and Errington 1999).

Real-estate developers strategically navigate this complex post-colonial dynamic, where the breath of colonialism lingers. Projects such as Paga Hill Estate are seen not merely as an episode in economic speculation, they are a crucial nation-building vehicle that will precipitate economic growth, jobs and a vaunted set of urban resources that will give Papua New Guineans a share in the cosmopolitan ideal. In its promotional literature, PHDC claims Paga Hill will host a K5 billion venture, arguably making it the country's most ambitious real-estate development to date (*The National*, 21/12/2016). 'The Estate', PHDC argues, 'will bring millions [sic] in direct investment and generate a plethora of employment opportunities, both during its construction, and in its ongoing operation well into the future' (2012a). The company insists:

> Paga Hill will become a focal point of Port Moresby and set new benchmarks for development within the region. The development will also send a message to the region that PNG is a progressive country leading the region in property development initiatives.
>
> (Anvil Project Services 2003)

This particular vision of progress is congruent with a national government led largely by business figures, who adeptly frame their commercial achievements – which are often tarnished by evidence of corruption and misappropriation – as part of a more benign contribution to a process of wealth creation and development essential to making Papua New Guinea an 'advanced' nation. Perhaps not surprisingly then, in the immediate aftermath of the demolition exercise at Paga Hill, which attracted considerable censure from civil society, the Minister for Tourism, Culture and Aviation came out in support of the company. He claimed: 'The proposed Paga Hill Estate constitutes an incredibly exciting development for the city of Port Moresby and PNG … perfectly aligned to our vision of developing Port Moresby as a tourism destination and not a transit point' (cited in *Post Courier*, 25/5/2012).

To ease investor concerns over further resident resistance, the government's private real-estate arm, National Housing Estate Limited (NHEL), announced it would partner in the Paga Hill Estate (*The National*, 3/12/2012). NHEL is a notably opaque commercial vehicle charged with managing public provision of commercial housing stock. To date it has refused to open its books to the Auditor General's Office (2014), despite facing serious allegations of misappropriation. With this private–public partnership at its base, the government declared Paga Hill Estate a project of 'national significance'.[2] This gave the resistance of residents opposing the development an almost seditious air.

The questions which this chapter interrogates, centre on the land acquisition, government approval and forced eviction processes at the heart of this major public–private megaproject.[3] To that end, we will examine how a developer coalition fused and leveraged its ties, assets, resources and expertise, to 'free' one of the most lucrative land portions in the South Pacific, from a range of encumbrances that protected this unique monopoly from market speculation. Close scrutiny will be paid to the illegitimate practices organised by the coalition, which became the subject of censure for a range of movements and organisations that spanned civil society and government, a clash which generated its own criminogenic momentum. When considering the outcomes of the ensuing struggle consideration will be given to the sinews of power that ultimately allowed the developer to prevail.

Through this empirical inquiry both here, and in the next chapter, we will begin to formulate a number of generalisable approximations that link illegitimate land and property market activity, to particular social network dynamics, commercial repertoires and political practices. In so doing, a basis will be forged to theorise the dynamism that gives these networks the capacity to unilaterally transform the urban landscape, and the vulnerabilities these drives contain, that open up new avenues for resistance. To begin, however, a brief history of the land at Paga Hill will be outlined, in order to identify the historical conditions that allowed this space to be stripped of long-standing communities and its national park status to make way for a luxury estate.

Land as an exchangeable asset: the commodification of Paga Hill

At the entry to Fairfax Harbour in the nation's capital is a small peninsula that hosts Port Moresby's more salubrious commercial and residential locations. At its heart is downtown, Port Moresby's central business district, where a modest grid of office blocks and hotels jut out from the landscape. Abutting the downtown area to the south-east is Ela Beach, a prime residential location populated by heavily fortified apartment and home compounds; rents here rival New York and London. To the southwest is Paga Hill. One side of this distinctive landmark faces the city, and rounds out the upmarket residential hub that stretches from Ela Beach; the other side is hidden from the downtown gaze by Paga's steep slope.

This secluded side of Paga Hill enjoys expansive ocean views, whilst being a five-minute walk from the bustling city centre. Until 2014 it was home to two residential communities containing a demographic which contrasted with neighbouring districts, where high prices exempt all but wealthy expatriates and local elites. On Paga Hill's peak lay a National Housing Corporation (NHC) residential complex, home to approximately 400 people (*The National*, 4/4/2012). Established in 1990, among a range of other objectives, the NHC is responsible for building and leasing public housing, which is a rare, much sought after resource for the capital's civil servants and professionals in search of affordable accommodation (*National Housing Corporation Act* 1990).

Beneath the NHC complex, along the harbour foreshore, lay Paga Hill settlement, an informal neighbourhood of around 3,000 people (Moses 2012). Like so much of Port Moresby, this land at the base of Paga Hill was initially occupied by rural migrants without any formal tenure arrangement (Thomas 2010). In the face of a prohibitive formal housing sector, the creation of legally insecure, but often intricately governed neighbourhoods such as this provide a critical living space for low wage earners in the capital, seeking access to employment and public services (Goddard 2005). However, because of their informal status settlements such as Paga Hill have limited tenure rights. While the courts are reluctant to define such communities as illegal, especially when evidence exists of landowner acquiescence to the arrangement, nonetheless informal settlements have few enforceable rights when confronted with eviction (*Koitaki Farms Ltd v Kenge* [2001] PGNC 59; *Ready Mixed Concrete Pty Ltd v The State, Samana and Kiamba* [1981] PNGLR 396).

The government of Papua New Guinea is the paramount titleholder over Paga Hill. However, it has distributed to private actors a large section of the land on the hill through the vehicle of state leases, while also reserving a portion for open space.[4] The NHC housing complex and the upper part of the settlement are located on portion 1597, a 13.7 ha plot of land. Until 1999 it was zoned open space, reserved as a national park.[5] Along the harbour foreshore is 4 ha of reclaimed land. Until 2013 this land had not been surveyed, registered or leased; nonetheless it hosted a large section of the settlement, including their school and church.

Of course, the survey and delineation of Paga Hill into discrete land portions, administered through a legal regime capable of underpinning a market in state leases, is not a 'natural' phenomenon, or even one that has precedent within the tenure system developed by the region's traditional owners. It signposts, rather, a complex legacy from Papua New Guinea's colonial period.

Prior to the 1880s the Port Moresby region was owned by two closely linked ethnic groups, the Motu and Koita peoples, commonly referred to as Motu-Koita. Membership of an *iduhu* – residential groupings linked by common descent – was the source of household land rights (see Goddard 2011a, 2011b). Land could be gifted under certain circumstances, while particular use rights could be allocated by primary right holders. As in Melanesia more broadly, land for the Motu-Koita has a deep range of meanings. It is not only a vital source of social security, where houses and gardens can be built, it possesses cultural and spiritual properties that are inextricably entwined with collective and individual identity. Accordingly, in this social system land is heavily bounded by socio-cultural encumbrances which make it a poor match for markets built along capitalist lines, where these significances must be extinguished if the land is to be freely exchanged through commercial mechanisms.

Had this customary system endured, PHDC would have no claim to Paga Hill. However, significant sections of Port Moresby were stripped from the Motu-Koita tenure system, including Paga Hill, during the 1880s. The impetus for this redistribution of land was the annexation of the southern coast of New Guinea by Britain in 1888. In preparation for this, during 1886 the Queen's Special Commissioner gave colonial officials instructions to survey and acquire land for a township, which would become known as Port Moresby (see *Administration of the Territory of Papua and New Guinea v Doriga and Guba* [1973] PGHCA 1). As part of this process, Paga Hill was acquired without payment to the original owners or any formal recording of the transaction.[6]

The acquisition's lawfulness to this day remains contested by Motu-Koita descendants. Nevertheless, when the matter was heard by the High Court of Australia, on appeal, the submission of the Motu-Koita was rejected. In the lead decision Chief Justice Barwick contended 'the Papuans … were singularly savage and given to reprisal raids on one another in which barbarous killings took place, frequently of women and children who were the easiest caught or waylaid' (*Administration of the Territory of Papua and New Guinea v Doriga and Guba* [1973] PGHCA 1). In contrast to the Papuans, colonial officers were deemed by the Chief Justice, 'competent, careful and just' (*Administration of the Territory of Papua and New Guinea v Doriga and Guba* [1973] PGHCA 1). He reasoned that had these officials erred in the acquisition, it would have triggered a swift, brutal reprisal:

> As I have said, these were belligerent people given to quite savage, at times quite inhuman, acts of revenge … I just cannot conceive that a proceeding with respect to the acquisition of land, publicly carried out because of the habit of walking the bounds, could have resulted in other than carnage if the rightful claimants were not satisfied parties to the transactions.
>
> (*Administration of the Territory of Papua and New Guinea v Doriga and Guba* [1973] PGHCA 1)

It was concluded that the land tracts around Port Moresby were acquired in accordance with local tenure norms:

> I am satisfied that it was possible according to the usages of the Papuans of the Port Moresby area as understood by them in 1886 for a stranger to their clans to have acquired land from individuals as well as from groups by outright sale and purchase for value in the form of 'trade' mutually agreed.
>
> (*Administration of the Territory of Papua and New Guinea v Doriga and Guba* [1973] PGHCA 1)

Although over 125 years ago, this transaction exhibits many of the traits we witness in contemporary land-grabs. The stigmatisation of those facing dispossession through pejorative labels that frame them as a barrier to the laudable process of development and modernisation. The transfer of land, through a semblance of legality, behind which often lies more opaque forms of illicit behaviour. And the selective enforcement of the law by courts, whose procedures, rules of evidence and legal rationales favour those abusing executive power over those resisting its abuse.

Nevertheless, in Paga Hill's case the events of 1888 led to a situation where by 1997 the land was owned by the Government of Papua New Guinea, who had inherited the holdings of the colonial administration. This meant that this demarked space, which had been surveyed and registered through a land titles regime, could be alienated to private actors for up to 99 years through a state lease, providing procedures set out in the *Land Act* 1996 and the *Physical*

Planning Act 1989 were adhered to. In other words, as a result of certain decisions taken during the colonial period, temporal monopolies over the land at Paga Hill could now be circulated through a leasehold market, regulated by post-colonial legal and administrative infrastructure. However, there were two critical barriers stopping this process of market alienation from taking place with respect to Paga Hill.

First, in 1987 the Lands Minister reserved portion 1597 'from lease for the purpose of Open Space for National Parks Board'.[7] A subsequent report issued by the Public Accounts Committee observes:

> There were good reasons for this to occur. The Land is of considerable historical importance to the nation, containing as it does, Wartime Bunkers, Gun Emplacements, tunnels and, apparently, significant prehistoric sites. Further, the situation of the land in the centre of a growing city offers superior recreational facilities to the occupants of Port Moresby.
>
> (2007: 61)

Second, the top of the hill and the harbour foreshore became occupied by two distinct communities, who had resided on the hill for over 30 years. Both had developed intricate informal governance structures, which made the hidden face of Paga Hill an important sanctuary for residents, who had access to affordable accommodation with close links to critical urban centres.

Accordingly, if this space was to become a tradeable asset, free of human encumbrances, an adept coalition of economic and political actors, with ambition, resources, skills and connections, would need to reverse the 1987 proclamation, acquire title to the land, and displace its residents. We will now trace the emergence of this network, including the biography of central actors, which provides a critical insight into the commercial repertoires that would inspire and facilitate the acquisition of Paga Hill.

The developer's commercial repertoire: a corporate biography

Arguably the most significant, single individual standing behind the networking buttressing Paga Hill Estate, is PHDC's CEO, Gudmundur Fridriksson. By his own account, Fridriksson has personally invested over ten million Kina in the project (Fridriksson 2012); in addition to being the mastermind driving the development since he first formulated a vision for Paga Hill's transformation back in 1995 (Anvil Project Services 2003; Fridriksson 2012). Fridriksson's position of centrality was not an accident, it signalled an individual with a particular set of skills, resources and repertoires, that gave him the capacity and motivation to organise and maintain a network capable of garnering the political support and informal cultural resources necessary for acquiring title to Paga Hill.

Originally from Iceland, Fridriksson settled with his wife in Australia during 1996 (O'Callaghan 1996). He would eventually become a prominent member of the Australian national policy making community, specialising in indigenous welfare reform. By 2012 Fridriksson had been appointed CEO of the Cape York Institute and a Director at Cape York Partnership. Both organisations were the principal private partners in a major welfare trial for indigenous communities funded by the Commonwealth and Queensland governments.

Perhaps not surprisingly, given these senior positions, Fridriksson's corporate resume boasts experience and respectability:

> He [Gudmundur] holds a Masters Degree in Business Administration and has nearly 25 years' management experience with major projects in Europe, China, Hong Kong, Australia and Papua New Guinea. Gummi is a member of the Papua New Guinea Institute of Management, Papua New Guinea Institute of Directors, Papua New Guinea Chamber of Commerce, and the Institute of International Project Management Association.
>
> (Cape York Partnership n.d.)

All apparent markers indicate that Fridriksson enjoys the right type of symbolic and commercial esteem to legitimately spearhead a project such as the Paga Hill Estate. Certainly throughout his ascendency in the policy making world, it appears no one had questioned or probed Fridriksson's distinguished resume. Yet employing the methodological techniques set out in chapters three and four, a process of biographical inquiry yielded data suggestive of a more complex backstory, featuring practices and techniques that had seen Fridriksson censured by a range of public oversight bodies, in addition to commercial actors and journalists.

Initial attempts to verify Fridriksson's corporate resume uncovered apparent inaccuracies. When contacted, the Papua New Guinea Institute of Directors claimed, 'we have never heard or come across anyone of that name. His claims that he is a member of the Institute are false and we hope that he ceases calling himself a member of the Institute' (PNG Institute of Directors 2012). Papua New Guinea's Chamber of Commerce maintained they did not have an individual membership.

These were not the only examples where preliminary inquiries yielded information that raised questions over Fridriksson's credibility. For example, as local opposition grew to the company's ambitions in Port Moresby, a partnership with Hilton Hotels – a potent symbol of western cosmopolitanism – was prominently featured in PHDC's corporate announcements (*Post-Courier*, 5/4/2012). When Hilton Hotels were approached to confirm this partnership, a public relations officer stated:

> I can confirm that Hilton Worldwide does not have an agreement to operate a Hilton Hotel & Resort with the developer of Paga Hill Estate. We

have asked the developer to remove any references to Hilton Hotels & Resorts in their marketing material.

(Hilton Worldwide 2012)

This offered *prima facie* evidence that certain aspects of the company's pitch for Paga Hill had been concocted or embellished, to buttress perceptions that it was a credible agent for building a 'progressive' Papua New Guinea. Deeper inquiry into Fridriksson's past offered critical insight into the origins of the repertoires being employed by PHDC in this respect.

His first significant public footprint was made in 1992 when Fridriksson's Icelandic company Sjónval, allegedly spearheaded an ambitious project to build a liquorice factory in China. Writing in the Icelandic newspaper *The Press*, it was reported by Jónsson (1992) that Sjónval had:

> announced that the production would be released onto the market in China but that first it would be necessary to teach the Chinese to eat liquorice! Markets would also be captured in many parts of the world, particularly in the USA.

(Jónsson 1992)

However, before this optimistic commercial strategy could be realised, Jónsson claims Fridriksson left the company; it was subsequently headed by a 'hot-dog seller from Akureyri' (Jónsson 1992). During this period, Fridriksson is also alleged to have imported '10,000 pairs of counterfeit Levi's jeans' which were impounded by Icelandic police (Jónsson 1992). However, Jónsson (1992) claims no charges were laid for want of evidence proving intent.

Shortly after the Sjónval feature, Fridriksson again made headlines, this time in *The South China Morning Post*, a respected Hong Kong newspaper. It was revealed that the proprietors of a five star Hong Kong hotel, and landlords at the Fairview Park apartments, were both suing Fridriksson for alleged unpaid tariffs and rents, amounting to HKD $425,000 (approx. US$54,500) (Laxton and Cheung 1993: 3; Ng and Wan 1993: 4). It was during his extended stay in Hong Kong that Fridriksson met Tauhura Asigau, an Air Nuigini hostess. The coupled married and established a company in Port Moresby, Destination Papua New Guinea.[8]

Destination Papua New Guinea turned heads in the national business community when the company secured a lucrative contract with the government to publish a book celebrating the twentieth anniversary of Papua New Guinea's independence. The deal was scrutinised by three respected regional correspondents, Sean Dorney (Australian Broadcasting Commission), Mary-Louise O'Callaghan (*The Australian*) and Rowan Callick (*The Australian Financial Review*).

Part of the controversy surrounded Tauhura Fridriksson's familial connections. O'Callaghan (1996) alleged: 'Mrs [Tauhura] Fridriksson is a relative of

Professor Renagi Lohia, who was chief-of-staff of the Prime Minister's Office of Sir Julius Chan, at the time Cabinet awarded the job'. Dorney uncovered that Cabinet had agreed to pay Destination Papua New Guinea K2.5 million (approx. US$1.92 million), for the book. According to Dorney (1996b) industry experts liberally estimated the market value of such a project at K500,000. When Professor Renagi Lohia was asked why the government agreed to a contract which was five times the estimated market rate, he remarked '[w]ho knows what these things cost?' (cited in Dorney 1996b).

O'Callaghan (1996) claims the book arrived five months late, 'sans its leather-bound and embossed cover, lacking captions for most of its badly reproduced photographs and full of sloppy mistakes' (see also Dorney 1996a). Despite these alleged issues, Fridriksson received a letter from the Minister for State, Arnold Marsipal, commending the book as the 'best recorded script of our last 20 years of our socio-economic and political system' (cited in Dorney 1996a). While politicians may have been supportive of the company, Papua New Guinean civil servants were apparently reluctant to action the K2.5 million payment, 'because proper tender procedures had not been followed' (Dorney 1996c). Faced with a significant barrier, Dorney alleges Destination Papua New Guinea 'signed a contract with a member of the Finance Minister's personal staff (he's since been sacked) offering him a percentage of the Government's contract price if he could help ensure the money was paid' (Dorney 1996c).

During the Destination Papua New Guinea affair, Fridriksson formulated his initial vision for Paga Hill. Having seen a prime landmark blighted by what he viewed as mismanagement and misuse, Fridriksson (2012) claims he felt there was an opportunity to create an urban icon all Papua New Guineans could enjoy. In Fridriksson's (2012) estimation the vision he had for Paga Hill was primarily about building a legacy for Papua New Guinea that his children could be proud of – commercial considerations were a secondary matter. Enacting this vision was given forward momentum by a chance event in Australia.

Following the considerable acrimony precipitated by the Destination Papua New Guinea affair, the Fridrikssons relocated to Cairns in Australia's north-east (O'Callaghan 1996). One of their new neighbours was Byron Patching, a corporate executive who worked for a major international property developer, Jones Lang Wootton. According to his resume, Patching had experience of 'major property and infrastructure developments in the South East Asia and South Pacific Rim' (Anvil Project Services 2003: 19). Having learnt of Patching's involvement in the property development industry, Fridriksson knocked on his door, and pitched his idea for Paga Hill over drinks (PHDC Official 2014).[9]

In Patching's view the project was feasible if the real-estate development could acquire political support at senior levels in Papua New Guinea, and an appropriate long-term tenure arrangement on financial grounds that would entice international investment (PHDC Official 2014). Demonstrating his political reach in Papua New Guinea, Fridriksson arranged a roundtable meeting between Patching and some of the country's most senior statesmen (PHDC Official 2014). The project's early vital signs were enough to fuse Patching's commitment to the project, with the backing of Jones Lang Wootton. This opened up to Fridriksson a wide range of commercial networks, resources and expertise, which once coupled to his political reach in Papua New Guinea, constituted a powerful conglomeration of forces buttressing a bid for Paga Hill.

Patching and Fridriksson also secured a local partner for the project, Ram Business Consultants Limited (Ram), who could undertake administrative legwork in Port Moresby (PHDC Official 2014). At the time, Ram was owned and managed by two businessmen from Papua New Guinea's Enga region,[10] Rex Paki and Ango Wangatau.[11] It was Rex Paki in particular who became a prime mover in the Paga Hill Estate during the project's early days.

Paki is a successful businessman in his own right who has accumulated indicia of centrality and prestige within corporate, civil society and political circles. For example, Paki has been appointed to the boards at the Bank of PNG, the PNG Sustainable Development Programme, the Civil Aviation Authority, and the University of Technology (Papua New Guinea Sustainable Development Program 2012). He also acted as the National Alliance Party's Highlands campaign manager, a party which led a governing coalition from 2002 to 2011 under the leadership of Prime Minister Somare.

On the other hand, his career has also prompted serious allegations, levelled by a range of key government organs. For instance, Paki featured prominently in the Commission of Inquiry into the National Provident Fund. The Commission concluded that Paki was party to a complex fraud, which he allegedly benefited from through charging excessive fees (Barnett 2002). Paki has also been reprimanded by the National and Supreme Court of Papua New Guinea, when he was sued for allegedly overcharging Motor Vehicle Insurance Limited by K792,512 (approx. US$213,000), as liquidator. The Supreme Court described Paki as 'evasive and dishonest' (*Paki v Motor Vehicle Insurance Ltd* [2010] PGSC 2, para.29). The Public Accounts Committee also found cause on two occasions to censure him for alleged illegal activities involving Ram (Public Accounts Committee 2006, 2007). During this approximate period, Ram was criticised by another Commission of Inquiry – into the Investment Corporation of Papua New Guinea – for failing to observe 'international standards on auditing' and neglecting its 'contractual obligations with the Auditor General when they undertook consultancy work' (Sawong 2007: 475). Like Fridriksson, Paki's business dealings are suggestive of a corporate figure with extensive political and commercial reach, who applies this power to establish highly profitable commercial ventures, that subsequently generate controversy owing to the inflated price charged, and the means through which these lucrative deals have been secured.

During the early phase of the Paga Hill development, the relationship between Fridriksson and Paki extended beyond this property deal, after

Fridriksson began working for Ram Business Consultants (Auditor General's Office 2005). During Fridriksson's tenure at the company, Ram was appointed by Papua New Guinea's Attorney General, Michael Gene, to both investigate allegations of corruption within the Office of the Public Curator, and modernise its accounting and filing systems (Auditor General's Office 2005; Public Accounts Committee 2006). The Public Curator's Office acts as a trustee for deceased estates in Papua New Guinea where there is either no will, or where there is no available executor.

Ram was paid K1,561,062 (approx. US$700,000) for 18 months' work between 1998 and 2000. Subsequently, during 2005–2006 the Public Accounts Committee initiated an inquiry into the office, after receiving 'a large number of very serious allegations of misconduct' (Public Accounts Committee 2007: 16). The Auditor General's Office (2005) assisted the inquiry by conducting a special investigation. Ram initially blocked the tabling of the special investigation report through an *ex parte* court order. However, this was subsequently overturned by the National Court (*Post-Courier*, 7/10/2005).

According to this special investigation report produced by the Auditor General the contract was awarded to Ram without public tender – which is required under the *Public Finances (Management) Act* 1995 – furthermore, there was no written contract, or certification of invoices (Auditor General's Office 2005). The hourly rate charged by Ram was also deemed 'excessive' (Auditor General's Office 2005: 45). The Auditor General observes, '[o]f particular concern must be that after eighteen months of paying for services of RAM the only result that could be reported to the Public Curator was a small amount of computer equipment' (Auditor General's Office 2005: 46).

On 12 May 2000, the Ram Business Consultants contract was revoked. The Acting Public Curator, Gamoga Jack Nouairi 'directed that all RAM staff depart by 6 June 2000' (Auditor General's Office 2005: 43). He then 'commenced negotiations with Anvil Project Services to provide similar advice and services' (Auditor General's Office 2005: 43). The Auditor General's report goes on to observe, 'Mr [Gudmundur] Fridriksson and Mr Ivan Demetrius, resigned from RAM Business Consultants shortly before May 2000 and along with several other expatriates formed Anvil Project Services in both Australia and PNG' (Auditor General's Office 2005: 53). Thus according to the Auditor General, Gudmundur Fridriksson left Ram and set up a company, which subsequently was awarded a contract to provide similar services to his previous employer, whose contract was cancelled on 12 May 2000.

Company registration documents held by the Investment Promotion Authority, indicate Anvil (PNG) Project Services Limited was formally incorporated in April 2001 and ceased operating during June 2005.[12] Notably its Directors were Gudmundur Fridriksson and Gamoga Jack Nouairi, the Acting Public Curator who 'commenced negotiations with Anvil Project Services' (Auditor General's Office 2005: 43). Looking to the shareholdings, Anvil (PNG) Project Services Limited was jointly owned by Asigau (PNG) Holdings

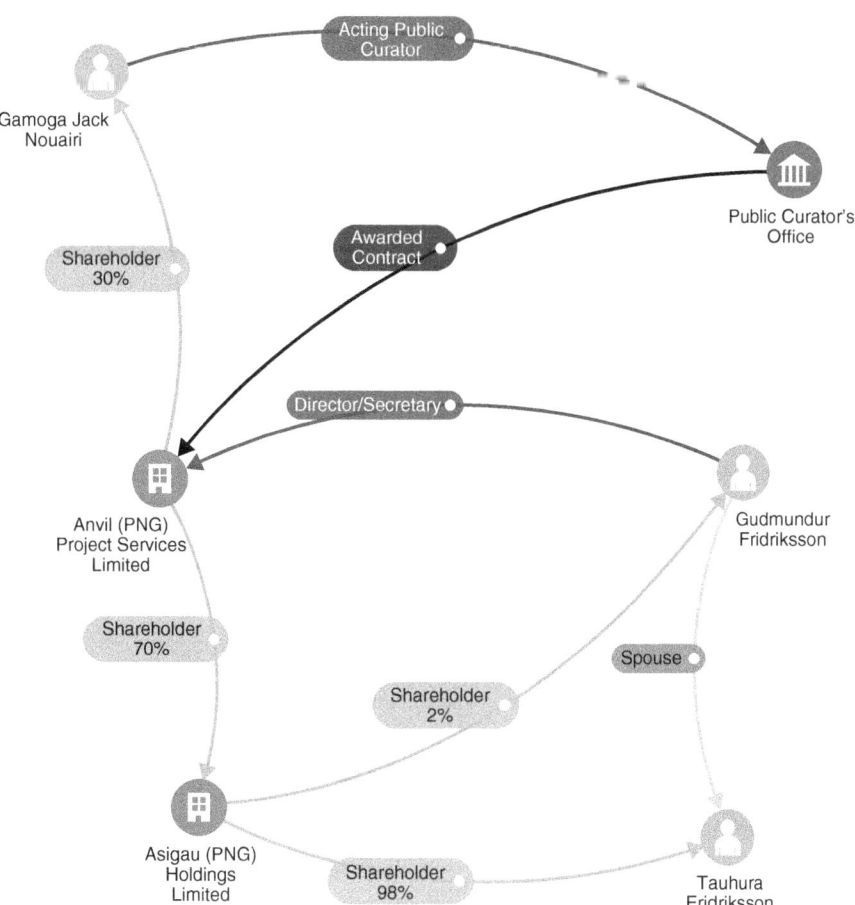

Figure 5.1 Anvil (PNG) Project Services Limited ownership structure

Limited (70%) and Gamoga Jack Nouairi (30%).[13] A search of Asigau (PNG) Holdings' share registry shows this company was owned by Gudmundur Fridriksson and his wife.[14] It would, therefore, appear Nouairi jointly owned with the Fridrikssons a private company that benefited from his public role as Acting Public Curator. In addition to their shared stake in Anvil (PNG) Project Services, the Fridrikssons and Gamoga Jack Nouairi owned and administered two other companies, Anvil Legal Services Limited and Anvil Commodities and Trading Limited.[15] It can be reasonably inferred this was a tightly knit commercial relationship (see Figure 5.1).

Like Destination Papua New Guinea, Anvil (PNG) Project Services received high praise for its work at the Public Curator's Office. Gamoga Nouairi's successor claimed the company had rectified 'years of neglect and mismanagement', often 'working for many months without payment' (Wagun cited in CCS Anvil n.d.). The Public Accounts Committee and Auditor General's Office, however, formed a more critical view of the arrangements. According to the Auditor General, on several successive occasions the Public Curator's Office attempted to have contracts with Anvil formally validated by the Central Supply and Tenders Board (CSTB) (Auditor General's Office 2005). This would allow payment for services rendered to be made from public funds. To validate the contracts, the CSTB was asked to retrospectively approve the agreements by issuing a certificate of inexpediency. The latter is an exceptional measure that allows the government to bypass the mandated public tendering process. In this case, the Public Curator's request was unlawful. Certificates of inexpediency are reserved for emergency situations, and a request for one must be made in advance of a contract being awarded (see *Robmos Ltd v Punangi* [2008] PGNC 70). Neither requirement was met here.

This strict public tender requirement – save for exceptional circumstances – is designed to combat 'the problem of corruption and misuse of public fund' (*State v Barclay Brothers (PNG) Ltd* [2001] PGNC 134). The state, in this respect, is a unique consumer whose officials apply funds on behalf of the public, for goods and services designed to benefit the latter. Given that we are talking about large, collectively consumed assets and services, these transactions can be sizable. Public tender procedures act as a safeguard designed to ensure officials make choices in observance with the principles of market discipline, value for money and avoiding conflicts of interest.

In this instance, the CSTB rightly refused all requests to issue the certificate of inexpediency. Nevertheless, the Public Curator's Office and Anvil (PNG) Project Services proceeded with the contract (Auditor General's Office 2005; Public Accounts Committee 2006). According to the Auditor General, K5,120,464 (approx. US$1.65 million) was paid to Anvil for consultancy services (Auditor General's Office 2005). The Auditor General also notes, with concern, that a large amount of money belonging to private estates appears to have been retained by Anvil (PNG) Project Services (Auditor General's Office 2005).

In a subsequent investigation conducted by Papua New Guinea's multilateral anti-corruption agency, Investigation Taskforce Sweep (ITFS), details were disclosed which potentially explain how the Public Curator circumvented the CSTB's decision. Drawing on information provided by the Public Curator's Office, ITFS (2014) note that when access to public funds was blocked by the CSTB the Public Curator's Office used its powers under the *Public Curator Act* 1951. Drawing on these trustee powers, the office allegedly expropriated assets from private estates to fund the contract with Anvil (PNG) Project Services Limited (ITFS 2014). Perhaps not surprisingly then the Public Accounts Committee (2006: 80) concluded 'the retainer [sic] of Anvil by the Public Curator was riddled by illegalities and an unlawful waste of Estate monies'.[16]

Yet, this is not the only occasion that a consultancy firm operated by Fridriksson has come under scrutiny for participating in questionable transactions. For example, in 2002 he set up a second consultancy company, CCS Anvil, which was managed with Byron Patching, a key collaborator in the Paga Hill Estate.[17] Later the business would include a young Australian graduate, George Hallit, who was brought in to help expand the company's IT expertise. CCS Anvil was awarded a number of high profile contracts. For instance, it was allocated K250,000 by the regional member of parliament for the National Capital District, Bill Skate,[18] to project manage a proposed fun park at Ela Beach (*Post-Courier*, 16/4/2003, p.1). Fridriksson assured the media it would become an iconic entertainment venue, noting it had already attracted strong investor interest. The project never materialised.

CCS Anvil also won a tender to head the National Parliamentary Efficiency Project. The project courted criticism in national media reports, when it was alleged that one of CCS Anvil's consultants was being 'paid K20,000 a fortnight almost three times the Prime Minister's salary' (*Post-Courier*, 25/4/2003, p.4). This move was again defended by Bill Skate who was Parliamentary Speaker at the time (*Post-Courier*, 13/5/2003, p.2). When the Public Accounts Committee (2003: 13) examined the arrangement, it found 'the payment of K375,779 to CCS Anvil had exceeded the original tender price of K200,000 and also exceeded the financial delegate limit for the Clerk of K300,000 Parliament set at by the Parliamentary Service Act'.

The last public forum featuring CCS Anvil centred on the Commission of Inquiry into the Department of Finance. Evidence tendered during the inquiry alleged CCS Anvil had aided a litigant to substantially inflate a compensation claim against the state – condemned as 'fraud' in the final report – in return for K1.4 million in payments (Davani et al. 2009: 267; see also Commission of Inquiry into the Department of Finance 2009).

However, around 2005 CCS Anvil's footprint disappears from Papua New Guinea. It was over this approximate period that Fridriksson's commercial interests begin to gravitate towards Australia's Cape York region (Fridriksson n.d.). Here he ascended to a number senior policy making posts, funded through public–private partnerships. During this period of ascendency in Australia, Fridriksson oversaw attempts to remove Paga Hill's residents as PHDC's CEO.

Before we return to PHDC, and the methods it employed to acquire and clear the land, a number of observations can be made about Fridriksson's commercial repertoire, which are echoed to an extent in the working methods of Rex Paki. Critically, from the evidence examined, it appears that Fridriksson regularly targets investment opportunities that do not necessarily have any connection with the technical expertise he may possess (in contrast, Paki tends to focus on opportunities more directly related to his financial and accountancy background). From liquorice factories, through to book publishing, project management, corporatisation services, property development and legal advisory services, this heterogeneous mix of ventures suggest an indifference to the project's technical content. Instead what appears to make these opportunities an attractive prospect – according to the evidence cited above – is certain speculative features they possess. Critically, pathways exist to circumvent

Table 5.1 Paga Hill Estate executives and their links to public inquiries

Company and personnel	Inquiry citations
Paga Hill Land Holding Company (1996–2009) Rex Paki – Director/Shareholder Gudmundur Fridriksson – Director Fidelity Management Pty Ltd* – Shareholder *Fidelity Management Pty Ltd is a Perth based holding company, which shared a registered address with Mr Gudmundur Fridriksson.	Public Accounts Committee Report to Parliament on the Inquiry into the Department of Lands and Physical Planning (2007)

Paga Hill Development Company (PNG) Limited (2000–Current)
Fidelity Management Pty Ltd* – Shareholder (2000–2005)
Gudmundur Fridriksson – Chief Executive Officer, Director and Shareholder** (2005–2009)
George Hallit – Chief Operations Officer
Stanley Liria – Director/Shareholder
Michael Nali – Shareholder (2011–2016)***
  * Fidelity Management Pty Ltd is a Perth based holding company, which shared a registered address with Mr Gudmundur Fridriksson.
  ** Through Anvil Holdings Limited and Palimb Holdings Limited
*** Through Kwadi Inn
	Public Accounts Committee Report to Parliament on the Inquiry into the Department of Lands and Physical Planning (2007)

Anvil (PNG) Project Services Limited (2001–2005) Gudmundur Fridriksson – Director/ Shareholder* Gamoga Jack Nouairi – Director/ Shareholder *Through Asigau (PNG) Holdings Limited	Auditor General's Office, Special Investigation into the Office of the Public Curator (2005) Public Accounts Committee Report to Parliament on the Inquiry into the Office of the Public Curator (2006)
CCS Anvil (PNG) Limited (2002–Current) Gudmundur Fridriksson – Director/ Shareholder* George Hallit – Shareholder** *Through Anvil Holdings Limited and Palimb Holdings Limited **Through Anvil Holdings Limited	Report of the Public Accounts Committee on the Parliamentary Services (2003) Auditor General's Office, Special Investigation into the Office of the Public Curator (2005) Public Accounts Committee Report to Parliament on the Inquiry into the Office of the Public Curator (2006) Report of the Auditor General on the Sepik Highway Roads and Bridges Maintenance and Other Infrastructure Trust Account (2006)

Table 5.1 (cont.)

Company and personnel	Inquiry citations
	Public Accounts Committee Report to Parliament on the Inquiry into the Sepik Highway, Roads and Bridges Maintenance and Other Infrastructure Trust Account (2007) Commission of Inquiry into the Department of Finance (2009)
Ram Business Consultants Rex Paki – Director/Shareholder Gudmundur Fridriksson – Former Employee* *According to the Auditor General's Office (2005) Mr Fridriksson left Ram Business Consultants shortly before May 2000 to set up Anvil (PNG) Project Services Limited	Commission of Inquiry into the National Provident Fund (2002) Auditor General's Office, Special Investigation into the Office of the Public Curator (2005) Public Accounts Committee Report to Parliament on the Inquiry into the Office of the Public Curator (2006) Commission of Inquiry into the Management of the Investment Corporation of Papua New Guinea and the Investment Corporation Fund of Papua New Guinea and all Matters Relating to the Conversion of the Investment Corporation Fund of Papua New Guinea to Pacific Balanced Fund, (2007) Commission of Inquiry into the Department of Finance (2009)

market competition, commercial pricing mechanisms and public governance, allowing the beneficiary company concerned to generate extremely high rates of profit.

Which is not to say these are enterprises devoid of skills, rather the skill lies in navigating complex fields of power, to secure the coalitions and approvals needed to make the venture happen. For instance, strategic vision is required to identify paths of influence, in both the political and commercial world, essential to securing requisite approvals and investment. This must be combined with the daring and drive to fuse together into a cohesive implementing subgroup, key actors at critical nodal points in the network. The adhesives that fuse actors together can be multiple, ranging from kinship ties through to financial incentives.

Certainly in the instances noted above, the subgroups concerned appear to have possessed the right bonds and characteristics to facilitate transaction chains capable of circumventing, to a degree, market competition, commercial pricing mechanisms and public governance. In a number of cases this led to serious allegations being levelled that the arrangements were illegal, with evidence of fraud and corruption being cited.

The speculative character of these investments, with their dependence on personal pathways of influence, also made them somewhat vulnerable to fracture. In one instance, for example, a large contract awarded to Ram Business Consultants – strongly condemned by the Public Accounts Committee – was rescinded, shortly after Fridriksson departed Paki's firm, only to set up a rival company, who secured a similar contract, initiated by a public official with a stake in the venture.

To justify these often controversial arrangements, the emerging networks proved adept at promoting a public face that extolled the project's legitimacy, and the professionalism of those driving it, even if the final asset proved elusive or of poor quality. While a range of authoritative reports issued by a number of oversight agencies have of course condemned these arrangements, they do not appear to have seriously impeded the activities. This would suggest informal networks of influence give actors greater influence over government in Papua New Guinea, versus formal lines of authority.

With that in mind, for a range of reasons, it can by hypothesised that Papua New Guinea's land and property market, as a field of practice, is congruent with the commercial habitus outlined above. For instance, as we noted in chapter one, some of the most lucrative landed assets in the country are distributed through the vehicle of long-term state leases, which are meant to be allocated by the Department of Lands and Physical Planning in conformity with provisions set out in the *Land Act* 1996, the *Physical Planning Act* 1989, in addition to other overlapping laws and regulations. These provisions are ostensibly designed to ensure land is allocated in ways that maximise the social use of space – in conformity with urban plans – while at the same time providing the state with an important revenue stream. However, if these provisions and associated processes can be circumvented to an extent, beneficiaries have the potential to acquire landed assets with high rental yields at a discounted price. This differential can facilitate land speculation, or it could be leveraged to improve the rate of return on property developments. Increasing the likelihood of such practices, the Department of Lands and Physical Planning has systemically demonstrated a willingness to ignore statutory processes, in the interests of private speculators (Davani et al. 2009; Numapo 2013; Public Accounts Committee 2007). However, again to achieve these types of outcome, lines of influence must be identified and enacted.

At first glance then, actors such as Paki and Fridriksson appear, from the evidence cited above, to enjoy skillsets which would place them in a strong position to take advantage of the institutional weaknesses within the Lands Department, to obtain high value leasehold titles at a discounted rate, under favourable operating conditions. Although neither actor boasts a wealth of experience in the property development sector, they have relevant professional expertise that could allow them to exploit the speculative potential latent in Papua New Guinea's land and property markets. On that note, we will now scrutinise the social relationships and associated transactions that ultimately saw PHDC acquire long-term leasehold title over Paga Hill, an area which had originally been designated a national park. This will lay the foundation for considering the broader struggle this acquisition precipitated, focusing of course on its criminogenic dimensions.

The acquisition of Paga Hill

The first steps which initiated the transaction chain that would eventually see a leasehold title over Paga Hill awarded to PHDC, began with the formulation of the Paga Hill Estate vision by Gudmundur Fridriksson. This appears to have taken place soon after he relocated to Port Moresby with his wife Tauhura during 1994/95. Then in 1996 Fridriksson formed ties with Byron Patching and Ram Business Consultants through its principal, Rex Paki.

The Paga Hill Land Holding Company (PHLHC) became the first corporate vehicle for this collaborative venture. The company was incorporated on 14 June 1996.[19] Both Fridriksson and Rex Paki acted as company Directors. The company had three shareholders, Rex Paki, Felix Leyagon and Fidelity Management Pty Ltd. The latter vehicle was owned by individuals based at a Perth accountancy firm in Western Australia.[20] This firm was apparently used to handle Fridriksson and Patching's interest in the company (PHDC Official 2014).[21] Initially PHLHC's Company Secretary was Tauhura Fridriksson, however, she was replaced in 1 July 1998 by Rex Paki, which signals the latter's centrality at this stage in the project.

As a prefatory step to gaining title over Paga Hill, PHLHC needed to instigate a rezoning of the land from open space to a form congruent with the proposed state lease. Accordingly, PHLHC's proposal for Paga Hill was pitched to the National Capital District Physical Planning Board, which was mandated with responsibility under the *Physical Planning Act* 1989 for approving development plans and rezoning land in Port Moresby. When considering applications in Papua New Guinea, planning boards have a legal duty to consider the broader social benefits of the proposal, and its potential impact on the urban environment. To that end, the National Court has emphasised the importance of consultation and public participation under the *Physical Planning Act*:

> The development and zoning of land are not simply matters affecting only a particular piece of land and its owner. The Act designates these matters as being of National importance and prescribes a code of practice to ensure transparency and public participation in the development of land.
>
> (*Steamships Trading Company Ltd v Minister For Lands and Physical Planning*
> [2000] PGNC 11)

The principles alluded to here by the National Court signal the fact that unlike some forms of production and commodity exchange, land alienated for a property development has the potential to directly impact upon the commercial, social and environmental interests of a wider set of stakeholders not involved in the transaction. Urban planning laws and land regulations, in this light, become machinery governments can employ to mediate interests and stimulate forms of urban transformation that bulwark overarching policy objectives. However, given the powerful interests and antagonisms bound up in change to the built environment, urban governance in reality is an intensive site of struggle, which is open to elite capture in ways that often depend on hidden modes of decision making and resource allocation.

PHLHC's initial planning proposal for Paga Hill was rejected. On 11 November 1996, the Physical Planning Board Chairman, Bill Skate, wrote to the company outlining the reasons behind their decision:

> (i) The proposal was a last minute submission to the Board and the members were not given enough time to assess the proposal critically. (ii) Proper procedures in relation to the processing of Planning applications were not followed. (iii) The Planners were not given time to properly assess the development.
>
> (National Capital District Physical Planning Board 1996)

In response to the decision, PHLHC began soliciting support for the project from a range of government departments, in addition to influential members of Cabinet. The Minister for Civil Aviation, Culture and Tourism, Michael Nali, became a critical patron of the project. On 27 February 1997 he wrote to PHLHC stating:

> It give [sic] me pleasure to confirm my full support to your proposed comprehensive mixed use development of Paga Hill … I am prepared to sponsor a submission to the National Executive Council [Cabinet] next month to have the project endorsed as a property of National Significance. It deserves the full support of Papua New Guinea.
>
> (Minister for Civil Aviation, Culture and Tourism 1997)

Company records suggest that PHLHC's relationship with Michael Nali was not at arm's length (see Figure 5.2). At the time this offer of support was issued, Michael Nali jointly owned, with Mary Nali, the company Waim No. 54 Limited. This concern shared a registered address with PHLHC, while its Directors were Rex Paki and Felix Leyagon, both PHLHC shareholders.[22] Subsequently in 2011, Nali would go on to acquire a 9% stake in the Paga Hill Estate – via his company Kwadi Inn Limited – after he lost office.[23]

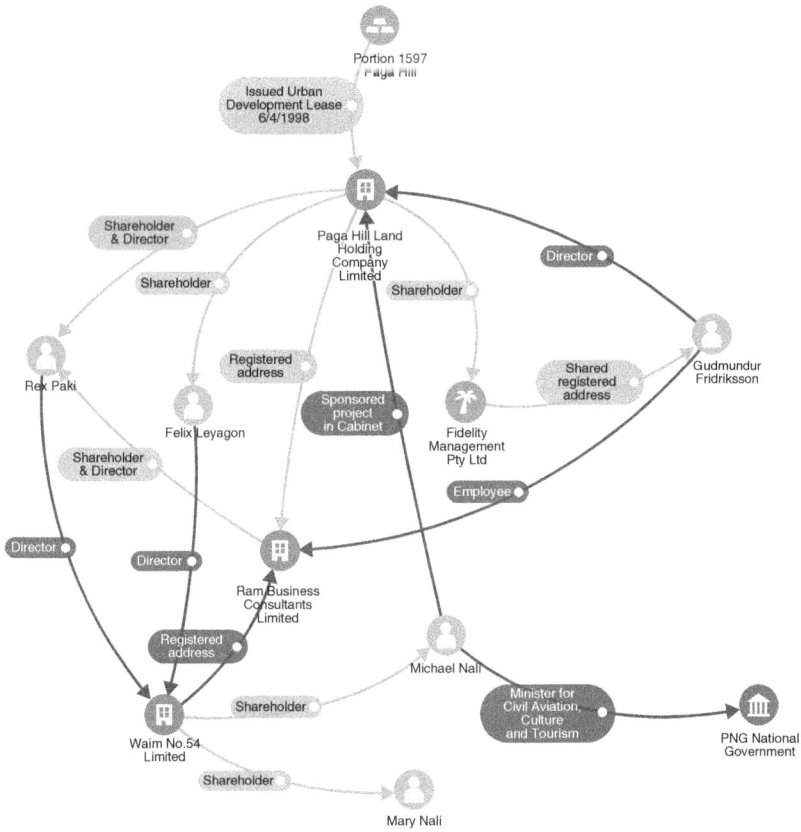

Figure 5.2 The Paga Hill Land Holding Company Limited commercial network

As this period of consultation and coalition building proceeded, Paga Hill's residents factored little into the deliberations. For example, in an exchange with the Department of Environment and Conversation, PHLHC state:

> Currently … the area is blighted with squatters and illegal uses, the war heritage sites have not been restored and the lookout points are not accessible or desirable to the general public … The proposal is to transfer ownership of the land to the Paga Hill Land Holding Company which would master plan the commercially viable development of the site.
>
> (PHLHC 1997)

In reply, the Minister for Environment and Conservation (1997) agreed, 'the proposal to comprehensively develop the site is a good solution to the squatting problem provided that the Department for Environment and Conservation is consulted during the master planning process'. The pejorative labelling of residents as squatters was inaccurate; residents in fact had a mixture of legal and equitable occupancy rights.

Once PHLHC successfully obtained departmental support and Cabinet sponsorship, an Urban Development Lease was finally issued to the company on 6 April 1998, following a Land Board hearing.[24] The lease included a series of covenants requiring the developer to conserve heritage sites, compensate the National Housing Corporation, produce a masterplan and obtain formal approvals from a number of state agencies. Annual rent was set at K30,000 (appox. US$16,500), which is 1% of the land's unimproved value. A mandatory improvement covenant was also inserted, 'to a minimum value of Three Hundred Million Kina (K300,000,000.00) [approx. US$165,000,000]. The structural construction shall commence within five (5) years from the date of grant and after fulfilment of conditions'.[25] The completion of these covenants would allow PHLHC to obtain a 99-year state lease over the site.

At the time the Urban Development Lease was issued, the area it covered was still zoned as open space. This presented a legal problem. PHLHC acknowledged that the arrangement breached the letter of the *Land Act* 1996 (s67), nonetheless, the company maintained their approach was 'consistent with the spirit of the legislation'. In the project's masterplan, PHLHC (1998: 25) observe:

> The application process for an Urban Development Lease, which would normally be required by the Land Act 1996 and the Physical Planning Act of 1989, has been altered in order to provide for the best development outcome for the Paga Hill site. None of the requirements of the existing process will be excluded, rather the timing of application and approval has been altered to provide for a more flexible and intuitive approach to the development of the site.[26]

However, PHLHC fail to identify legal provisions which would exempt them from the sequencing set out in the *Land Act* 1996 (the courts have adopted a strict compliance approach, see *Kalem v Yumi Yet Trading* [2016] PGNC 278). In a subsequent investigation into the Department of Lands and Physical Planning, the Public Accounts Committee (2007: 65) raises other concerns over the award to PHLHC:

> i) There was no quorum at the original Land Board. The Solicitor General advised the Department of Lands that the Grant of the Lease was illegal for this reason, but the Department ignored the advice. ii) The Land Board could not have been reasonably satisfied that the applicant could raise K300 million in five years. Indeed, the Committee finds that the Lessee cannot pay the Land Rental and has sought relief from that obligation,

much less fund a development of the magnitude required. iii) The land was a National Park zoned Open Space.

The Land Board Chair was Ralph Guise, an official subsequently censured by the Commission of Inquiry into the National Provident Fund (NPF) for 'fabricating and gazetting false documents, preparing and signing false Land Board minutes and signing false and fictitious approvals' (Barnett 2002). According to the Commission of Inquiry, both Guise and the Lands Minister, Viviso Seravo, were 'bribed' to ensure a company, Waim No.92, was granted a lease over prime Port Moresby land 'cheaply and on favourable conditions' (Barnett 2002).

This is noteworthy not only because these officials were in position when the Urban Development Lease was awarded to PHLHC – which in itself raises governance concerns – but also because there were direct ties between Waim No.92 and those standing behind PHLHC.

According to the Commission of Inquiry, Waim No.92 Limited was owned by Phillip Mamando and Philip Eludeme, who it argues were proxy shareholders for Jimmy Maladina, Chairman of the National Provident Fund (Barnett 2002).[27] The conspiracy, according to the Commission of Inquiry, was to acquire land at Waigani for a discounted price and then sell it to the National Provident Fund for an inflated sum. To that end, Eludeme is alleged to have acted as a key fixer: 'Prior to the Land Board hearing, Mr Eludeme had approached Minister Seravo seeking favourable consideration for Waim No. 92's application and, at Mr Seravo's request, had performed, free of charge, accountancy services for Minister Seravo valued at K100,000' (Barnett 2002). The Commission continues:

> The records of the Land Board indicate it notified Waim No. 92 that it had been recommended as the successful applicant and on September 28, 1998, Waim No. 92 received notice that a corruptly reduced purchase price of K1,724,726.10 was payable before title would issue, with annual rent to be K17,000 (instead of the legally correct amounts of K2,866,000 and K143,000 respectively).
>
> (Barnett 2002)

According to the company's Annual Return for 1998, Waim No.92's registered address during this period was Ram Business Consultants, ADF House – this is also the registered address for Waim No.92's two shareholders.[28] Furthermore, during 1998 Philip Eludeme and Felix Leyagon – a PHLHC shareholder – were Directors of the company Sulawei Limited, whose registered address was again Ram Business Consultants, ADF House.[29] It would thus appear there were multiple links between two networks alleged to have been involved in similar style illicit land deals, by the Public Accounts Committee and the Commission of Inquiry into the National Provident Fund respectively.

In the Paga Hill case it is also notable that on 25 October 1998, six months after PHLHC obtain the Urban Development Lease, Guise purchased Noko

No.96, a company holding state leases over shorefront land abutting portion 1597 (*Noko No. 96 Ltd v Temu* [2012] PGSC 27).[30] It cannot be assumed, without further evidence, there is any direct link between this acquisition and the April award to PHDC, but at the very least it would appear Guise was trading on inside information.

Yet these irregularities were discrete, technical matters, that were easily overshadowed by more alluring promises in the media of a world-class cosmopolitan development at a prime Port Moresby location. The *Australian Financial Review*, for instance, reported: 'The [now] Deputy Prime Minister, Mr Michael Nali, said Paga Hill would convert "an eyesore" overlooking the entrance to Port Moresby harbour into "an icon"' (Pettafor 1998: 41). When questions were raised over the legality of PHLHC's title, Papua New Guinea's Attorney General, Michael Gene, defended the company, writing on 5 October 1998: 'I am satisfied that there has been substantial compliance of all statutory and technical requirements by Paga Hill Land Holding Company' (cited in *The National*, 23/10/1998). Two months later, Gene contracted Ram Business Consultants to investigate the Office of the Public Curator (Auditor General's Office 2005). Thus at a time when PHLHC was being accused of breaching the law, its principals appear to have been in receipt of strong public support from powerful political figures.

Almost two years after the Urban Development Lease was issued, the National Capital District Physical Planning Board (2000) granted PHLHC planning permission. Then on 22 May 2000, a gazettal notice was published stating that portion 1597 would be rezoned from open space to part commercial, part residential, part public institutional and part public utilities.[31] However, just as Paga Hill Estate began to acquire the requisite approvals which would allow investors to be approached, critical schisms were opening up within PHLHC between its local and foreign executives. For instance, Fridriksson departed Ram Business Consultants in early 2000 and set up a rival firm, which is alleged to have taken over Ram's responsibilities at the Public Curator's Office (Auditor General's Office 2005). Then on 14 August 2000, Fidelity Management Pty Ltd – an Australian corporate vehicle linked to Fridriksson and Patching – acquired a recently renamed holding company, Paga Hill Development Company (PNG) Limited (PHDC), from its Papua New Guinean owner.[32] Tauhura Fridriksson and Byron Patching were appointed Directors of PHDC, while Gudmundur Fridriksson became Secretary.[33] A company representative would later claim that PHDC was a mere rebranding of PHLHC (PHDC 2012b). In fact, registry records clearly show it was an entirely new corporate vehicle, where Rex Paki and Ram Business Consultants are notable by their absence (see Figure 5.3).

On 1 September 2000, the new corporate vehicle PHDC was awarded a 99-year Business (Commercial) Lease over portion 1597 – in effect PHLHC lost its only asset.[34] As with the Urban Development Lease, this transaction was marked by numerous irregularities. First, PHDC was now a foreign owned entity. In order

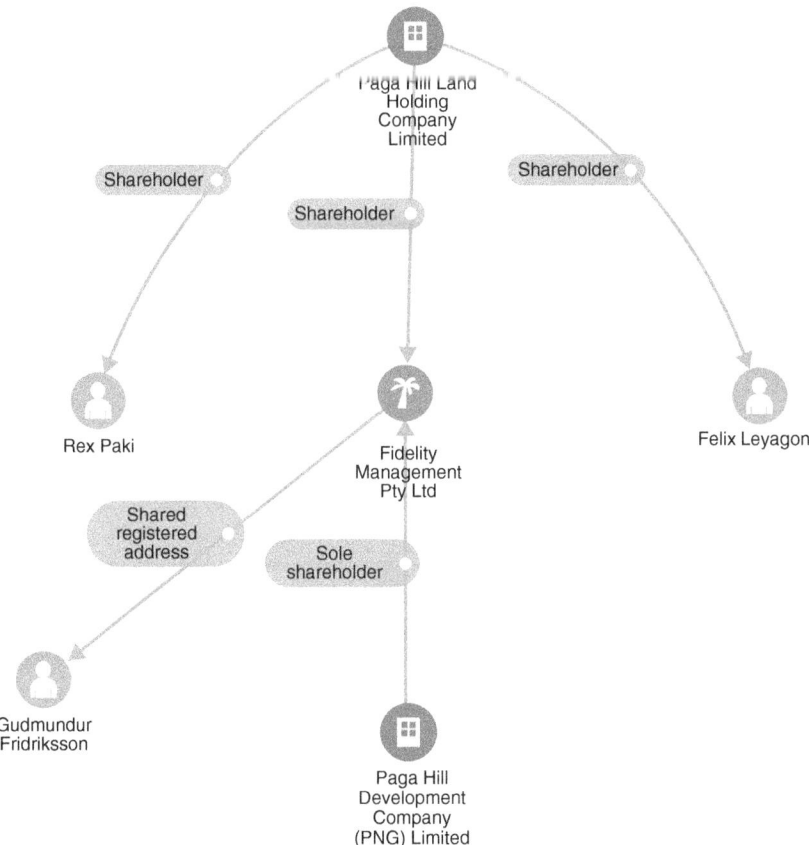

Figure 5.3 Ownership structure of Paga Hill Land Holding Company Limited and Paga Hill Development Company (PNG) Limited

to lawfully conduct business in Papua New Guinea it required certification from the Investment Promotion Authority (see 32(4), *Investment Promotion Act* 1992). There is no record on the foreign enterprise registry that this took place. Second, the 99-year business lease should have only been issued once the conditions of the Urban Development Lease had been complied with; most notably in this respect, the K300 million improvement covenant had not been observed. Third, once the covenants had been completed, the 99-year lease should have ordinarily been issued to PHLHC, the existing title holder (see s110, *Land Act* 1996; PHLHC 1998). Fourth, the state lease was for commercial purposes, whereas the land was zoned mixed purpose.

In addition to these irregularities, the new lease reduced the improvement covenant set out in the Urban Development Lease from K300 to K10 million (approx. US$3.85 million). On the other hand, annual rent increased from

K30,000 per annum to K250,000 (approx. US$96,000). This was in line with the *Land Regulation* 1999, which requires rent to be set at 5% of the land's unimproved value. However, according to the Public Accounts Committee, during 2001 this amount was illegally reduced to K50,000 by a Lands Department official, Romilly Kila Pat,[35] through a hand written amendment to the lease title (Public Accounts Committee 2007).[36]

Perhaps not surprisingly then, when this second award was considered by the committee it was equally damning of the above breaches of law and due process. The Public Accounts Committee notes, 'the State has lost a minimum of approximately K900,000 from 2000 until 2005' as a result of these alleged illegal actions (2007: 68). It adds, 'the Committee was advised that the Lessee could not pay even this reduced amount' (2007: 68).

Despite these failings, no substantive attempt was made by the Lands Department to cancel PHDC's title. We know from court records that the Lands Department has been prepared to forfeit other state leases where rent is in arrears, or even when relatively minor improvement covenants – for as little as K100,000 – have been breached (see *Lavongai Equities Ltd v Allan* [2016] PGNC 171). The Public Accounts Committee concluded its inquiry into Paga Hill noting a 'prime land and a National Park, has been illegally given to a private, foreign speculator with no ability to even pay the Land Rental, much less build anything on the site' (2007: 70). Furthermore, they assert, the award was marred by 'corrupt dealings' (Public Accounts Committee 2007: 60).

Although the Lands Department made no serious effort to execute the recommendations of the Public Accounts Committee, the bad publicity generated by the inquiry did impact on PHDC's 'ability to secure investment' (PHDC 2006). In particular, any investor conducting due diligence would have serious concerns over PHDC's security of tenure at Paga Hill, in light of the official reporting. With assistance from its lawyer, during 2008 PHDC attempted to calm investor concerns by lobbying the Public Accounts Committee's new Chair, Timothy Bonga (Public Accounts Committee 2008). They asked Bonga to overturn the findings of his predecessor.

Bonga had recently returned to public life after being dismissed from office for breaches of the Leadership Code (Ketan 2007).[37] Despite having no legal power to personally review or indeed overturn a previous finding tabled in Parliament by the committee, Bonga issued the requested letter on 17 July 2008. He stated:

> it is now confirmed that all documents relating to the grant of the State Lease for the land are in order … please advise your Client that they may go ahead with the development they have for the land … I urge that your Client take heed of the recommendations put forward by the PAC [Public Accounts Committee].
>
> (Public Accounts Committee 2008)

Subsequently, the Parliamentary Member for Moresby South, Dame Carol Kidu, inquired into the circumstances surrounding the letter. She claims:

> I know for a fact, I spoke to the legal adviser for the Public Accounts Committee, one of the foreign legal advisers, who said that they actually advised that subsequent Chairman [Timothy Bonga] not to do it, it was wrong, the public accounts committee report was extremely thorough and it was correct, because they had been working on the report with the Chairman, John Hickey. They actually drafted a letter for him to respond to the company, but he sent something drafted separately.
>
> (Kidu 2012c)

However, the governance reality in Papua New Guinea is such that public officials rarely face consequences for ignoring legal procedure, even where criminal sanctions are attached. Indeed, on the few occasions when public officials have been successfully prosecuted, the Courts have shown a willingness to suspend their custodial sentences when the offender agrees to repay the stolen assets (see *State v Maladina* [2015] PGNC 146). Therefore, a permissive system has emerged which allows informal and often illegal deals to be set up between politicians, public officials and the private sector. Even when these deals are exposed, there is negligible chance of those censured being prosecuted. It is perhaps not surprising then in this broader institutional environment that Bonga was allegedly prepared to ignore the legal advice solicited by his committee secretariat.

During this contentious period, PHDC underwent a number of important changes in personnel. One of its founding members, Byron Patching, grew tired of the commercial environment in Papua New Guinea, with its uncertainty and particular brand of entrepreneurial risk-taking (PHDC Official 2014). His departure removed from Fridriksson's immediate network an actor who brought vital commercial connections, industry prestige and technical knowledge. This absence triggered critical changes in the ownership structure of PHDC, as attempts were made to rebuild a coalition of actors who could steward the Paga Hill Estate into being. Shares in the company became a vital adhesive for strategically binding influential actors to the project.

Initially Fidelity Management Pty Ltd transferred its shares to Anvil Holdings Limited.[38] At this stage Anvil Holdings Limited was owned by George Hallit, and the Fridrikssons.[39] However, between 2008 and 2011 there were a series of further changes to PHDC's ownership structure. Most critically the Fridrikssons divested their stake in the company, despite sinking a significant amount of personal funds into the project. When Gudmundur Fridriksson was asked why he would do this, when he no longer had a beneficial stake in the company, Fridriksson stated his hope that PHDC's board would see fit at a later stage to reward him for the investment (Fridriksson 2012). In place of the Fridrikssons, a number of Australian investors – mainly from the business and construction community – took up minority stakes in the company, including Gregory Harrison-Ward (6%), George Hallit (11%), John Dale Martin (5%), Barry James Cheshire (5%) and Tracey Veronica Kluck (3%).[40] Kluck is the wife of Noel Pearson, a prominent indigenous Australian lawyer who is the principal architect of Cape York Partnership and the Cape York Institute, where Fridriksson had senior roles between 2009 and 2012.

However, arguably the most significant change to PHDC's ownership structure, was the acquisition of a 61% stake by Stanley Liria, the company's lawyer. Liria is from the Southern Highlands of Papua New Guinea, and enjoys ties with the current Prime Minister and leader of the People's National Congress Party, Peter O'Neill. According to Dame Carol Kidu, Liria 'grew up in the same household as the [current] Prime Minister [Peter O'Neill]'.[41] Liria also enjoys ties with another People's National Congress Party powerbroker, the Southern Highlands Governor, William Tipi, through the company Sharp Hills Investment Limited, whose registered address is Liria's law firm.[42]

Another prominent Southern Highlands figure, Michael Nali, joined PHDC during this period through his company Kwadi Inn, which obtained a 9% stake in the developer. During 1997, it will be recalled, Nali had originally endorsed the Paga Hill Estate as a 'as a property of National Significance' (Minister for Civil Aviation, Culture and Tourism 1997). Nali lost his seat in the 2007 national elections, and then unsuccessfully contested the 2011 elections on a People's National Progress Party ticket. Since then Nali has concentrated on his considerable business interests.

In addition to being an important Southern Highlands powerbroker, Nali enjoys strong commercial ties with Prime Minister O'Neill through NIU Finance Limited. According to Investment Promotion Authority records, Nali's company Kwadi Inn obtained a significant stake in this company during 2009, joining a select cast of executives and investors.[43] The company's last annual return states its Managing Director is Peter O'Neill.[44] Peter O'Neill again appears as the largest shareholder in NIU, through his companies LBJ Investments Limited (28%), Paddy's Hotel & Apartments Limited (12.5%) and Remington Technology Limited (25%).[45]

Nali also has commercial ties to PHDC's Stanley Liria. Both sat together on the board at Southern Highlands Holding Limited.[46]

It would thus appear that the new national shareholders of PHDC, who acquired a stake in the company during this 2009–2011 period, are notable because of their common ties to the Southern Highlands region, the People's National Congress Party (although mediated in Liria's case), and Prime Minister Peter O'Neill, one of the Southern Highlands most successful politicians. These overlapping entities have been a critical locus of power in Papua New Guinea over the past six years, particularly now that the Southern Highlands hosts the country's most significant natural resource project, the Papua New Guinea Liquefied Natural Gas venture operated by ExxonMobil.

Of course, nothing improper can necessarily be inferred from these links. Nonetheless, it can be surmised that PHDC enjoyed multiple ties to the largest power centre in government, with direct lines of communication to the Prime Minister. The assiduous acquisition of these links echoes the past commercial strategy of PHDC's CEO, recounted in the previous section. Given the contention that would soon emerge over Paga Hill between 2012 and 2014, the company was now seemingly well positioned to defend its interests.

However, it is important that PHDC's ownership structure – as recorded within Papua New Guinea's corporate registry – is treated with caution. For instance, between 2000 and 2005 PHDC shares were held by Fidelity Management Pty Ltd, a holding company legally owned by executives associated with the Western Australian firm, Sothertons Chartered Accountants. Evidence indicates that these shares were held on behalf of certain beneficiaries, which is alleged to have included Gudmundur Fridriksson and Byron Patching (PHDC Official 2014).[47] Therefore, it is possible in light of past practices that the legal shareholding structure currently registered with the Investment Promotion Authority, is different from the structure of those who stand to ultimately benefit from the returns yielded by the Paga Hill Estate.

Indeed, during the final edit of this volume it was discovered that Papua New Guinea's Minister for State Enterprises, William Duma,[48] had acquired a beneficial interest in the Paga Hill Estate during 2015/16.[49] This equitable interest in the venture was in exchange for Duma's company, Kopana Investments Limited,[50] signing over five state leases to a PHDC subsidiary, which covered critical land adjacent to portion 1597. From National Court records it appears Kopana Investments Limited acquired this land without public tender, under contested conditions (*Noko No.96 Ltd v Temu* [2012] PGSC 27).

Accordingly, in light of the above examples, it is difficult to specify with any completeness the full range of actors with an interest in the venture. Nevertheless, from the evidence we do have it can be concluded a number of those with a stake in the venture, enjoy considerable political capital.

Cementing the overarching forward motion this new ownership structure gave PHDC, the company also managed to acquire a new Business (Commercial) Lease over Paga Hill in 2009.[51] This replaced the 2000 lease – which featured an illegal rent reduction written on the title – with a clean copy that now formally assessed the annual rental at K50,000 (approx. US$18,500). In addition to the rent reduction, the improvement covenant dropped from K10 million to K5 million (approx. US$1.85 million) – given that the original Urban Development Lease had promised K300 in improvements back in 1997, PHDC had been relieved of a substantial burden. That said, past failures to meet improvement covenants had not attracted sanction.

Now that the company possessed a new state lease, influential shareholders and a letter of exoneration from the Chairman of the Public Accounts Committee, the security of its title over Paga Hill was significantly enhanced.

The main impediment confronting PHDC was the three and a half thousand people resident on the hill, a matter to which we will now turn.

Clearing Paga Hill of 'squatters', 'settlers' and 'criminals'

During April 2012 PHDC's principal shareholder and lawyer, Stanley Liria, visited the settlement along Paga Hill's foreshore, accompanied by police, police dogs and private security guards. Residents were given three options (Kidu 2012a). They could dismantle their homes and relocate to the area of 6-Mile, where PHDC claimed it had purchased land for the community. The company promised titles to individual plots at 6-Mile would be signed over to house-holds. In addition, they would be paid a K2,000 hardship allowance, along with a tent and mosquito net. Investigations revealed that the area at 6-Mile was customarily owned. Moreover, the legal steps required to register the land and issue formal leasehold title had not been taken by PHDC (Fridriksson 2012). Instead an agreement with a member of the customary landowner community had been reached. As a result, no household would be issued with registered title, as had been claimed. Any resident who chose to relocate would face inse-curity of tenure, in an area where they possessed none of the community links enjoyed at Paga Hill (Radio New Zealand International 2014).

As an alternative to the above proposal, Liria advised residents they could find their own land, and PHDC would compensate them at a rate of K10,000 for permanent houses, K5,000 for semi-permanent houses and K2,000 for shanties and bunkers (Kidu 2012a). These sums appear to be well below the price homes at Paga Hill were fetching in the informal housing market, which is a critical part of the capital's urban economy. If residents declined to accept options one or two, they were informed police would be authorised to carry out an eviction exercise (Kidu 2012a).

The Member for Moresby South, Dame Carol, condemned PHDC's pro-posal on the floor of parliament, insisting the land had been 'obtained fraudu-lently' (*The Post-Courier*, 5/4/2012, p.4). Following this intervention, Prime Minister O'Neill assured his government would respond to the matter (*The Post-Courier*, 5/4/2012, p.4). There is no evidence the Prime Minister followed through on this. To the contrary, subsequent events indicate PHDC enjoyed strong support from within government quarters.

The precise sequence of events leading up to the first major eviction exer-cise on 12 May 2012 is not clear. However, residents claim PHDC convened a private meeting with two community leaders, who are accused of signing consent orders for the eviction exercise, without the knowledge of the commu-nity, in return for payment (Moses 2012). When Paga Hill residents learnt the District Court had subsequently approved the signed consent order, a coalition of community representatives emerged, coordinated by Joe Moses. Moses is an anthropology graduate, and university administrator at the University of Papua

New Guinea. Although lacking a legal background, Moses possessed the skills, contacts and community standing to steer a campaign to save Paga Hill. Under his leadership, the community obtained a special sitting of the National Court for 12 May 2012 to hear an injunction request. On the morning of the twelfth, a Saturday, while community leaders waited to be heard at the National Court in Waigani, 10 police Landcruisers arrived at Paga Hill with heavy demolition equipment hired by PHDC (Moses 2012; Sepuna 2012).

A prominent Papua New Guinea artist, Ratoos Haoapa, who lived in the settlement, contacted Dame Carol Kidu, who was a personal friend. She arrived at Paga Hill as the demolition began, accompanied by an Australian documentary filmmaker, Hollie Fifer. While Dame Carol appealed for a cessation of the exercise, residents were beaten by officers, with a range of weapons, as homes were flattened by the demolition equipment (Moko 2012; Mua 2012). During one particularly tense moment in the demolition exercise police opened fire on residents. Fortunately, no one was struck by the bullets (Fifer 2016). When lawyers finally arrived at Paga Hill with a National Court injunction, several hundred residents had been left homeless. They remained on the site under tarpaulins and scraps salvaged from the demolition site.

The forced eviction exercise triggered a struggle to save Paga Hill, which would last just over two years. This movement was spearheaded by the Paga Hill Heritage Association, a resident's advocacy group, which lobbied to have the hill reinstated as a national park (Moses 2012). It was joined by another resident's group, the Paga Hill Arts Resistance, which raised the struggle's public profile through art, song and performance, while also lobbying for the settlement to be instated as the city's first cultural precinct (Haoapa and Wasi 2013). These efforts attracted considerable media interest and support from a number of influential public intellectuals. Alongside these efforts, residents legally contested the eviction order.

Wider support for the movement was garnered from members of the national arts community, in addition to human rights organisations such as Amnesty International and the International State Crime Initiative. Dame Carol Kidu also continued to support residents, bringing considerable prestige as a politician and well known human rights advocate, in addition to her resources, technical knowledge and background as a key architect of the country's national urbanisation policy (Kidu 2012c). She agreed to earmark some of her parliamentary discretionary funds, to support the legal action (Kidu 2012c).

Shortly after the demolition exercise Dame Carol (2012a) released a damning media statement claiming: 'This is not a development of national significance. It is purely a commercial venture by a company that has no fundamental rights to this prime real estate ... The so called relocation plan put forward by the company was disgusting' (Kidu 2012a). She also informed Radio Australia: 'On my last knowledge (earlier this year when I had records checked), they [PHDC] have still not paid [the] PNG government millions of kina for outstanding land tax and their company was behind with submitting annual returns to the state' (cited in Pacific Beat 2012a).

The movement to save Paga Hill won international attention during October 2012, when the International State Crime Initiative released its findings on the demolition exercise, including evidence on the commercial repertoires previously employed by PHDC's executives (Lasslett 2012). The report featured on the front page of Australia's national broadsheet, *The Australian* (Robinson 2012a; see also Robinson 2012b, 2012c), and was given generous air time by Australia's public broadcaster, the ABC (Pacific Beat 2012a). This put a spotlight on Fridriksson's role at the government funded Cape York Institute and Cape York Partnership – where concerns had already been raised over financial management (Department of Finance and Deregulation 2009) – organisations closely connected to Noel Pearson, a prominent indigenous lawyer of considerable national standing, with close ties to successive Australian Prime Ministers. A week after the report's release, it was announced Fridriksson was going on 'extended leave without pay' from the Cape York Partnership and the Cape York Institute, to pursue his 'business interests' in Papua New Guinea (four years on, Fridriksson has not returned to either organisation) (Robinson 2012c: 5). Three months later, Noel Pearson's wife Tracey Kluck sold her shareholdings in PHDC.[52]

To counteract the growing momentum of the resident's movement, PHDC executives fell back on established repertoires. However, now the challenge was to build links with actors who could marshal forms of esteem and legitimacy that might neutralise the stigmatising effect of the residents' campaign, and the public reporting on the demolition exercise, while at the same time easing potential investor concerns over the developer's 'social license'.

To that end, in December 2012 it was announced that the government's private real estate arm, National Housing Estate Limited, would partner with PHDC. The National Housing Estate Limited's Managing Director, John Dege (see chapter seven), informed ABC Radio, 'NHEL is … a major proponent in the Paga Hill housing development project undertaken by Paga Hill Development Company (PNG) Limited' (Pacific Beat 2012b). PHDC also recruited a public relations and corporate social responsibility team, to buttress a more sophisticated public face for the company, after the CEO made a series of callous remarks to the Australian media (see Robinson 2012a). Arguably, however, PHDC's most visible victory during this period was the successful negotiation of a consultancy contract with Dame Carol Kidu through her company CK Consultancy Limited.

Dame Carol had retired from politics in July 2012, after a distinguished career that had garnered her a range of international awards, honorary doctorates and positions at respected NGOs, charities and think tanks. This prestige, combined with her wide-ranging ties to civil society, state bodies and international human rights organisations, made Dame Carol a highly sought after commodity for those in the corporate community looking to access her considerable symbolic and cultural capital. On 7 April 2013, for instance, Bougainville Copper Limited appointed Dame Carol an independent, non-executive Director with annual remuneration of K150,000 (approx. US$69,000) (Bougainville Copper Limited 2014, 2015). At the time, Bougainville Copper Limited stood accused of aiding the Papua New Guinea Defence Force, during a decade long war on the island of Bougainville, an outfit who were responsible for authoring a range of war crimes and gross human rights abuses. Dame Carol also helped administer the Porgera Remediation Program on behalf of Canadian miner, Barrick Gold (Barrick Gold 2014). The programme was initiated to deal with a large number of women who alleged they had been sexually assaulted by the company's security force. It was heavily criticised by civil society and human rights researchers for making victims sign legal waivers, in return for relatively small compensation awards (Columbia Law School Human Rights Clinic and Harvard Law School International Human Rights Clinic 2015).

However, in contrast to the cases of Barrick and Bougainville Copper Limited, Dame Carol had been a vocal critic of PHDC during her political career, and had supported the community's legal struggle. Indeed, during the 12 May 2012 demolition exercise she rebuffed police efforts in stark terms, stating, 'why should some f★★★ing foreign company get our hill' (*Carol Anne Kidu v Hollie Fifer* [2016] NSWSC 982, para. 27). 'This is a national park for the future generations of Papua New Guinea', Dame Carol maintained, 'this is not a development, tell me how the people are going to benefit? They say there's going to be a marina cruise liner wharf. That's the big people – right' (*Carol Anne Kidu v Hollie Fifer* [2016] NSWSC 982, para. 27). When she was criticised for her 'emotional' reaction, Dame Carol responded in the national press: 'Yes I am emotional about the blatant corruption, greed and land theft in "modern" PNG and I am emotional when I personally witness gross abuse of human rights' (Kidu 2012b).

Given the broadsides launched by Dame Carol against PHDC in parliament, the press and public, her decision to act as a consultant for the company came as a surprise to many involved in the struggle to save Paga Hill. So sharp was the reversal, Dame Carol published a formal letter of apology. In it she repudiates her previous position, whilst applauding PHDC for its 'incredible patience' and 'determination' (CK Consultancy Limited 2015).

Under the contractual agreement signed with PHDC, Dame Carol's company, CK Consultancy Limited, would assist the developer to relocate residents from Paga Hill to the site at 6-Mile. It was later disclosed during a Supreme Court trial in Australia, CK Consultancy was paid A$178,000 by PHDC (*Carol Anne Kidu v Hollie Fifer* [2016] NSWSC 982, para. 41).

Rejecting allegations she had been bought off, Dame Carol strongly defended her relationship with the developer, claiming: 'The development of Paga Hill has been declared a project of national significance by NEC [National Executive Council – Cabinet]' (Kidu 2014a). This contrasted with her 2012 position, where Dame Carol maintained, 'this is not a development of national significance' (Kidu 2012a). Addressing the question of Paga Hill's residents, Dame Carol's 2014 position also contrasted with her 2012 stance, where she had labelled PHDC's relocation strategy, 'laughable' (Kidu 2012b). Dame Carol now claimed 'some [residents] will have alternatives [alternative accommodation] when the next eviction occurs if they choose not to leave voluntarily. However, for others 6-Mile is their only option and my task is to help them settle there' (Kidu 2014b). She warned

> I fear for those who choose not to move because Paga has always been marked as a settlement for relocation in the NCD Urban Development Plan … I will do the best that I can to honour our obligations under the various UN Conventions but I will also have to pragmatically deal with the reality of PNG.
>
> (Kidu 2014a)

The new relationship between CK Consultancy Limited and PHDC, cemented through a six figure consultancy agreement, was a blow to the residents' movement at Paga Hill. Not only had they lost access to Dame Carol's professional knowledge, political connections and social esteem, these assets were now potentially at the disposal of PHDC. Compounding matters, PHDC was busy building relationships with key government agencies, in addition to prestigious bodies within civil society. On 24 April 2014, for instance, the Royal Papua New Guinea Constabulary issued a press release thanking the company for a K20,000 (approx. US$7,200) donation (Royal Papua New Guinea Constabulary Media Unit 2014a). It would help send policewomen to the Australasian Police & Emergency Services Game in Melbourne, Australia. PHDC (2016) also claims in March 2014 it 'became Police Legacy's first Platinum Corporate Sponsor to the Commandant's Scholarship Fund which provides educational grants for primary, secondary and tertiary students of deceased officers'. Then in December 2016, the company announced it had donated a K1.2 million (approx. US$380,000) property to Police Legacy (PHDC 2016).

The company's philanthropic donations extended to Papua New Guinea's only annual literary prize, where they sponsored the award for children's books (Kora 2016). PHDC even established their own story-writing competition for displaced residents. The winning short story declared:

> What PHDC was doing was truly a blessing in disguise … I believe without a shadow of doubt that God answers prayers in many ways and uses people like those with PHDC and Carol Kidu Consultancy (CKC) for his will and purpose in life. I would be doing an injustice if I ended my story without expressing my gratitude to PHDC, and especially CKC for a job well done.
>
> (Mamondo 2014)

In addition to these charitable endeavours, effort was also plumbed into ensuring a positive face for the project was presented in the Papua New Guinea media. A growing number of pieces supporting the development appeared in the national dailies during 2014. For instance, on 27 May the *Post-Courier* reported, 'a unique gesture was shown by a developer who has gone out of its way to provide a relocation solution for illegal settlers living on its land to move out and allow for a development project to take place' (Kelola 2014a: 17). The paper approvingly outlines PHDC's plans to relocate residents to 6-Mile, adding: 'Former Moresby South MP Dame Carol Kidu, who had earlier supported the settlers, has now shown support for the company after realising the genuine efforts put in by the company, for a win–win situation for all concerned' (Kelola 2014a: 17). The effusive tone of the reporting is not unusual for the national media, where promotional pieces for corporate and political actors are regularly published as impartial news.

The company also utilised its social and digital media presence, to distribute promotional material. In one video featured on PHDC's website the Member of Parliament for Moresby North East, Labi Amaiu, lends the company his support, stating: '[I] congratulate and thank the CEO of Paga Hill development for a successful venture, this is what we call legacy, and I am proud to be part of that legacy' ('PHDC handover of Tagua Six Mile – speech by Hon Labi Amaiu MP' 2014). In a re-emerging theme, corporate records reveal Amaiu and PHDC's CEO enjoyed historical commercial ties through Anvil Marine Limited, a company which they jointly owned until it was deregistered in 2005.[53] PHDC also released its own documentary film in which 'Gudmundur Fridriksson celebrates the achievement of Paga Hill Development Company's vision for a harmonious relocation solution' ('Humanitarian Resettlement in Papua New Guinea' 2015). The documentary featured at Papua New Guinea's 2014 Human Rights Film Festival.

Later, when an Australian production house entered a less sympathetic documentary on the Paga Hill development to Canada's Hot Docs Film Festival, Dame Carol Kidu took injunctive action against its creators in the New South Wales Supreme Court (*Carol Anne Kidu v Hollie Fifer* [2016] NSWSC 982). Although she had originally encouraged the Director, Hollie Fifer, to expose the Paga Hill issue internationally, and had signed a release form for her own footage, Kidu now alleged she had been misled. During the trial it was revealed that PHDC had 'agreed to indemnify the Plaintiff [Kidu] in respect of her costs of these proceedings and also has paid the [required] $250,000.00' in security (*Carol Anne Kidu v Hollie Fifer* [2016] NSWSC 982, para. 41). Justice Rein found in favour of the filmmaker. In a scathing 38 page judgement, he opined, 'the impression gained is that the Plaintiff [Dame Carol] is prepared, for her own benefit and that of PHDC, to say anything to stop the footage taken of her by Ms Fifer being broadcast' (*Carol Anne Kidu v Hollie Fifer* [2016] NSWSC 982, para. 59).

In addition to funding the Australian litigation, PHDC also marshalled its considerable financial resources to neutralise the legal campaign mounted by residents. The legal team representing residents – which went through a number of iterations – chose not to have the administrative decision awarding title to PHDC judicially reviewed, despite the many irregularities documented by the Public Accounts Committee, the International State Crime Initiative and a local land expert. Instead, they argued the lease was wrongly awarded under the *War Surplus Material Act* 1952. This unorthodox and fraught argument was rejected by the National Court (*Paga Hill Development Company (PNG) Ltd v Kisu* [2014] PGNC 27). As a result, the Court now merely had to be satisfied PHDC was indeed named as the title holder on the state lease over portion 1597, in order to enforce the eviction order. This was clearly the case. Accordingly, on 29 May 2014, the National Court dismissed the appeal launched by National Housing Corporation residents (Kelola 2014b). However, a reprieve was offered to settlement residents, when the Supreme Court agreed on 1 July that the reclaimed land along the harbour foreshore lay outside portion 1597 (*Moses v Paga Hill Development Company (PNG) Limited* [2014] PGSC 18). As a result, the eviction order did not apply to households resident in this area.

However, this decision had in effect been nullified before it was delivered. During 2013/14, PHDC was in the process of obtaining title over the reclaimed land. Neither the settlement residents nor the courts were apparently made aware of these efforts. Obscuring matters further, the National Gazette report advertising the relevant Land Board hearing over the reclaimed land, featured the applicant company Andayap No.5 Limited, rather than PHDC.[54] An inspection of the company records reveal Andayap No.5 was incorporated on 31 May 2013, and is fully owned by PHDC.[55] Six weeks later on 16 July 2013 the 4.402 ha of reclaimed land was surveyed and registered as portion 3149 by the Lands Department.[56] On 4 June 2014, it was announced that a special purpose lease over the land had been awarded to Andayap No.5 Limited.[57] In effect, settlement residents could now be evicted by PHDC, who had state title over the land through its subsidiary.

The first community removed from Paga Hill and relocated to 6-Mile was the National Housing Corporation residents. This group of approximately 400 people was evicted from the site over the weekend starting 31 May 2014, by police officers and PHDC employees. Shortly after, the Royal Papua New Guinea Constabulary issued a media release, stating 'the relocation exercise was successful largely due to the humane and responsible actions of the lease holder of Paga Hill, the Paga Hill Development Company Limited' (Royal Papua New Guinea Constabulary Metropolitan Superintendent 2014). Superintendent N'dranou Perou is quoted in the media release, saying:

> I must commend the Chief Executive Officer of the Paga Hill Development Company, Mr Gudmundur Fredrickson [sic] for not only having the vision

to develop what will become a PNG landmark, but also for having the heart for the former tenants of the National Housing Corporation.

(Royal Papua New Guinea Constabulary Metropolitan Superintendent 2014)

The United Nations Development Program also came out in support of the company and the landmark character of the forced relocation process, claiming they were 'thrilled' by the exercise ('UN at PHDC's Official Handover to the Tagua Community' 2014).[58]

Witnesses, however, volunteered a different account. The British head of Papua New Guinea's Institute of National affairs, Paul Barker (2014), warned in the social media on 31 May: 'I observed some of the heavy looking young men with bushknives this morning [at Paga Hill], who were certainly intending to intimidate and didn't seem to appreciate observers (let alone poor residents)'. A settlement resident concurred, alleging:

> Today is not like before, the developers are with weapons, like long bush knives and axes, people are already scared about them. Right now we are planning to move to somewhere. We are trying to take some pictures but its not allowed, they said 'if we see anyone taking picture we'll cut them with knives'.
>
> (Paga Hill Settlement Resident 2014)[59]

Both accounts echoed testimony from a National Housing Corporation resident who claimed:

> [I]ts [a] scary scenario when you are not given enough time to prepare your house-hold stuff with policemen with their guns … the developer hired certain ethnic group of people with no civilised mindset clearing the land … Policemen would not allow us take pictures and they even confiscated our tenants' chairman's phone for taking shots.
>
> (National Housing Corporation Resident 2014)[60]

Following the eviction exercise, police issued a second media release (Royal Papua New Guinea Constabulary Media Unit 2014b). This one announced that the Royal Papua New Guinea Constabulary had launched a manhunt for Joe Moses – Chairman of the Paga Hill Heritage Association – who was considered to be armed and dangerous. Police accused the university administrator of discharging a firearm in public, and escaping police custody (Royal Papua New Guinea Constabulary Media Unit 2014b). Amplifying matters, Moses faced numerous anonymous death threats, including a drawing of his impending death which was left on his desk at work. His public standing was further damaged when Dame Carol Kidu (2015) took to the social media and alleged that his 'faction' had 'intimidated' and 'bashed' other residents. As a result of the growing danger to his safety, Moses went into hiding. This provoked anxiety within the Paga Hill community. A settlement resident observed:

> we are in a timebomb now … Joe Moses's life is in risk … now he is not here with us, he just left on Friday … the Paga developers are looking for him, they said if they found him he's going to jail, that's the latest of what happened in Paga.
>
> (Paga Hill Settlement Resident 2014)[61]

Adding to the community's woes, the National Capital District Commission (NCDC) – the city council for Port Moresby – was spearheading the construction of a ring road which was set to pass through the reclaimed land at Paga Hill. During July 2014, the NCDC and the ring road contractor, Curtain Brothers, became directly involved in the Paga Hill eviction issue. On 9 July 2014, the Royal Papua New Guinea Constabulary's Principal Legal Officer noted that police officers and NCDC agents were now intimidating residents at Paga Hill:

> We have perused and verified that the Plaintiffs have a legitimate Supreme Court Order in place that restricts us from doing so and the actions of our members whether regular or reserve will be seen to be in breach of these orders and we could be cited for contempt.
>
> (Miviri 2014)

Despite this warning a demolition exercise was implemented on 22 July 2014, allegedly by the NCDC and Curtain Brothers (Nianfop 2014). Homes, heritage sites, a church and school were destroyed along the foreshore area. One prominent Seven Day Adventist, Rtd Supreme Court Judge Mark Sevua (2014), condemned the exercise stating: 'The demolition and destruction of the Church and the Settlers' shelters were carried out without any consideration of human dignity and the interest and welfare of the affected citizens. This is a blatant violation of the Constitution!'. Rather ironically, given the 12 May 2012 demolition exercise, PHDC (2014) joined the chorus of criticism, tweeting: 'Worse fears realised – NCDC & Curtain Bros demolish homes & belongings whilst residents were out' – these are the same residents labelled 'criminals' and 'squatters' by PHDC's CEO in 2012.

As a result of the May and July eviction exercises, Paga Hill was no longer 'burdened' by human 'encumbrances'. The developer, and its partners, now possessed a monopoly over Paga Hill. During 2015 it was announced that PHDC would work with Sydney based architect Studio GA to develop the site – Studio GA had previously collaborated with CCS Anvil on the short-lived fun park venture at Ela Beach. Glossy media pieces accompanied the announcement. According to the *Post-Courier*, their escorted visit to the Paga Hill site was a 'breath-taking moment for media personnel' (*Post-Courier* 25/9/2015, p.15).

The lead architect promised that the 'Paga Hill project will be an icon of a modern and progressive PNG' (*Post-Courier* 25/9/2015, p.15).

Another favourable article appeared in *Business Advantage*, where PHDC's CEO boasts the forthcoming development will create 'a whole new economy' (Business Advantage PNG 2015). *Business Advantage* also note, the Paga Hill Estate will be 'the venue for the Leaders' meetings at the Asia-Pacific Economic Co-operation (APEC) summit in Port Moresby in November, 2018', a major regional event organised by the Papua New Guinea government with financial and logistic support from Australia (Business Advantage PNG 2015). More recently the project is reported to have been dubbed Port Moresby's 'tourism city' by the Minister of Trade, Commerce and Industry (Ikuavi 2016).

Added to this it appears PHDC reached a cooperation agreement with State Enterprises Minister William Duma during 2015 in order to absorb his adjacent landholdings into the project; in return Duma will be granted an equity interest in the venture (Tlozek 2017b). More recently in 2016, PHDC revealed that it had entered a partnership agreement with the National Capital District Commission, Papua New Guinea national government and Chinese investors to collaboratively develop the site in time for APEC (PHDC 2017). To help facilitate this objective, the national government of Papua New Guinea has promised considerable tax relief (PHDC 2017).

It remains to be seen, however, whether this ambitious objective can be achieved. The evidence presented in previous sections, when tracing the commercial biography of key executives associated with the venture, would suggest that the project's future execution may be a turbulent affair.

Conclusion

Power in the urban field does not operate in a broad brush stroke manner. Coalitions of actors prevail over others, because their dominance is negotiated on a day to day basis, upon historical structures that create asymmetries and inequalities. At the most elementary, these processes can be broken down into the units of actors, ties and transactions, which form the build blocks for more complex economies of power.

In the Paga Hill case, a close study of evidence obtained from a range of credible sources, appears to reveal a developer coalition motivated by inflated profits yielded by an investment repertoire that circumvents, to varying extents, market competition, commercial pricing mechanisms and urban governance regimes. It is clear, however, that to successfully prosecute such transactions a supportive social architecture needed to exist. Such an architecture rested upon the adeptness with which key fixers were able to strategically tie their clique, through a range of material adhesives, to actors with relevant forms of political power, technical expertise and esteem. When moments of rupture and rivalry fractured the prosecuting coalition, the centrality, prestige, resource base and skill of fixers became important determinants of which faction prevailed.

Because the ties and transactions underpinning these coalitions had illegiti-mate characteristics – owing to the contravention of legally enshrined norms governing land, urban planning, public administration and human rights – efforts were made to shield them from the public gaze. However, even when the public gaze penetrated, whether through the authority of oversight agencies or a sophisticated social movement, it was not fatal in the Paga Hill case. Critical to PHDC's success was the adept way in which company executives marshalled political capital behind their objectives, whether it be through material adhe-sives or by possessing strategic paths of communication to power centres in government. It also required organising public relations expertise, so a positive image of the company and project could be projected through the mass media, social media and public events. Notably these are resources, assets, ties and trans-actions that are structurally biased towards those with monetary capital, who are in the best position to access and deploy them.

Of course, violence is a persistent theme in this case study, administered by both the police and private security personnel. The currency of violence was heightened when it became apparent that the proposed estate would be opposed by a coherent social movement, with ties to national and international civil society. Violence, in this respect, was multi-faceted. Demolition exercises brutalised and demoralised residents; the targeting of key leaders by police disrupted residents' capacity to organise political and legal activities; and the threat of violence, backed up by precedent, was employed to control informa-tion flows during eviction exercises, so there was no repeat of 12 May 2012. These efforts were insulated by the complicity of organisations like the UNDP, who further buffered the venture's less salubrious features from the public gaze, through upbeat public statements that belied reality – although subsequently, in 2017, the UNDP has taken welcomed steps to repudiate their previous stance (Aston 2017).

Structurally speaking, none of the above activity could have taken place without certain asymmetries and inequalities being built into the fields of politics, public administration and law. For instance, in Papua New Guinea a Lands Department has come into being that contravenes laws and regula-tions with impunity, and fails to consult public stakeholders on major urban projects. This works in the favour of commercial actors who have failed to secure landed interests/property developments in conformity with national legislation, and to the notable disadvantage of government agencies and pub-lic stakeholders who wish to see this law enforced.

The police have also prove indifferent to the law. Their activities have been informed by a range of haphazard, devolved institutional objectives – unat-tached to broader law and order strategies. The lawfulness of police activities appears a matter of convenience rather than necessity. When eviction orders had been sanctioned by the court, police prosecuted demolitions at Paga Hill citing their judicial mandate. On the other hand, when court orders were deliv-ered outlawing further demolitions, they were simply ignored.

Compounding matters, Papua New Guinea's corporate regulator has proven inept at overseeing the *Companies Act* and *Investment Promotion Act*; corporations can thus breach regulations with apparent impunity. Politically speaking, the National Executive Council when alerted to evidence of serious illegitimate activity, was adept at paying lip-service to these concerns, while employing the machinery of the state to ensure that censure from government accountability agencies did not affect the commercial interests of those targeted.

However, the network architecture, commercial repertoires and structural environments critical to understanding the Paga Hill case are not anomalous. In the following chapter we will scrutinise a seemingly quite different example, taken from Madang on Papua New Guinea's north coast. In contrast to Paga Hill, it involves a large tract of rural land belonging to customary land-owners, which is adjacent to a proposed special economic zone. Moreover, those companies vying for title possess different characteristics to PHDC. Yet many core features of the commercial repertoires, networking techniques, institutional mechanisms and structural inequalities observed here can again be identified, which suggests a set of generalisable processes underpin speculative activity in national land and property markets, that functions in part through illegitimate and deviant practices. That said, the Madang case study will evidence these processes from a different angle. If the Paga Hill case study offers unique insights into the precise ways the commercial repertoires and networks facilitative of speculative activity gestate over time, the Madang case study offers rich insights into how illegitimate state–corporate practices essential to inflated speculative profits, are organised and concealed by key actors at a day to day level.

Notes

1 Paga Hill is situated within the Moresby South electorate.
2 National Executive Council, Decision No: NG 101/2012, 24 October 2012.
3 Flyvbjerg (2014: 6) observes: 'Megaprojects are large-scale, complex ventures that typically cost US$1 billion or more, take many years to develop and build, involve multiple public and private stakeholders, are transformational, and impact millions of people.'
4 Survey of Portion 1597, Milinch of Granville, Fourmil of Moresby, Cat. No. 49/2332, 17 March 1998.
5 Papua New Guinea National Gazette, No. G59, 10 September 1987.
6 This acquisition was later formally registered under provisions of the *Land Ordinance* 1899.
7 Papua New Guinea National Gazette, No. G59, 10 September 1987.
8 Destination Papua New Guinea Ltd, Company Extract, Investment Promotion Authority, accessed 5 July 2015.
9 PHDC Official is a senior executive source who worked for the company over a prolonged period. Their identity has been anonymised, as a precaution.
10 Bonds of ethnic solidarity are an important adhesive for political and economic cliques in Papua New Guinea.

11 Ram Business Consultants, Annual Return 1998, Investment Promotion Authority, 6 January 2003.
12 Anvil (PNG) Project Services Limited, Company Extract, Investment Promotion Authority, accessed 16 January 2015.
13 Anvil (PNG) Project Services Limited, Company Extract, Investment Promotion Authority, accessed 16 January 2015.
14 Asigau (PNG) Holdings Limited, Company Extract, Investment Promotion Authority, accessed 16 January 2015.
15 Anvil Commodities and Trading Limited, Company Extract, Investment Promotion Authority, accessed 16 January 2015; Anvil Legal Services Limited, Company Extract, Investment Promotion Authority, accessed 16 January 2015.
16 Despite the Public Accounts Committee findings, Investigation Taskforce Sweep declined to prosecute the matter. A subsequent evaluation of Sweep's case report revealed significant errors in fact, law and method, that were so egregious it was concluded the investigation was severely compromised (see International State Crime Initiative 2015).
17 CCS Anvil (PNG) Limited, Company Extract, Investment Promotion Authority, accessed 16 January 2015.
18 Skate had served as Prime Minister between 1997 and 1999. His Prime Ministership became synonymous with a secret recording, aired by the Australian Broadcasting Corporation, in which Skate 'claimed he was the Godfather of Port Moresby's infamous raskol [criminal] gangs and that he'd ordered a killing' (7.30 Report, 1999). While his stint as Prime Minister was short, Skate remained a powerful figure in national politics and a mentor to Papua New Guinea's current Prime Minister, Peter O'Neill.
19 Paga Hill Land Holding Company Limited, Company Extract, Investment Promotion Authority, accessed 4 July 2012.
20 Fidelity Management Pty Ltd, Current and Historical Company Extract, Australian Securities & Investment Commission, accessed 9 February 2014.
21 Corroborating this claim, Fridriksson's registered address as Director of Asigau (PNG) Holdings Limited – a holding vehicle he co-owned with his wife – is the same as Fidelity Management Pty Ltd.
22 Waim No. 54 Limited, Current and Historical Company Extract, Investment Promotion Authority, accessed 24 March 2016.
23 Paga Hill Development Company (PNG) Limited, Notice of Change of Shareholder (Share Transfer), Investment Promotion Authority, 16 December 2011.
24 Independent State of PNG, Urban Development Lease (portion 1597), issued to Paga Hill Land Holding Company (PNG) Pty Limited, 6 April 1998.
25 Independent State of PNG, Urban Development Lease (portion 1597), issued to Paga Hill Land Holding Company (PNG) Pty Limited, 6 April 1998.
26 Subsequently the company has been less inclined to acknowledge fault. In 2012 executives claimed 'PHDC has a history with the site that dates back to 1996, when an application was first submitted for its rezoning from what was then a National Park' (PHDC 2012a). They neglect to add the application was rejected.
27 Waim No.92 Limited, Annual Return 1998, Investment Promotion Authority, 1 August 2000.
28 Waim No.92 Limited, Annual Return 1998, Investment Promotion Authority, 1 August 2000.
29 Sulawei Limited, Current and Historical Company Extract, Investment Promotion Authority, accessed 24 March 2016.

30 Noko No.96 Limited, Notice of Change of Shareholder (Share Transfer), Investment Promotion Authority, 26 January 1999.

31 Papua New Guinea National Gazette, No. 234, 22 May 2000.

32 Paga Hill Development Company (PNG) Limited, Notice of Change of Shareholder (Share Transfer), Investment Promotion Authority, 14 August 2000.

33 Paga Hill Development Company (PNG) Limited, Notice of Change of Directors and Particulars of Directors, 24 August 2000; Paga Hill Development Company (PNG) Limited, Notice of Appointment or Change of Secretaries or Particulars of Secretaries, 27 September 2000.

34 Independent State of Papua New Guinea, Business (Commercial) Lease (portion 1597), issued to Paga Hill Development Company (PNG) Limited, 1 September 2000.

35 At the time of writing, Kila Pat has been arrested and charged with misappropriation K208,569, after ascending to the position of Lands Secretary (Nero 2016).

36 This hand written amendment is apparent on the owner's copy of the state lease: Independent State of Papua New Guinea, Business (Commercial) Lease (portion 1597), issued to Paga Hill Development Company (PNG) Limited, 1 September 2000.

37 The Leadership Code sets out the ethical standards governing the conduct of senior office holders. Breaches of the code can lead to dismissal and potentially criminal prosecutions.

38 Paga Hill Development Company (PNG) Limited, Notice of Change of Shareholder (Share Transfer), Investment Promotion Authority, 22 May 2005.

39 Anvil Holdings Limited, Company Extract, Investment Promotion Authority, accessed 16 January 2015.

40 Paga Hill Development Company (PNG) Limited, Annual Return 2012, Investment Promotion Authority, 4 December 2014; Paga Hill Development Company (PNG) Limited, Notice of Change of Shareholder (Share Transfer), Investment Promotion Authority, 13 September 2011.

41 This allegation was made by Dame Carol Kidu during a meeting with Dr Thomas MacManus, an International State Crime Initiative Executive Board member on 30 October 2015 (MacManus 2015).

42 Sharp Hills Investment Limited, Company Extract, Investment Promotion Authority, accessed 29 March 2016.

43 NIU Finance Limited, Company Extract, Investment Promotion Authority, accessed 6 May 2016.

44 NIU Finance Limited, Annual Return 2009, Investment Promotion Authority, 2 July 2010.

45 NIU Finance Limited, Company Extract, Investment Promotion Authority, accessed 6 May 2016.

46 Southern Highlands Holding Limited, Current and Historical Company Extract, Investment Promotion Authority, accessed 1 February 2017.

47 Fidelity Management Pty Ltd, Current and Historical Company Extract, Australian Securities & Investment Commission, accessed 9 February 2014.

48 At the time of writing, Duma has been implicated in a major land scandal. The Australian Broadcasting Commission reports that Duma, along with his Ministerial colleague Fabian Pok:

> are accused of benefitting from the purchase of land by government corporation Kumul Consolidated Holdings, for a new naval base west of Port Moresby. Mr Duma

is the minister responsible for Kumul Consolidated Holdings, but is alleged to own or have a proxy interest in a parcel of land purchased by that company.

(Tlozek 2017a)

49 The existence of this agreement was uncovered when the author observed a short period in March/April 2016, when Duma held shares – via Kopana Investments – in Malaga No. 7 Limited, a company cited in a 2017 investor memorandum for the Paga Hill Estate (PHDC 2017). When PHDC's Chief Financial Officer was questioned about this by the Australian Broadcasting Commission he acknowledged the existence of a cooperation agreement with Duma, giving the latter a beneficial interest in the estate (Tlozek 2017b).

50 Kopana Investments Limited, Company Extract, Investment Promotion Authority, accessed 12 February 2017.

51 Independent State of Papua New Guinea, Business (Commercial) Lease (portion 1597), issued to Paga Hill Development Company (PNG) Limited, 22 June 2009.

52 Paga Hill Development Company (PNG) Limited, Notice of Change of Shareholder (Share Transfer), Investment Promotion Authority, 25 January 2013.

53 Anvil Marine Limited, Company Extract, Investment Promotion Authority, accessed 3 May 2016.

54 Papua New Guinea National Gazette, No.G551, 5 December 2013.

55 Andayap No. 5 Ltd, Company Extract, Investment Promotion Authority, accessed 29 July 2014.

56 Survey of Portion 3149, Milinch of Granville, Fourmil of Moresby, Cat. No. 49/3107, 16 July 2013.

57 Papua New Guinea National Gazette, No.G220, 4 June 2014

58 Later this position was reversed by the UNDP's Papua New Guinea head, who informed the media, 'I've asked the company to stop using my name to endorse something I haven't seen [relocation site at 6-Mile]' (Trivedy cited in Aston 2017).

59 Paga Hill Settlement Resident, Personal Communication, 31 May 2014. The source has been anonymised to protect their identity.

60 The source has been anonymised to protect their identity.

61 The source has been anonymised to protect their identity.

Bibliography

7.30 Report. (1999). ABC, 7 July.

Anvil Project Services. (2003). *Information Memorandum – Investment Opportunity*, Port Moresby: Author.

Aston, H. (2017). 'Port Moresby settlers evicted to make way for Australian-backed development "abandoned"'. Sydney Morning Herald, 11 June. [Online]. Available at: www.smh.com.au/federal-politics/political-news/port-moresby-settlers-evicted-to-make-way-for-australianbacked-development-abandoned-20170609-gwodh2.html (accessed: 12 June 2017).

Auditor General's Office. (2005). *Special Investigation into the Office of the Public Curator*, Port Moresby: Author.

Auditor General's Office. (2014). *Report of the Auditor-General 2013 – Part 4*, Port Moresby: Author.

Barker, P. (2014). 'Paul Barker', *Facebook*, 31 May. [Online]. Available at: www.facebook.com/paul.barker.54943 (accessed: 1 March 2017).

Barnes, C. E. (1969). 'Business and investment opportunities in New Guinea', *Current Notes on International Affairs*, 40(6), 333–334.

Barnett, T. (2002). *Report of the Commission of Inquiry into the National Provident Fund.* [Online]. Extracts available at: web.archive.org/web/20060923050634/http://www.post-courier.com.pg/NPF%20inquiry/npf116 (accessed: 16 February 2017).

Barrick Gold. (2014). The Porgera Joint Venture Remedy Framework. [Online]. Available at: www.barrick.com/files/porgera/Porgera-Joint-Venture-Remedy-Framework-Dec1-2014.pdf (accessed: 13 February 2017).

Bougainville Copper Limited. (2014). Annual Report 2013. [Online]. Available at: www.bcl.com.pg/wp-content/uploads/2014/05/Annual-Report-Release-March-14.pdf (accessed: 13 February 2017).

Bougainville Copper Limited. (2015). Annual Report 2014. [Online]. Available at: www.bcl.com.pg/wp-content/uploads/2015/03/BCL-Annual-report-20141.pdf (accessed: 13 February 2017).

Business Advantage PNG. (2015). 'Paga Hill development to transform Papua New Guinea's capital', Business Advantage, 21 October. [Online]. Available at: www.businessadvantagepng.com/paga-hill-development-to-transform-papua-new-guineas-capital/ (accessed: 9 March 2017).

Cape York Partnership. (n.d.). 'Gudmundur Fridriksson'. Available at: http://web.archive.org/web/20110219202419/http://www.capeyorkpartnerships.com/gudmundur-fridriksson (accessed: 3 March 2017).

CCS Anvil. (n.d.). 'Public Curator's Efficiency Project'. [Online]. Available at: web.archive.org/web/20070212053626/http://www.ccsanvil.com.pg/Project_PC.htm (accessed: 3 March 2017).

CK Consultancy Limited. (2015). Letter from Dame Carol Kidu, CK Consultancy Limited, to Mr Gudmundur Fridriksson, Mr Stanley Liria, Mr George Hallit, Paga Hill Development Company (PNG) Ltd, 19 June.

Columbia Law School Human Rights Clinic and Harvard Law School International Human Rights Clinic. (2015). Righting Wrongs? Barrick Gold's Remedy Mechanism for Sexual Violence in Papua New Guinea. [Online]. Available at: hrp.law.harvard.edu/wp-content/uploads/2015/11/FINALBARRICK.pdf (accessed: 13 February 2017).

Commission of Inquiry into The Department of Finance. (2009). *Transcript of Proceedings*, 6 July, Waigani: Author.

Connell, J. (1997). *Papua New Guinea: The Struggle for Development*, London: Routledge.

'Dame Carol Kidu Arrest Threat'. (2012) YouTube video, added by Taukorema. [Online]. Available at www.youtube.com/watch?v=ovPdiIJNynU (accessed: 2 March 2017).

Davani, C., Sheehan, M. and Manoa, D. (2009). *The Commission of Inquiry Generally into the Department of Finance: Final Report*, Port Moresby: The Commission.

Department of Finance and Deregulation. (2009). *Performance Audit of Money Management Service Strategies*. Canberra: Author.

Donaldson, M. and Good, K. (1988). *Articulated Agricultural Development: Traditional and Capitalist Agricultures in Papua New Guinea*, London: Aldershot.

Dorney, S. (1996a). 'Two and a half million kina for this? Errors!!', *The Independent*, 20 January.

Dorney, S. (1996b). 'Destination – land of the unexpected publishing coup', *The Independent*, 27 January.

Dorney, S. (1996c) 'Destination PNG claims the moral high ground', *The Independent*, 13 April.

Fifer, H. (2016). *The Opposition*. Australia: Media Stockade.

Flyvbjerg, B. (2014). 'What you should know about megaprojects and why: An overview', *Project Management Journal* 45(2), 6–19.

Fridriksson, G. V. (n.d.). 'About me'. [Online]. Available at: www.gudmundurfridriksson. com/ (accessed: 3 March 2017).

Fridriksson, G.V. (2012). Chief Executive Officer of the Paga Hill Development Company, Personal Communication, 1 August.

Gewertz, D. B. and Errington, F. K. (1999). *Emerging Class in Papua New Guinea: The Telling of Difference*, Cambridge: Cambridge University Press.

Goddard, M. (2005). *The Unseen City: Anthropological Perspectives on Port Moresby, Papua New Guinea*, Canberra: Pandanus Books.

Goddard, M. (2011a). 'Historicizing Edai Siabo: A contemporary argument about the precolonial past among the Motu-Koita of Papua New Guinea'. *Oceania*, 81(3), 280–296.

Goddard, M. (2011b). 'Bramell's rules: Custom and law in contemporary land disputes among the Motu-Koita of Papua New Guinea', *Pacific Studies*, 34(2/3), 323–349.

Haoapa, R. G. and Wasi, P. J. (2013). Paga Hill Arts Resistance, Personal Communication, 14 July.

Hawksley, C. (2007). 'Constructing hegemony: Colonial rule and colonial legitimacy in the Eastern Highlands of Papua New Guinea', *Rethinking Marxism*, 19(2), 195–207.

Hilton Worldwide. (2012). Email from Charlotte Seymour, Senior Manager, Corporate Communications, Asia Pacific, to Dr Kristian Lasslett, Ulster University, 13 July.

'Humanitarian Resettlement in Papua New Guinea'. (2015) YouTube video, added by Paga Hill Estate [Online]. Available at www.youtube.com/watch?v=g-8Zvus8pCA (accessed: 11 August 2017).

Ikuavi, J. (2016). 'Tourism city', *Post-Courier*, 20 December.

International State Crime Initiative. (2015). *An Evaluation of Task-Force Sweep's Case Investigation into 'Allegations against Public Curator, CCS Anvil, Paga Hill Development Company Ltd etc.*, London: Author.

Investigation Taskforce Sweep. (2014). *Allegations against Public Curator, CCS Anvil, Paga Hill Development Company Ltd etc.*, Port Moresby: Author.

Jónsson, S. M. (1992). 'The liquorice factory in China turned out to be empty illusion', *The Press*, 10 September.

Kelola, T. (2014a). 'Company provides for squatter settlement', *Post-Courier*, 27 May, p.17.

Kelola, T. (2014b). 'Court rules in favour of developer', *Post-Courier*, 30 May, p.10.

Ketan, J. (2007). 'The use and abuse of electoral development funds and their impact on electoral politics and governance in Papua New Guinea', CDI Policy Papers on Political Governance, Canberra: Centre for Democratic Institutions.

Kidu, C. (2012a). 'Statement by Dame Carol Kidu on the Paga Hill Scandal'. 14 May. [Online]. Available at: http://asopa.typepad.com/files/statement-by-dame-carol-kidu-on-the-paga-hill-scandal.pdf (accessed: 24 February 2017).

Kidu, C. (2012b). 'Get the facts right on Paga Hill', *Post-Courier*, 23 May, p.10.

Kidu, C. (2012c). Member of Parliament Moresby South, Personal Communication, 25 June.

Kidu, C. (2014a). CK Consultancy Limited, Personal Communication, 30 March.

Kidu, C. (2014b). CK Consultancy Limited, Personal Communication, 6 April.

Kidu, C. (2015). 'Academic's comments on Paga Hill were incorrect & irrelevant', *PNG Attitude Blog*, 16 February. [Online]. Available at: http://asopa.typepad.com/asopa_people/2015/02/academics-comments-on-paga-hill-were-incorrect-irrelevant.html (accessed: 4 March 2017).

Kora, A. (2016). 'PHDC sponsor literary competition', Loop, 9 October. [Online]. Available at: www.looppng-sb.com/content/phdc-sponsors-2016-literary-competition (accessed: 13 February 2017).

Lasslett, K. (2012). *The Demolition of Paga Hill*, London: International State Crime Initiative.

Laxton, A. and Cheung, I. (1993). 'Mandarin files writ for $350,000 bill', South China Morning Post, 12 December, p.3.

MacManus, T. (2015). International State Crime Initiative Executive Board, Personal Communication, 31 October.

Mamondo, J. (2014). 'Paga Hill Development Company'. [Online]. Available at: www.paga-hill.com/a-personal-story-of-paga-hill-resettleme (accessed: 1 March 2017).

McCasker, A. W. (1966). 'Economic development in Papua and New Guinea', *Australian Territories*, 6(3), 2–13.

Minister for Civil Aviation, Culture and Tourism. (1997). Letter from Hon. Michael Nali, Minister for Civil Aviation, Culture and Tourism, to Mr Byron Patching, Manager, Jones Lang Wootton International Property Group, Central Plaza One, 345 Queen Street, Brisbane, 4000, Australia, 27 February.

Minister for Environment and Conservation. (1997). Letter from Hon. Paul Mambei MP, Minister for Environment and Conservation, to Sir Albert Kipalan KBE LLB MP, Minister for Lands, Aopi Centre, Waigani Drive, PO Box 5665, Boroko, 8 May.

Miviri, N. (2014). 'SCA 18/2014 – Joe Moses & Ors -v- Paga Hill Development Ltd', Minute, 9 July.

Moko, S. (2012). Paga Hill resident, Personal Communication, 26 June.

Moses, J. (2012). Chairman of the Paga Heritage Association, Personal Communication, 19 June.

Mua, R. (2012). Paga Hill resident, Personal Communication, 1 July.

National Capital District Physical Planning Board. (1996). Letter from Bill Skate (Governor), Chairman, N.C.D. Physical Planning Board, to The Managing Director, Paga Hill Land Holding Company (PNG), PO Box 269, Badili, NCD, 11 November.

National Capital District Physical Planning Board. (2000). Letter from Jack Livinai Patterson, Chairman, National Capital District Physical Planning Board, to Paga Hill Holding Company, Ram Business Consultants, PO Box 1648, Port Moresby, NCD, 6 March.

National Housing Corporation Resident. (2014). Personal Communication, 6 June.

Nero, T. (2016). 'Kila Pat committed to trial', The National, 17 June. [Online]. Available at: www.thenational.com.pg/kila-pat-committed-to-trial/ (accessed: 1 March 2017).

Ng, E. and Wan, M. (1993). 'Landlord sues man in Mandarin writ', *South China Morning Post*, 19 December, p.4.

Nianfop, S. (2014). 'WWII site fears', The National, 24 July. [Online]. Available at: www.thenational.com.pg/wwii-sites-fear/ (accessed: 1 March 2017).

Numapo, J. (2013). *Commission of Inquiry into the Special Agriculture and Business Leases: Final Report*, Port Moresby: Commission of Inquiry into the Special Agricultural and Business Leases.

O'Callaghan, M. (1996). 'Icelandic author in PNG's bad books', *The Australian*, 15 February.

Pacific Beat. (2012a). ABC Radio. [Online]. Available at: www.abc.net.au/news/2012-10-11/an-png-paga-hill-report/4306520 (accessed: 26 February 2017).

Pacific Beat. (2012b). ABC Radio. [Online]. Available at: web.archive.org/web/20131207081054/http://www.radioaustralia.net.au/international/radio/program/pacific-beat/pngs-dysfunctional-housing-corporation-privatised/1055576 (accessed: 26 February 2017).

'Paga Hill at Night, Aftermath of Eviction'. (2012) YouTube video, added by Jeffry Feeger. [Online]. Available at: www.youtube.com/watch?v=oiyNkCo9Wtw (accessed: 2 March 2017).

Paga Hill Development Company (PNG) Limited. (2006). Letter from George Hallit, Director, Paga Hill Development Company (PNG) Limited, to Pepi Kimas, Secretary, Department of Lands and Physical Planning, Boroko NCD, Papua New Guinea, 29 March.

Paga Hill Development Company (PNG) Limited. (2012a). 'Paga Hill looks to the future', The National, 13 April.

Paga Hill Development Company (PNG) Limited. (2012b). *'Response' to the Forced Eviction at Paga Hill – A Brief History of Portion 1597 Granville*, Port Moresby: Act Now! PNG.

Paga Hill Development Company (PNG) Limited. (2014). 'Paga Hill Estate', Twitter, 24 July. [Online]. Available at: https://twitter.com/PagaHillEstate (accessed: 6 March 2017).

Paga Hill Development Company (PNG) Limited. (2016). 'Paga Hill Development Company donates house to Police Legacy', Media Release, 22 December.

Paga Hill Development Company (PNG) Limited. (2017). *Information Memorandum*, Port Moresby: Author.

Paga Hill Land Holding Company Limited. (1997). Letter from Byron Patching, Project Manager, Paga Hill Land Holding Company, to Mr Pius Y Pundi, Secretary, Department of Environment and Conservation, PO Box 6601, Boroko PNG, 18 March.

Paga Hill Land Holding Company Limited. (1998). Masterplan Submission: NCD Physical Planning Board, Port Moresby: Author.

Paga Hill Settlement Resident. (2014). Personal Communication, 31 May.

Papua New Guinea Sustainable Development Program. (2012). *2011 Annual Report*, Port Moresby: Author.

Pettafor, E. (1998). '$450m boost for Port Moresby', *Australian Financial Review*, 14 April, p.41.

'PHDC handover of Tagua Six Mile – speech by Hon Labi Amaiu MP'. (2014). Youtube video, added by Paga Hill Estate. [Online]. Available at: www.youtube.com/watch?v=PoN93EQ7sCM (accessed: 1 March 2017).

PHDC Official. (2014). Personal Communication, 17 February.

PNG Institute of Directors. (2012). Email from Eileen Samoa-Simet, Executive Officer, PNG Institute of Directors, to Dr Kristian Lasslett, University of Ulster, 19 July.

Public Accounts Committee. (2003). *Report of the Public Accounts Committee on the Parliamentary Service*, Waigani: National Parliament of Papua New Guinea.

Public Accounts Committee. (2006). *Public Accounts Committee Report to Parliament on the Inquiry into the Office of the Public Curator*, Waigani: National Parliament of Papua New Guinea.

Public Accounts Committee. (2007). *Public Accounts Committee Report to Parliament on the Inquiry into the Department of Lands and Physical Planning*, Waigani: National Parliament of Papua New Guinea.

Public Accounts Committee. (2008). Letter from Hon Timothy Bonga, Chairman Public Accounts Committee, to Mr Stanley Liria, Liria Lawyers, PO Box 82, Konedobu, NCD, 17 July.

Radio New Zealand International. (2014). Dateline Pacific. [Podcast]. Available at: www.radionz.co.nz/international/programmes/datelinepacific/audio/2598597/a-controversial-resettlement-in-png's-capital-cops-flak (accessed: 3 March 2017).

Robinson, N. (2012a). 'Champion of aborigines Gummi Fridriksson "evicts" PNG's poor', *The Australian*, 9 October, p.1.

Robinson, N. (2012b). 'Paga link to "profits from PNG deceased"', *The Australian*, 10 October. [Online]. Available at: www.theaustralian.com.au/national-affairs/indigenous/paga-link-to-profits-from-png-deceased/news-story/20a595c8b1df3fa8c20bf580519daa91 (accessed: 3 March 2017).

Robinson, N. (2012c). 'Fridriksson "to focus on PNG"', *The Australian*, 16 October, p.5.

Royal Papua New Guinea Constabulary Media Unit. (2014a). 'Policewomen thank Paga Hill Development Company for timely donation of K20,000', Media Release, 24 April.

Royal Papua New Guinea Constabulary Media Unit. (2014b), 'NCD Police on hunt for Joe Moses for unlawful discharge of firearm', Media Release, 3 June.

Royal Papua New Guinea Constabulary Metropolitan Superintendent. (2014), 'Police pleased with Paga Hill resettlement exercise', Media Release, 1 June.

Sawong, D. (2007). *Report of the Commission of Inquiry into the Management of the Investment Corporation of Papua New Guinea and the Investment Corporation Fund of Papua New Guinea and all Matters Relating to the Conversion of the Investment Corporation Fund of Papua New Guinea to Pacific Balanced Fund*, Port Moresby: Commission of Inquiry.

Sepuna, L.T. (2012). Chairman of the National Housing Corporation Residents' Association, Personal Communication, 24 June.

Sevua, M. (2014). 'Paga Hill demolition in blatant violation of Constitution says retired judge', *PNG Exposed*, 4 August. [Online]. Available at: https://pngexposed.wordpress.com/2014/08/04/paga-hill-demolition-in-blatant-violation-of-constitution-says-retired-judge/ (accessed: 4 March 2017).

Thomas, D. R. (2010). *A Social Mapping Report of Paga Hill, National Capital District*, Port Moresby: Author.

Tlozek, E. (2017a). 'PNG ministers suspended amid inland naval base corruption scandal', ABC News, 6 February. [Online]. Available at: www.abc.net.au/news/2017-02-06/papua-new-guinea-ministers-suspended-over-corruption-scandal/8245796 (accessed: 2 March 2017).

Tlozek, E. (2017b). Australian Broadcasting Commission Papua New Guinea Correspondent, Personal Communication, 23 February.

'UN at PHDC's Official Handover to the Tagua Community'. (2014). YouTube video, added by Paga Hill Estate. [Online]. Available at: www.youtube.com/watch?v=oJ60h-bATUc (accessed: 1 March 2017).

Cases

Administration of the Territory of Papua and New Guinea v Doriga and Guba [1973] PGHCA 1

Carol Anne Kidu v Hollie Fifer [2016] NSWSC 982

Kalem v Yumi Yet Trading [2016] PGNC 278

Koitaki Farms Ltd v Kenge [2001] PGNC 59

Lavongai Equities Ltd v Allan [2016] PGNC 171

Moses v Paga Hill Development Company (PNG) Limited [2014] PGSC 18

Noko No. 96 Ltd v Temu [2012] PGSC 27

Paga Hill Development Company (PNG) Ltd v Kisu [2014] PGNC 27

Paki v Motor Vehicle Insurance Ltd [2010] PGSC 2

Ready Mixed Concrete Pty Ltd v The State, Samana and Kiamba [1981] PNGLR 396

Robmos Ltd v Punangi [2008] PGNC 70

State v Barclay Brothers (PNG) Ltd [2001] PGNC 134

State v Maladina [2015] PGNC 146

Steamships Trading Company Ltd v Minister For Lands and Physical Planning [2000] PGNC 11

Chapter 6

A land-grab in the world's 'tuna capital'

Introduction

On Papua New Guinea's north coast lies the town of Madang. Its surrounds have become the site of a thriving fisheries industry dominated by RD Tuna, which is a subsidiary of the Filipino multinational, RD Corporation. Punctuating rural villages, with their artisanal houses and plump food gardens, are processing plants, wharves, trawlers and the environmental footprint of an industrial trade. Impacted communities have frequently complained of poor labour conditions, racism, intimidation, land-grabs and toxic dumping (Havice and Reed 2012; Sullivan et al. 2003). However, community opposition has been diluted to an extent by influential local actors with a direct or indirect stake in the fisheries industry.

In a controversial turn, Papua New Guinea's Minister for Commerce and Industry, Gabriel Kapris, announced during November 2007 that his government had bold plans to transform Madang into the 'tuna capital' of the world (Albanial 2007: 6). This would be facilitated through the construction of a special economic zone, named the Pacific Marine Industrial Zone (PMIZ). The Minister later noted that the project would be built on state land 20 minutes north of Madang town, known as Vidar plantation. The site would 'house up to 10 tuna factories, capable of creating more than 30,000 jobs and hundreds of spin off opportunities' (Kaiok 2008: 5).

RD Tuna was a vocal supporter of the proposal. For example, the company hosted a Papua New Guinea political delegation in the Philippines during 2008, so they could witness first-hand the benefits special economic zones deliver (*Post-Courier* 26/2/2008, p.27). The company was also leaseholder over the 200 ha Vidar plantation, which the Papua New Guinea government reacquired at a reported cost of K20 million (approx. US$7.7 million) (Bashir 2010). To fund the project's construction costs, a tied loan from the Chinese government was acquired (Bashir 2010). Loan conditionalities include the use of Chinese contractors in the PMIZ's construction and operation.

However, one local company, Aces Ventures, has proven particularly adept at seizing the new commercial opportunities opened up by the PMIZ.

Incorporated on 3 October 2008, initially Aces Ventures was owned by a Papua New Guinea citizen, Ernesto Bautista (51%), along with Filipino national, Jeanie Nieva (49%).[1] During its infant years Aces Ventures was awarded lucrative contracts to prepare the Vidar plantation for the PMIZ development (Albaniel-Evera 2013). In addition to this, it has been the beneficiary of other large government contracts (Mathias 2014; Tapakau 2010). For example, Aces Ventures was awarded K8 million to build a bridge in the Commerce Minister's electorate, funded through the District Support Improvements Program. According to the *Post-Courier*, Commerce and Industry Minister Gabriel Kapris 'said the contractor had delivered on past projects and he was confident that they would again deliver on the bridge project' (Tapakau 2010: 35).

In the 2012 national elections Kapris lost his parliamentary seat. However, the former Minister's vision for the PMIZ has been maintained by the government of Peter O'Neill. Shortly after the loss of his seat, Kapris acquired a 26% stake in Aces Ventures, which he evidently purchased from Ernesto Bautista for K300,000.[2] The deal was a particularly good one for Kapris. By 2012 the infant company had a stated net worth of K3,448,560;[3] in effect he had purchased a K896,625.60 stake for K300,000. Kapris also became the company's Managing Director and Chairman.

One of the most valuable assets on Aces Ventures' books is a leasehold title they possess over state land at Mililat, a rundown plantation abutting Vidar, the chosen site for the PMIZ. The company purchased the land in 2009 from Selon Limited. Because of its close proximity to the PMIZ, it is reasonable to predict that the title's value will increase significantly once construction begins.

The vendor, Selon Limited, held itself out to be a landowner company, representing a range of kinship groups with a customary stake in the Mililat land. In Papua New Guinea only a select number of mechanisms exist for customary landowners to convert their informal title, which cannot be alienated in any form, into registerable titles, that can then be transferred to a third party through market exchange. In this case, landowners acquired a formal state lease over their customary land through the mechanism of a short lived Plantation Redistribution Scheme (Department of Lands and Physical Planning 1990). The scheme allowed land alienated during the colonial period to be returned to its traditional owners (Turner 1990). In effect, customary participants could regain their land, in a form congruent with certain forms of formal market exchange. When this indeed took place at Mililat, the subsequent transfer of leasehold title to Aces Ventures meant that the large tract of land concerned would not be available to its customary owners for at least 90 years.[4]

Up until recently, this type of transaction has rarely garnered national attention in Papua New Guinea. To the contrary, the formalisation of customary title has been vaunted as the means through which 'poor' rural communities, can convert 'locked' assets into capital that can be used to advance development goals (AusAID 2006; Gosarevski, Hughes and Windybank 2004). In really existing capitalism, this objective has proven to be elusive. The reasons why are acutely demonstrated in the Mililat case. Behind this increasingly routine transaction between Selon Limited and Aces Ventures – which saw leasehold title over customary land transfer to a third party – lay a fraud (*Kais v Tagau* [2016] PGNC 1). This fraud permitted a local strongman, Sali Tagau, to seize the leasehold title's financial value, while relinquishing ownership rights to private interests enmeshed in the PMIZ project, at the cost of surrounding clans who were losing a vital part of their landed heritage.

Because these transactions are commonplace, discrete, localised and removed from the limited arenas where civil society oversight exists, they are hidden, yet at the same time the registration of customary title through state leases, represents a core thrust behind a 'land-grab' in Papua New Guinea which has seen the mass-transfer of landed assets from customary landowners to private interests for up to 99 years (Mousseau 2013; Numapo 2013). These transactions are frequently prosecuted through deceptive practices, which deliver title at prices far below market price (Numapo 2013). If the previous chapter alerts us to the dynamics supporting a wider illegitimate economy in state owned land, this chapter examines the possibilities that emerge for illicit speculative activity when customary tenure acquires a registered form that can be circulated through market exchange.

Of course, the different ownership structure customary holdings entail, creates a distinct set of challenges that must be navigated. In the instance of Paga Hill foreign fixers navigated informal systems of power within the Papua New Guinea state, in order to secure support for the venture. However, where customary landowners are a critical feature in the transaction chain, a space is opened up for locally embedded fixers to acts as a bridge between government, commercial and clan power brokers, a dynamic which is underpinned by a range of structural asymmetries. This network architecture and structural asymmetry generates potent opportunities for the illicit transfer of land from customary ownership to private hands. In some instances local fixers are a key financial beneficiary of this process, while in others they are a secondary stakeholder who works for the primary beneficiary, such as private developers and/or state officials.

In the Mililat case we will be considering an example where an influential local speculator, possessing strong connections within the business community and provincial government, leveraged customary standing to acquire land fraudulently and deliver it to a private developer, closely connected to the PMIZ's ministerial architect. By carefully controlling lines of communication and information flows, this local speculator was able to acquire the land for a discounted price, and then sell it at market value, creating an inflated rate of return.

To begin this case study, a short history of the land will be provided. The complex weave of actor coalitions vying for Mililat will then be scrutinised, focusing on the way each was tied into different power centres. Consideration will also be given to how these competing coalitions prosecuted their interests, looking at the role illicit practices played. Critically in this case intimate data is available on the way in which the fraud was organised, with the complicity of state officers. The chapter will conclude by looking at how these efforts were challenged and censured from below by the landowner community.

A short history of the Mililat plantation

In its entirety Mililat plantation is a 416.9 ha property 19 km north of Madang town. The land's potential rental yield was apparent well before the PMIZ project had been announced. A valuation report produced in 2001 notes:

> Due to virtually nil supply of vacant land in Madang Town for any kind of development, people are now looking to land outside of town to establish their business or simply a place to stay. Subject land [Mililat] is ideally located with good access and suitable for any kinds of development for such/type size land.
>
> (Siwat 2001)

Like many fertile tracts in Papua New Guinea located near accessible transport corridors, Mililat was acquired from its customary owners during the colonial period under contested conditions. According to one elder from the landowning community, when a foreign settler purchased the land, 'payments were in forms of things like metal pot, bow knife and cement armband' (Koli 2012). While no detailed account exists of the land acquisition process, such imbalanced exchanges frequently occurred, as the example of Paga Hill demonstrates (see chapter five).

To relieve some of the tensions triggered by unjust land transfers during the colonial period, a short-lived Plantation Redistribution Scheme was introduced by the national government in 1974. According to Muroa (1998), the scheme allowed the state to acquire plantations owned by foreign entities, and redistribute them to 'original customary landowners or their descendants, for subsistence farming purposes where land for such purposes is in short supply, or for economic development purposes so that they may participate in and benefit from the economic development of the country'.

Through this scheme Mililat plantation was reacquired by the government, with a view to signing a state lease over to an umbrella customary landowner company. A vehicle for this transaction, the Mililat Development Corporation Limited, was incorporated on 14 August 1975. To complete the transfer, the state needed to be compensated for the reacquisition costs. An initial payment of K90,000 was made, before the company went into liquidation (Gadens Lawyers 2000). Then in 1982 the Plantation Redistribution Scheme was abolished before a final settlement could be reached. Nevertheless, during 1990 the Lands Department signalled its continued willingness to issue customary landowners with leasehold title, once the final outstanding amount – which came to K65,545 – was paid (Department of Lands and Physical Planning 1990).

It was the local businessman and strongman, Sali Tagau, who would go on to acquire the land through his company Selon Limited. The transaction chain underpinning this transfer took place within a heavily balkanised political context, where a number of landowner factions were vying for title, some of whom wanted to see the land returned into the customary tenure system, while others, like Tagau, had aspirations to realise the considerable price that subdivision and sale could garner.

These heterogeneous goals are a reflection of an ongoing process of rural differentiation in Papua New Guinea, which has seen divisions emerge between those seeking to convert land into assets that can buttress local accumulation strategies rooted in a capitalist logic, and those who wish to retain land as a device for sustaining rural livelihoods and preserving community bonds (Donaldson and Good 1988; MacWilliam 2005). The former actors often tie their aspirations to a vision for the future rooted in modernisation and progress, which is set against a pejorative narrative of otherwise static rural communities mired in a primitive way of life (Gewertz and Errington 1999). In the case of Mililat, two factions emerged whose aspirations were rooted in 'development' discourses and fiscal accumulation, while a third faction would later seek title to the land, grounding their claim in a social justice narrative. On that note, we will now examine how these competing claims to the land at Mililat were organised and prosecuted.

The contest for portion 237, Mililat

After the Mililat Development Corporation went into liquidation during the 1970s, landowner efforts to reacquire Mililat temporarily ceased. Over the next two decades the plantation fell into disrepair. However, by the late 1990s Madang province was emerging as an important commercial hub, with a growing stake in global fisheries. Added to this, Madang town had become a popular location for international NGOs with offices in Papua New Guinea. Accordingly, registerable land in close proximity to the township, with good access to roads, sea and electricity, was an increasingly valuable quantity. The state leasehold title over portion 237, which encompassed Mililat plantation, fitted this description. Moreover, the cost of acquiring the land was exceedingly low, a mere K65,545 (approx. US$19,300). Given that the plantation was potentially worth up to K10 million (approx. US$3 million),[5] there was a compelling commercial case for acquiring the title at this heavily discounted price. However, the procedures governing portion 237's transfer – which prioritised customary owners – was a core impediment to outside speculators.

Given Mililat's historical association with the Plantation Redistribution Scheme, the successful applicant needed to convince Lands Department officials that their organisation represented customary landowners, before title could be signed over. This precondition precipitated a complex struggle between two landowner factions. Both factions were dominated by private, speculative interests.

Contention between the two began in 1999. The first coalition involved two corporate actors, Selon Limited and Tropic Timbers Limited. At the time, Selon Limited's principal driver was Sali Tagau and his Filipino business partner Jacob Zabala.[6] Tagau was a member of the Panufun clan which had customary claims over Mililat (Selon Limited 2000d). Furthermore, Tagau had previously served as a village councillor, before establishing Savolon Security Services Limited with Zabala, which won a lucrative security provision contract with RD Tuna (*The National*, 19/8/2013).[7] By 1999 Tagau was emerging as one of the landowning community's more successful business figures. However, like many aspiring rural entrepreneurs in Papua New Guinea, lack of capital meant he was not in a position to acquire portion 237 unaided. In order to finance the acquisition, Tagau turned to an Australian businessman, John Davidson, who was looking to relocate his timber processing business to Madang. According to a 2003 affidavit, Tagau (2003) claims he and Davidson were friends.

John Davidson enjoyed a long association with Papua New Guinea. He had been brought to the country in 1949 by missionary parents (Davidson 2013). Davidson subsequently established himself in the construction and forestry trades, with experience both in Papua New Guinea and Australia. During 1998 he set up Tropic Timbers Limited, a foreign enterprise certified by the Investment Promotion Authority to work in Papua New Guinea's forestry industry. According to Davidson, 'the prime objective of the company is to assist the small people in PNG get more value for their timber resources' (Tropic Timbers Limited 1998). He claims:

> in the short term of its operations the company has learnt that the small people have been badly losing out on their timber resources. At the same time the destruction that has been made to the eco system has been damaging to their well being.
>
> (Tropic Timbers Limited 1998)

During August 1999, Davidson and Tagau agreed that Tropic Timbers would loan a landowners' company K65,545 secured against the leasehold title over portion 237.[8] Once title had been assigned to the landowner vehicle, the land would then be subdivided. A small plot of 4–5 ha would be given to Davidson for his timber processing business, while another modest plot would be sold to pay back the principal (Selon Limited 2000a). The remainder of the land could then be retained by the customary landowning community. At this stage, Davidson believed Tagau was acting as a representative of the different clans with a customary interest in the land at Mililat – Tagau's legitimacy, in this respect, was attested to by Lands Department officials stationed in the provincial government (Department of Lands and Physical Planning 2000c).

To action the plan, Sali Tagau and John Davidson flew to Port Moresby during November and December 1999, accompanied by two advisers from the Madang Provincial Government's lands branch, Zebedee Zosingao and Michael Larry. In Port Moresby they met with the Lands Department's Northern Director, Daniel Katakum, and his Deputy, Allan Bolla. According to Tagau: 'They advised that a traditional land owner company be incorporated to act as an umbrella company for the traditional land owners to replace Mililat Development Corporation. Only then, the title will be transferred to the Land owner company' (Selon Limited 2000a). It was on the basis of this advice, Tagau contends, 'Selon Limited was incorporated with [the] IPA [Investment Promotion Authority] to represent the Landowners and to replace Mililat Development Corporation' (Selon Limited 2000a).

However, company records show Selon Limited was actually incorporated on 2 September 1998, over a year before this meeting with Lands Department officials.[9] The records also reveal that Sali Tagau (50%) and his business partner Jacob Zabala (50%), were joint owners. In contrast to this arrangement, the Lands Department's Northern Director envisioned title going to a company whose shares were held by incorporated landowner groups representing the different clans/subclans with a stake in the property. Incorporated landowner groups are a particular organisational vehicle available in Papua New Guinean law, that give clans formal corporate status (Mousseau 2013). In this case, the relevant stakeholder communities could have incorporated and taken up shares in a vehicle like Selon Limited to meet Lands Department stipulations – however, corporate records show this did not take place.

Nevertheless, Tagau wrote to Daniel Katakum at the Lands Department, telling him 'Selon Limited is a registered company under the names of all clans namely; Panufun Clan, Timiso Group, Matanan Clan, Abo Clan and Gamarmatu Clan' (Selon Limited 1999). Representatives from each clan signed the letter, confirming 'we the undersigned hold an interest in Selon Limited and hereby agree that Mililat land, on payment of the overdue amount to be transferred into the name of Selon Limited' (Selon Limited 1999).

Later on 22 March 2000, Selon Limited produced a statutory declaration signed by representatives of the Panufun, Sousia, Maksil Mot, Tilu, Asonanen and Abo clans. It stated:

> we the following principal Clan Leaders do solemnly and sincerely declare that Selon Limited is the true Land Owner Company put in place of Mililat Development Corporation to act on Behalf of its people, to safeguard the interests of its members and the people of Kananam/Malmal/ Riwo and Mabonob villages.[10]

It appears, however, that clan representatives signed this declaration and the earlier letter under the erroneous belief that Selon Limited was in fact a landowner company, which collectively represented their different clan groupings. They were unaware it was a private company, over which they had no control. This signalled a broader inequality. Evidence suggests (see below) that Tagau was carefully guarding corporate information on Selon Limited. Compounding matters, landowner communities lacked the resources and expertise to independently inquire into Selon Limited's affairs. This created the structure upon which Tagau could solicit local support, without conceding actual control over Selon's affairs to the broader community. However, the fact Selon Limited supplied Lands Department officials with signed declarations, rather than a company extract certified by the Investment Promotion Authority should have put them on guard.

Competing with Selon Limited and Tropic Timbers for leasehold title over portion 237, was a coalition ostensibly led by Panuluan Holdings. Panuluan was owned by Jacob Sagui Masai (50%), Kubai Bibei (25%) and Solop Kalbai (25%), who were 76, 75 and 77 respectively at the time of incorporation in 1999.[11] According to the company's lawyer, Panuluan Holdings' three shareholders are 'Chiefs of Malmal, Kananam and Mabonob Villages, which villages are the principal landowners of Milinat [sic] Plantation' (Jacobus Puringi Lawyers 2000b). Although the individuals involved in Panuluan may have had a customary stake in the land, there is no evidence they were holding these shares in a representative capacity.

Panuluan Holdings' bid for portion 237 was financially backed by Gudi Investments. Gudi Investments was willing to pay the outstanding amount owed to the Lands Department (K65,545). At the time, Gudi Investments was jointly owned by Madang businessman Gus Tibong (50%), and Lae businessman Dian Roo (50%).[12] It was Sali Tagau's allegation that Gudi Investments ultimately aimed to acquire the land for itself. In a letter to the Lands Secretary, Tagau alleged certain inducements had been given by Gudi Investments to Panuluan Holdings' largest shareholder: 'Gus Tibong of Gudi Investment purchased an outboard motor with a dingy and gave it to Mr Jacob Sagui Masai in November, 1999' (Selon Limited 2000d). He adds, 'Jacob Sagui is very sick with mouth cancer and he has isolated himself from the Public' (Selon Limited 2000d).

As a witness Tagau lacks credibility, however, there is in this instance evidence to support his overarching claim that Gudi Investments was the primary driver in this rival coalition. For example, both Panuluan Holdings and Gudi Investments were incorporated on the same date. This indicates they were created for the principal purpose of acquiring title to portion 237. Furthermore, the relevant incorporation documents for both vehicles were lodged by an accountancy firm, Maquela Limited, which is based in the capital of Morobe Province, Lae.[13] Lae is a considerable distance from Madang, but the city of residence of Dian Roo, one of Gudi Investments' principals.[14] Added to this, the owners of Gudi Investments were over 25 years younger than Panuluan Holdings' shareholders, and had become established businessmen with a large range of commercial interests in Madang and Lae respectively.[15] In contrast, the elderly shareholders of Panuluan Holdings were seated in rural Madang, and do not appear to have had any commercial training or notable business experience which would have allowed them to spearhead the corporatisation and conveyancing process. Accordingly, while the latter figures may have possessed signifiers of legitimacy as members of the customary landowning community, they appear to have lacked the technical knowledge and financial capital possessed by Gus Tibong and Dian Roo. Thus, it would seem reasonable to infer that Gudi Investments was in all likelihood the primary driver behind this faction.

Like their rivals, Panuluan Holdings and Gudi Investments petitioned the Lands Department to grant them title over Mililat. Indeed, while senior officers from the department's Northern Division were aiding the Selon–Tropic Timbers coalition, the Lands Secretary attempted to settle the matter in favour of Panuluan Holdings. To that end, on 26 November 1999, the Lands Secretary wrote to Panuluan Holdings' Jacob Sagui, *care of* Gus Tibong (Gudi Investments), stating 'it is of the paramount importance that the Panuluan Holdings Group which is believed to be the landowners immediately settle the outstanding debts to proceed with necessary documentation' (Department of Lands and Physical Planning 1999). A month later Gudi Investments paid the outstanding amount (Jacobus Puringi Lawyers 2000a).

Over the Christmas period Selon Limited learnt of the payment, and began rallying political support. A distinct feature of Selon Limited's commercial repertoire, during this period of contention, involved the recruitment of champions from within the provincial government who lobbied for the company at a national level. For example, Joe Maira, Chairman of the Madang Provincial Government's Natural Resources Department, wrote to the Lands Minister on 4 January 2000 stating: 'It is very disappointing to note that someone has seen fit to bypass the provincial office and deal directly with HQs to settle the amount' (Madang Provincial Government 2000). An adviser from the provincial government's lands branch, Michael Larry, was equally critical in a letter to the Lands Secretary:

> [I]t was very disturbing while they [Selon Limited] were doing these arrangements [to acquire Mililat] somebody was approved to make a payment, the company that is not an umbrella company nor does it represent the interest of majority of clans.
>
> (Department of Lands and Physical Planning 2000a)

In the correspondence from Maira and Larry, both provincial officials vouch for Selon Limited's legitimacy as a landowner vehicle. For instance, Larry informs the Lands Secretary that 'the group company this office has been entertaining in the purchase of plantation is Selon Limited which accommodates interests of all customary clans and is the umbrella company for all clans' (Department of Lands and Physical Planning 2000a). Similarly, Maira advised the Lands Minister that Mililat should be transferred to Selon Limited because they had 'gone through all administrative formalities to acquire this property' (Madang Provincial Government 2000). In further correspondence with the

Lands Secretary, Larry went so far as to claim he had 'carried out an internal investigation to determine the former traditional owners of Mililat Land' (Department of Lands and Physical Planning 2000d). The investigation, Larry maintained, found those behind Panuluan Holdings were not the rightful owners. Accordingly, he concluded that 'Selon Limited is [the] true representative of the Land Owner Company and that the Lease Title [should] be prepared on behalf of Selon Limited' (Department of Lands and Physical Planning 2000d).

It is difficult to accept that an internal investigation, conducted with any rigour, could reach this conclusion. While landowners at the time certainly laboured under the belief that they enjoyed a stake in Selon Limited, owing to Tagau's representations – which landowners later discovered were false – government officials were in a position to verify these claims through a check of the company records held by the Investment Promotion Authority. Indeed, when Lands Department officials were explicitly advised by lawyers representing Panuluan Holdings of the fraud being perpetrated by Selon Limited, nothing was done in response (see below). According to the Public Accounts Committee, this type of irregular behaviour was becoming endemic within a Lands Department that had 'become an arm of private enterprise responsible for allocating Leases regardless of the Law and to the very considerable cost of the State and the citizens of Papua New Guinea' (2007: 23).

Following the intervention of provincial government officials, and a further visit by Tagau in January 2000, the Lands Secretary retracted the offer to Panuluan Holdings (Department of Lands and Physical Planning 2000b). In response, Gudi Investments petitioned the Madang Provincial Government to drop its support for Selon Limited, and applied legal pressure to the Lands Department claiming their conduct was illegal (Jacobus Puringi Lawyers 2000a, 2000b). However, the documentary records suggest Gudi Investments failed to secure any government backing. Indeed, in a meeting with Sali Tagau on 26 April 2000, Lands Department officials Daniel Katakum and Allan Bolla, went so far as to advise Selon Limited on how to shore up their position vis-à-vis Panuluan Holdings, by incorporating representatives of the Matanan Panuluan subclan – the group backing the latter company – into their coalition (Selon Limited 2000c).

Although Tagau had previously argued that this clan-group had no rightful claim over Mililat, a meeting was nonetheless convened with a number of Matanan Panuluan representatives on 14 May 2000 (Selon Limited 2000b). It was agreed they would withdraw their support for Gudi Investments Limited and back Selon Limited. Following on from this meeting two of Panuluan Holding's shareholders, Kubai Bibei and Solop Kalbai, backed Selon Limited, after Tagau agreed to give them equivalent shareholdings in Selon Limited (2000d) – although there is no evidence in the share registry that this transfer ever took place.

Selon Limited had now in effect built a coalition of customary and political supporters, which gave it a prime position to acquire portion 237. However, the company still needed to remove one commercial impediment. Before the state would issue the lease, Gudi Investments needed to accept a K65,545 refund. Selon Limited, Tropic Timbers, the provincial government, the Lands Department (including the Lands Secretary) and customary landowners all forcefully petitioned Gudi Investments to accept this refund.

These efforts elicited a strong response from Jacobus Puringi Lawyers, which acted for Gudi Investments and Panuluan Holdings. In a letter to the Lands Secretary, Jacobus Puringi reminded the Department of the chiefly status enjoyed by Panuluan Holdings' shareholders. He also revealed the results of a company registry search – Selon Limited was not a landowner company, in fact it was owned by two private individuals: Sali Tagau and his business partner Jacob Zabala (Jacobus Puringi Lawyers 2000b). Puringi noted, 'the above particulars speak for itself. Is this what you call "the true representatives of the original landowners"'. Having laid what appeared to be a damning piece of evidence on the table, Puringi informed the Lands Secretary, 'you must accept this as a notice to complete from us, as failure to do so will result in us suing the State and yourself in person for damages and for a mandamus order to compel you to do so' (Jacobus Puringi Lawyers 2000b).

This factual revelation failed to disrupt the arrangements. In fact, Lands Department officials made no attempt to alert the wider landowning community. It also appears no direct line of communication existed between Gudi Investments' lawyers and customary leaders, which could have seen this critical detail directly relayed.

In the aftermath of Gudi Investments' intervention, Sali Tagau consolidated his position in government by informing the Lands Secretary that a form had in fact been lodged with the registrar of companies on 28 June 2000, appointing a Board of Directors, which would include Sali Tagau (Panufun clan), Joseph Balim (Panufun clan), Augistine Wingiak (Gamaratu clan), Paul Masai Basan (Panuluan clan), Andrew Nak (Tilu clan), Philip Leik (Abau clan) and Jacob Zabala (N/A) (Selon Limited 2000d). There is no record at the company registry that this form was lodged on 28 June, or thereabouts. Tagau also promised, 'the directors will hold a meeting at a later date to discuss issuing of additional shares to recognized landowners to contribute capital by taking up shares' (Selon Limited 2000d). There is no evidence to suggest this took place either.

Despite being alerted to Selon Limited's misleading representations, the Lands Department did not delay the transfer of title so an independent investigation could be conducted. Indeed, on 21 September 2000, a gazettal notice was published advertising the proposed leasehold award to Selon Limited.[16] Then on 27 September 2000, a 99-year agricultural lease was issued to the company.[17] This lease had no rental requirement, 'as the Leaseholder is the Traditional Land Owner'.[18] In effect, Selon Limited acquired portion 237 at a price set in the 1970s, that is, K155,545, while enjoying special concessions meant for the traditional owners as a collective unit. Furthermore, by passing itself off as a landowner company Selon Limited was able to channel, for its own benefit, the initial K90,000 paid off by the Mililat Development Corporation. As a result, a mere K65,545 (approx. US$19,300) remained outstanding for a property worth up to K10 million (approx. US$3 million), which Selon Limited had paid through credit supplied by Tropic Timbers Limited, a company that was operating under the belief that Selon represented the wider customary community.

If Selon Limited was to now realise the significant difference between the heavily deflated purchase price, and the amount portion 237 could fetch on contemporary land markets, it needed to be in a position to contract with prospective purchasers. To that end, three impediments needed to be eliminated. First, the mortgage attached to the leasehold title in favour of Tropic Timbers had to be repaid and the encumbrance removed. Second, landowner groups who had banded behind Selon Limited – having been told it was a landowner company – now believed that they were at liberty 'to develop this land by our own means and ways' (Kodii et al. 2000). Selon Limited thus needed to conceal from customary backers the company's actual ownership and control structure, so commercial negotiations could be concluded with purchasers. Third, the land housed two distinct residential communities. Customary landowners had already reclaimed some of the land for village homes during the 1960s. In addition to this, former plantation workers resided in an informal settlement located on the land. Selon Limited had been aware of this during 1999, although it was not flagged as a significant problem. On that note, we will now examine how Selon Limited navigated these challenges in order to release onto the market, leasehold titles over the Mililat land.

Courting profit: the subdivision and sale process

To start the sale process, Selon Limited wrote to Allan Bolla, a Lands Department official based in Port Moresby. Alongside Daniel Katakum, Bolla had been closely involved in the events of 1999/2000. Selon informed Bolla on 10 October 2000 that the Board of Directors – which consisted of Sali Tagau and Jacob Zabala – had 'resolved to seek your approval for the above proposal mainly to generate enough capital for the development of the same [portion 237] to a sound economic and commercial property' (Selon Limited 2000e). It was explained, 'our proposal is to subdivide portion 237 … and sub-lease the blocks to genuine companies or organisations with proven financial capabilities and good standard operational records' (Selon Limited 2000e). Bola was assured, only 11.3% of the total land mass would be alienated to outside actors. A month later, on 9 November 2000, Selon Limited was advised the Lands Minister had accepted their application for subdivision (Department of Lands and Physical Planning 2000e).

While the subdivision process was taking place, Selon Limited began soliciting buyers. One interested party was New Tribes Mission, a US based missionary organisation that specialises in 'converting' remote indigenous communities.

Tagau informed New Tribes Mission on 19 October 2000 that 'Selon Limited is happy to know that your Mission is interested in some land to establish your PNG Headquarters' (Selon Limited 2000f). The letter continues:

> We understand that you would require about 12 hectares. We have no objection. The price given is about K20,000 per hectare. We ask that, you do a down payment of 50% initially in order that the subdivision of the land will commence immediately.
>
> (Selon Limited 2000f)

The correspondence concludes, 'we trust that you will understand us and we will give you the support required to establish the mission station knowing that you are carrying on God's vision as we are God fearing people' (Selon Limited 2000f). Eventually a price of K230,800 (approx. US$80,000) was settled upon for the 12 ha plot (Acanufa & Associates Lawyers 2001).

This initial attempt to subdivide and sell the land was done without the approval of Tropic Timbers Limited. The company's owner-manager John Davidson was concerned by the deal. Although Davidson supported a sale to recoup the loan principal, he was adamant that all subdivided land must be encumbered by the loan, until the owing amount had been repaid in full. As a result of this position, Tropic Timbers made it clear to Selon that the owner's copy of the state lease would only be released on condition that the new sub-divided titles were encumbered by the mortgage (Selon Limited 2000g). This placed a brake on Tagau's ambition to quickly convert the land into liquid funds.

Complicating matters, in March 2001 the group banding behind Selon Limited began to fracture as a result of two events. First, contention between Tagau and local landowner leaders emerged over a K30,000 (approx. US$10,400) deposit paid by New Tribes Mission. Two-thirds of the deposit was employed to defray the Tropic Timbers loan, while the remainder was allegedly kept by Selon Limited without account being made to landowner leaders (Sungai and Kubak 2001). According to Davidson, 'the K10000.00 which Selon Ltd received as deposit has disappeared without trace. Only Jack [Zabala] and Sali [Tagau] know where it is and will not say'. As a result, he claims, 'the people are up in arms and ready to kill' (Tropic Timbers 2001a). Tensions over the management of Selon Limited were heightened when Davidson learnt, 'Selon Ltd has only two Directors Sali Tagau and Jack Sibala [sic] (a Filipino). These two are also the Directors of Savolon Security Ltd. The other [landowner] "Directors" were never registered' (Tropic Timbers 2001a).

To resolve matters Davidson considered exerting his rights as mortgagor in order to repossess the land, and then transfer title to a genuine landowner company, as had been originally envisaged (Tropic Timbers 2001a). An invoice was sent to Selon Limited for K95,000, in addition to a further K70,000 in lieu of the 4–5 ha plot Selon had promised Tropic Timbers Limited (Selon Limited 2001a). By this stage, Tropic Timbers had also begun adding those expenses to the principal which the company felt it had incurred as a result of Selon Limited's improper manoeuvring.

In response to the actions of Tropic Timbers, Selon Limited looked to shore up its local support base at a meeting of customary landowner representatives on 21 March 2001. At the meeting it was acknowledged that landowner leaders had not in fact been appointed Selon Limited directors, despite the fact Tagau had previously promised to do just that. To diffuse matters, Jack Zabala elected to stand down as a director – although he maintained his shareholdings – while it was agreed 'the following persons [would] be elected as directors of Selon Ltd. 1. Sali Tagau 2. Joseph Balim. 3. Paul Basan 4. Augistine Wingiak 5. Boin Gain 6. Andrew Nak 7. Matei Kaut' (Selon Limited 2001a).

Yet even were these latter parties to be appointed directors – as representatives of the different clan groups – Selon Limited could not then be described as a landowner vehicle. The principal beneficiaries would remain the two shareholders Sali Tagau and Jacob Zabala. Crucially, under the *Companies Act* 1997 both men as shareholders would retain the power to remove directors. The proposed arrangement, in effect, would only give customary landowner leaders certain executive functions and responsibilities. They would, therefore, incur the risks associated with being responsible for a corporate body engaged in questionable commercial activities, without standing to benefit from the sizable profits this activity could elicit. It would appear from subsequent events, that landowner representatives were unaware of the significant disadvantages associated with the proposed corporate arrangement. This deficit in commercial knowledge allowed Tagau to dissipate growing tensions in the short term, while steps were being taken to unencumber the land titles and find a purchaser.

To that end, Selon Limited attempted to resolve its dispute with Tropic Timbers by giving the company access to the plot of land they had agreed to sign over following subdivision. This allowed Tropic Timbers to begin making the necessary improvements for its timber processing business. However, an agreement over the legal arrangements which would secure the loan following subdivision still could not be reached. Matters came to a head on 21 July 2001 at a meeting between Selon Limited, landowner representatives, and Tropic Timbers, at Savolon village. John Davidson revealed to landowners that despite its repeated representations Selon Limited had failed to register landowner representatives as company directors (Selon Limited 2001b). In response, Tagau's close ally Joseph Balim – an accountant, formerly employed by Ram Business Consultants (see chapter five) – claimed the forms had been lodged, and registration was pending (Selon Limited 2001b). Davidson made clear to those in attendance at the meeting that his company would not release the portion 237 title for subdivision until landowner representatives were listed on the company registry as directors.

The meeting outcomes are disputed. According to Tagau, 'it was resolved that the chairman [Tagau] will proceed with the court action to force Mr John Davidson to release the original land Title for Selon Ltd to Lands Department to carry out subdivision of 6 portions' (Selon Limited 2001b). Davidson, on the other hand, maintains that his alternative proposal to foreclose the mortgage, subdivide the land, and allocate titles to a new landowner company that excluded Sali Tagau, received widespread support (Tropic Timbers Limited 2001b). Landowner representatives, he insists, 'heartily agreed, as they are sick of Sali Tagau and his cunning tactics' (Tropic Timbers Limited 2001b).

Following the 21 July 2001 meeting Tagau went on the offensive. He advised Davidson, 'to immediately cease all building works, also you are not to enter the Plantation, upon being liable for trespass, as the sub-division has yet to be finalised by your hand' (Selon Limited 2001c). Tagau added, 'the [Selon Limited] Board of Directors will not be held responsible if any materials go missing from Portion 1060 whilst you are in the process of releasing and finalising the subdivision' (Selon Limited 2001c). During August 2001 Tropic Timbers was served with court papers by Selon Limited, in a bid to force the subdivision. Steps were also taken to distance John Davidson from the landowner community. Selon had by this stage employed an Australian manager, David Monks, in a bid to avail itself of business expertise that could give the company an edge over Tropic Timbers. Davidson was instructed that all communications were to go through Monks (Tropic Timbers Limited 2001d). Tightly controlling communication lines again proved an important practical issue.

Davidson would later blame David Monks for spearheading Selon Limited's efforts to significantly restrict the landed assets encumbered by the mortgage arrangement. As a result of Monk's perceived role, Tropic Timbers considered trying to remove the expatriate manager from the rival coalition by reporting him for visa condition violations. To that end, Davidson informed his lawyers:

> David Monks apparently has a work permit with Akanufa [a company], but none with Selon. You have evidence on file that he is working for Selon as he has signed official letters as 'manager'. He has given Sali a bill for K20,000 for his commission for stealing everything from me.
>
> (Tropic Timbers Limited 2001f)[19]

On this occasion, it appears Davidson did not follow through on the proposed action.

To the contrary, as the legal action proceeded, Tropic Timbers attempted to break the impasse outside court. To that end, Davidson offered to release the title over portion 237 on condition that:

> a properly authorised representative of Selon Ltd be sent to I.P.A. [Investment Promotion Authority] Port Moresby with full documentation for the registration of Joseph Balim, Paul Masai Basan, Augistine Wingiak, Philip Leik, Andrew Nak, Matael Kaugh, Gileng Sabub. a) As board members of Selon Ltd. b) As shareholders of Selon Ltd.
>
> (Tropic Timbers Limited 2001c)

Once this had been done, Davidson stated that 'the representative [must] bring evidence to Tropic Timbers Pty Ltd, within one week of the date of this proposal' (Tropic Timbers Limited 2001c).

This proposal, if complied with, would legally empower the customary land-owning community to share in any revenues earned by Selon Limited through sale of the subdivided land. However, Tagau and Zabala were unwilling to forfeit their position as the principal beneficiaries. Tagau responded to the proposal observing, 'we have had [a] legal opinion on [this matter] and we are of the view that the allocation of shares is an internal matter for the Board to decide on not an outside person or company' (Selon Limited 2001d). He adds:

> Selon Limited has complied with the registration of the correct Directors of which was faxed and sent to IPA on Tuesday the 18th of September, 2001. The registration of these correct Directors shall satisfy the Department of Lands and should also satisfy yourself.
>
> (Selon Limited 2001d)

By this stage, Davidson had been approached on numerous occasions by clan leaders who feared 'Sali Tagau would take everything as soon as the mortgage was paid off' (Tropic Timbers Limited 2001e). He nonetheless conceded to Tagau's proposal after the same leaders allegedly claimed 'that they are now happy for Sali Tagau to be the only shareholder'(Tropic Timbers Limited 2001e). As a result, Davidson notes 'I have now accepted this wish of theirs' (Tropic Timbers Limited 2001e).

Tropic Timbers' lawyer, Bruce Apana – on the instruction of his client – agreed to hand over the portion 237 leasehold title to Lands Department officials for subdivision on 11 October 2001. According to Apana, 'we further instructed Mr Malo [Northern Region Leases Officer], that it was imperative that the subdivision Portions note our client's encumbrances' (Gadens Lawyers 2001). It was expected that portion 237 would be subdivided into six new titles, portions 1056, 1057, 1058, 1059, 1060 and 1061 which were 368.25 ha, 22.23 ha, 11.54 ha, 4.83 ha, 4.562 ha and 3.744 ha respectively. The mortgage would then be registered against each of these titles, until the principal was repaid.

However, in a curious move the Lands Department issued a title over portion 1058 the following day, without the registered encumbrance. An owner's copy of the new leasehold title was given to Selon Limited, allowing the contract of sale with New Tribes Limited to be completed (Department of Lands and Physical Planning 2001b). Tropic Timbers learnt of the manoeuvre, and immediately complained to the Registrar of Titles, Lands Secretary and the Director of the Department's Northern Division (Tropic Timbers Limited 2001b). In response, the Registrar ordered Selon Limited to return the improperly issued state lease over portion 1058. Additionally, the registrar advised Lands Department colleagues that the titles over portions 1056, 1057, 1059, 1060 and

1061 must be encumbered by the mortgage (Department of Lands and Physical Planning 2001b).

To prevent the Registrar's request from being actioned, Selon Limited petitioned the courts to relieve the company of its obligations to Tropic Timbers. In a sign of its enduring support from within the Lands Department – even if not universal – Selon again solicited the backing of Lands officials to see off this new impediment. On this occasion it was Allan Bolla, the Deputy Director of Northern Division, who rallied behind the company. Bolla stated, in a letter to the trial judge, that his department initially thought 'Tropic timbers offer was genuine' (Department of Lands and Physical Planning 2001a). However, he now believed the company was trying to 'manipulate the ignorance of the people to gain' (Department of Lands and Physical Planning 2001a). Of course, by late 2001 the Lands Department had received evidence Selon Limited was in fact the one exploiting inequalities in information, knowledge and power, to acquire Mililat for the benefit of private interests. Nevertheless, Bolla advised the judge that the new titles being issued to Selon Limited should come unencumbered by Tropic Timbers' loan (Department of Lands and Physical Planning 2001b).

While the case was before the courts, New Tribes Mission contracted with Selon Limited on 17 November 2001 to purchase portion 1058, seemingly unaware of the legal contention. Over half the sale price was transferred to Selon Limited, K130,400, leaving a remainder of K100,400 owing (Warner Shand Lawyers 2004). Drawing on the sale proceeds, Selon Limited sent a cheque to Tropic Timbers on 5 December 2001. In the attached letter, Tagau notes: 'Please find enclosed our PNGBC Bank Chq no 0519336 for K49,661.94 being the principal owed, a cheque for about K16,312.47 being the interest on the total amount borrowed shall be forward to you in due course' (Selon Limited 2001e). This attempt to settle the debt, however, was rejected by Tropic Timbers. Davidson, its Managing Director, contested the outstanding amount. In addition to the loan principal and interest, Tropic Timbers now wanted to be compensated for extra expenses that had been incurred as a result of Selon Limited's conduct, including legal costs, denial of property (access to portion 1060), and the rental paid to acquire alternative premises for its timber processing activities.

With both parties seemingly at loggerheads, on 6 December 2001 the National Court delivered judgement in favour of Tropic Timbers (*Selon Limited v John Davidson & Tropic Timbers Limited* OS No. 514 of 2001). An order was issued requiring Selon Limited to surrender portion 1058 to the Lands Department Registrar; the sale to New Tribes Mission was injuncted until this condition was fulfilled. Once the leasehold title over portion 1058 had been corrected and the sale completed, the Court declared that the proceeds were to be set aside for settling the mortgage. Selon Limited was also restrained from obstructing the registration of encumbrances over the remaining titles.

The National Court order was served on Selon Limited's Directors during 27 January 2002 (Tropic Timbers Limited 2002a).

Balkanisation within the landowner community

As embittered relations between Selon Limited and Tropic Timbers appeared to worsen, a new front of contention emerged when representatives from Mabonob, Riwo, Kananam and Malmal villages challenged Selon Limited's title to portion 237, arguing they instead represented the true customary landowners. To prosecute this claim, the new landowner faction established a corporate vehicle, Masuba Limited, which was owned and administered by Vitus Kai, David Kem, Adolf Nuvo, Francis Masu Mui, Mathias Ambura and Theodore Bamatu of Mabonob village.[20] The company wrote to Papua New Guinea's Public Solicitor appealing for support, claiming:

> With no proper or good mediations and investigations, the relevant authorities of the land department had given away the customary land known as Mililat plantation … The customary landowners were not given a privilege to talk and have been neglected by this relevant authorities.
>
> (Masuba Limited 2001)

Masuba Limited argued they were confronting those 'in love for money'. It was suggested, in contrast, that those standing behind Masuba formed part of the 'grassroots of this country … in pain for our land in outside hands' (Masuba Limited 2001).

This new front against Selon Limited signalled a wider loss of confidence in Tagau from within the landowner community, especially by those who felt that they had been excluded altogether from the arrangement spearheaded by Selon. Indeed, while some landowner representatives had been given Selon Limited directorships – due in large part to the insistence of John Davidson – it was becoming increasingly apparent that other clan representatives with a claim over the land had been ignored. This hints at the difficulty of solidifying backer networks in customary contexts marked by complex tenure arrangements, that involve a range of distinct ethnic groups and subgroups. In this case, to facilitate a sale of the land it was not so much a matter of binding all players into the Selon coalition, rather it just had to be enough to form a critical mass that could produce the requisite stability while the commercial transactions were completed.

Previously, in 2000, Selon Limited had successfully soldered hostile Matanan Panuluan subclan representatives to its coalition with the offer of equity interests. On this occasion, however, the landowner front opposing Selon was couching its interests in the language of social justice (J. Bamatu 2013; W. Bamatu 2013). This signalled that it was populated by landowner representatives inclined towards employing the land as a long-term community resource, rather than as a financial instrument which could be converted into money through market alienation. In the face of clashing economic motives, there was seemingly less scope for co-optation of rivals.

Of course, this was not a problem peculiar to Mililat. Speaking more broadly, rural contention in Papua New Guinea tends to be more marked when the commodification of landed resources is opposed by organised customary groupings looking to advance a model of development that sustains rural landholdings through a mixture of subsistence farming and cash cropping (Lasslett 2014). This is juxtaposed against development models built on significant injections of foreign capital into large-scale extractive enterprises, which have found favour with national politicians, certain foreign donors and those aspiring local businessmen capable of monopolising spin off benefits.

In the case of Mililat, with internal landowner tensions emerging upon more rigid and fraught fault lines, allegations were made that Selon Limited was now shoring up its position through violence and intimidation. In an appeal for support to Tropic Timbers, one Kananam villager observed:

> Our garden stuffs have been stolen, vandalism has been taking place for too long with our properties and now the act of arson (burning of the house). Please can you do something now! Put Sali Tagau and his directors behind bars immediately. The more we delay the more they'd ruin us. Please do something.
> (Bilson 2002)

During January 2002 John Davidson himself allegedly became a target of the Selon Limited faction. The Tropic Timbers Managing Director informed his lawyers:

> [On] Tuesday 29th of January 2002 Simon of Mabonob [village] reported that … our Morota house on portion 1058 was burned down by Philipus Tagau last night. Some personal possessions belonging to Simon were also burned; Simon was looking after the house for us.
> (Tropic Timbers 2002b)

Despite the growing violence and tension within the landowning community, during the early months of 2002 Selon Limited continued with its efforts to sever ties with Tropic Timbers. On 13 May 2002, a K14,000 cheque was delivered to Tropic Timbers (Tropic Timbers 2002c). In the eyes of Selon Limited this finally settled the mortgage in its entirety. Davidson, however, continued to insist a much larger sum was owed. Tropic Timbers' position was seemingly strengthened on 24 May 2002, when the National Court re-endorsed its 6 December 2001 order, after it was discovered that the Lands Department had issued new leases without the encumbrance (in violation of the instructions given by the Registrar of Titles) (*Selon Limited v John Davidson & Tropic Timbers Limited* OS No. 514 of 2001).

The National Court demanded that new leases be issued with the registered encumbrance, thus replacing the improperly issued titles. It also repeated previous advice that any proceeds from the New Tribes Mission sale were to be kept in trust to settle the outstanding debt with Tropic Timbers Limited. When Selon Limited again failed to comply with this court order, Davidson successfully prosecuted a case of civil contempt against Selon Limited's directors. Justice Sawong claimed:

> there is no doubt that you have disobeyed the orders of a National Court judge. You were present and your lawyers were present when the orders were made. Many of you are well educated persons and successful businessmen in your own right and in my view there is little excuse for your actions.
>
> (*Selon Limited v John Davidson & Tropic Timbers Limited*
> OS No. 514 of 2001)

All Selon directors were convicted and fined K500.

Despite the court order and contempt case, evidence suggests the May 2002 decision was still not complied with by Selon Limited. Furthermore, Davidson continued to find resistance from within the Lands Department. Tropic Timbers' lawyers again petitioned the Department to act, stating: 'Your prompt action is required on this matter in light of the fact that it has already taken the Lands Department nearly 8 months to carry out a Court Order' (Gadens Lawyers 2003). After further requests from Tropic Timbers, new titles were eventually issued over portions 1056–1061 and handed to the company as security. However, the Lands Department, it appears, failed to reclaim the old titles held by Selon Limited. As a result, two sets of titles were circulating, one encumbered by the mortgage and one free of encumbrances. The circulation of multiple leasehold titles to the same plot is not uncommon in Papua New Guinea, creating a fertile context for fraud and protracted legal action (Land Consultant 2013).[21]

At the time that Tropic Timbers was petitioning the Lands Department to action the most recent National Court order, Selon Limited was contending with a major internal rupture as the landowner community began to balkanise further. On 11 May 2003 a special meeting was held of four villages, Riwo, Malmal, Mabonob and Sek, with approximately 60 people in attendance, including Selon Limited directors Gileng Sabub and Philip Leik (Saurin 2003). Philip Leik informed the crowd he had been used by Tagau as a 'window curtain' (Saurin 2003). Others at the meeting expressed concerns over Sali Tagau and the opaque management of Selon Limited's finances. It was concluded that 'the four villages which form Mililat Development Corporation Ltd [the initial landowner vehicle incorporated in 1975], the Principals, need urgent action to be taken against Selon Ltd for corruptions and [mis]management' (Saurin 2003). It was also agreed that the leasehold titles over Mililat must be reissued to a new landowner company.

In a clear sign of Tagau's slipping position within the landowner community, two months later on 4 July 2003, Selon Limited's Directors met and decided to remove him as Chairman (Selon Limited 2003). Gileng Sabub was appointed interim Chairman. On 19 February 2004, a former ally of Tagau, Joseph Balim, was elected as his permanent replacement, with support from Selon Directors Gileng Sabub, Matei Kaug and Philip Leik. Effectively this faction was attempting to oust Tagau from the Board, along with his two remaining backers, Paul Masai Basan and Andrew Nak (Selon Limited 2004b).

To leverage their position, the Balim-led faction placed their support behind Tropic Timbers, in a bid to recruit John Davidson over to their side. This perhaps was not surprising, after all Davidson appeared to possess the financial resources and commercial savvy to counteract Tagau's commercial manoeuvres. To tie Davidson into their subgroup, the Balim-led Board faction resolved on 18 March 2004 to transfer portion 1060 to Tropic Timbers, as originally agreed back in 1999 (Selon Limited 2004c). Additionally, this faction also agreed to review Tropic Timbers' invoices and settle the outstanding amount. However, by this stage in the elongated process, Tropic Timbers was demanding K771,911.01 (approx. US$255,600) for the expenses it had incurred and other economic hardships resulting from Selon Limited's actions (Tropic Timbers 2005a).

Complicating matters further, yet another landowner faction formed, this time from Sek village. The Sek village faction opted to form their own company, Kilimat Holdings (2004). Kilimat Holdings would, it was proposed, work with Tropic Timbers and the Balim-led faction to reclaim the land from Sali Tagau.

Accordingly, by 2004 the customary landowners had visibly split into at least four factions. Two of which banded behind their own corporate vehicles Kilimat Holdings and Masuba Limited, while Selon Limited itself had become divided between a Balim-led faction, and a smaller faction led by Tagau. The Balim faction, allied with Kilimat Holdings, attempted to strengthen their position by teaming with Tropic Timbers. On the other hand, Masuba Limited wanted to circumvent the entire Selon Limited/Tropic Timbers arrangement, which it saw as illegitimate. Meanwhile, Tagau's faction was looking to sever all ties with Tropic Timbers and the rival factions, so they could finally sell off the leasehold titles without encumbrances.

Despite the balkanisation, tension, rivalry and loss of standing, Tagau was still at a distinct advantage. Most critically he continued to monopolise a position of centrality and political prestige within the commercial network he had put together to acquire Mililat. This privileged position had a number of key dimensions.

First, Tagau and his business partner Jacob Zabala were the sole shareholders of Selon Limited. Under the *Companies Act* 1997 they had the legal power to remove company directors, and veto all major decisions affecting Selon Limited. In a letter to the directors and certain landowner representatives, Tagau was explicit in this regard:

> There is no obligation for me to report to you all while I being the 100% share and sole owner [sic] of the company. For this reason I should be the authority who should be advising you people and any other interested party to conduct any meeting relating to the business activity of Selon Ltd.
>
> (Selon Limited 2004a)

Second, Tagau's faction apparently retained the old leasehold titles to Mililat, which had been issued by the Lands Department in contravention of the National Court order. While Selon was ordered to return the titles, the Lands Department failed to take any notable action when the company failed to do so. As a result, Selon appears to have retained old leasehold titles which were free of the registered encumbrance that would impede a sale.

Third, in addition to enjoying longstanding support from within the Madang Provincial Government, Tagau also enjoyed strong backing from the Lands Department's Northern Division. The Northern Division had lobbied the National Court on Selon's behalf, and then failed to comply with successive National Court decisions in favour of Tropic Timbers. In a government where informal lines of influence hold sway over formal lines of authority, it appears that the Tagau faction possessed the right form of political capital to prosecute their interests, while frustrating Tropic Timbers' actions.

The sale of Mililat, and legal resistance

Tagau pressed home his advantageous position to sever ties with Tropic Timbers Limited and the other landowner factions. Matters came to a head on 2 February 2005. Tropic Timbers delivered a default notice on the Tagau and Balim factions, which relayed the company's intention to sell portions 1056–1061 in 30 days unless the mortgage debt was repaid in full (Tropic Timbers 2005b). In response, Tagau launched a National Court action against Tropic Timbers in Port Moresby, evidently unbeknownst to John Davidson, the company's Managing Director (Davidson 2013). Having shifted forums from Madang to the capital Port Moresby, Tagau succeeded in obtaining an *ex parte* order[22] on 11 August 2005 (*Selon Limited v Tropic Timbers Limited & John Davidson* OS No.89 of 2005). Tropic Timbers maintains this was an abuse of process (Davidson 2013). The *ex parte* order discharged the mortgage and restrained Tropic Timbers from interfering with Selon Limited's business. Following this decision, on 3 November 2005, Selon Limited's Board of Directors was dismissed by the company's shareholders, leaving Sali Tagau the sole director.[23] Zabala's 50% stake in the company was transferred to Tagau on the same date.[24]

The company records executing these decisions were lodged with the Investment Promotion Authority by Ram Business Consultants, whose principal is Rex Paki, a Port Moresby business figure who featured in the Paga Hill case study (see chapter five). It will also be recalled, Tagau's former ally, Joseph Balim, had worked as an accountant at Ram, creating a bridge between the two organisations. In this instance Rex Paki and a business partner, the prominent politician Peter Yama, were looking to acquire portion 1056. According to Paki he purchased the portion from Selon Limited, but the company failed to honour the contract.[25]

A critical intervening event, in this respect, was deliberations over the PMIZ. Launching a new 'megaproject' on land adjacent to Mililat had the potential to substantially increase the market price of Selon Limited's leasehold titles. Certainly the speculative value of Mililat increased on 8 November 2007, when the Minister for Commerce and Industry, Gabriel Kapris, boldly predicted the PMIZ would establish Papua New Guinea as the tuna capital of the world through a project that would inject 30,000 jobs, 10 tuna factories, hundreds of spin off opportunities and government revenues valued at K2 billion (Albaniel 2007).

The company Aces Ventures succeeded in winning contracts to initiate prefatory PMIZ groundwork, a fact noted in the introduction. This complemented other big ticket projects awarded to the company, such as a bridge building contract valued at K8 million in Kapris' electorate (Mathias 2014; Tapakau 2010). Aces Ventures was also acquiring prime Port Moresby land through Special Agricultural and Business Leases (SABLs), a legal mechanism which had come under significant scrutiny and criticism by a Commission of Inquiry for their role in facilitating a wave of illicit land-grabs (Aces Ventures' leasehold titles were not investigated by the commission, or subject to censure).

Once finance for the PMIZ's construction had been secured by the Commerce and Industry Minister, through a tied loan from China, Aces Ventures looked to expand its landed interests to Madang. Mililat's close proximity to the proposed PMIZ site at Vidar plantation, coupled to its good transport and communication links, made it an obvious choice for auxiliary infrastructure. Not surprisingly then, it was eyed by Aces Ventures. At this stage the company was jointly owned and managed by Ernesto Bautista and Jeanie Nieva,[26] although the Commerce and Industry Minister, Gabriel Kapris, would go on in 2013 to acquire a 26% stake in Aces Ventures – after he left office – for a price that was less than half its book value.[27] In addition Kapris assumed the positions of Managing Director and Chairman.

To facilitate a sale with Aces Ventures, Selon Limited subdivided portion 1056 into several smaller plots, which included portions 1214 (36.11 ha), 1215 (16.92 ha), 1216 (100.48 ha) and 1217 (204.21 ha). Selon initially aimed to facilitate subdivision by seizing the new set of lease titles that were in Tropic Timbers' possession. To that end, on 6 January 2008 five police officers served a search warrant on Tropic Timbers, demanding the titles be handed over. The warrant was overturned on appeal to the courts. The National Court argued this was not a criminal matter, accordingly it was an abuse of process by police to employ a search warrant (*Kikoli v Tropic Timbers Ltd* [2008] PGDC 115). The company nonetheless managed to have portion 1056 subdivided on 17 February 2009, although it is not clear whether the old title was used to enact the administrative process. Shortly before the new leases were issued, a contract of sale for portions 1214 (36.11 ha) and 1215 (16.92 ha) was signed with Aces Ventures for the amount of K558,700 (US$221,700).[28] The sale was witnessed by RD Tuna's Managing Director, a company Tagau provided security services to RD Tuna was also a key lobbyist for the PMIZ project.

Completion of the landsale faced a final hindrance. Portion 1214 housed a residential settlement made up of former plantation workers, who had lived on the location for over two decades. According to subsequent court proceedings, settlement households were given several hundred Kina each by Aces Ventures to vacate the land. When residents refused, the National Court contends that police were sent to the site by Aces Ventures on 8 December 2010. Then, without

> warning or notice … [police] conducted an eviction exercise: the Police forced them out of their houses and burned down their houses and destroyed their food gardens. As a result, their houses, which were made of bush materials, were destroyed together with their personal possessions and they had nowhere to live and no food to eat.
>
> (*Samoua v Aces Venture Ltd* [2013] PGNC 149)

The National Court found in favour of evicted residents in tort. It was noted that the police had razed the site at the behest of Aces Ventures, without a court order, and then proceeded to unlawfully destroy homes and personal property (*Samoua v Aces Venture Ltd* [2013] PGNC 149).

While Selon Limited had now successfully alienated portions of Mililat plantation to Aces Ventures and New Tribes Mission, realising K789,500 in revenues (approx. US$302,000), the remaining land in its possession still contained villages populated by customary owners associated with Masuba Holdings. These residents adamantly maintained Mililat was a part of their customary heritage. It was not a commodity for sale to outsiders. Indeed, they opposed in its entirety the arrangement made between Selon Limited and Tropic Timbers.

In a bid to dislodge them from the site Selon Limited acquired an ejectment order from the District Court.[29] This paved the way for a police raid conducted on 6 October 2009. According to medical reports a number of residents sustained injuries as a result of police violence. For example, 'Walter Bamatu was assaulted in which he was hit with a pistol on the left side of the mouth then punched twice at the left nasal ridge and right eye' (Madang Medical Centre 2009); while Ruben Markus 'was hit with a gun butt on the left eye in which he almost blacked out … the gun butt was quite wide therefore also caused injury to the left maxilla and left angle of the mouth' (Madang Medical Centre 2009).

In response to the violence customary residents organised themselves into an incorporated landowner group, and petitioned the National Court to injunct the eviction order and cancel Selon Limited's title. On 6 April 2010, the National Court issued an order allowing residents to remain on the land.[30] Additionally, Selon Limited was injuncted from selling, mortgaging, leasing or commercially dealing with the land, while the legitimacy of the company's title was determined.

In the subsequent proceeding, the plaintiffs argued that the leasehold title over portion 237 was issued on 'the basis of fraudulent misrepresentations of the First Defendant [Sali Tagau]', making the transfer 'null and void' under section 33(1)(a) of the *Land Registration Act* 1981.[31] On the basis of this argument the Court was asked by residents to issue an order transferring the remaining land held by Selon Limited, to a company registered with 'shareholding and representation from Kananam, Malmal, Riwo and Mobonob villages'.[32] They also requested that all proceeds from the sale to New Tribes Mission and Aces Ventures be transferred to this landowner company. In effect, this was the culminating effort of those groups and interests that had been marginalised and excluded by the Tagau faction.

In a decision delivered on 15 January 2016, Justice Canning observed 'that under Papua New Guinea's Torrens Title system of land registration the general principle is that once a lease of land from the State to a person is registered, an indefeasible title is conferred on the registered proprietor' (*Kais v Tagau* [2016] PGNC 1, para. 15). An exception, he notes, is where fraud can be evidenced. In this respect, Justice Canning notes, drawing on documentary records cited in this chapter:[33]

> There is ample evidence before the Court from the Company Register to show that the shareholdings and directorships of Selon Ltd are not consistent with it being a customary landowner company. It is reasonably to be inferred from the evidence that Selon Ltd was granted the State Lease over Portion 237 because it was regarded by the relevant authorities (the fourth and fifth defendants) as the genuine corporate representative of the traditional owners of the land. I find that the Lease was granted on that false premise … Mr Tagau has testified that Selon Ltd was granted the Lease following a tender process, but provides no details and no evidence of that process … I am satisfied in these circumstances that the plaintiffs have proven a case of 'fraud'.
>
> (*Kais v Tagau* [2016] PGNC 1, para. 21–23)

As a result of this determination, at the time of writing the Court has resolved that the fraudulently obtained titles be 'set aside, forfeited or transferred or subject to such other orders of the Court as are necessary to do justice in the circumstances of this case' (*Kais v Tagau* [2016] PGNC 1, para. 31).

The decision appears to offer residents a reprieve from forced eviction. However, it remains to be seen whether the final court order will be honoured by the Lands Department and police. Both agencies have an evidenced history of non-compliance with court decisions. In the case of Mililat, we have seen numerous instances where they have unlawfully lent their support to Selon Limited. A National Court order may not, therefore, be enough to secure customary interests in the long term.

Finally, it is also not clear whether Tropic Timbers will attempt to assert any residual interest in the property. Its Managing Director remains aggrieved over the actions of Selon Limited (Davidson 2013). Having repeatedly been disappointed when efforts have been made to enforce the law through formal lines of governmental authority, Tropic Timbers recently tied into its network a former MP and government Minister, Thompson Harokaqveh, who acquired a 20% stake in the company for a nominal sum of K200.[34] He was also appointed Director and Secretary. This decision, it appears, has only served to court internal fissures within Tropic Timbers. It is alleged by Davidson that Harokaqveh subsequently attempted to take over the business through the use of force and fraud (Tropic Timbers Limited 2014).

At an extraordinary shareholders' meeting held on 29 June 2014, Davidson alleged, 'Thompson Harokaqveh has done a lot of irreparable damage' to the company (Tropic Timbers Limited 2014). The meeting minutes continue:

> due to Thompson Harokaqveh's illegal and fraudulent 'ceasing' of John Lawrence Davidson as director of Tropic Timbers Ltd though John Lawrence Davison is 80% shareholder, Thompson Harokaqveh is to be removed as unfit for any position at all in Tropic Timbers Ltd.
>
> (Tropic Timbers Limited 2014)

To oust Harokaqveh, Davidson recruited prominent businessman Chris Kundul Alu. Alu has become the new company Director and Secretary (Tropic Timbers Limited 2014). In addition, he has taken up a 20% interest in the company for K20.[35] It remains to be seen whether Alu can reverse Tropic Timbers' fortunes. However, it appears the company is now in a weakened state, with low capacity to reengage with the Mililat issue.

Conclusion

From a speculative perspective, portion 237 was an extremely attractive proposition. For a mere K65,545 the prospective owner could obtain a leasehold title whose total market value is potentially 100 times that sum. However, in this case certain procedures needed to be adhered to, to ensure the property transactions were conducted with landowner consent, and for their benefit.

In Papua New Guinea safeguards designed to protect customary stakeholders have not proven an insurmountable barrier for illegal forms of land acquisition. To the contrary, with illicit repertoires permeating into all levels of the nation's business culture, combined with a permissive regime of land administration, customary land is a prime target for illegitimate forms of transfer. The risk of illicit transfer is heightened when this land hosts, or is adjacent to, major economic projects, whether it be the PMIZ, a mining venture or logging project.

Given the complex fault lines that must be navigated in order to illicitly alienate customary land, an opportunity structure is opened up for local fixers to mediate relations with government and developers. Drawing on inequalities in capital, information, knowledge, resources and access, local fixers are in a position to facilitate the fraudulent transfer of land, without necessarily requiring acts of commission from partners in government and business. In the case of Mililat we can observe that this demands a degree of social dexterity and authority.

For example, Sali Tagau, through Selon Limited, needed to construct a network architecture that could finance the acquisition, and legitimate it in the eyes of local communities. This involved in some instances being able to solder key actors into his circle, who at first sharply opposed Selon Limited's ambitions. However, it was done in a way that denied newly recruited opponents a position of centrality that could have undermined Tagau's ambitions.

All of these manoeuvres demanded that careful control be exercised over communications and access to corporate records. This control meant information could be selectively distributed, and leveraged further by the resource and knowledge differentials Tagau enjoyed vis-à-vis landowner representatives. It also required the accumulation of patrons within the provincial government and Lands Department. On numerous occasions, Tagau relied on supporters from both institutions to vouch for Selon Limited, in the face of evidence suggesting that the company was not a landowner vehicle. When other actors in the network, principally Tropic Timbers Limited, began to seize positions of centrality, steps were taken by Selon Limited to sever them from the commercial network.

Of course, because of the delicate and convoluted transactions these processes involved, the constellation of landowner factions tied to Mililat simply could not be stabilised over a prolonged period of time. Therefore, the network which Tagau established to acquire portion 237 in 2000, began to balkanise into rival factions over subsequent years. It is alleged that Selon Limited's Managing Director turned to violence as a tool for managing relations in the aftermath of multiple internal ruptures.

In the end, Selon Limited was indeed able to convert a number of leasehold titles into money through sales to Aces Ventures and New Tribes Mission. However, legal action by customary owners may now impede the company's unmitigated enjoyment of the proceeds, and remaining land. Yet it must be said this is an exceptional case where residents have been able to evidence the fraud and administer a prolonged legal action. More often than not such challenges prove insurmountable. Not only is it rare to obtain access to 'smoking gun' documents in the volume possessed here, the legal resources and professional expertise needed to properly administer a legal action over a prolonged period, is simply not within the budget of most communities facing forced eviction by better resourced opponents.

So far in chapters five and six our focus has been on setting out rich, narrative based accounts of the two exemplary case studies. However, clearly once we begin to think about illicit land transactions more generally, deploying units of analysis focused on actors, ties, networks and transaction chains, a complex, patterned regime of social practice can be observed, facilitated through certain underpinning commercial and governance structures. Indeed, despite certain key differences, Paga Hill and Mililat evidenced numerous shared traits with respect to the commercial repertoires, motivations and opportunity structures underpinning speculation. With that in mind, the next chapter will undertake a criminological analysis of the land and property market activity observed here, in order to build a generalisable framework that can aid future investigation into land and property market speculation.

Notes

1 Aces Ventures Limited, Annual Return 2009, Investment Promotion Authority, 30 June 2011.
2 Aces Ventures Limited, Notice of Change of Shareholder (Share Transfer), Investment Promotion Authority, 8 August 2013.
3 Aces Ventures Limited, Annual Return 2012, Investment Promotion Authority, 20 March 2013.
4 Contract for the Sale of Land between Selon Limited (the 'Vendor') and: Aces Ventures Limited (the 'Purchaser'), 27 January 2009.
5 For instance 4.562 ha of land held within the plantation was valued at K114,000 in September 2001 (Siwat 2001), while a neighbouring 200 ha plantation was reacquired by the national government in 2010 for K20 million (Bashir 2010).
6 Selon Limited, Current and Historical Company Extract, Investment Promotion Authority, accessed 1 February 2015.
7 Savolon Security Services Limited, Company Extract, Investment Promotion Authority, accessed 1 February 2015.
8 Mortgage Facility Agreement between Tropic Timbers Limited (Lender) and Selon Limited (Borrower), 7 February 2000.
9 Selon Limited, Current and Historical Company Extract, Investment Promotion Authority, accessed 1 February 2015.
10 Statutory Declaration, Madang, 22 March 2000, signed by Joseph Balim, Maksil Mot, Andew Nak, Sir Angmai Bilas and Philip Like.
11 Panuluan Holdings Limited, Company Extract, Investment Promotion Authority, accessed 12 June 2015.
12 Gudi Investments Limited, Company Extract, Investment Promotion Authority, accessed 12 June 2015.
13 Maquela Limited, Company Extract, Investment Promotion Authority, accessed 3 April 2017.
14 Gudi Investments Limited, Company Extract, Investment Promotion Authority, accessed 12 June 2015.

15 This assessment is based off Investment Promotion Authority records and publicly available corporate reporting.

16 Papua New Guinea National Gazette, No. G117, 11 September 2000.

17 Independent State of Papua New Guinea, Agricultural Lease (portion 237), issued to Selon Limited, 27 September 2000.

18 Independent State of Papua New Guinea, Agricultural Lease (portion 237), issued to Selon Limited, 27 September 2000.

19 There is no evidence to suggest David Monks was actually involved in theft.

20 Masuba Limited, Company Extract, Investment Promotion Authority, accessed 1 February 2017.

21 To protect the identity of this source, the reference has been anonymised. They are a land consultant with several decades' experience of property conveyancing in Papua New Guinea.

22 *Ex parte* orders are court orders that have been issued without the presence of a party to the litigation.

23 Selon Limited, Notice of Change of Directors and Particulars of Directors, Investment Promotion Authority, 3 November 2005.

24 Selon Limited, Notice of Change of Shareholders (Share Transfer), Investment Promotion Authority, 3 November 2005.

25 Caveat, Lodged by Rex Paki, Against Portion 1215, Milinch Kranket, Fourmil Madang, Province Madang, 22 February 2011.

26 Aces Ventures Limited, Annual Return 2009, Investment Promotion Authority, 30 June 2011.

27 Aces Ventures Limited, Notice of Change of Shareholder (Share Transfer), Investment Promotion Authority, 8 August 2013.

28 Contract for the Sale of Land between Selon Limited (the Vendor) and Aces Ventures Limite (the Purchaser), 27 January 2009.

29 Writ of Summons, *Vitus Kais, Peter Siarup, Tom Bamatu, Wolff Bamatu, Manuel Ambat, Julius Bamatu, John Sapuri, Sim Sipiel, Mepi Vitus, Erlberth Siarup, Tarisu Siarup, Juackim Bunam, Jaul Sagui and John Dap (first plaintiffs), Masuba Land Group Incorporated (Second plaintiff) v Sali Tagau (first defendant), Selon Limited (second defendant), Tropic Timbers Limited (third defendant), Pepi Kimas (fourth defendant), the Independent State of Papua New Guinea, (fifth defendant)*, WS No 301 of 2010, in the National Court of Justice at Madang Papua New Guinea, 23 March 2010.

30 Court Order, *Vitus Kais, Peter Siarup, Tom Bamatu, Wolff Bamatu, Manuel Ambat, Julius Bamatu, John Sapuri, Sim Sipiel, Mepi Vitus, Erlberth Siarup, Tarisu Siarup, Juackim Bunam, Jaul Sagui and John Dap (first plaintiffs), Masuba Land Group Incorporated (Second plaintiff) v Sali Tagau (first defendant), Selon Limited (second defendant), Tropic Timbers Limited (third defendant), Pepi Kimas (fourth defendant), the Independent State of Papua New Guinea, (fifth defendant)*, WS No 301 of 2010, in the National Court of Justice at Madang Papua New Guinea, 6 April 2010.

31 Amended statement of claim, *Vitus Kais, Peter Siarup, Tom Bamatu, Wolff Bamatu, Manuel Ambat, Julius Bamatu, John Sapuri, Sim Sipiel, Mepi Vitus, Erlberth Siarup, Tarisu Siarup, Juackim Bunam, Jaul Sagui and John Dap (first plaintiffs), Masuba Land Group Incorporated (Second plaintiff) v Sali Tagau (first defendant), Selon Limited (second defendent), Tropic Timbers Limited (third defendant), Pepi Kimas (fourth defendant), the Independant State of Papua New Guinea, (fifth defendant)*, WS No 301 of 2010, in the National Court of Justice at Madang Papua New Guinea, 4 April 2012.

32   Amended statement of claim, *Vitus Kais, Peter Siarup, Tom Bamatu, Wolff Bamatu, Manuel Ambat, Julius Bamatu, John Sapuri, Sim Sipiel, Mepi Vitus, Erlberth Siarup, Tarisu Siarup, Juackim Bunam, Jaul Sagui and John Dap (first plaintiffs), Masuba Land Group Incorporated (Second plaintiff) v Sali Tagau (first defendant), Selon Limited (second defendent), Tropic Timbers Limited (third defendant), Pepi Kimas (fourth defendant), the Independant State of Papua New Guinea, (fifth defendant),* WS No 301 of 2010, in the National Court of Justice at Madang Papua New Guinea, 4 April 2012.

33   The author and residents collaboratively researched the land transfer process. The author was given copies of documents signed by landowners during 1999–2000. Following further fieldwork during 2013, the author in turn provided landowners with copies of internal Selon Limited documents obtained from a number of sources.

34   Tropic Timbers Limited, Notice of Change of Shareholders (Share Transfer), Investment Promotion Authority, 14 May 2013.

35   Tropic Timbers Limited, Notice of Change of Shareholders (Share Transfer), Investment Promotion Authority, 7 July 2014.

Bibliography

Acanufa & Associates Lawyers. (2001). Letter from Lawrence Acanufa, Principal, Acanufa & Associates Lawyers, to Bruce Apana, Messrs Gedens Ridgeway Lawyers, PO Box 1042, Port Moresby 121, NCD, 6 July.

Albaniel, R. (2007). 'Madang tuna capital of PNG', *Post-Courier*, 8 November, p.6.

Albaniel-Evara, R. (2013). 'PMIZ contracts irk landowners', *Post-Courier*, 20 September, p.4.

AusAID. (2006). *Australian Aid: Promoting Growth and Stability*, Canberra: Author.

Bamatu, J. (2013). Personal Communication, 2 August.

Bamatu, W. (2013). Personal Communication, 2 August.

Bashir, M. (2010). 'Chinese seal deal over PMIZ construction', *Post-Courier*, 30 September, p.15.

Bilson, J. (2002). Letter from John K. Bilson, Kananam Village, to John Davidson, Tropic Timbers PO Box 525, Madang, 9 January.

Davidson, J. (2013). Managing Director of Tropic Timbers Limited, Personal Communication, 7 August.

Department of Lands and Physical Planning. (1990). Minute, Daniel P. Katakum, Regional Manager – Northern Region, p.11/509, 14 February.

Department of Lands and Physical Planning. (1999). Letter from Morris Alaluku, Secretary Department of Lands and Physical Planning, to Mr Jacob Sagui, C/-G. Tibong, PO Box 1179, Madang, Madang Province, 26 November.

Department of Lands and Physical Planning. (2000a). Letter from Michael Larry, Advisor, Lands Department (Madang Provincial Administration – Lands Branch), to the Secretary, Department of Lands, PO Box 5665, Borko NCD, 5 January 2000.

Department of Lands and Physical Planning. (2000b). Letter from Morris Alaluku, Secretary Department of Lands, to the Director Gudi Investment Ltd, PO Box 1179, Madang, Madang Province, 12 January.

Department of Lands and Physical Planning. (2000c). Letter from Michael Larry, Advisor, Lands Department (Madang Provincial Administration – Lands Branch), to Gadens Lawyers, PO Box 1042, Port Moresby, National Capital District, 20 January.

Department of Lands and Physical Planning. (2000d). Letter from Michael Larry, Advisor, Lands Department (Madang Provincial Administration – Lands Branch), to the Secretary, Lands Department, PO Box 5665, Boroko, National Capital District, 15 March.

Department of Lands and Physical Planning. (2000e). Letter from Guao K. Zurenuoc OBE, Secretary, Department of Lands and Physical Planning, to the Chairman, Selon Limited, PO Box 1158, Madang, Madang Province, 9 November.

Department of Lands and Physical Planning. (2001a). Letter from Allan Bolla for Guao K. Zurenuoc, Secretary, Department of Lands, to [address crossed out], 10 October.

Department of Lands and Physical Planning. (2001b). Letter from Raga Kavana, Registrar of Titles, to Sali Tagau, Selon Limited, PO Box 1158, Madang, Madang Province, 20 November.

Donaldson, M. and Good, K. (1988). *Articulated Agricultural Development: Traditional and Capitalist Agricultures in Papua New Guinea*, London: Aldershot.

Gadens Lawyers. (2000). Facsimile Transmission from Bruce Apana, Gadens Lawyers, to John Davidson, Tropic Timbers Limited, 27 March.

Gadens Lawyers. (2001). Letter from Bruce M. Apana, Gadens Lawyers, to the Director, Northern Region, Department of Lands and Physical Planning, Level 2, Aopi Centre, Waigani, 19 October.

Gadens Lawyers. (2003). Facsimile Transmission from Christine Bai, Gadens Lawyers, to Mr Romilli Kila, Department of Lands & Physical Planning, 14 February.

Gewertz, D. B. and Errington, F. K. (1999). *Emerging Class in Papua New Guinea: The Telling of Difference*, Cambridge: Cambridge University Press.

Gosarevski, S., Hughes, H. and Windybank, S. (2004). 'Is Papua New Guinea viable with customary land ownership?', *Pacific Economic Bulletin*, 19(3), 133–136.

Havice, E. and Reed, K. (2012). 'Fishing for development? Tuna resource access and industrial change in Papua New Guinea', *Journal of Agrarian Change*, 12(2/3), 413–435.

Jacobus Puringi Lawyers. (2000a). Letter from Jacobus Puringi, Principal, Jacobus Puringi Lawyers, to the Advisor, Madang Office, Department of Lands & Physical Planning, PO Box 2072, Yomba, Madang 511, Madang Province, 23 June.

Jacobus Puringi Lawyers. (2000b). Letter from Jacobus Puringi, Principal, Jacobus Puringi Lawyers, to the Secretary, Department of Lands & Physical Planning, Aopi Centre, PO Box Boroko, National Capital District, 28 June.

Kaiok, M. (2008). 'Kapris announces marine park plans', *Post-Courier*, 3 March, p.5.

Kilimat Holdings. (2004). Letter from Kilimat Holdings, Malmal Village, to [recipient unclear], 21 February.

Kodii, B., Barui, L., Kamos, S. and Pau, O. (2000). Letter from Bolo Kodii (Bared Clan), Lill Barui (Abo Clan), Sambun Kamos (Nuho Clan) and Oromda Pau (Makel Clan), to the Manager, Gudi Investment, PO Box, Madang, 19 June.

Koli, B. (2012). *Statutory Declaration*, Madang Province, 16 August.

Land Consultant. (2013). Personal Communication, 23 July.

Lasslett, K. (2014). *State Crime on the Margins of Empire*, London: Pluto Books.

MacWilliam, S. (2005). 'Post-war reconstruction in Bougainville: Plantations, smallholders and indigenous capital', in Regan, A. J. and Griffin, H. M. (eds) *Bougainville: Before the Conflict*, Canberra: Pandanus Books.

Madang Medical Centre. (2009). Letter from Dr C. Kalanam, MBB, DGO, Madang Medical Centre, 7 October.

Madang Provincial Government. (2000). Letter from Joe Maira, Chairman, Natural Resources, Madang Provincial Government to the Honorable Minister for Lands, PO Box 5665, Boroko, NCD, 4 January.

Masuba Limited. (2001). Letter from Mr Mathias Ambera and Philip Bell, Masuba Ltd, to the Public Solicitors Office of Sub-Branch Madang, 10 October.

Mathias, A. (2014). 'Contractor signs deal to fix highway', *Post-Courier*, 24 November, p.21.

Mousseau, F. (2013). *On Our Land: Modern Land Grabs Reversing Independence in Papua New Guinea*, Oakland: Oakland Institute.

Muroa, G. M. S. (1998). 'The extent of constitutional protection of land rights in Papua New Guinea', *Melanesian Law Journal*, 26. [Online]. Available at: www.paclii.org/journals/MLJ/1998/ (accessed: 10 March 2017).

Numapo, J. (2013). *Commission of Inquiry into the Special Agriculture and Business Leases: Final Report*, Port Moresby: Commission of Inquiry into the Special Agricultural and Business Leases.

Public Accounts Committee. (2007). *Public Accounts Committee Report to Parliament on the Inquiry into the Department of Lands and Physical Planning*, Waigani: National Parliament of Papua New Guinea.

Saurin, A. (2003). Meeting Minutes – Special Meeting, Milinat Plantations, Four Villages: Riwo, Malmal, Mabenob and Sek, held at Riwo Village, 11 May.

Selon Limited. (1999). Letter from Sali Tagau, Chairman of Selon Limited, to Mr Daniel Katakum, Department of Lands – Northern Region, PO Box 5665, Boroko, National Capital District, 9 December.

Selon Limited. (2000a). Letter from Sali Tagau, Director of Selon Limited, to the Provincial Administrator, Department of Madang, PO Box, Madang, Madang Province, 29 March.

Selon Limited. (2000b). Meeting Minutes, Savolon Village, Kananam, 14 May.

Selon Limited. (2000c). Letter from Sali Tagau, Director, Selon Limited, to Daniel Katakum, Department of Lands, Apopi Centre, PO Box 5665, Boroko, National Capital District, Papua New Guinea, 16 May.

Selon Limited. (2000d). Letter from Sali Tagau, Director, Selon Limited, to the Secretary, Department of Lands & Physical Planning, PO Box 5665, Boroko, Port Moresby, National Capital District, 12 July.

Selon Limited. (2000e). Letter from Selon Limited, to Mr Allan Bolla, Department of Lands & Physical Planning, PO Box 5665, Boroko, National Capital District, 10 October 2000.

Selon Limited. (2000f). Letter from Sali Tagau, Managing Director, Selon Limited, to New Tribes Mission, no address, 19 October 2000.

Selon Limited. (2000g). Letter from Sali Tagau, Managing Director, Selon Limited, to the Manager, Tropic Timbers Limited, Madang, Madang Province, 1 November.

Selon Limited. (2001a). Meeting Minutes, Directors Meeting – Office of Corporate Management and Business Consultants, 21 March.

Selon Limited. (2001b). Meeting Minutes, 4th Meeting of Directors, Savolon Village, Kananam, 21 July.

Selon Limited. (2001c). Letter from Sali Tagau, Managing Director, Selon Limited, to John Davidson, Managing Director, Tropic Timbers Pty Ltd, PO Box 525, Madang 511, Madang Province, 31 July.

Selon Limited. (2001d). Letter from Sali Tagau, Chairman, Selon Limited, to the Managing Director, Tropic Timbers Ltd, PO Box 525, Madang 511, Madang Province, 20 September.

Selon Limited. (2001e). Letter from Sali Tagau, Chairman, Selon Limited, to The Managing Director, Tropic Timbers Ltd, PO Box 525, Madang 511, Madang Province, 5 December.

Selon Limited. (2003). Draft letter from Directors, Selon Limited, to Andrew Maipson, Pato Lawyers, PO Box 2126, Port Moresby, National Capital District, 11 July.

Selon Limited. (2004a). Letter from Sali Tagau, Chairman, Selon Limited, to the Landowner Elders, 3 January.

Selon Limited. (2004b). Meeting Minutes, Joe Balim's Office, 19 February.

Selon Limited. (2004c). Directors' Resolutions, Selon Limited, 18 March.

Siwat, V. (2001). *Valuation and Report, Portion 1060, Milinch Kranket, Fourmil Madang*, Madang: Author.

Sullivan, N. J. Warr, T., Rainbubu, J., Kunoko, J., Akauna, F., Angasa, M. and Wenda, Y. (2003). *Tinpis Maror: A Social Impact Study of Proposed RD Tuna Cannery at Vidar Wharf, Madang*, Madang: Nancy Sullivan Ltd.

Sungai, J. and Kubak, M. (2001). Meeting Minutes, Kananam community, 11 March.

Tagau, S. (2003). Affidavit, *Selon Limited v John Davidson & Tropic Timbers Limited*, OS No. 514 of 2001, 12 March.

Tapakau, E. (2010). 'Filipino firm to build K8m bridge', *Post-Courier*, 26 July, p.32.

Tropic Timbers Limited. (1998). *Proposed Business Plan*.

Tropic Timbers Limited. (2001a). Facsimile Transmission from John Davidson, Managing Director, Tropic Timbers Ltd, to Bruce Apana, Gadens Lawyers, 19 March.

Tropic Timbers Limited. (2001b). Facsimile Transmission from John Davidson, Managing Director, Tropic Timbers Ltd, to Bruce Apana, Gadens Lawyers, 23 July.

Tropic Timbers Limited. (2001c) Proposal by John Davidson, Managing Director, Tropic Timbers Ltd, to Resolve Deadlock, 8 September.

Tropic Timbers Limited. (2001d). Letter from John Davidson, Managing Director, Tropic Timbers, to Selon Limited, North Coast Road, PO Box 1158, Madang, 14 September.

Tropic Timbers Limited. (2001e). Statement by John Davidson, Managing Director of Tropic Timbers Pty Ltd, 21 September.

Tropic Timbers Limited. (2001f). Facsimile Transmission from John Davidson, Managing Director, Tropic Timbers Ltd, to Bruce Apana, Gadens Lawyers, 11 November.

Tropic Timbers Limited. (2002a). Facsimile Transmission from John Davidson, Managing Director, Tropic Timbers, to Bruce Afana, Gadens Lawyers, 28 January.

Tropic Timbers Limited. (2002b). Facsimile Transmission from John Davidson, Managing Director, Tropic Timbers, to Bruce Afana, Gadens Lawyers, 30 January.

Tropic Timbers Limited. (2002c). Letter from John Davidson, Managing Director, Tropic Timbers Ltd, to Selon Ltd, PO Box, Madang, 3 June.

Tropic Timbers Limited. (2005a). Statement of Account, 30 January.

Tropic Timbers Limited. (2005b). Letter from John Davidson, Managing Director, Tropic Timbers Limited, to the Directors, Selon Limited, Section 10, Allotment 21, Binnen Road, Madang. Delivered to Joe Balim at 10:20am by Constable Peter Mores. 2 February.

Tropic Timbers Limited. (2014). Meeting Minute – Extraordinary Shareholders Meeting, Port Moresby, 29 June.

Turner, M. (1990). *Papua New Guinea: The Challenge of Independence*, Harmondsworth, UK: Penguin.

Warner Shand Lawyers. (2004) Facsimile Transmission from Nigel Merrick, Warner Shand Lawyers, to Young Wada Lawyers, PO Box, Madang, Madang Province, 23 September.

Cases

Kais v Tagau [2016] PGNC 1
Kikoli v Tropic Timbers Ltd [2008] PGDC 115
Samoua v Aces Venture Ltd [2013] PGNC 149
Selon Limited v John Davidson & Tropic Timbers Limited OS No. 514 of 2001
Selon Limited v Tropic Timbers Limited & John Davidson OS No.89 of 2005

Chapter 7

State–corporate wrongdoing in land and property markets

Forging an analytical framework

The two exemplary case studies presented in chapters five and six illuminate the actors, ties, networks, resources, repertoires and transaction chains, used to prosecute land transfers, real-estate ventures and massed forced eviction, in addition to the institutional, legal, political and economic environments in which these activities are facilitated. Evidence was presented which suggests the relevant economic and governance terrains were marked by systematic, illegitimate practices. In this chapter, the patterns observed in the investigative data-sets is going to be transformed into an analytical framework for further testing, as part of a broader attempt to theorise organised wrongdoing within land and property markets. To that end, through a series of theses, core drivers of illicit activity in land and property markets are going to be identified and explained. The replicability of this framework to the wider data-set collected for this study will be demonstrated through its application to two further case studies conducted in Papua New Guinea, presented at the end of this chapter.

It ought to be emphasised that the theses employed to construct the theoretical framework are primed for conceptualising land speculation and real-estate developments involving larger estates, relative to the urban scale being examined.[1] The type of illicit repertoires captured by this focus includes, for instance, anti-competitive practices, price manipulation, fraud, corruption, regulatory non-compliance, forced evictions, property destruction, and acts of violence directed at residents, activists and civil society.

Because this framework is grounded most immediately in six case studies conducted in one country, its transferability will need to be tested through subsequent research. However, it establishes an agenda for this research, creating hypotheses that can be tested, refined and reformed, as a larger body of data emerges. All of which is critical if applied resources are to be developed that can guide resistance initiatives looking to establish counter-networks and resistance-repertoires that can successfully challenge those illicit dynamics underpinning the urbanisation process, which spark exclusion and contention.

Before the framework is presented, one final caveat must be noted. A distinction is made here between criminological theory on the organisation and prosecution of land and property market misconduct, and political-economic theory, which was the focus of chapter two. With that in mind, this chapter's objective is to better understand the sustained, patterned dynamics underpinning illicit state–corporate conduct within land and property markets. In chapter two, on the other hand, our theoretical lens was adjusted to think about the broader set of historical relationships that have emerged, which make this illicit conduct possible and desirable.

Ten theses on state–corporate misconduct in land and property markets

1. Established land and property markets

Land is not a natural commodity. Paper documents or digital files entitling the named holder to certain monopoly rights over space, which can be traded on markets – an important precondition for commercial misconduct – requires a complex, historically constructed institutional and regulatory edifice, backed by organised expressions of sovereign power. At a minimum, land must be freed of personal, political or customary encumbrances that would prevent the holder from enjoying monopoly rights over land, that can be traded on an open market to a third party. There must be in place a recognised system of land surveying, that permits portions to be systematically identified and demarcated. Legal mechanisms must exist that give the surveyed land a registerable form, so a title can be produced. Furthermore, the proprietary rights this title gives the holder over a particular land portion must be enforceable, which assumes a court system, executive apparatus and, where needed, certain coercive tools.

If land titles are then to be traded onwards to a third party, conveyancing rules and procedures must be established. Also, because this particular form of market activity can have a wide range of consequential impacts on the surrounding social landscape, some form of regulatory order will generally be needed, through mechanisms such as zoning, development approval procedure, land tax and ownership requirements.

The critical point is, for land to assume a commodified form, an expansive edifice is needed to confer on titleholders tradable monopoly rights that can attract revenue flows (rental yield), which permit a process of market price formation to take place. This historically developed framework, in turn, creates the possibility of commercial repertoires that profit from price shifts rooted in property yields, which title-holders can influence through landed improvements and by lobbying for changes to the broader urban environment (see chapter two). It is at this social juncture that a range of illicit practices are frequently deployed to amplify returns.

Of course even today not all land is necessarily encompassed by such a legal, administrative and commercial edifice. A case in point is Papua New Guinea, where a significant portion of the national estate continues to be distributed through kinship networks, according to custom. However, on occasions when the national government has engineered schemes which selectively convert customary estates into formalised systems of titles that can be traded to a third party in leasehold form, it has opened the door to speculative activity and forms of dispossession underpinned by corruption and fraud. Therefore, it is essential that the creation and expansion of land and property markets is seen as an active, historical moment – not an assumed fact – often marked by a prehistory of contention and violence, which is an important driver for the illicit activity being analysed here.

2. Opportunity structure for price manipulation

While the historical expansion of land and property markets creates the possibility of speculative activity, there is heightened risk that market transactions will take an illicit form, when opportunity structures exist that permit agents to illegitimately obtain titles at a discounted rate, or sell them at an inflated price.

The former transaction can occur in a number of different ways. For example, state land may be acquired at a discount through corrupt transactions that allow the purchaser to circumvent procedures and regulations – such as public tender – designed to enforce market discipline and competition. Equally, privately held titles can be the subject of illegitimate forms of devaluation, for instance, when land is undersold by an asset management firm or a trustee, on behalf of a beneficiary. We also observed in the previous chapter that customary land, owned collectively by kinship groups, can be acquired at a discount, especially when a group member employs their position of centrality to defraud the larger collective, covertly selling on a communal resource at a reduced price to a private third party.

It is also important to keep in mind that property sales – particularly when it is large scale – will have a range of built-in expenses, which add to the overall acquisition cost in real terms. For instance, the process may demand that the purchaser obtain development approval, a potentially costly and time-consuming process which if bypassed – illicitly – can deflate acquisition costs. There may be certain taxes levied on the sale, which can be waived or reduced through the payment of a bribe. The key point is, property acquisitions – particularly on a larger scale – are complex affairs, where there exist multiple avenues for reducing acquisition costs through illegal means.

Illicit forms of manipulation may, of course, be directed at the other side of the sales transaction, leading to an inflated purchase price. We have witnessed companies illegitimately increasing sale prices in the UK through land banking schemes, where consumers are mis-sold land through fraudulent representations exaggerating its development potential. Price inflation may also be precipitated, for example, when a vendor and the purchaser's agent conspire – sometimes aided by professional middlemen (such as valuers). This type of conspiracy can precipitate an illicit transfer of revenue from the purchaser, to their agents, the seller and the relevant middlemen. In Papua New Guinea the most well-known example of this dynamic was uncovered by the Commission of Inquiry into the National Provident Fund (NPF). The inquiry found that managers stationed within the latter superannuation fund, worked with public officials and conveyancing professionals to illicitly organise the sale of land held by a private individual – a senior NPF executive – at an inflated price to the fund. The augmented proceeds this fraud would produce was then to be shared between the complicit actors.

Illegitimately influencing urban governance regimes can be another lucrative conduit for price manipulation. For instance, where powerful developer coalitions emerge, they can leverage their political connections and economic weight, to illicitly steward through changes to the urban environment that increase the value of their existing property holdings, or bring new assets onto the market at a discounted rate. For instance, bribery or other forms of illicit influence can be employed to rezone an area creating a price spike, or it can be used to free 'moribund' land through the issue of demolition orders over rundown properties.

Of course, it is impossible to predict the exact arrangements which will underpin price manipulation in any one instant, owing to different regulatory, institutional and market regimes. Clearly systemic corruption, speculative investment cultures, weak oversight and bullish markets – matters which will be returned to in a moment – are all, broadly speaking, potentially part of such an opportunity structure. Nevertheless, the point being underlined here is that illegitimate repertoires are not intrinsically desired. Rather, it is their instrumental value as a tool for augmenting returns that gives them appeal for those actors looking to valorise capital through land and property market activity. It can be hypothesised then that illegitimate repertoires will more likely exist in land and property markets where there are relatively accessible means for price manipulation, with low levels of risk for the actors involved, and potentially high rewards.

3. The construction and maintenance of diversified social networks

The network architecture underpinning illegitimate land deals and property developments usually includes a diverse range of actors, who as a whole bring together the financial, technical, political and public administrative resources necessary to prosecute the requisite transactions. However, for these networks to successfully operate, the architecture must be designed and managed in such a way as to connect the right actors, manage tensions, maintain network integrity, and where necessary exile/convert actors who threaten to destabilise the transaction chain. This often involves the application of considerable effort by fixers and middlemen.

First, people possessing appropriate forms of knowledge, capital and power need to be identified. This demands that network architects are literate enough in the commercial and political landscape, to strategically identify and access relevant actors. Then adhesives need to be applied, that can fuse strategically important actors to the emerging network. The adhesives will be stronger where they take multiple forms, such as shared pecuniary interests and a personal relationship of some enduring sort, whether it be friendship, marriage or ethnic solidarity.

To be effective, the network architecture needs to maintain its integrity for a sustained period of time, without rupturing. Accordingly, network architects need to be able to carefully manage relationships, control flows of information, regulate communication lines, and identify dangerous nodes within the network which need to be suppressed or excised. Because networks often feature actors who are deviating beyond the norms governing their public or private roles, network architects must also be discrete players, who can conceal these deliberations from the public.

Therefore, we can expect to find when examining or indeed confronting illicit land and property market activity, intricate networks of actors who bring together a strategic mix of resources, assets, expertise and power, congruent with the transaction chains being employed. Such networks do not emerge organically; rather a range of material adhesives are applied to solder the actor constellation into place. Accordingly, behind a prosecuting network will generally stand an architect or architects essential to its construction and maintenance, who may also be among the principal beneficiaries of the transaction. Their distinguishing skill is a capacity to identify and wed together strategic actors, in a discrete fashion, while being astute to potential dangers in need of excision.

Because there is an intrinsic connection between transaction chains – which generate certain expertise, power and resource needs – and the qualitative features of the actors threaded together to execute these chains, concretely documenting this relationship can potentially enhance short and long term resistance efforts. In the instance of broader reform agendas, understanding this relationship can inform interventions designed to prevent the soldering together of actor constellations essential to illicit transaction chains. More immediately speaking, however, strategic appreciation of this relationship can strengthen grass-roots resistance movements challenging a particular venture. If steps can be taken to break ties between the requisite actors in the constellation – such as a politician or financier – there is a possibility that the transaction chain can be delayed or potentially prevented, depending on the resources and agility of the network architects.

4. Competition and contention between rival groups

Even once a durable, diversified coalition has been established, there is the persistent problem of rival groups. Indeed, given the considerable profits that can be generated from illicit land and property market activity, rivalry between speculative cliques appears to be an endemic feature of this field of practice. Such a dynamic can trigger a range of illicit tactics, particularly when they give a competitor an edge in the race for resources (financial, expert, cultural), and contacts (professional, administrative, political), that can enhance the group's position vis-à-vis rivals. It can also precipitate strategic offensives, marked by illegitimate practices. For example, a rival clique can be sabotaged by removing a key actor from its network architecture, whether it be through incentivising them to change sides (bribery), or by excising them from the equation entirely through forceful measures (use of violence).

However, the critical point to underline here is the existence of rivalry as a common determinant in speculative land and property market activity, which makes such activity a heated, contested affair. This, in turn, can precipitate illicit practices designed to increase a group's institutional leverage and undermine their rivals. Such dynamics also alerts us to a significant test network architects contend with – to succeed they must be adept at assessing their rivals' strengths and weaknesses, deploying tactics that can strategically decimate the latter's resources, expertise, contacts and access to capital. Furthermore, when looked at from the vantage point of resistance, episodes in rivalry can create cleavages which if harnessed may strengthen the movement's social, legal or political efforts, particularly when an embittered party reaches out to civil society in an effort to enhance their position – albeit obviously in these situations caution and care must be exercised.

5. Permissive land administration regimes

The sustained forms of illicit activity discussed in the previous sections, prosper when permissive land administrations exist whose structures and processes prove amenable to such activities, and the improper relations they involve. Aid, in this respect, may come in many forms. For example, it could occur through ignoring tendering requirements; providing development approvals and permits without due diligence; ignoring contractual and regulatory breaches; failing to act on complaints made by the public; politically defending illegitimate proposals; and harassing opposition movements.

These permissive dynamics encompass a range of government agencies which form a direct or indirect part of the land administration edifice. In the cases researched for this volume, there was evidence to suggest all key nodes in the land regime under examination were permissive of illegal market activity. Regulations relating to zoning, planning and sale were routinely ignored by the national Land Board; Lands Department officials actively participated in illegal transactions and frauds; when departmental officers were alerted to improper processes, no redress occurred; senior political figures championed projects marked by illegal transactions; some public officials obtained a direct or indirect stake in landed developments they had helped approve; certain civil society actors were willing to lend their esteem to illegitimate transactions/ ventures; and the police routinely executed evictions, and harassed opposition movements, without lawful authority, using excessive forms of violence.

However, we must be cautious when describing such behaviour as a 'breakdown' in governance. More accurately it may signal the emergence of shadow governance regimes that supersede and subordinate formal lines of administrative authority. In the cases researched here, it was certainly apparent that an informal institutional structure and culture had developed by design over a prolonged period, which exerted weight over formal lines of authority and regulatory processes. With good reason, this informal system allowed market actors, wielding particular forms of leverage and power, to employ the machinery of government to manipulate prices, circumvent competition and unlawfully remove impediments, all of which could accrue to beneficiaries an often considerable financial windfall. Such practices had been vividly brought to the government's attention on numerous occasions by anti-corruption agencies. However, this had no identifiable effect, in part because Ministers were themselves either instigators or facilitators of land sales and property developments marked by illegal conduct.

Accordingly, it may be hypothesised that illegal land and property market activity will take place more vigorously when shadow regimes have historically emerged, which can circumvent formal administrative and regulatory processes, creating a permissive environment for illicit investment repertoires. Furthermore, because the land administration landscape is often marked by unevenness in this respect – that is, some organisational points in the administration will be more permissive than others – we would expect to see dialectical synergy between permissive nodes and the type of illicit market repertoires being employed in a jurisdiction. In other words, permissive nodes are carved out by adept state–corporate actors looking to achieve certain economic goals through illicit means. In turn, these permissive nodes will entice further rounds of like illicit activity from market actors looking to gain a competitive edge or augmented returns using this historically developed opportunity structure.

6. Permissive corporate and financial governance

When diversified networks pursue speculative landed ventures or large scale property developments employing illicit repertoires, the joint nature of this enterprise requires organisational vehicles that can discretely manage collaborations, while minimising the personal risk borne by members. These ventures will also often involve questionable financial transactions, including the laundering of proceeds from crime and the payment of bribes. These financial flows must be free to circulate between individual and corporate bank accounts without being detected or impeded by regulatory authorities. Therefore, it may be hypothesised that illicit land and property activity will be simpler to conduct when network actors have access to corporate forms and banking networks operating within 'light touch' governance regimes.

The latter regimes can have both national and transnational dimensions. At a national level there will be company laws setting out the duties, rights and powers of different stakeholders, such as shareholders, directors and liquidators, in addition to the rules that must be observed with respect to particular transactions, such as share transfers or producing annual returns. In some cases, foreign investors may be subject to a set of more specific requirements designed to vet inward investment. Additionally, financial institutions handling individual and corporate accounts will have certain due diligence obligations with respect to their clients, including verifying identity and reporting suspicious transactions. The rigour of this corporate and financial regime, and the vigour with which it is enforced, will shape the opportunities available for illicit land and property market transactions, given their likely dependence on the corporate form and banking institutions.

However, it must be kept in mind that evidence is emerging from a range of regions, which suggests commercial activities marked by corruption and other illicit transactions are increasingly facilitated through transnational corporate and financial infrastructure. This infrastructure allows illicit financial transactions to take place in multiple, lax regions featuring banks that specialise in laundering money for clients. Adding another layer of protection, these illicit financial flows can be enacted by companies incorporated in secrecy jurisdictions, where the identity of beneficial owners may be concealed. Accordingly, when evaluating the permissive corporate and financial infrastructure available to network actors, it is important to consider the transnational opportunities that may exist for concealing ownership, laundering assets, escaping oversight and transferring funds without triggering due diligence checks.

We should not ignore either, the mandate and resources of regulatory authorities responsible for enforcing company, foreign investment and finance regulations at a national and transnational level. Even when robust legal provisions govern corporate conduct and financial transparency, their impact can be negated by a weak enforcement culture. The latter may reflect resource constraints which significantly reduce a regulator's investigative and prosecutorial capacities, or it may signal a business friendly 'compliance' culture. Certainly when researching Papua New Guinea, regulations enumerated in the *Companies Act* 1997 were breached serially by many of the corporate actors examined. These breaches were never detected by the Investment Promotion Authority, and even when the authority's attention was drawn to breaches by outside parties, they failed to prosecute violations. Of course, where a robust enforcement culture exists at a national level, the transnational corporate and financial context may be so complex and replete with barriers, that only a small proportion of cases can be investigated, thus substantially lowering the risk of detection or prosecution.

Taking these considerations into account, it may be hypothesised that illicit land and property market activity will be easier to prosecute when there exists national and transnational regimes that allow joint enterprises to assume a limited liability corporate form, where beneficial ownership can be hidden, and minimal obligations are placed on the company, in law or practice, to account for its business and interests. The same principle applies to financial regimes which permit banks, in law or practice, to facilitate financial transactions without vetting clients or conducting rigorous due diligence.

7. Central agents experienced in speculative repertoires

Profitably employing fraud, corruption, violence and other illegal techniques to circumvent competitive pressures, manipulate prices, avoid governance regimes and remove impediments, requires technical proficiency and bespoke expertise. For instance, prosecuting agents must identify potent investment opportunities, forge ties with key power brokers, manage information flows and lines of communication, locate permissive administrative nodes, exploit governance weaknesses, eradicate opponents and rivals, all while maintaining an outward face of legitimacy. The repertoires this necessitates can be profitably practised in a range of sectors. Consequently, we can expect that illicit land and property market activity will frequently involve central actors who have honed their abilities through a range of speculative activities, giving them a diverse portfolio of interests.

Indeed, during the Papua New Guinea research it soon emerged that key figures driving the relevant land and property ventures did not have a professional background in the sector. Instead, their careers were built around a generalisable skill-set that had been deployed in wide range of fields, through projects that were often coupled to serious allegations of illegal conduct by oversight agencies, in addition to civil society actors. Perhaps the most obvious example – but certainly not the only one – is Gudmundur Fridriksson (see chapter five), who, over a period of two decades, had run businesses involved in building a liquorice factory, publishing a book for the Papua New Guinean government, project managing a fun park venture, providing legal services, consulting with a range of government agencies, implementing a welfare reform programme, and overseeing a property development at Paga Hill. Many of these ventures became the subject of censure; the most serious allegations being levelled by government oversight agencies in Papua New Guinea, who accused Fridriksson's businesses of employing corruption and other illegal practices.

With this overarching point in mind, we should expect to see when examining illicit land and property market activity, on a frequent basis, central actors who are adept at spotting opportunities in diverse fields, with modest upfront investment costs but significant potential gains. These opportunities are then exploited through a repertoire – that includes illicit dimensions – honed in a range of commercial pursuits that enable practitioners to build networks, out-manoeuvre rivals, utilise permissive regimes and remove impediments.[2]

8. Accumulating indicia of legitimacy

Although land and property market activity prosecuted through illicit repertoires relies to an extent on discrete networks and transactions, the material impact these ventures have on the built environment invariably elicits some public attention. How heavy a project's public footprint is, and the attention it is likely to attract, will depend in part on the venture's size and location, and the type of physical changes it might prompt. The public footprint will also be affected by the strength and vibrancy of civil society actors, in addition to the vigour of public agencies charged with oversight responsibilities. The stronger both are, the greater is the likeliness that these activities will generate substantive public attention. Where this occurs, a burden is placed on the coalition prosecuting these activities to legitimise their efforts.

Of course, legitimacy is a socio-historically rooted phenomenon that hinges on context specific norms. These norms give certain types of activity a permissible quality in the eyes of a wider social audience, while framing other practices as improper. However, in the cases documented so far the normative criteria governing transaction legitimacy has been subtly different in each instance. For example, the legitimacy of Mililat's transfer was framed by post-colonial norms which emphasised the importance of returning alienated land to customary owners. As a result, the group which organised itself through Selon Limited needed to marshal support from clan leaders and selectively circulate corporate information, which would reinforce the public appearance that it was a collective vehicle for customary landowners with a stake in the land's return. On the other hand, in the case of Paga Hill, PHDC's proposal to construct a luxury estate on national park land in Papua New Guinea's capital, evoked debates over the developer's suitability, background, project aims and eviction methods. To counter these objections, PHDC appealed to normative values centring on the desirability of 'modernisation' and 'development', in order to frame its real-estate venture as an iconic vehicle for converting Port Moresby into a respected cosmopolitan hub, whilst creating jobs and generating economic growth. This pitch was eventually married to a corporate social responsibility narrative, following a failed forced eviction exercise. These efforts were further enhanced by public statements of support from government agencies, relevant Ministers and certain civil society actors.

Therefore, it may be hypothesised that for contentious forms of land and property market activity to succeed, facilitating agents will need to be conversant in the norms governing land use, and capable of accumulating the associated hallmarks of legitimacy. How demanding this process will be depends on the rigour of public oversight, the vibrancy of civil society and the visibility of the particular activity under examination.

9. Strategic fusion of legal and illegal processes

It is unusual to find large scale land and property market transactions that are purely illicit in content. The acquisition/sale process, subsequent construction efforts, and where relevant, forced evictions, tend to be of a mixed nature, where some laws are observed, while others are not. However, it can be hypothesised that the balance in this respect is not an accidental affair, but rather, reflects strategic decisions taken by the actors prosecuting the transactions concerned.

So, while zoning, public tender or other conveyancing regulations may be violated in order to acquire title at a discounted price, nonetheless, once the property is obtained it can be strategically used to facilitate a range of lawful transactions such as acquiring a mortgage, or evicting residents. Where title holders wish to sit on land without honouring legal obligations such as rental or land tax payments, or improvement covenants, agencies charged with oversight may be incentivised, through illegitimate means, to derogate from their duties. On the one hand, while this is taking place, land title holders may wish the same government officials to lawfully approve development plans, so funding can be solicited from private investors. Where residents impede a venture, land titles and court orders can be selectively employed to stigmatise resistance and garner support from the courts and police. On the other hand, where residents are able to successfully prosecute their interests in the courts, illicit forms of violence, intimidation or influence, may be employed to quash opposition.

Clearly it is difficult to predict in advance the precise consistency of lawful and unlawful activity each venture will involve. It will depend on the prevailing opportunity structure, characteristics of the land administration regime, corporate oversight, the integrity of the courts and police, the vigour of resistance, to name just a few determinants. Nevertheless, when examining land and property market activity, it is unlikely we will see interests solely prosecuted through illicit means. Quite often, indicia of legality will front the project, behind which stands a more opaque set of illicit practices. This is not surprising, given that the commercial agendas driving projects tainted by illicit conduct will often be dependent for their success on unhindered participation in legitimate markets, so capital can be acquired, partners secured and the property leased/sold.

10. Resistance and counter-resistance

Because illicit land and property market activity will often impact upon human communities and natural phenomena, opposition from organised grass-roots movements is a constant threat. The precise socio-ecological makeup of the property/space sparking contention, and the relative capacity of interested parties to form networks of resistance, will condition the form and strength of the opposition experienced. In the cases researched for this volume, resistance was mounted largely by economically marginalised communities, who were not well positioned – at least initially – to fuse into their network of resistance, influential government, corporate, legal or indeed civil society actors. Nevertheless, despite being in a position of structural disadvantage innovative activist repertoires were witnessed, rooted in community solidarity and an emerging set of norms championing housing rights.

Over time, multi-faceted public awareness campaigns, boosted by community fundraising activities, enabled residents resisting displacement to construct meaningful ties with human rights organisations, researchers, politicians, lawyers and journalists, who each brought certain resources, expertise and forms of influence. Although soldered together under austere conditions, these coalitions helped buttress a series of legal, social and political interventions which questioned the legitimacy of the land and property market transactions being contested, while building support for alternative land use projects congruent with resident rights and livelihoods.

However, given that the actors behind illicit land and property market activity specialise in building networks that can successfully navigate complex political processes, and see off commercial rivals, they are well equipped to mount counter-resistance campaigns. For instance, opposition movements can be stigmatised and marginalised through a fusion of symbolic and physical actions, including political lobbying, court proceedings, public statements, benevolent activities, media attacks and of course violence, whether it be privately organised, publicly organised or a mixture of both. This type of adversarial behaviour can be strategically married to more discrete interventions that aim to co-opt key individual or organisational actors within the resistance movement, who are integral to its influence, resource base or organisational capacities.

It may be hypothesised, therefore, that when illicit land and property market activity impinges on the interests of communities, it will prompt organised resistance. This resistance will likely be mounted from a position of structural disadvantage, owing to diminished access to capital, decision makers and strategic resources. Nevertheless, resistance movements can to an extent overcome structural forms of disadvantage through frenetic, multi-dimensional activism strengthened by ties with sympathetic local, national and international parties, such as NGOs, religious institutions, trade unions or influential politicians. When these actions are executed with distinction, networks banding behind the contested property transactions will have to deploy counter-resistance tactics that are congruent and proportionate to the threats posed. The latter actors will likely enjoy advantages with respect to capital, resources and influence, stemming from a privileged position that has been carved out in the economic, social and political landscape. Therefore, we should expect to see state–corporate actors prevail over community opponents. However, victory will rarely be absolute. Consequently, even when communities fail to achieve core objectives, their conduct can attract important concessions. The more effective their resistance is, in terms of technique, weight and impact, the greater the concessions.

Summary

The preceding sections advanced ten theses which conceptualise generalisable dynamics found to be critical drivers of illicit activity in land and property markets. These are:

1. *Established land and property markets*
2. *Opportunity structure for price manipulation*
3. *The construction and maintenance of diversified social networks*
4. *Competition and contention between rival groups*
5. *Permissive land administration regimes*
6. *Permissive corporate and financial governance*
7. *Central agents experienced in speculative repertoires*
8. *Accumulating indicia of legitimacy*
9. *Strategic fusion of legal and illegal processes*
10. *Resistance and counter-resistance*

This list is not intended to be exclusive or definitive. Clearly if we are to conceptualise the systemic characteristics of the networks and transaction chains underpinning illicit activity in land and property markets, the generalisability of these theses must be confirmed through further testing. In addition, there is scope for new concepts to be developed.

Beyond the intrinsic importance of theory as a tool of explanation, this endeavour has a number of practical benefits. In the case of urban reform, policy makers and civil society need a theory 'heat map' that can identify the most criminogenic dynamics underpinning state–corporate deviance in land and property markets, so resources and efforts can be strategically prioritised (see chapter eight). Furthermore, movements of resistance contesting particular ventures can more effectively prosecute their interests, when capable of strategically targeting network and transaction vulnerabilities. Accordingly, the theses presented here go beyond giving conceptual form to generalisable dynamics, they also constitute an applied resource for reform and resistance efforts.

To tease out, and further evidence the generalisability of these theses, two shorter case studies will now be presented. Each case study offers up its own unique set of determinations that differentiate them from the exemplary studies presented in chapters five and six. Yet as we will see, the dynamics conceptualised here continue to be key illicit drivers.

A K300 million development by Parliament House

The Port Moresby suburb of Waigani is home to some of Papua New Guinea's most important political, legal and cultural institutions. The National Parliament, National and Supreme Court, National Museum, National Library and the University of Papua New Guinea, all lie in close proximity to each other. Alongside these iconic national institutions are a range of government departments, diplomatic offices and the city's most popular entertainment and shopping complex. It was in this important urban hub that the Arts Centre Settlement could once be found, until its demolition in 2014.

Situated on portion 1564, a 12.13 ha plot of state land abutting the scenic grounds of Parliament House, the Arts Centre Settlement was a growing multi-ethnic neighbourhood. Established in the late 1980s, by 2014 it had approximately 4,000 residents who lived in a mixture of permanent and semi-permanent houses (Yalbees 2013c, 2013d). The Arts Centre Settlement was home to white-collar professionals through to unskilled labourers. Although no survey has been conducted that would permit authoritative statements on the settlement's social demography, observations from multiple site visits during 2013 suggested many residents worked in lower-paid areas of the formal economy, or in the informal economy.

As with many Port Moresby settlements, a vibrant local economy could be observed made up of community traders, in addition to an informal real-estate market, overseen by a local governance structure coordinated by settlement leaders. Of course, in a city facing extreme forms of urban poverty and structural inequality, street crime, anti-social behaviour and alcohol abuse were enduring challenges for the settlement, along with the management of refuse and other services. However, there was evidence of a strong leadership structure, and innovative efforts to deliver services drawing on local resources.

The first major attempt to demolish this residential community and displace its members occurred on 8 March 2013. Armed officers, accompanied by police dogs, entered the settlement. Residents were informed they had 25 minutes to collect their belongings and vacate the property (Yalbees 2013a). Homes and businesses were then demolished, under police watch. Portion 1564's title-holder, a private company, Macata Enterprises Limited, informed journalists that the demolition would pave the way for a K300 million real-estate investment (approx. US$143 million) (Kelola 2013: 6). The venture would consist of a 'world-class hotel, villas and apartments' (cited in Muri 2013a: 11). The company also maintained that the project was going to 'directly employ scores of Papua New Guineans and boost the country's economy' (cited in Kelola 2013: 6). When approaching the topic of the already existing residents on portion 1564, Macata Enterprises claimed that the settlement was 'a nerve centre for criminal activity' ('Former MP's Company to Develop Arts Settlement' 2013), populated by 'illegal settlers' (cited in Muri 2013a: 11).[3]

At this stage, Macata Enterprises was owned by Tom Amaiu (40 shares) and his wife Cathy (34 shares). Tom Amaiu also acted as Macata Enterprise's Managing Director.[4] He had entered the private sector following a truncated political career. Amaiu's first steps in public life took place during the late 1970s, when he was elected Member of Parliament (MP) for Kompiam-Ambum, an electorate situated in Enga Province. Amaiu's tenure, however, was cut short by a theft conviction. He was sentenced to five years imprisonment with hard labour (*Amaiu v The State* [1979] PNGLR 576). According to the Supreme Court of Papua New Guinea, Amaiu had stolen a K10,120 timber royalty cheque, belonging to Wagop Korowai (*Amaiu v The State* [1979] PNGLR 576). Following his release from custody, Amaiu was re-elected and served somewhat ironically as Minister for Prisons. According to Transparency International (2003: 45), Amaiu then resigned from parliament in 1992, after a Leadership Tribunal was appointed to investigate allegations of public misappropriation.[5]

During his political career, Amaiu is reported to have been heavily involved in the alluvial mining industry at Mt Kare, where he 'did well as a gold buyer' (Callick 1992: 7). Mt Kare was then the site of a Papua New Guinea 'goldrush'. An estimated K50 million was extracted by alluvial miners from a rich, easily accessible ore body (Connell 1997). However, 'the principal beneficiaries were the middlemen, some of whom were politicians, paying on site little more than half the world market price' (Connell 1997: 126–127). Rowan Callick alleges that Tom Amaiu was one of these middlemen, and that 'his success has been such that he has acquired special status as a high roller at Queensland's casinos [in Australia]' (1990: 17).

It was during this period of commercial success that Macata Enterprises was incorporated on 15 July 1991. Annual returns list the company's principal activity as 'management agency'.[6] Unusually, Macata's assets, liabilities and employees have remained notably static since 2000. They are consistently declared to be K100,000, K10,000 and 10 respectively. Of course, it is impossible to definitively contest the accuracy of these financial statements, without an independent audit. Nevertheless, it is worth noting that during this period Macata Enterprises held a 99-year state lease over prime land with significant development potential, in one of the capital's most expensive suburbs. At the very least, this would appear to cast some doubt over the company's statement of assets. If an annual return contains false statements, it is an offence under section 420 of the *Companies Act* 1997. However, given the lax enforcement culture within the national corporate regulator, the risk of prosecution is negligible.

We also know from National Court records that Macata Enterprises has been involved in the gambling industry. According to Justice Hartshorn, police seized 180 gaming machines owned by Macata, after it was revealed that the company did not have a licence under the *Gaming Machine Act* 1993 (*Macata Enterprises Ltd v Independent State of Papua New Guinea* [2009] PGNC 278). The National Court rejected Macata Enterprises' request for compensation, awarding costs to the state. Nevertheless, Public Accounts Committee (2009a) reporting indicates that Macata was paid K100,000 out of Trust Fund Suspend Account No.2. The transfer reference notes the payment was for 'WS 68 2002', which corresponds to the National Court case number where Macata's request for compensation had in fact been dismissed. This fact needs to be read alongside other concerns raised by the Public Accounts Committee. In particular, the committee observe, 'this [Trust] Account was used as a conduit for misappropriated and illegally applied monies [which were] at the complete discretion of unelected and unrepresentative officers of the Department of Finance' (Public Accounts Committee 2009a: 182–183). A subsequent Commission of Inquiry similarly discovered, 'funds to process settlement payments of claims against the State on numerous instances were illegally sourced from other appropriation such as the Trust Fund Suspense Account No. 2' (Davani et al. 2009: 59). Neither inquiry specifically commented on whether the payment to Macata Enterprises was illegal.

If we widen our lens, and consider Amaiu's activities beyond Macata, it is apparent that he has a significant range of commercial interests. Over the past 30 years, the former politician has owned or managed 35 companies, some of which are tied to Ministers, public officials and international business people from Malaysia, China and Australia. For example, Amaiu had a 40% stake and directorship in Data Enterprises Limited, which was active between 2000 and 2005.[7] During this period the company was also part owned (40%) by Francis Damem, who was then Attorney General. Damem would later meet disgrace when a Commission of Inquiry put him at the centre of a multi-million dollar scheme designed to defraud the government of Papua New Guinea, a scheme which in fact abused the same trust account employed to pay out Macata Enterprises (Davani et al. 2009).

Amaiu was also director and majority owner (59%) of Bless Corporation, a concern in which former Public Services and Lands Minister, Sir Albert Kipalan, enjoyed a 19% stake.[8] And for a period between 2002 and 2005, Amaiu partnered with Icelandic-Australian businessman Gudmundur Fridriksson, through Anvil Marine Limited.[9] Fridriksson was profiled in chapter five; it was noted there that he has run companies censured in four Public Accounts Committee inquiries, two Auditor General reports, the Department of Finance Commission of Inquiry and a range of media investigations.

If we now reflect on the public footprints left by Macata Enterprises' principal it would appear Amaiu's emergence as a national figure began when he acquired a position of political centrality as MP for Kompiam-Ambum. Following a period in prison, Amaiu successfully converted his political capital into commercial success, with interests in a wide range of sectors – including mining, gaming, real-estate, fisheries, automotive and forestry. Through these business dealings, it is apparent Amaiu enjoyed close ties to influential individuals within government and the private sector. Accordingly, these networks and positions signal an actor well poised to prosecute their interests.

We have also observed evidence that Amaiu sought to obtain profit through illicit means, most notably theft and unlicensed gambling, with questions also raised over his link to a government trust account found to be a routine subject of misappropriation. Compounding matters, Amaiu has consorted with figures censured for corruption and fraud by a range of oversight bodies. Given the commercial and governance structure underpinning land and property markets in Papua New Guinea, Amaiu in principle appears to have been well positioned to take advantage of the illegitimate opportunities they systematically present.

On that note, we will now turn to the landed transactions buttressing Macata's real-estate venture.

Court and Lands Department records suggest Macata Enterprises first acquired a Town Subdivision Lease over portion 1564 during the early 1990s.[10] The Town Subdivision Lease was a precursor to the Urban Development Lease. In effect, they are short term titles issued by the state, attached to which are certain covenants, such as improvements of a certain amount. If observed, these covenants lead to the award of a longer leasehold title, usually 99 years in duration. Because the original leasehold title could not be accessed, it is unclear what conditions were attached to Macata's Town Subdivision Lease, or whether they were observed. Nevertheless, in 1995, the Land Board awarded Macata a 99-year Business Lease over portion 1564, commencing on 24 August 1995.[11]

There are a number of facts surrounding this award worth noting. First, the Land Board which awarded the 99-year lease was led by Sir Ralph Guise,[12] an individual who later met disgrace for his involvement in a range of illegal activities as Chair, including bribery and fraud (Barnett 2002). Second, the Lands Minister during 1995 was Sir Albert Kipalan. Kipalan would subsequently become Tom Amaiu's business partner, through the jointly owned company Bless Corporation. Finally, the Lands Department records suggest annual rent for portion 1564 was set at just K100 (approx. US$77).[13] However, under the *Land Regulation* 1999, rent on a business lease should be levelled at 5% of the unimproved land value, unless a special Ministerial dispensation has been applied for, and approved, under section 83 of the *Land Act* 1996. Of course, none of these facts prove that the lease was wrongfully awarded to Macata Enterprises. They do, however, point to notable irregularities and weaknesses marking the institutions and processes underpinning the award.

Between 1995 and 2011, when Macata Enterprises appears to have held portion 1564 at a nominal rent, property prices throughout Port Moresby increased significantly, with Waigani, Paga Hill and Ela Beach being among the principal beneficiaries of upward price shifts (see chapter one). This precipitated a construction boom on the limited supply of registrable land in Port Moresby's more desirable locations. Consequently, by 2011 the rental yield of Macata's Waigani landholdings had increased significantly, and could be further accentuated through built improvements. To that end, Macata Enterprises claimed during 2013 it had successfully negotiated a K300 million investment (approx. US$143 million), which it said will transform the vacant land into a luxury estate, featuring a hotel and apartments (Kelola 2013). Company records show that a development agreement has indeed been signed with China Railway Construction Engineering Group (PNG) Real Estate Limited (2015), a Papua New Guinea subsidiary of the Hong Kong based China Railway Construction Engineering Group (H.K.) Co., Limited.

Up until 2014, one major barrier preventing the agreement's implementation, was the 4,000 people resident on portion 1564 (Yalbees 2013c). To clear the land of this sizable community, Macata Enterprises initiated eviction proceedings, filing an originating summons on 9 September 2011. On 22 October 2012 a consent order was entered into with Kelly Palleyo, endorsed by the National Court (Maeokali 2013). According to Macata Enterprises, Palleyo was appointed site caretaker in 1998. He then 'invited his relatives to settle on the land and then [an] influx of illegal settlers moved in' (Macata Enterprises Limited 2013). Settlement leaders reject this claim. Instead, they argue, the community predates Palleyo's arrival by a decade (Kuyako 2013; Yalbees 2013c).

Nevertheless, the 22 October consent order required that all people resident on portion 1564 vacate the land within 14 days from the date of service, removing all built structures. The consent order also stated, in the event that this condition was not observed, police officers were empowered:

> to enter the property by force and remove the Defendant including his family, relatives and those other persons illegally living on the property with necessary force by demolishing, breaking down and removing any illegal buildings, houses, shelters and makeshifts that have been illegally erected.
>
> (*Macata Enterprises Limited v Kelly Palleyo* OS No.727 of 2011)

During this period of contention over the Waigani land, Tom Amaiu's son, Labi Amaiu, was elected Member of Parliament for Moresby North East. This electorate includes the Waigani land and Arts Centre Settlement. That said, there is no evidence in Macata's share registry to suggest that Labi Amaiu had a stake in the company at the time, although his father claims Labi had initially been a shareholder/director (Amaiu 2015). Furthermore, Tom Amaiu continues to describe Macata Enterprises as a 'family company' (Amaiu 2015). Residents also allege that Labi Amaiu was present at one of the eviction exercises, and that they have 'received death threats from the member of Port Moresby North-East' (Yalbees 2013b).

In light of their considerable investment in the neighbourhood, and the absence of a relocation strategy, arts centre residents contested the consent order. To delay the eviction and obtain compensation from Macata, settlement leaders initiated court proceedings on 29 October 2012. The court issued an *ex parte* restraining order, staying the eviction so the matter could be considered in further detail. In a subsequent decision entered into on 19 February 2013, Justice Kariko stated: 'The other Settlers were not a party to that proceeding [on 22 October 2012] nor did Mr Palleyo represent them, which means the consent order cannot apply to the present plaintiffs' (*Lunge v Macata Enterprises* OS No.704 of 2012).

Despite Justice Kariko's explicit statement that the 22 October 2012 consent order did not apply to the settlement, the company 'warned the settlers to move out as it wanted to develop the property' (Macata Enterprises Limited 2013). According to Macata's legal representative:

The settlers were ignorant and were very stubborn and did not want to move out. The Defendant then after many warnings moved into its property on the 7th of March, 2013 and moved the settlers with force with the assistance of the police force pursuant to the Orders of 22nd 2012.

(Macata Enterprises Limited 2013)

Before the March 2013 eviction exercise took place, a lawyer for the settlement alleges that 'policemen in police vehicles and private cars … frequented the site and have warned the squatters [sic] that they will be evicted anytime. Those policemen have on one instance fired police issued guns on squatters [sic]' (Kombri & Associates Lawyers 2013). Then on, or around, 8 March 2013, armed police officers, police dogs and private security were trucked to the settlement, in order to conduct home demolitions. Residents were informed that the exercise would begin in 25 minutes (John 2013). Police alleged they were acting with Supreme Court authorisation (Yalbees 2013a).

While settlement leaders attempted to verify this claim, bulldozers demolished homes and businesses. According to the community's Chairman, Thomas Yalbees (2013c):

When they gave this 25 minutes [warning], the dogs barked, guns were being fired, the bulldozer started working and the people lost all their things, a lot of men outside too came and damaged a lot of our things. The bulldozer bulldozed our things, people came and stole our belongings, damaged them, they brought chainsaws, cut down the trees, damaged the houses, all our things. We didn't even save one thing.

Police then left the site. Residents remained, however, living under sheet metal and tarpaulins provided by the Catholic Church.

Several days later, on 14 March 2013, community leaders obtained a restraining order from the National Court, preventing Macata Enterprises and the police from conducting further demolitions, or harassing residents. According to a settlement leader, Wilson Kuyako, the Court Order was served on Macata's legal representative, Japson and Associate Lawyers, on 14 March 2013, along with the Police Commissioner, Deputy Police Commissioner, NCDC Central Police Commander, NCDC Metropolitan Superintendent and all local Police Station Commanders, including Six Mile, Badili, Waigani, Gerehu, Hohola and Gordons (Kuyako 2013). Japson and Associate Lawyers dispute the legality of the service, claiming under the *Companies Act* 1997, the papers needed to be served on a Macata Enterprises' office holder, or employee (Macata Enterprises Limited 2013).

Over the ensuing year residents claim they were subjected to constant harassment and violence, while their case was proceeding through the National Court. For instance, Thomas Yalbees states that on 17 March 2013 police officers from Gordons Police Station entered homes on the site and assaulted residents

(Yalbees 2013b). The following day, Yalbees notes, Macata employees visited the settlement to erect a large fence around the property. Shortly thereafter, on 3 April 2013, six Toyota 10-seater vehicles visited the site. Three were private vehicles containing individuals said to be associated with Macata Enterprises, the remainder contained officers from the Police Dog Unit. Residents again claim community members were assaulted; additionally, money was evidently stolen from a trade store, a power generator was destroyed, and temporary canvas shelters were demolished (John 2013; Yalbees 2013c).

Home burnings, intimidation and arrests are said to have persisted throughout 2013. As a result of the violence, residents were eventually forced off the land and 'scattered all over the city' (James 2014). On 13 December 2013 the National Court finally dismissed the community's legal action, a result which signals the limited right of recourse available to informal settlements in Papua New Guinea (Muri 2013b). While settlements are a critical part of the urban landscape, providing affordable housing to city residents, there are no substantive laws protecting residents' rights, or governing the eviction/relocation process. As a result, when it comes to informal settlements the courts have only been willing to recognise the limited equitable right of receiving adequate notice prior to eviction (*Koitaki Farms Ltd v Kenge* [2001] PGNC 59; *Ready Mixed Concrete Pty Ltd v The State, Samana and Kiamba* [1981] PNGLR 396). In a small number of cases, communities affected by illegal demolitions have also succeeded in obtaining compensation for property damage (*Alep v Madang Provincial Government* [2011] PGNC 149).

The legal resistance mounted by Arts Centre Settlement residents was, therefore, always going to be a staying exercise, rather than an avenue for achieving a solution that accords with international norms dealing with development based evictions. The only exception would have been if a judicial review action had been mounted, questioning the administrative process standing behind the award of leasehold title to Macata. However, the cost and complexity of such an action limits it largely to well-resourced commercial entities.

With residents removed, and the court decision to hand, the development agreement between Macata Enterprises and Chinese investors was free to be enacted. However, the sizable sums now in play precipitated a schism within Macata Enterprises, between its husband and wife owners. Each one competed for the 'substantial' access-payment the Chinese developer had offered (KK Charlthom Lawyers 2015).

By this stage, Tom Amaiu had increased his holdings in Macata to 64 shares, through a transfer from his wife. This left Cathy Amaiu with 10 shares. However, on 17 March 2015, a special Board of Directors meeting resolved to transfer 35 of Tom Amaiu's shares back to his wife (Macata Enterprises Limited 2015a). This gave Cathy Amaiu a 61% controlling stake in the firm. Just over a month later, on 4 May 2015, she obtained a restraining order preventing Macata Enterprises from conducting any business, or enacting change to its corporate structure (*Catherine Pis Amaiu v Tom Amaiu, Alex Tongayu, and the Investment*

Promotion Authority, DC No.47 of 2015). Cathy Amaiu's lawyer alleged that a 'substantial amount of money ha[s] been paid to Thomas Amaiu without the knowledge of our client who is the holder of the majority of shares in Macata Enterprises Limited' (KK Charlthom Lawyers 2015). As a result:

> Our client maintains that those payments were illegally received by Thomas Amaiu as he acted without the consent and authority of our client who is also a director and chairlady of Macata Enterprises Limited … Our client has also lodged [a] formal complaint with Police (National Fraud and Anti-Corruption Directorate) for alleged fraud and stealing against Mr Thomas Amaiu. The complaint has been registered as [a] Fraud Crime Report (FCR 79/150).
>
> (KK Charlthom Lawyers 2015)

In response to these allegations, Tom Amaiu insisted that the 17 March 2015 share transfer was illegally executed by his wife:

> The purported Macata Board of Directors meeting is illegal. I was in Singapore Hospital, the date 17th March, 2015 on which the meeting was conducted on, [there are] only two Directors and shareholders of Macata and I was not present on that meeting. I never signed on the Company resolutions and there was no board meeting.
>
> (Amaiu 2015)

Tom Amaiu thus argued, 'the company Form 13 was lodged with [the] IPA to effect [a] share transfer … illegally without my consent, knowledge and authority' (Amaiu 2015).

On 29 June 2015, the District Court set aside the restraining order awarded to Cathy Amaiu. It was stated in the decision that the originating court lacked jurisdiction over the matter owing to the sizable amounts of money involved (*Catherine Pis Amaiu v Tom Amaiu, Alex Tongayu, and the Investment Promotion Authority*, DC No.47 of 2015). Following this decision on 30 July 2015, Tom Amaiu unilaterally dismissed his wife as Company Secretary, Director and shareholder. He informed the Investment Promotion Authority:

> Cathy Pis Amaiu is terminated as shareholder, Director and the company Secretary for tempering [sic] company records with the Registrar of Companies (IPA) by defrauding illegal share transfer and for filing illegal documents with IPA and also instituting DC No. 47 of 2015 to cover up her illegal activities.
>
> (Macata Enterprises Limited 2015c)

According to company minutes, this decision to terminate Cathy Amaiu's involvement and stake in Macata Enterprises was made at a meeting held on

22 July 2015 (Macata Enterprises 2015b). The 15 minute meeting involved one individual, Tom Amaiu. Company records also show that the Investment Promotion Authority subsequently enacted this meeting outcome, despite having no lawful mandate to do so.[14] Under section 67 of the *Companies Act* 1997, a form of transfer signed by the current share owner must be submitted to the company before a share transfer can take place. Given the unilateral character of Tom Amaiu's actions, which is apparent in the records submitted to the Investment Promotion Authority, it should have been realised that this procedure had not been observed. Furthermore, under section 71 of the *Companies Act* 1997, only the Courts have the power to issue an order rectifying a share registry, where shares are alleged to have been wrongfully transferred. The Court Order of 29 June 2015 contains no such direction. Accordingly, it would seem on the basis of the records submitted by Macata Enterprises, that the Investment Promotion Authority has implemented a decision incongruent with *Companies Act* 1997 requirements.

At the time of writing, however, Cathy Amaiu has not sought legal redress over her removal from Macata Enterprises. As a result, Tom Amaiu is seemingly in prime position to realise the substantial sums being paid by Chinese investors for access to the Waigani land, which Macata holds at an annual rent of K100.[15]

If we return now to the 10 theses set out in the beginning of this chapter we can see there is evidence to suggest that many of the themes conceptualised, were directly or indirectly at play in this case. For instance, the land title was acquired under conditions which at the very least signal concerns over the award's legitimacy, especially in light of the nominal rent being paid, the evidenced governance weaknesses within the Land Board and Lands Department, combined with the beneficiary's criminal record and subsequent partnerships with the Lands Minister. Furthermore, Macata Enterprises' primary motivation for acquiring the land appears to have been speculative in character. That is, the company saw an opportunity to acquire a prime piece of urban real-estate at a discounted price, with a view to capitalising on price shifts.

The primary organiser of these transactions in this case, is the principal owner of Macata Enterprises, Tom Amaiu. The biography set out above reveals a man who has honed his professional abilities through careers in politics and a wide range of commercial sectors. Both careers have been marked by evidence of illegal behaviour. We also observed that Amaiu has, during his career, forged ties with a number of prominent actors, including Sir Albert Kipalan, Francis Damem and Gudmundur Fridriksson, in addition, of course, to his familial connection with Labi Amaiu, the MP for Moresby North-East. This suggests that Amaiu enjoyed a wealth of ties to actors with resources and influence in a wide range of areas. In the political climate of Papua New Guinea, being able to tap such powerful circles gives actors the capacity to influence procedural outcomes. Accordingly, on the basis of his biography, Amaiu at least in principle had the expertise and network position to take advantage of a permissive land administration.

Table 7.1 The 10 theses, applied to the Arts Centre Settlement case

The establishment of land-titles markets	✓
A favourable opportunity structure for price manipulation	✓
The construction and maintenance of diversified social networks	✓
Competition and contention between rival groups	✓
Permissive land administration regimes	✓
Central agents experienced in speculative repertoires	✓
Permissive corporate and financial governance	✓
Accumulating the indicia of legitimacy	✓
Strategic fusion of legal and illegal processes	✓
Resistance and counter-resistance	✓

The proposed improvements to the Waigani land – which would deliver a significant access payment – were legitimised by the company, drawing on a cosmopolitan urban vision, combined with the promise of job creation. Residents contesting displacement were dismissed as squatters and criminals. Macata Enterprises also drew on the court's symbolic power to legitimise resident evictions through a certified consent order. However, even when an injunction was acquired by residents staying the proposed demolition exercise, police nonetheless deployed illegal violence to clear the land, allegedly with company involvement.

Finally, following the successful eviction exercise, the family network underpinning Macata Enterprises began to fracture as the husband and wife owners competed to monopolise the sizable payments being offered by foreign developers. This has led to accusations of criminal conduct and unilateral actions which violate the *Companies Act* 1997.

It would appear, therefore, on the basis of the evidence examined that the dynamics conceptualised in the 10 theses were important drivers of the transactions documented in this case (see Table 7.1). On that note, attention will now be turned to a second example, which involves a different set of circumstances. In this second case, the focal point is a public housing estate which was the subject of a privatisation effort.

Status is no barrier: the North Waigani apartment complex

Since 1990 the National Housing Corporation (NHC) has been the primary public vehicle for addressing housing shortages in Papua New Guinea. Established by the *National Housing Corporation Act* 1990, the NHC has a mandate to address Papua New Guinea's housing situation through building and maintaining public housing stock, which can be leased or sold to eligible persons. The corporation is also empowered to conduct housing research, and report back to the Minister. Underpinning these different roles, is the NHC's overarching mission 'to promote orderly and economic urban development' (s28, *National Housing Corporation Act* 1990).

The NHC's current housing stock is unknown. According to the Auditor General's Office (2014), the corporation has been unable to supply auditors with a fixed assets register for verification. A Public Accounts Committee inquiry conducted during 2008 and 2009 – with assistance from the Auditor General's Office – paints a bleak picture of the NHC. The committee observes, 'political patronage and appointment on grounds other than merit has characterized the appointment of Senior Managers to the Corporation for many years' (2009b: 33). It adds, 'the National Housing Corporation's systems of accounting and recording public monies, property and stores collapsed at least twenty years ago' (Public Accounts Committee 2009b: 1). The significance of these failings are underlined: 'this would be serious in any Corporation but in a Corporation managing a huge property portfolio and complicated and complex Housing Schemes, it was clearly a prescription for failure and misconduct' (Public Accounts Committee 2009b: 30).

Although the NHC's organisational environment could be framed as a breakdown in governance, viewed from a different angle the Public Accounts Committee findings signal the successful development of a permissive environment for illicit forms of speculative activity. Certainly the Public Accounts Committee notes, 'controls and systems for the sale of properties have been abused [by NHC personnel] for personal gain in collaboration with outside interested parties' (2009b: 42). It adds, 'there is no valuation report [for NHC properties] prepared or presented to the Auditor. In the absence of such a Register, properties can be undervalued and sold out cheaply thereby causing a loss of revenue' (2009b: 50).

Despite requests from the Public Accounts Committee for drastic, immediate reforms to the NHC, little has been done. Mungu (2013: 1) explains the inertia:

> One prime reason is that many people in higher public and political circles have vested interests in that organization. It is also strongly believed that any investigations conducted into the affairs of NHC would reveal the dealings of several political leaders, bureaucrats and their associates who have plundered that organization of its assets and resources. It has been used as a cash cow for politicians, cronies and officials over the years at the expense of ordinary Papua New Guineans where their rights to affordable shelter have been abused through such dealings.

One example which appears to accord with this general dynamic, involves an NHC apartment block situated on Pitpit street in Waigani North, close to the nation's parliament and bureaucratic hub. Designed to accommodate up to 240 people, the apartment complex, known as the North Waigani Hostel, was completed in 1997, at a cost of K7 million (approx. US$4.3 million) (Ako 2013). It was the NHC's first major development since its creation in 1990, accordingly the apartment block was opened with a degree of fanfare by the Prime Minister, Sir Julius Chan (Watta 2013).

The North Waigani Hostel became home to a range of public and private sector employees looking to take advantage of the reasonable rents charged by the NHC, in an otherwise prohibitive rental market. However, just 13 years after the property's opening, on 16 April 2010 tenants were served with a notice instructing them to cease rental payments (National Housing Corporation 2010). The NHC then claimed the property needed to be temporarily vacated for renovations (Watta 2013). It was later revealed that the NHC's actual intention was to sell the property.

In response, residents launched the North Waigani Hostel Working Committee (Wellin 2013). The committee enjoyed a considerable body of expertise – its members included senior civil servants, an experienced lawyer and an engineer (Watta 2013; Wellin 2013). A court injunction was soon acquired, staying the eviction process. Nevertheless, the property sale went ahead. A tender for sale was issued on 14 November 2011 (National Housing Corporation 2011), although formal news of the result was not made public until 2013, when it was announced that the apartment complex had been sold to DAC Real Estate for K11.1 million (approx. US$5.3 million) (Ako 2013). Records held by the Investment Promotion Authority indicate DAC Real Estate is a business name registered to Platinum Investment Limited – a company owned by Shirley Lylang Yip (50%) and Jason Neil Yip (50%).[16] A legal adviser to the residents' committee claims, 'Jason Yip is a Malaysian businessman. He owns a lot of the properties around here. He is a very popular guy around here' (Watta 2013).

The North Waigani Hostel Working Committee (2013a), in particular, has raised concerns over the valuation process underpinning the sale. The committee argues that the apartment block was priced by an unregistered valuer, working on behalf of the NHC. When a registered valuer's opinion was sought by residents, the report concluded that the apartment complex was worth approximately K37 million (approx. $US17.6 million). Given the prime location, significant increases in Port Moresby's rental yields between 1997 and 2013, and improvements made to the land in 1996–1997, this would appear a feasible assessment.

The NHC's Managing Director, John Dege, nonetheless defended the sale in a media statement, claiming: 'The initial cost of the money to erect the hostel in 1997 was K7 million so we made about K4.1 million profit' (cited in Ako 2013). Of course, the apartment complex's construction cost is only one determinant of the property's market value. Excluded from Dege's calculation is the land's capitalised rent yield, which appreciated significantly between 1997 and 2013. Dege also argued that the sale was needed to cover the considerable rent arrears owed by North Waigani residents. He failed to note that the NHC had refused to accept rents since April 2010.

At the very least, there is reasonable evidence which indicates that the North Waigani property was sold to a private investor for a price well below its market value. This would appear to be in violation of the NHC's mandate as prescribed in the *National Housing Corporation Act* 1990. Of course, without further evidence, it is impossible to identify who benefited from the irregular arrangement, or to attribute any blame to DAC Real Estate.

Given the lack of meaningful daily oversight of public authority in Papua New Guinea, residents proved to be the only force challenging this under-valued sell off to the private sector. To that end, tenants at the North Waigani Hostel refused to leave the property until their case had been heard by the National Court. In a bid to hasten their departure, the residents' working committee alleges that a range of extra-legal tactics were employed (North Waigani Hostel Working Committee 2013b). First, on 31 May 2010, the NHC closed the hostel's administrative office, in effect leaving the property unmanaged except for security personnel charged with guarding the property (North Waigani Hostel Working Committee 2013b). The working committee claims security guards threatened and intimidated tenants. They also allegedly permitted illegal squatters, who have used the hostel to engage in a range of illegal activities including prostitution, gambling and drug use (North Waigani Hostel Working Committee 2013b).

Then on 3 December 2011, shortly after the North Waigani property was tendered for sale, police entered the premises to post eviction notices – officers are alleged to have threatened residents and cocked their firearms (North Waigani Hostel Working Committee 2013b). In subsequent legal action, the National Court warned the NHC against implementing an eviction exercise. According to the working committee's legal adviser, 'Justice Davani in open Court [stated] on the 24th of December 2012 that no evictions may be threatened and carried out between 24th December 2012 and [the] hearing of the Tenant's application for reinstatement of their case' (North Waigani Hostel Working Committee 2013b). The hearing date was set down for 1 March 2013.

Residents also successfully solicited support from the Prime Minister. Peter O'Neill is reported to have declared that the 'eviction of tenants at the Waigani Hostel in NCD and other assets in the country [are to] be halted' (cited in Elapa 2013), until a long term public housing strategy had been developed.

While the court hearing was pending, and contrary to the Prime Minister's statement, a forced eviction exercise was initiated by the NHC. A leaked corporation memorandum dated 13 February 2013, signed by the NHC board, recommends 'that the K10,000 requested by Mr Kama [North Waigani Hostel Manager] be approved and a further K20,000 be made available for contingencies because the eviction will need massive police and manpower presence to carry out successfully. Therefore a total of K30,000' (National Housing Corporation 2013). The residents' legal adviser observes:

> They requested funding, the funding was approved and just paid the same day, that is unusual in government. This is so unusual you know … We were

saying you know, the state cannot fund a criminal act. This is criminal. And it has been funded by a government entity.

(Watta 2013)

Two days after the funds were approved, it is alleged that senior NHC officials visited the tenants at North Waigani:

> Just before 4pm, John Dege [NHC Managing Director] accompanied Philip Kama (Hostel Manager) and other NHC Officials to the Hostel to issue threats to the tenants. John Dege said the tenants have not been paying rent and therefore must leave the hostel premises as the hostel has been sold.
>
> (North Waigani Hostel Working Committee 2013b)

An eviction exercise was actioned on 23 February 2013. The residents' working committee produced a detailed account of the event:

> Between the hours of 12–1pm on the 23rd of February, more than ten vehicles convoyed into the North Waigani Hostel's car park. The first four vehicles were Toyota Land cruisers, 10 seaters loaded with armed men in civilian clothes. As soon as the vehicles drove into the car park, men got out of the vehicles and ran and shouting wielding weapons towards the tenant's living quarters. The Acting Managing Director of the National Housing Corporation, John Dege came out of the 1st Toyota Land Cruiser (dark blue five door BDS 814) with a loud hailer announcing … 'I am the MD; no-one is above the law. We are all Melanesians, we have our wantoks [extended family], don't pretend and stay here, you go and look for your wantoks' … With Police presence and John Dege's supervision, control, physical presence and encouragement the gangers [gangs] then went from door to door of the tenants breaking down [doors] with iron bars and axes and throwing tenants belongings out of the rooms onto the corridors … weapons used includes; high powered firearms, long knives, axes, iron bars, sharp metal rods, baseball bats, coffee sticks, bottles, bricks, rocks, chains, police dogs, tear gas … About 300 people are now on the streets, they lost a lot of valuables, money, laptops, computers, fridge, washing machine, personal files, clothes etc.
>
> (North Waigani Hostel Working Committee 2013b)

The committee's legal adviser adds: 'They didn't have an eviction order … They don't have an eviction order, they never had! … They provided this letter here, which is an eviction notice, but you have to get an eviction order from the court' (Watta 2013).

Despite the illicit use of force, and the apparent lack of a legal mandate, residents were successfully displaced from the site. At the time of writing, tenants are continuing with their legal struggle to quash the sale. Additionally, Prime

Minister O'Neill expressed 'disappointment' that the eviction was carried out against his express wishes, however, no formal action has been taken by the national government to support residents or reprimand those responsible (*Post-Courier* 26/3/2013, p.5).

As a result, after a mere 18 years of life the NHC's first major development, designed to tackle systemic housing shortages in Port Moresby, has been successfully sold off to a private company, seemingly at a heavily discounted price. Because the NHC fails to maintain adequate records no public account has been made of the sale proceeds. However, it is alleged that some of the sale price, K6 million, was transferred to the National Housing Estate Limited (NHEL) (*The Sunday Chronicle* 9/12/2012, p.4). NHEL is a shadowy organisation set up by the national government to take ownership of NHC properties, with a view to operating them along strict commercial lines. Incorporated as a private company, with no clear oversight or controls, the Auditor General's Office (2014) has been unable to access any of NHEL's financial records, nor has NHEL submitted annual returns to the Investment Promotion Authority, as is required under the *Companies Act* 1997.

Accordingly, it is unlikely that any concrete evidence will ever emerge documenting what happened to the K11.1 million. Nevertheless, the decision to sell a relatively new property, at a discounted sale price with a lack of transparent documentation, backed by an illegal eviction process, set against an evidenced background of systemic corruption within the NHC, including the misappropriation of public assets, all indicate that NHC officials have wrongfully traded a public asset at a heavily discounted price. Given the corporation's past conduct, it is likely that the proceeds of the sale have been privately appropriated in whole or part by fixers, NHC staff and political power brokers.

Clearly there are gaps in the case study data for North Waigani owing to the secretive nature of the networks and organisations under examination. Nevertheless, the transaction chain documented here is such that we can reasonably find evidence pointing to eight out of the ten theses (see Table 7.2). For instance, we observed price manipulation taking place in an established property market, which was used to offload state assets at a discounted price,

Table 7.2 The 10 theses, applied to the NHC North Waigani case

The establishment of land-titles markets	✓
A favourable opportunity structure for price manipulation	✓
The construction and maintenance of diversified social networks	?
Competition and contention between rival groups	?
Permissive land administration regimes	✓
Central agents experienced in speculative repertoires	✓
Permissive corporate and financial governance	✓
Accumulating the indicia of legitimacy	✓
Strategic fusion of legal and illegal processes	✓
Resistance and counter-resistance	✓

facilitated through a permissive land and corporate governance regime, by public officials experienced in trading away public assets for private gain. These transactions were underpinned by a mixture of legal and illegal processes, which sparked resident resistance. In this case residents were not only legitimate tenants, they collectively had a considerable accumulation of professional expertise, resources and contacts, which enabled them to mount legal action underpinned by robust documentary evidence. Nevertheless, this did not ultimately stop their displacement, a fact which exemplifies the significant challenges even legal tenants face, given the government's demonstrated willingness to act without lawful authority, and the cumbersome, expensive processes that must be negotiated when resisting through litigation.

Conclusion

The literature on land-grabbing, megaprojects and development induced displacement, has tended to focus on macro-social currents and their intricate impacts (see chapter one). Less attention has been given to the organisational drivers of this activity, owing in part to the significant barriers researchers face when investigating such opaque processes. However, as the preceding chapters demonstrate, intricate social forces are at play, which have certain consistencies that are capable of being conceptualised. While research into these forces is indeed beset by a range of difficulties, nevertheless, through the use of certain methodological tools and analytical techniques, data-sets can be generated, upon which a series of theoretical hypotheses may be produced. These hypotheses are critical for identifying criminogenic environments, engaging in strategic reforms, and buttressing resistance.

Of course, for reasons already set out in chapter two, theory must also be employed to think about broader, historically developed structures and processes, which make these illicit transactions a profitable and desirable activity. Indeed, so far we have surveyed a number of case studies where organisational actors have accrued significant returns from largely unproductive activities, where no value has been generated. This pattern of state–corporate conduct could only be sustained on a durable basis – via continued, significant rates of profit – owing to the existence of certain historically developed social conditions conceptualised through the theories of capital, monopoly rents and governmentality discussed in chapter two.

On that note, we will now draw together the methodologies, theory and empirical data-sets set out in this volume to explore their implications for future crimes of urbanisation research.

Notes

1 It is difficult to define large estates in purely numerical terms, given the relativity of scales. In this instance, the term large-scale is deployed to capture land of sufficient scale to house major real-estate developments or industrial-scale economic projects.

2 When opposition movements and researchers attempt to gauge the credibility of actors driving contentious ventures, it is important to investigate potential past commercial activity in other sectors, where their commercial repertoire may have been honed, including any censure it elicited. Given that land and property ventures enacted through illicit repertoires, depend to an extent on maintaining a palatable public face, evidence of previous misconduct can prove an important asset for resistance efforts.

3 This virtually mirrors the legitimising narrative documented in chapter five. It is worth noting, therefore, that Macata's Managing Director had previously partnered with PHDC's CEO in a company, Anvil Marine Limited.

4 Macata Enterprises Limited, Company Extract, Investment Promotion Authority, accessed 6 September 2013.

5 Leadership Tribunals can only scrutinise public officials in office. Therefore, Amaiu's decision to quit aborted the investigation.

6 Macata Enterprises Limited, Annual Return 2011, Investment Promotion Authority, 26 April 2013.

7 Data Enterprises Limited, Company Extract, Investment Promotion Authority, accessed 1 April 2017.

8 Bless Corporation Limited, Company Extract, Investment Promotion Authority, accessed 5 January 2016.

9 Anvil Marine Limited, Company Extract, Investment Promotion Authority, accessed 3 May 2016.

10 Papua New Guinea National Gazette, No. G43, 11 May 1995.

11 Portion 1564, Milinch Granville, Fourmil Moresby, LAGIS Land Extract, Department of Land and Physical Planning, checked 16 February 2011.

12 Papua New Guinea National Gazette, No. G78, 24 August 1995.

13 Portion 1564, Milinch Granville, Fourmil Moresby, LAGIS Land Extract, Department of Land and Physical Planning, checked 16 February 2011.

14 Macata Enterprises Limited, Company Extract, Investment Promotion Authority, accessed 1 April 2017.

15 On the basis of a land record search conducted in 2013.

16 Platinum Investment Limited, Company Extract, Investment Promotion Authority, accessed 27 September 2014.

Bibliography

Ako, W. (2013). 'North Waigani hostel sold', The National, 15 February.

Amaiu, T. (2015). 'Affidavit', Catherine Pis Amaiu v Tom Amaiu, Alex Tongayu, and the Investment Promotion Authority, DC No.14 of 2015, 24 June.

Auditor General's Office. (2014). *Report of the Auditor-General 2013 on the Accounts of Public Authorities and Statutory Bodies Established under the Act of Parliament and Government Owned Companies Established under the Companies Act*, Waigani: Author.

Barnett, T. (2002). Report of the Commission of Inquiry into the National Provident Fund. [Online]. Extracts available at: web.archive.org/web/20060923050634/http://www.post-courier.com.pg/NPF%20inquiry/npf116 (accessed: 16 February 2017).

Callick, R. (1990). 'Puzzling politics of never never land', *Australian Financial Review*, 31 August, p.17.

Callick, R. (1992). 'Aust mavericks' grab for PNG', *Australian Financial Review*, 24 December, p.7.

China Railway Construction Engineering Group (PNG) Real Estate Limited. (2015). Correspondence from The Director, China Railway Construction Engineering Group (PNG) Real Estate Co. Ltd to The Principal, KK Charlthom Lawyers, Section 53 Allotment 22, Soare Street, Gordons Industrial Area, and The Managing Director, Macata Enterprises Ltd, Section 75 Lot 15 Kuku Place, Korobosea, PO Box 55, Boroko, National Capital District, PNG, 18 May.

Connell, J. (1997). *Papua New Guinea: The Struggle for Development*, London: Routledge.

Davani, C., Sheehan, M. and Manoa, D. (2009). *The Commission of Inquiry Generally into the Department of Finance: Final Report*, Port Moresby: The Commission.

Elapa, J. (2013). 'PM stops NHC evictions', The National, 20 February.

'Former MP's company to develop arts settlement' (2013) YouTube video, added by EMTV Online. [Online]. Available at: www.youtube.com/watch?v=AZ95BdMbAW4 (accessed: 28 March 2017).

James, M. (2014). Arts Centre Settlement Resident, Personal Communication, 25 April.

John, A. (2013). Arts Centre Settlement Resident, Personal Communication, 19 July.

Kelola, T. (2013). 'Title holder supports eviction', *Post-Courier*, 14 March, p.6.

KK Charlthom Lawyers. (2015). Correspondence from Charles W Kaki, KK Charlthom Lawyers, to the Project Manager, China Railway Construction Engineering Group (PNG) Real Estate, PO Box 397, Waigani, National Capital District, 20 May.

Kombri & Associates Lawyers. (2013). Letter from Martin Kombri, Kombri & Associates Lawyers, to Jim Andrews, Assistant Commissioner of Police, PO Box 1910, Boroko, National Capital District, 1 March.

Kuyako, W. (2013). 'Affidavit of service', *Thomas Yalbees, Wilson Kuyako, Graham Wambi, Ken Irabe for and on behalf of themselves and 3,754 others v Macata Enterprises Limited*, OS No.121 of 2013, 2 April.

Kuyako, W. (2013). Arts Centre Settlement Community Representative, Personal Communication, 19 July.

Macata Enterprises Limited. (2013). 'Defendant's submission', *Thomas Yalbees, Wilson Kuyako, Graham Wambi, Ken Irabe for and on behalf of themselves and 3,754 others v Macata Enterprises Limited*, OS No.121 of 2013, April 2013.

Macata Enterprises Limited. (2015a). Meeting Minutes – Special Board of Directors Meeting No.01/2015, 17 March.

Macata Enterprises. (2015b). Meeting Minutes, Korobosea – Section 72 Lot 15, 22 July.

Macata Enterprises Limited. (2015c). Letter from Thomas Amaiu, Company Secretary, Macata Enterprises, to The Registrar of Companies, Investment Promotion Authority, PO Box 1281, Port Moresby, National Capital District, 22 July.

Maeokali, N. F. (2013). 'Affidavit in support', Newman Freeman Maeokali for himself and on behalf of the 3053 Settlers of Portion 1564, Milinch Granville, Port Moresby, National Capital District v Macata Enterprises Limited, OS No.121 of 2013, 8 March.

Mungu, E. (2014). *The Reality of Housing Situation in PNG*, Port Moresby: National Research Institute.

Muri, D. (2013a). 'Picket fence vandalised', *Post-Courier*, 16 January, p.11.

Muri, D. (2013b). 'Court settles long land battle', *Post-Courier*, 19 December, p.6.

National Housing Corporation. (2010). Notice to Tenants of the North Waigani Hostel, 16 April.

National Housing Corporation. (2011). Public Tender Notice – Sale of North Waigani Hostel, Tender No: PM 01-11-11, 14 November.

National Housing Corporation. (2013). Memorandum from Geroge L. Pera, National Housing Corporation, to the Managing Director, National Housing Corporation, 13 February.

North Waigani Hostel Working Committee. (2013a). Media Release – Rex Wellin, Chairman, North Waigani Hostel Working Committee, for and on behalf of Tenants of North Waigani Government Hostel and Tenants of all NHC Properties Nationwide, 21 February.

North Waigani Hostel Working Committee. (2013b). Letter from Rex Wellin, Chairman, North Waigani Hostel Working Committee, to the Chairman, Investigation Task Force Sweep, PO Box 391, Waigani, National Capital District, 12 March.

Public Accounts Committee. (2009a). *Inquiry into the Public Accounts of the Government of Papua New Guinea for the Financial Year 2004: Report to the National Parliament*, Waigani: National Parliament of Papua New Guinea.

Public Accounts Committee. (2009b). *Inquiry into the National Housing Corporation and State Home Ownership Schemes*, Waigani: National Parliament of Papua New Guinea.

Transparency International. (2003). *National Integrity Systems, Country Study Report – Papua New Guinea*, Berlin: Transparency International.

Watta, I. (2013). NHC North Waigani Working Group, Personal Communication, 19 July.

Wellin, R. (2013). NHC North Waigani Working Group, Personal Communication, 28 July.

Yalbees, T. (2013a). 'Affidavit in support', Ben Lunge for and behalf of Applicant v Macata Enterprises Limited, OS no. 121 of 2013, 10 March.

Yalbees, T. (2013b) 'Affidavit', Thomas Yalbees, Wilson Kuyako, Graham Wambi, Ken Irabe for and on behalf of themselves and 3,754 others v Macata Enterprises Limited, National Court, OS No.121 of 2013, 22 April.

Yalbees, T. (2013c). Arts Centre Settlement Community Representative, Personal Communication 15 July.

Yalbees, T. (2013d). Arts Centre Settlement Community Representative, Personal Communication 19 July.

Cases

Alep v Madang Provincial Government [2011] PGNC 149

Amaiu v The State [1979] PNGLR 576

Catherine Pis Amaiu v Tom Amaiu, Alex Tongayu, and the Investment Promotion Authority, DC No.47 of 2015.

Koitaki Farms Ltd v Kenge [2001] PGNC 59

Lunge v Macata Enterprises OS No.704 of 2012

Macata Enterprises Ltd v Independent State of Papua New Guinea [2009] PGNC 278

Macata Enterprises Limited v Kelly Palleyo OS No.727 of 2011

Ready Mixed Concrete Pty Ltd v The State, Samana and Kiamba [1981] PNGLR 396

Chapter 8

Crimes of urbanisation research and social resistance

Conclusions and the task ahead

Industrialisation, and more recently financialisation, have both been recognised – at least within critical criminological tracts – as processes where wealth is realised on a global scale through techniques and practices that are frequently illicit and socially harmful (Barak 2012; Tombs and Whyte 2007). To date, however, urbanisation is yet to attract the same levels of criminological critique. Nevertheless, there is a growing body of evidence which clearly indicates that urbanisation – a process just as integral to everyday social life – is no less marked by socially harmful, illicit conduct.

Indeed, once our lens broadens to encompass geography and cognate areas, we find scholarly examples on the critical margins, which point to the forms of corruption, dispossession, social marginalisation and abuse that urbanisation can generate in both its concentrated and extended forms. Furthermore, this critical literature, as a whole, reminds us that not all of this illicit activity is necessarily motivated by profit. Research from Israel/Palestine, for instance, emphasises that apartheid and ethnic cleansing can be executed in subtle, but no less exacting forms, through the technocratic apparatus of physical planning and urban governance (Green and Smith 2016; Smith and Green 2014).

Whether the motive force is economic, political or a blend of both, it nevertheless follows that if the birth pangs of our built environment are marked by violent forms of dispossession, marginalisation and illicit activity, the concrete edifice that emerges from these processes will solidify the injustices, and convert them into a permanent feature of our built world. In chapter five, for instance, the inception of a luxury megaproject was catalogued, which will capture the southern face of Port Moresby's iconic Paga Hill. Removed from the hill, through a range of illegitimate techniques, was a national park, and affordable accommodation for working class households. If this megaproject indeed comes to fruition, hotel and residential accommodation tariffs will be at a level significantly out of reach for those who used to call the harbourside location, home.

Indeed, Port Moresby residents – like many city dwellers in the current neoliberalised global political economy – are seeing the most exclusive spaces become spaces of exclusion; centres of luxury and ostentatious wealth open only to those with high disposable incomes. Added to this, the eye-catching exterior fronting these spaces of exclusion often conceal a period of gestation marked by illegal transactions and human rights abuses.

It is one of the core contentions underpinning this intervention that criminology is in a unique position to shine light on the crimes of urbanisation, in a way that sits sympathetically and symbiotically with critical urban research being conducted in other disciplines. Criminology can investigate the intricate social patterns which underpin illicit forms of concentrated and extended urbanisation. And in so doing it can document and conceptualise the social networks, transaction sequences, organisational interplay, institutional schisms, elite competition, resistance, counter resistance, synthesis of legal and illegal tactics, profiteering, and political agendas, which as a whole cohere to underpin illicit forms of state–corporate activity in the urban sphere.

But to do this, criminology requires specialised methodologies that are capable of systematically collecting, collating and analysing data, employing tools which will ensure high degrees of rigour and comparability. In chapters three and four of this book, a framework was introduced which has been specifically designed to: interrogate, across an extended temporal expanse, complex networks and transactional sequences; detect evidence of illicit activity; and produce data-sets that can underpin longitudinal and comparative analysis, in addition to theory development. Of course, there is ample scope for further innovation on this front, and for mixed-methodological approaches, that blend quantitative and qualitative methods, to track patterns and experiences, for instance, of development-based forced displacement. It might also be asked how drone and satellite technology can be usefully employed to track the illicit frontiers of urban change.

It ought to be underlined – as both chapters two and seven demonstrate – that while intricate fieldwork methods, that capture the granular social processes which drive illicit forms of concentrated and extended urbanisation, are essential for building rigorous data-sets, theoretical understandings are equally dependent on their successful execution. Indeed, unless we have to hand data that tracks the business models, political agendas, social networks, organisational techniques, permissive state–corporate governance regimes and associated forms of social contention that frame the crimes of urbanisation, theoretical innovation will be of a speculative character.

For example, an exacting analysis of the empirical data was an essential precondition for the extended engagement with Marx's theory of fictitious capital, presented in chapter two. Indeed, while the types of speculative repertoire documented in chapters five, six and seven were never explicitly discussed by Marx in any detail, a rereading of *Capital* during 2014, set against the backdrop of the study's preliminary findings, indicated that his theories of value, industrial capital and fictitious capital, offered a powerful scaffold through which to understand the sanctifying structures that sustain the deviant state–corporate activity chartered in this book.

And from this theoretical analysis, it must be underlined, important conclusions follow. At first glance, the urbanisation process and the heterogeneous built environments it generates, often appear to be commodities in the conventional sense, no different say from cotton or a pair of shoes. For instance, whether it be an apartment block or a hotel, both structures emerge from a labour process, through which surplus value is extracted. And for this surplus value to be realised the developer capitalist must offer the built commodity – through lease or sale – to a consumer possessing value in its money-form. However, this profit generating sequence notably does not match the actual commercial metabolism or speculative repertoires chartered in the empirical chapters.

Here the turn to David Harvey proves productive. Once real-property is liquidated of its political or communal form, with the associated encumbrances that heed free market exchange, an exclusive type of private property is created. There is pregnant in this arrangement the potential for a new speculative economy. The exclusive spatial monopoly a property titleholder possesses under such a real-property regime, supports a new commercial logic. Here investors do not apply a portion of industrial capital in order to capture a share of surplus value generated by labour. Instead, their investment is valorised through an unproductive set of mechanisms (unproductive in the sense that it is not generating surplus value). Specifically, the monopoly charge property titleholders can levy through exclusive, private property regimes, offer investors an opportunity to make a claim on the revenues emerging from the circuit of industrial capital, without actually participating in it.

This generates two important vectors of commercial activity. First, we observe investors who acquire the property title, much in the same way as any piece of financial paper, such as a share certificate or bond. That is, they do so with a view to speculating on upward market shifts – growing their claim on future revenues – which increases the title deed's price. Second, we also observe those who court property-development capital, and influence urban governance, in order to enhance the exclusive nature of their spatial monopoly. This can increase – often in league with upward market shifts – the charge levied on consumers for access to the spatial monopoly.

Neither vector is necessarily illegitimate in nature. However, we have certainly seen in the empirical chapters that it creates the conditions for market activity and regimes of governmentality which use nefarious means in order to both expand, and capture, the revenues being switched into land and property markets, through the mechanism of monopoly rents.

For example, we observed evidence in chapters five and seven which indicates that anti-competitive practices, corruption and state–corporate violence can be used both to give market actors an edge in acquiring high-value real-property, and to do so in a way that reduces acquisition costs. Furthermore, through political fixing and market rigging – enacted through the networks and repertoires theorised in chapter seven – private actors are able to engorge their share of the revenues captured by state leasehold titles, for instance, through obtaining political concessions that increase the property's value, or by decreasing the share of monopoly rents claimed by the state. In addition to this, we also observed in chapters six and seven, that once property titles assume the historical form of financial paper, which gives the holder a claim over future revenues, an opportunity structure is created for fraudulent practices designed to cheat vulnerable owners of this asset. Whether the victim is customary landowners, or the citizens of Papua New Guinea who rely on the state to manage public property on their behalf, corruption within the Lands Department has generated a lucrative opportunity structure for fraud and misappropriation.

And, of course, it has been noted that this opportunity structure, and the rewards it produces, have been enlarged in Papua New Guinea by a regime of governmentality that dispossesses – often violently – customary landowning communities of their natural resources. This helps to stimulate muscular streams of revenue, through circuits of industrial capital operating in the resource extraction sectors. These revenues, which come in the form of profits and taxation receipts, in turn oxygenate auxiliary circuits of fictitious capital, in which a national elite play core roles as fixers and speculators, alongside an international class of investors.

However, it is clear, theoretically speaking, that if concepts drawn from the writings of Marx, Foucault, Harvey, and so on, are to have effect, careful diagnostic work is required. Indeed, deceptive state–corporate conduct and opaque market transactions, in their outward form, do not necessarily connect in any obvious way to appropriate sets of explanatory concepts. Accordingly, investigative inquiry is required in order to dissect this outward form, and enter the interior of the social processes and transactions under examination. For the conduct chartered in the previous chapters, this demanded a new methodological framework. Yet even once the interior of the processes under scrutiny had been drilled into, their relationship to different theoretical canons remained ambiguous. For example, some of the more fertile answers to questions emerging from the case study data did not come from Marx's chapters on industrial capital, or indeed ground rent – although both proved essential to framing the answer. Instead, it was Marx's embryonic writings on fictitious capital which offered the most relevant and congruent conceptual matter, for making sense of commercial repertoires and governance arrangements, documented in the data-sets.

Certain generalisable lessons can be pointed to based on this experience of empirical inquiry and conceptualisation. Most critically, Marx's theory of value remains a potent instrument for engaging with diverse forms of criminogenic phenomena emerging out of the global political economy. However, its saliency is not always obvious. For its explanatory potential to bear fruit, a considerable amount of *mediated* analysis is required that draws on the intricate weave of theoretical categories set out in *Capital*, which operate as a progressive bridge into a 'rich [empirical] totality of many determinations and relations' (Marx 1973: 100). This demands engaging dialectically with the carefully sequenced categorical development in Marx's work, which begins by defining the universal characteristics that form the essence of capitalism, before examining mediating determinations that condition the way in which this essence becomes expressed concretely in our lived realities.

The framework set out in chapter two, for example, could not emerge simply by taking an essential insight extracted from volume I of *Capital* and applying it to dissect land and property markets. Indeed, there was no clear line between the speculative repertoires documented in chapters 5–7, and the theories of value, surplus value and industrial capital set out in volume I. The explanatory potential of Marx's ideas depended, rather, on more concrete categories from volumes II and III being incorporated, thus connecting the lived realities documented in the case study data, with the mediated trajectories of value circulation that emerge under capitalist conditions of production as a rich totality.

Equally, as an unfinished work, there is ample scope to consider how the categories Marx developed in *Capital*, would work once we include new conceptual mediations, such as theories which articulate how the exercise of political power shapes the circuit of industrial capital, and those auxiliary estuaries that feed off it. Certainly in this study, such steps helped concretise the mediated way in which surplus value extracted from the worker at the moment of production, oxygenates auxiliary circuits of speculation.

Of course, here again there is further scope for innovation and cross-pollination between theoretical paradigms. This volume drew guidance from Foucault's late work – but we have also seen a range of other theoretical paradigms being employed to explain contentious forms of urban change, ranging from Lefebvre through to Agamben and Tilly (see Brenner 2000, 2013; Hammar 2008). Cutting across each application is one similar goal – social theory is utilised to enrich our appreciation of the intricate web of intersecting forces on which urban contention and the crimes of urbanisation pivot, rather than as a set of theoretical abstractions that seek to disclose isolated causes of events, in a style closer to empiricist traditions of scholarship. When theory is applied in the former way, namely as a vehicle for teasing out the subtle empirical nuance which escapes analysis unmediated by theory, there is greater scope for innovative combinations of approaches, that offer different vantage points for thinking in greater depth about the conduct under examination.

If we move now beyond method and theory, another challenge that confronts crimes of urbanisation research is the uncertain status of the category 'crime' within critical strands of criminological scholarship (Hillyard and Tombs 2007; Lasslett 2010; Pemberton 2007). For heuristic purposes the word crime has at times been employed in this book with perhaps a degree of clarity that it does not enjoy in social life. This is an issue that needs to be acknowledged and dealt with.

Indeed, when the label *crimes* of urbanisation is employed, it does not specify conduct that is inherently criminal – that is, an ontological fact that transcends historical epochs. To the contrary, crime is a category which, once dialectically defined, draws attention to the contested way in which criminalising forms of stigma are unevenly applied in particular historical conjunctures. While a vast institutional edifice exists – that bridges the state and civil society – for directing disproportionate levels of stigma towards deviant activity we might label street crime, there is a notable absence of such institutional weight or activity when it comes to the deviant activity of powerful corporate and state actors.

Nevertheless, as critical criminologists have pointed out, this does not negate the possibility that powerful organisational actors, engaged in deviant conduct, may still be subjected to stigmatisation at comparable levels (Green and Ward 2000; Lasslett 2014). However, it generally requires systematic grass-roots organisation, mass social mobilisation, strategic institutional fusions and longevity. From Bhopal to the Vietnam war, history offers up examples where social movements have gradually amassed the capacity to direct stigma at such levels, that the criminal nature of the targeted activity begins to assume hegemonic status, despite the best efforts of the offender organisation(s) to fracture, and suppress, resistance.

Certainly the case studies presented in chapters five, six and seven, point to nascent currents of social mobilisation that are taking place in Papua New Guinea, in order to resist and censure deviant state–corporate conduct facilitating unwanted forms of concentrated and extended urbanisation. The struggle to save Paga Hill is arguably the most mature and explicit example in Papua New Guinea's recent history of such a social movement. Rooted in a tight network of grass-roots organisations that possessed strong ties to a broader international coalition of civil society actors, this movement succeeded, to an extent, in stigmatising the illegitimate and abusive practices underpinning the Paga Hill Estate. However, most notably, it did not succeed in triggering sympathetic reactions from centres of state power, that have a monopoly over some of the most potent forms of symbolic capital which attach stigma to events and actors, primarily through criminal prosecution (Bourdieu 1994).

Nevertheless, even without the symbolic capital wielded by such state organs, enough stigma has attached to the megaproject – through exposé, activism and advocacy – that the developer coalition's capacity to mobilise wider commercial and social support for the project has been constrained. In the other cases examined, resistance was more localised. Residents mobilised and censured the deviant state–corporate activity, primarily through litigation, media interventions and political protest. In the Mililat case, Papua New Guinea's National Court lent its symbolic capital to the customary landowners, labelling the censured state–corporate activity, fraud. Notably, however, the Royal Papua New Guinea Constabulary has not prosecuted the offenders, despite being notified of the conduct, and provided with documentary evidence. Law enforcement inaction is certainly not unusual. As each case presented in this volume demonstrates, police in Papua New Guinea largely act as agents for developer coalitions, a loyalty that is sealed through 'donations', and other forms of patronage.

For reasons that were noted in chapter one, only summary attention could be devoted to the deeper sets of principles and discourses that inspired resistance in each case, in addition to the mechanisms and organisational methods communities employed to stigmatise state–corporate actors. Nevertheless, even in summary form, it is apparent from the contention and conduct surveyed that the illicit state–corporate activity documented in each case is not intrinsically criminal. It only has the potential to exhibit such a social quality, under certain historical conditions. However, for this potential to be realised, there must be hegemonic norms governing the urbanisation process, and a potent groundwork for sanctioning deviant conduct when detected.

In Papua New Guinea, norms enshrined in the *Land Act* 1996, *Physical Planning Act* 1989, *Companies Act* 1997, *Criminal Code* 1974, the national *Constitution*, the UN *Basic Principles and Guidelines on Development Based Evictions and Displacement*, in addition to broader human rights discourses, provide a framework for executing censure. And to an extent, grass-roots community networks and broader international coalitions, have succeeded in attaching moderate levels of stigma to the transactions concerned, by vigorously censuring their deviant characteristics employing these norms. However, the impact of such actions could be more potent, were this normative framework articulated in a more coherent, succinct form, possessing greater levels of symbolic capital – and had the social movements concerned enjoyed more resources to organise censure, including through support from centres of power within the state.

Which, of course, alerts us to the complex challenges that lie ahead when confronting the crimes of urbanisation. We not only require hegemonic norms that are capable of more equitably governing the process of concentrated and extended urbanisation – norms which must emerge and fuse across multiple scales – we also need forms of social mobilisation capable of delivering prohibitive levels of stigma. Yet such activity invariably takes place in contexts marked by the class antagonisms of capitalism, where centres of state power are occupied by governmentalised regimes, that are not only incapable of delivering this stigma, but are often centrally involved in disrupting social movements which are attempting to confront the crimes of urbanisation. Further interrogating such contradictions is a critical part of a future research agenda.

Indeed, crimes of the powerful researchers have an important role to play in documenting, conceptualising and confronting the crimes of urbanisation. In the first instance, robust data-sets are needed that evidence the intricate ways in which dispossession, marginalisation, abuse, fraud and corruption in the urban sphere are organised. Clearly, there are many vectors to explore in this respect.

Land-grabbing is one notable arena, another is contested megaprojects. The criminological spotlight can also be usefully shone on the forms of social cleansing being meted out through often lauded gentrification processes – whose outward normative cleanliness often collapses once subjected to forensic scrutiny. Additionally, we have witnessed urban governance and physical planning regimes being utilised as tools for persecuting different, distinct groups, and rigging democratic processes. Nor should we overlook the fact that the sphere of urbanisation often interlinks with other arenas of criminality. For instance, the edifice of fraud exposed by the global financial crisis was intimately linked to illicit financial instruments, and deviant forms of market activity, that centred on real-property assets. Also, of late, we have seen more attention focused on the way western housing markets have become permissive hot-spots for money laundering.

Crimes of the powerful scholarship is well positioned to shine light on all these different vectors, which as a whole make up the crimes of urbanisation. It can also usefully evidence, and conceptualise, the role which grass-roots networks and social mobilisation play in resisting the crimes of urbanisation. Of course, investigating state–corporate deviance and the resistance it triggers, can be a complementary affair. Indeed, the more incisively the crimes of urbanisation can be documented and publicly exposed, the greater practical value criminological research will have to civil society movements resisting such illicit activity and violence. With this symbiosis come enhanced opportunities for collaboration, solidarity and access to grass-roots experience and knowledge.

For scholars rooted in radical traditions, research into the crimes of urbanisation cannot be divorced from a broader process of class struggle. In his 1902 classic, *What is to be Done*, Lenin argues that exposing the crimes of the powerful plays an important role in the 'awakening of class-consciousness ... [and] developing the political consciousness of workers' (1970: 162–164). These crimes were, for Lenin, visceral examples of the contradictions lying at the heart of the capitalist mode of production, which could unsettle hegemonic forms of common-sense, that saturate societies underpinned by ideologies designed to legitimise and dehistoricise capitalism.

Fast forward a century, it is David Harvey who has most forcefully argued that capitalism in its current unstable iteration – typified by globalised production chains and neoliberal governance structures – has cultivated an urban sphere where these contradictions are often experienced with most potent force (Harvey 1976, 1985, 2012). It is here that fractured members of the working class share a common experience of marginalisation, dispossession, exploitation and immiseration – through price gouging, debt bondage, market exclusion, inequality in services and pollution. Equally, we see rural communities and indigenous peoples struggle against violent forms of dispossession and ecocide, precipitated by more intensive tracts of extended urbanisation, set up to service urban centres marked by their own fault lines of structural violence. Urbanisation, in other words, shares its pain and benefits in an uneven way, which closely correlate with class power. Extended and concentrated urbanisation is thus a powerful trigger for new forms of solidarity, mobilisation and revolutionary praxis.

Against this fractious context, placing a forensic spotlight on those illicit activities taking place at the coalface of concentrated and extended urbanisation, offers one powerful means for linking the everyday urban experience of labouring populations, to the harmful contradictions at the heart of the capitalist mode of production. Contradictions which, it would appear, can ultimately only be unravelled through forms of praxis capable of reimagining and enacting a post-capitalist future, from which new forms of urbanisation and urban justice can emerge.

Bibliography

Barak, G. (2012). *Theft of a Nation: Wall Street Looting and Federal Regulatory Control*, Plymouth: Rowman & Littlefield.

Bourdieu, P. (1994). 'Rethinking the state: Genesis and structure of the bureaucratic field', *Sociological Theory*, 12(1), 1–18.

Brenner, N. (2000). 'The urban question as a scale question: Reflections on Henri Lefebvre, urban theory and the politics of scale', *International Journal of Urban and Regional Research*, 24(2), 361–378.

Brenner, N. (2013). 'Theses on urbanization', *Public Culture*, 25(1), 85–114.

Green, P. and Smith, A. (2016). 'Evicting Palestine', *State Crime*, 5(1), 81–108.

Green, P. and Ward, T. (2000). 'State crime, human rights, and the limits of criminology', *Social Justice*, 27(1), 101–115.

Hammar, A. (2008). 'In the name of sovereignty: Displacement and state making in post-independence Zimbabwe', *Journal of Contemporary African Studies*, 26(4), 417–434.

Harvey, D. (1976). 'Labor, capital, and class struggle around the built environment in advanced capitalist societies', *Politics and Society*, 6(3), 265–295.

Harvey, D. (1985). *The Urbanization of Capital: Studies in the History and Theory of Capitalist Urbanization*, Baltimore: John Hopkins University Press.

Harvey, D. (2012). *Rebel Cities: From the Right to the City to the Urban Revolution*, London: Verso.

Hillyard, P. and Tombs, S. (2007). 'From "crime" to social harm?', *Crime, Law and Social Change*, 48(1–2), 9–25.

Lasslett, K. (2010). 'Crime or social harm? A dialectical perspective', *Crime, Law and Social Change*, 54(1), 1–19.

Lasslett, K. (2014). 'Understanding and responding to state crime: A criminological perspective', in Bantekas, I. (ed.) *International Criminal Law and Criminology*, Cambridge: Cambridge University Press.

Lenin, V. (1970). *Selected Works*: Volume 1, Moscow: Progress Publishers.

Marx, K. (1973). *Grundrisse: Foundations of the Critique of Political Economy*, Harmondsworth, UK: Penguin Books.

Pemberton, S. (2007). 'Social harm future(s): Exploring the potential of the social harm approach', *Crime, Law and Social Change*, 48(1–2), 27–41.

Smith, A. and Green, P. (2014). Forced Evictions in Israel-Palestine, June. [Online]. Available at: statecrime.org/data/2014/07/20140709_ForcedEvictionsInIsraelPalestine.pdf (accessed: 17 February 2017).

Stanley, E. and McCulloch, J. (eds) (2012). *State Crime and Resistance*, Abingdon: Routledge.

Tombs, S. and Whyte, D. (2007). *Safety Crimes*, Cullompton, UK: Willan Publishing.

Whyte, D. (2012). 'Between crime and doxa: Researching the worlds of state–corporate elites', *State Crime*, 1(1), 88–108.

Index